H·E·A·R M·Y V·O·I·C·E

H·E·A·R M·Y V·O·I·C·E

A multicultural anthology of literature from the United States

LAURIE KING, *Editor*

 ADDISON-WESLEY PUBLISHING COMPANY

Menlo Park, California • Reading, Massachusetts • New York
Don Mills, Ontario • Wokingham, England • Amsterdam • Bonn • Sydney
Singapore • Tokyo • Madrid • San Juan • Paris • Seoul, Korea
Milan • Mexico City • Taipei, Taiwan

This book is published by Innovative Learning, an imprint of Addison-Wesley's Alternative Publishing Group.

Project Editor: *Rachel Farber*
Production Manager: *Janet Yearian*
Senior Production Coordinator: *Karen Edmonds*
Design Manager: *Jeff Kelly*
Permissions Editor: *Marty Granahan*
Photo Editor: *Lindsay Kefauver*
Design and Production: *Seventeenth Street Studios*

✺ This book is printed on recycled paper

ISBN 0-201-81839-5

3 4 5 6 7 8 9 10 - ML - 97 96 95

Cover Art: Linda Lomahaftewa (Hopi/Choctaw), *New Mexico Sunset*, 1978. Acrylic on canvas, 130 x 104 cm. The Heard Museum, Phoenix. Photo courtesy of Linda Lomahaftewa.

ACKNOWLEDGMENTS

Lynda Barry, "Seventh Grade" from *The Good Times Are Killing Me*, copyright © 1991 by Lynda Barry, first Harper Perennial edition. Reprinted by permission of The Real Comet Press, 1463 E. Republican St., #126, Seattle, WA 98112.

Dwight Okita, "In Response to Executive Order 9066: All Americans of Japanese Descent Must Report To Relocation Centers," copyright © 1983 by Dwight Okita, from *Crossing With The Light* by Dwight Okita (Chicago: Tia Chucha Press, 1992).

Wilma Elizabeth McDaniel, "Who Said We All Have To Talk Alike," from *The Things That Divide Us: Stories by Women*, Faith Conlon et al, eds., copyright © 1985 by The Seal Press. Reprinted by permission of The Seal Press.

Tahira Naqvi, "Paths Upon Water," from *The Forbidden Stitch: An Asian American Women's Anthology*, Shirley Geok-Lin Lim and Mayumi Tsutakawa, eds., copyright © 1989 by Calyx Books. Reprinted by permission of the publisher.

Elena Tajima Creef, "Notes from a Fragmented Daughter," from *Making Face, Making Soul*, copyright © 1990 by Gloria Anzaldua. Reprinted by permission of Aunt Lute Books, San Francisco, CA.

Peter DeVries, "Different Cultural Levels Eat Here," from *Without A Stitch in Time*, copyright © 1972 by Peter DeVries. Reprinted by permission of Little, Brown & Co.

(Continued on page 393)

✳ CONSULTANTS

Gabino Tlamatini Aguirre
Principal
Community High School
Moorpark, California

David Alcoze
Teacher
Gaston Middle School
Dallas School District
Dallas, Texas

Jane Braunger
Language Arts Specialist
Curriculum Department
Portland Public Schools
Portland, Oregon

Marie Duffey
Teacher
San Leandro High School
San Leandro, California

Sandra E. Gibbs
Educational Consultant
Urbana, Illinois

Angie Ginty
Second Language Coordinator
New York City Public Schools District 15
Brooklyn, New York

Edna Lisbon
English Department Chairman
Westlake High School
Fulton County School System
Atlanta, Georgia

Norman McRae
former Director of Social Studies
Detroit Public Schools
Detroit, Michigan

Brenda Rudman Padial
Teacher
Phillips Exeter Academy
Exeter, New Hampshire

Shawn Wong
Director, Asian American Studies
Department of American Ethnic Studies
University of Washington
Seattle, Washington

I want to thank my family, friends, students, and colleagues who have taught me about cultures and about teaching. Thank you for bringing so much love and fun into your "lessons." You made this anthology and teacher's guide possible. To Manuela Apparicio Ryce, Gail Harter, Ginny Cotsis, Gabe Serrano and family, Gabino Aguirre and family, Luzma Espinoza and others in *Lucha*, Michael Mora, Linda Van der Wyck, Andy Sawyer, Jane Braunger, Linda Christiansen, Carlin Syvanen, Maxine Rock and family, Carmen Meler and family, Gloria Johnson, Alice Goldfarb, Paul Artega and others at Chase Bag Company, Ted Cline, Ron Herndon and others in the Black United Front, my family on the East coast, and my students at Fillmore High School. Special thanks to Carol Mazer. To the hundreds of political and social activists with whom I have worked—at kitchen tables and on picket lines—and to our goal of making this a multicultural, classless, nonsexist society.

To Robert Mangus, who was principal of Fillmore High School, thanks for boldly promoting heterogeneous grouping in English classes.

To Rachel Farber, my editor at Addison-Wesley, who is so intelligent, diplomatic, and fun to work with. I feel fortunate to have been able to work with you.

My special gratitude to Judith Wild, Jackie Ellenz, and my mother Sylvia Goldfarb, who all patiently listened to me through my writing process and gave me the precious gifts of their support, ideas, and care.

Dave King, my husband and partner for life . . . Your encouragement, inspiration, your ideas and outlook are in this project. You have been my partner in *Hear My Voice*.

To the memory of my father, Jack Goldfarb.

L.K.
Portland, Oregon

✳ CONTENTS

FAMILY AND GENERATIONS

SOCIETY: CONFLICT, STRUGGLE, AND CHANGE

PERSONAL IDENTITY

CELEBRATIONS

✳

VISIONS AT A CROSSROADS

*I*taught English in Fillmore, a small town northeast of Los Angeles. After my students read some of the poems in this anthology, I asked them to write a poem about a place they knew using at least three words from a language other than English to help them evoke the feeling of this place. A junior in the class wrote the following poem about his home town.

FILLMORE/FILTROS[1]

*F*illmore is just a town
with not much to do
Half Hispanic and half Anglo
No one cares who is best,
or who is worst.
Las fiestas[2] are the only things that come alive.
Las calles[3] seem deserted at night
with the wind blowing the leaves
from place to place.
A few people gather, but not much to do.
It's another day
in el pueblo[4] de Fillmore.

Though years have passed, the author, Eric Rangel, still remembers his pleasure at having expressed his unique way of seeing the world.

Your own story is unique. It includes who you are and how you got to be the person you are. It tells about the people who raised you and influ-

---

1. Fillmore's nickname in Spanish is "Filtros."
2. Las fiestas—the parties.
3. Las calles—the streets
4. el pueblo—the town

enced you. Your story begins before your birth; your family's history is also part of it. How has your relative's past shaped them? How does it continue to shape you? In addition to the people in your life, the places where you have spent your time are telling parts of your narrative, whether you have lived in a small agricultural or industrial town, a bustling inner city, or a suburb. Your story provides a glimpse of your beliefs and traditions, your problems, fears, loves, and dreams, and the special way you relate to the world.

For too long, we have not been able to hear the individual voices expressing the diversity of the United States. Movies, mass media, and school texts have omitted or compressed beyond recognition the rich histories and contemporary cultures of Native Americans, African Americans, Asian Americans, many European Americans, and Latinos.

For too many generations, young people were expected to assimilate, or be absorbed into, the mainstream. People were expected to cast aside or at least downplay their own cultural heritage and blend into the "melting pot" of the United States. Many now feel that the rush to assimilate has to a significant degree homogenized culture in the United States, resulting in a loss of valuable history, science, art, music, and literature. In recent years, however, people have begun to redefine what it means to live in the United States. The image of a "salad," in which individual flavors remain distinct but contribute to the overall taste of the dish, is more apt and widely accepted than the "melting pot" metaphor. In other words, many have begun to recognize and value diversity within the United States.

In an enlightened multicultural society, individuals would be able to choose to retain their original cultures as well as enrich their lives through exposure to other cultures. If Spaceship Earth is to survive, we will need to make real the vision of a multicultural society in which individuality is encouraged, a variety of cultures flourish, and yet teamwork is demanded.

I hope that the stories you "hear" in this anthology will help you become more familiar with people of cultures other than your own, some of whom you may see daily, but may not really know. As you read this book, let the characters inform you of the circumstances of their lives and help you to understand the voices of those around you.

One last word before the stories begin: Storytelling is often contagious; it brings out the desire and power in the listener to tell stories of his or her own. I hope the literature in this volume will help inspire you to tell your own story.

B·O·R·D·E·R·S

SEVENTH GRADE
FROM *THE GOOD TIMES ARE KILLING ME*
Lynda Barry

Lynda Barry grew up in Seattle, Washington. At Evergreen State University she began producing cartoon strips that reflected her youth: her neighborhood, family, school, romances, and friends. Now a syndicated cartoonist and a novelist, she still writes about the complex emotions of teenagers. "Seventh Grade," excerpted from the novel The Good Times Are Killing Me, *explores how prejudice and group pressure affect friendships between black and white students.*

FROM THE FIRST DAY OF SEVENTH GRADE EVERYONE WAS NEW. Even if you had known them all of your whole life they were still new. And from the second we walked through the doors we all automatically split apart into groups of who was alike. Everyone knew exactly what to do, like someone was whispering instructions to our hands and eyes and feet and hair. Every kid from my old school, all of us who had ever lived on the same street together and played together all our lives stopped talking and walking with each other and never talked or walked with each other again.

This was our new main rule of life even though it wasn't us who created it. It just grew there, like big permanent teeth after baby teeth.

We had to constantly read books and poems about equality in English, and I wondered sometimes if Bonna ever thought of me the way I thought of her when I read them. *To Kill a Mocking Bird. A Raisin in The Sun:* "What happens to a dream deferred?"

If she didn't that's OK. It wouldn't hurt my feelings.

And we had to write our own stories and poems and discuss them and they would put us in a mood that felt so real and true to us because we could each write the answer and the answer was always the same: love each other, love each other, love each other. And we would really believe things could change until the bell would ring and we would go back out into the hallway and know there was no way some puny poem or story could ever touch this huge big thing. This Kal-Tiki The Immortal Monster.

There were a lot of fights. You would get pushed in the back on your way to class or pushed at your locker. One day I got shoved so bad I cracked my head against a toilet stall and when I turned around I saw who did it was a girl I didn't know standing with two other girls, and one of them was Bonna. For a second I forgot the rule of Bonna and me not talking anymore and I said "Why didn't you tell her? What'd you let her do it for, stupid?" And we both froze. Bonna didn't have a choice. By the time I tried to run it was too late. She pushed me into the corner and her friends stood there watching and I remember looking at her and not believing she would really hit me because I had been to her house, because I knew her mother, because inside we were still friends, we were, I knew it, and I knew she knew it, rules or no rules. When she raised up her hand and slapped my face hard I told her so, I said "Remember? Don't you even remember?" and I started crying, I couldn't help it, and she slapped me again and kept slapping me until I started naming everything in her house—the lamps, the chairs, the TV, the color of the walls, the couch, the rug, and I couldn't shut up and I couldn't shut up and the next thing I knew a teacher was yanking both of us by the arms and dragging us down the hall to the office just like I had seen girls being dragged every day since I got there.

We sat on two chairs in front of the secretary, waiting for the vice principal to come. I turned to look at Bonna and she was staring straight ahead and I could see the streaks on her face.

In the vice principal's office we acted like we had never met. Like all it was was any black girl slapping any white girl who had mouthed off to her, something that happened every single day and would just keep on happening world without end.

When he called my mother to tell her, she never knew the girl was Bonna, just like Bonna's father never knew the other girl was me.

FOR DISCUSSION AND WRITING

1. Did you and your classmates experience a transformation similar to the one Lynda Barry describes when you began junior high school or middle school? What changes in friendship patterns, if any, occurred when you left elementary school? I lost touch with all but 3 or 4 of my friends, they all just stopped calling me & stuff.

2. Why do you think the girls' friendship changed in the seventh grade and not earlier? because in seventh grade you start to really kind of understand the

3. What do you think would happen if the speaker in the story and Bonna were to meet again as adults? They probably wouldn't even say Hi, I think they'd ignor each-other.

4. In what ways can schools help slay "Kal-Tiki The Immortal Monster"? What books and materials might be useful? What could teachers and administrators do to help? Can dances, sporting events, or assemblies be structured to create friendships between groups? I think the school should do more group activities where the kids could really get to know each other and their personalities, I don't know that anything would change but they might. The teachers and stuff could teach more about other races and all the bad

IN RESPONSE TO EXECUTIVE ORDER 9066:
ALL AMERICANS OF JAPANESE DESCENT
MUST REPORT TO RELOCATION CENTERS

Dwight Okita

During World War II President Franklin D. Roosevelt signed Executive Order 9066 that mandated people of Japanese ancestry on the West Coast be confined in internment camps. Dwight Okita's parents were among the 120,000 Japanese-American citizens forced to go to such camps. His father was released to fight in Europe with the Japanese-American 442nd Regiment, the most decorated Army brigade in United States history, while Okita's mother remained in the camp. This poem shows how experiences of internment are still vivid for many Japanese-American families.

DEAR SIRS:
Of course I'll come. I've packed my galoshes
and three packets of tomato seeds. Denise calls them
"love apples." My father says where we're going
they won't grow.

I am a fourteen-year-old girl with bad spelling
and a messy room. If it helps any, I will tell you
I have always felt funny using chopsticks
and my favorite food is hot dogs.
My best friend is a white girl named Denise—
we look at boys together. She sat in front of me
all through grade school because of our names:
O'Connor, Ozawa. I know the back of Denise's head very well.
I tell her she's going bald. She tells me I copy on tests.
We're best friends.

I saw Denise today in Geography class.
She was sitting on the other side of the room.
"You're trying to start a war," she said, "giving secrets away
to the Enemy, Why can't you keep your big mouth shut?"
I didn't know what to say.

I gave her a packet of tomato seeds
and asked her to plant them for me, told her
when the first tomato ripened
she'd miss me.

FOR DISCUSSION AND WRITING

1. Why does the speaker in the poem have no response to Denise?

2. Do you think the seeds are an appropriate gift? Why or why not?

3. To whom is this poem written? Is the poem effective in letter form?

4. Do you think that a situation like the Japanese internment could happen today in the United States? Who might be targeted as enemies of the United States? What could you do to prevent such an incident?

Photographer unknown, Japanese-American Neighborhood, Sienega, California, 1932

WHO SAID WE ALL HAVE TO TALK ALIKE
Wilma Elizabeth McDaniel

Wilma Elizabeth McDaniel was raised in rural Oklahoma. She moved to California in the dust bowl migration of the Great Depression and lives in California's San Joaquin Valley. The heroine of the following story is from the Ozark Mountains of Arkansas, just east of the Oklahoma state line. She, too, tries to begin a new life in California, but she finds that linguistic obstacles hinder the fulfillment of her dream. This story raises several questions about dialects and accents, including the one asked in the title: "Who Said We All Have to Talk Alike."

WHO KNOWS HOW NEFFIE PIKE'S SPEECH PATTERN WAS FORMED? Her Ozark family had talked the same way for generations. They added an "r" to many words that did not contain that letter. In spite of this, or because of it, their speech was clear and colorful and to the point. Most people understood what they were talking about, exactly.

Neffie was her parent's daughter. She called a toilet, "torelet," and a woman, "worman," very comfortably. The teacher at the country school never attempted to change Neffie's manner of speaking. She said that Neffie had a fine imagination and should never allow anyone to squelch it. In fact, Neffie never really knew that she talked different from most other people.

People in the tiny community of Snowball really loved Neffie. She was a good neighbor, unfailingly cheerful and helpful. The appearance of her tall and boney figure at the door of a sickroom or a bereaved family meant comfort and succor. A great woman, everyone in Snowball agreed.

She would have probably lived her life out in the same lumber house if her husband had not died. In the months that followed his death she developed a restless feeling. Home chores, church and charity work did not seem to be enough to occupy her mind. She started to read big town newspapers at the library in nearby Marshall, something new for her. She became especially interested in the out of state employment want ads. She mentioned to neighbors, "They are a lot of good jobs out there in the world."

One day she came home from Marshall and stopped at old Grandma

Meade's house. She sat down in a canebottom chair and announced, "I have got me a job in California. I am a selling my house and lot to a couple of retired people from Little Rock. They will be moving in the first of June."

Grandma Meade sat in shocked silence for several seconds, then said, "Honey, I do not believe it. I mean that I never in the world imagined that you would consider leaving Snowball. You and Lollis was so happy together here." Her voice trailed off, "Of course nobody could foretell the Lord would call him so young."

Neffie looked stonily at her and said with her usual clarity, "A widder worman is a free worman, especially if she don't have no children. She ought to be free to come and go like she pleases. After all, I am only fifty-one years old. I can do as much work as I ever did. This job is taking care of two little girls while their mother works at some high paying job. She has already sent me a bus ticket. I would be a fool not to go. Everyone has been to California except me. I always hankered to see the state for myself. Now is my chance to see some of the rest of the world. It may sound foolish, but it will sort of be like having a dorter of my own and grandchildren. I aim to write you a long letter when I get settled down out there."

Neffie left for California on schedule. After two weeks Grandma Meade began to worry a bit. She said, "I thought that Neffie surely would have dropped us a line by now. The last thing she told me was that she would write me a long letter. Well, maybe she hasn't got settled down yet."

A month passed without any word from Neffie.

Bug Harrison was at Grandma Meade's house when Neffie returned the day after Snowball's big Fourth of July celebration.

Neffie put her suitcases down and began at the beginning. "Grandma, you was so right about so many things. I knowed I was in trouble hock-deep, only one minute after I stepped off that bus in California. A purty young worman come forward to meet me and said she was Beryl. I busted out and told her, 'My, you are a purty worman, even purtier than your pitcher.' She kinda shrunk back and looked at me like I had used a cussword. She stood there holding her little girls' hands and asked me, where on earth did you hear a word like worman, was it a female worm of some kind? She said, 'Worman is woe-man,' like you say woh to a horse.

"Her remark nearly knocked me off my feet. I felt like a fool, and I didn't even know why. My stomach started churning. I durst not say anything to defend myself, because I hadn't done anything wrong.

"We started walking to Beryl's station wagon in the parking lot. I told her that I never was blessed with a dorter or son, either. That set her off again. She said that her children were at a very impressionable age, that I would have to watch my speech and learn the correct pronunciation of words. She did not want them picking up incorrect speech patterns and something she called coll-oke-ism, something I had, and didn't even realize. I decided to shut up and get in the car. The worman had already paid for my fare. I felt that I had to at least give her a few months' service, if I could stand the punishment at all.

"On our way to Beryl's house, she stopped at a drive-in restaurant and ordered cheeseburgers and milkshakes for all of us. I decided to just eat and listen.

"It was sure a pleasurable drive on to Beryl's home. We followed the same county highway for the entire seven miles. The road was lined on both sides with pams, tall with them fronds waving in the breeze. It reminded me of pitchers I have seen of The Holy Land, really touched my heart. I forgot myself again and said that I never had seen pams before except in pitchers. Quick as a flash Beryl told me, 'They are pall-ms, not pams. There is an l in the word.' After that, I sure buttoned up my mouth. I just said yes or no to anything she asked me.

"Her house turned out to be a real nice place, bright and modern with every type of electrical gadget you could think of. There were four bedrooms, each with a bath. I was so tired and upset over Beryl's attitude that I begged off sitting up to visit with her and the little girls. I ran me a full tub of warm water and took me a long soaking bath. I fell into bed and went sound asleep. Worman, I plumb died away, slept all night without waking up. To show you how hard I slept, there was a fairly severe earthquake in the central part of California where Beryl lived. It even shook a few things off a living room shelf. I tell you, I wouldn't have heard Gabriel blow his horn that night.

"I woke up feeling relieved that it was Monday. Beryl left for work promptly at seven-thirty. That meant the girls and I had the house to ourselves. Worman, I am a telling you, they was two living dolls, Pat and Penny. I made them bran muffins for breakfast and scrambled some eggs. They ate until they nearly foundered. It seemed like they had never seen a bran muffin before, asked me if I would cook them the same thing each day.

"I told them I knew how to cook other good old homely dishes, too. Every day, I tried something new on them, biscuits and sausage and milk gravy, buttermilk pancakes, waffles, popovers, french toast, corn dodgers, fried mush. You name it, worman, I cooked it for those dolls. It wouldn't be no big deal for the kids here in Snowball, they was raised to eat like that, but it was hog heaven to Pat and Penny."

Grandma Meade had been listening intently, her eyes pinned on Neffie's face. Now she asked, "How did Beryl like your cooking?"

Neffie laughed heartily. She said, "To put it plain, she LOVED it. I can say that she never found any flaw in my cooking, only made one complaint connected with it. I boirled her a fine big cabbage and hamhock dinner and made cornbread for our supper one evening. When we started to sit down at the table, I said that it was a nice change to have a boirled dinner now and then. That set her off like a firecracker. She said, 'That is boil-ed, not boirled.' I decided to let that snide remark pass. I saw she started dishing up the food—she lit in on it like a starving hounddog. That showed what she thought of my cooking, didn't it? My cooking sure helped me get through them weeks as good as I did."

Bug Harrison broke in, "What were your duties during the day?"

Neffie said, "I was hired to take care of the two little girls. That is what I done. I cooked because people have to eat. I always have, always will. That didn't put no extra strain on me. The girls and I played the most of the day. They would sit on each arm of my chair and listen to me tell them about my life back in Arkansas. I didn't hold back nothing. I told them about haunted houses, ghosts, robbers, bank holdups, tornadoes, snakes, tarantulas, times when the river flooded and we had to float on a rooftop to save our lives. Lordy, worman, they just ate it up. They would listen to me with their eyes as big as saucers. I don't quite know why I done it, but I asked the girls not to tell their mother about my stories. They were as secretive as little private detectives until a week ago. They got so excited over one of my stories that they forgot theirselves. I was busy in the kitchen putting some homemade noodles into a pot of chicken broth. I heard Pat tell her mother, 'Mom, back in Arkansas where Neffie used to live, they are wormans that can tell fortunes for people. They can look right through your face and tell if you are telling the truth or a lie. They can rub your warts with skunk oirl and say some words and all the warts will fall off, never ever come back.' I figured I was in bad trouble, but I kept on dropping the noodles into the broth. I was a hundred percent right about the trouble.

"Beryl blowed her stack. She marched right back to the kitchen with the girls at her heels. She stood in the door and said, 'I have been afraid of this very thing. Neffie, I just can't keep you on any longer.'

"At that point Pat and Penny throwed themselves down on the floor and started bawling like two young calves. Pat sobbed out real angry-like, 'Yes, you CAN keep Neffie! She is the best storyteller in the whole world and the best cooker. If she goes home to Arkansas, we won't never have no more biscuits and sausage and gravy.' The tears began to run down her little face.

"Beryl stood there with her face like a flintrock. It looked like she wanted to be nice to me, but that her duty come first with her. She drawed in her breath and said, 'Neffie, you are as good and kind and honest as you can be, exceptional, but your speech is totally unacceptable. My children are at a very impressionable age. I have tried to overlook it, but they are definitely being influenced in the wrong direction. They say dorter and orter with regularity. This pattern must be eradicated immediately. I shall be happy to pay your traveling expenses home. You can look on this trip out West as my vacation gift to you.' I could see that her mind was made up and she wasn't going to change it.

"I did think to ask her if she had some other babysitter in mind. I didn't want to run out and leave her in a bind without one. She said there was a young girl from the college who wanted day work, so she could attend night classes. She thought that would work out great. I got her point. The college girl would be different from me, more to suit Beryl.

"Well, to shorten my story, she bought me a big box of real expensive chocolates and put me on the bus with my paid ticket, just like she had promised. She and the girls stood there beside the bus waiting for it to pull out. Penny looked up at me and blew me a kiss. I heard her say as plain as plain could be, 'Neffie, you are a sweet worman.' Then I saw Beryl put her hand over Penny's mouth. Right then, the bus pulled out of the depot and I lost sight of them.

"Worman, I done a lot of thinking as that bus rolled along the highway. I would eat a chocolate and think over my experience with Beryl. Things kind of cleared up in my mind, like having blinders taken off of my eyes. I saw I had really been ignorant of some things that other folks knowed. I didn't talk right to suit some of them, but that wasn't my fault. *I didn't know we was all supposed to talk the same way.* I thought people hadn't all talked the same since before God tore down their tower at Babel and confused all their tongues. Folks all over the world have talked different ever since then. I guess some of them like Beryl want to go back to pre-Babel days. Anyway, it was sure an eye-opener to me, hurt me, too. Beryl just plain separated herself from me. It was like she took a sharp knife and cut a melon in half, and throwed away the half that was me. You know what you do with a piece of melon you don't want. You throw it with the rinds into the garbage can. Worman, who said that we all have to talk alike? Can anyone tell me that?"

FOR DISCUSSION AND WRITING

1. Do you agree with Beryl that Neffie was not suitable to take care of the children? What would you do if you were in Beryl's situation? How would you feel if your children learned to speak like Neffie? What qualities are important in taking care of children? Explain your views.

2. Who decides whether a certain form of English is correct? Who speaks proper English? What do you think should be the standards for correct English?

3. Do people in your area speak with a particular accent or style of grammar? Can you think of ways of speaking that are different from the English television newscasters use?

4. Can you think of a time you have felt prejudice toward a person based only on his or her speech pattern? Have you assumed someone was ignorant or intelligent without knowing anything else about them besides their accent?

5. Why do you think people are sensitive when criticized about their accents or dialects?

PATHS UPON WATER
Tahira Naqvi

Tahira Naqvi immigrated to the United States from Pakistan and currently lives in Connecticut. In the following story, Sakina Bano, also from Pakistan, visits her son in the United States and confronts styles of dress and behavior that are very different from her own traditions.

THERE HAD BEEN LITTLE WARNING, actually none at all to prepare her for her first encounter with the sea. At breakfast that morning, her son Raza said, "Ama, we're going to the seaside today. Jamil and Hameeda are coming with us." She had been turning a *paratha* in the frying pan, an onerous task since she had always fried *parathas* on a flat pan with open sides, and as the familiar aroma of dough cooking in butter filled the air around her, she smiled happily and thought, I've only been here a week and already he wants to show me the sea.

Sakina Bano had never seen the sea. Having lived practically all her life in a town which was a good thousand miles from the nearest shoreline, her experience of the sea was limited to what she had chanced to observe in pictures. One picture, in which greenish-blue waves heaved toward a gray sky, she could recollect clearly; it was from a calendar Raza brought home the year he started college in Lahore. The calendar had hung on a wall of her room for many years only to be removed when the interior of the house was whitewashed for her daughter's wedding, and in the ensuing confusion it was misplaced and never found. The nail on which the calendar hung had stayed in the wall since the painter, too lazy to bother with detailed preparation, had simply painted around the nail and over it; whenever Sakina Bano happened to glance at the forgotten nail she remembered the picture. Also distinct in her memory was a scene from a silly Urdu film she had seen with her cousin's wife Zohra and her nieces Zenab and Amina during a rare visit to Lahore several years ago. For some reason she hadn't been able to put it out of her mind. On a brown and white beach, the actor Waheed Murad, now dead but then affectedly handsome and boyish, pursued the actress Zeba, who skipped awkwardly before him—it isn't at all proper for a woman to be skipping in a public place. Small foam-crested waves lapped up to her, making her *shalwar* stick to her skinny legs, exposing the outline of her thin calves. Why, it was just as bad as baring her legs, for what cover could the wet, gossamer-like fabric of the *shalwar* provide?

The two frolicked by an expanse of water that extended to the horizon and which, even though it was only in a film, had seemed to Sakina Bano frightening in its immensity.

"Will Jamal and his wife have lunch here?" she asked, depositing the dark, glistening *paratha* gently on Raza's plate. She would have to take out a packet of meat from the freezer if she was to give them lunch, she told herself while she poured tea in her son's cup.

"No, I don't think so. I think we'll leave before lunch. We can stop somewhere along the way and have a bite to eat."

"They'll have tea then." She was glad Raza had remembered to pick up a cake at the store the night before (she didn't know why he called it a pound cake), and she would make some rice *kheer*.

If she had anything to do with it, she would avoid long trips and spend most of her time in Raza's apartment cooking his meals and watching him eat. The apartment pleased her. The most she would want to do would be to go out on the lawn once in a while and examine her surroundings.

Bordering each window on the outside, were narrow white shutters; these had reminded her of the stiffened icing on a cake served at her niece Amina's birthday once. And on the face of the building the white paint seemed impervious to the effects of the elements. Discolorations or cracks were visible, and she had indeed craned her neck until it hurt while she scrutinized it.

The apartment building was set against a lawn edged with freshly green, sculptured bushes, evenly thick with grass that looked more like a thick carpet than just grass. Located in a quiet section of town, the apartments overlooked a dark, thickly wooded area, a park, Raza had told her. Although tired and groggy on the evening of her arrival from Pakistan, she had not failed to take note of the surroundings into which she found herself. Her first thought was, 'Where is everybody?' while to her son she said, "How nice everything is."

Looking out the window of his sitting room the next morning, she was gladdened at the thought of her son's good fortune. The morning sky was clear like a pale blue, unwrinkled *dupatta* that has been strung out on a line to dry. Everything looked clean, so clean. Was it not as if an unseen hand had polished the sidewalks and swept the road? They now glistened like new metal. 'Where do people throw their trash?' she wondered when she went down to the lawn again, this time with Raza, and gazed out at the shiny road, the rows and rows of neat houses hedged in by such neat white wooden fences. In hasty answer to her own query, she told herself not to be foolish; this was *Amreeka*. Here trash was in its proper place, hidden from view and no doubt disposed of in an appropriate manner. No blackened banana peels redolent with the odor of neglect here, or rotting orange skins, or worse, excrement and refuse to pollute the surroundings and endanger human habitation.

She had sighed in contentment. Happiness descended upon her tangibly like a heavy blanket affording warmth on a chilly morning. Once again, she thanked her Maker. Was He not good to her son?

"Is the sea far from here?" she asked casually, brushing imaginary crumbs from the edges of her plate. Raza must never feel she didn't value his eagerness to show off his new environment. This was his new world after all. If he wanted to take her to the seaside, then seaside it would be. Certainly she was not about to be fussy and upset him.

"No, *Ama*, not too far. An hour-and-a-half's drive, that's all. Do you feel well?" His eyes crinkled in concern as he put aside the newspaper he had been reading to look at her.

She impatiently waved a hand in the air, secretly pleased at his solicitude. "Yes, yes, I'm fine son. Just a little cough, that's all. Now finish your tea and I'll make you another cup." She knew how much he liked tea. Before she came, he must have had to make it for himself. Such a chore for a man if he must make his own tea.

The subject of the sea didn't come up again until Jamil and his new bride arrived. Jamil, an old college friend of Raza's, angular like him, affable and solicitous, was no stranger to Sakina Bano. But she was meeting his wife Hameeda for the first time. Like herself, the girl was also a newcomer to this country.

"*Khalaji*, the sea's so pretty here, the beaches are so-o-o-o large, nothing like the beaches in Karachi," Hameeda informed Sakina Bano over tea, her young, shrill voice rising and falling excitedly, her lips, dark and fleshy with lipstick, wide open in a little girl's grin. There's wanderlust in her eyes already, Sakina Bano mused, trying to guess her age. Twenty-one or twenty-two. She thought of the girl in Sialkot she and her daughter had been considering for Raza. Was there really a resemblance? Perhaps it was only the youth.

"Well child, for me it will be all the same. I've never been to Karachi. Here, have another slice of cake, you too Jamil, and try the *kheer.*"

For some reason Sakina Bano couldn't fathom, sitting next to the young girl whose excitement at the prospect of a visit to the seaside was as undisguised as a child's preoccupation with a new toy, she was suddenly reminded of the actress Zeba. The image of waves lapping on her legs and swishing about her nearly bare calves rose in Sakina Bano's mind again. Like the arrival of an unexpected visitor, a strange question crossed her mind: were Hameeda's legs also skinny like Zeba's?

Drowned in the clamor for the *kheer* which had proven to be a great hit and had been consumed with such rapidity she wished she had made more, the question lost itself.

"*Khalaji*, you must tell Hameeda how you make this," Jamil was saying, and Hameeda hastily interjected, "I think you used a lot of milk."

"Have more," Sakina Bano said.

Tea didn't last long. Within an hour they were on their way to the sea, all of them in Raza's car. Jamil sat in the front with his friend, and Sakina Bano and Hameeda sat in the back, an unfortunate arrangement, Sakina Bano discovered after they had driven for what seemed to her like an hour. It wasn't Hameeda's persistent prattle that vexed her, she realized, it was her perfume. So pungent she could feel it wafting into her nostrils, it irritated the insides of her nose, and then traveled down her throat like the sour after-taste of an overripe orange. But her discomfort was short-lived; soon she became drowsy and idled into sleep.

. . .

To be sure she had heard stories of people who swam in the ocean. She wasn't so foolish as to presume that swimming was undertaken fully clothed. After all, many times as a child she had seen young boys and men from her village swim, dressed in nothing but loincloths as they jumped into the muddy waters of the canal that irrigated their fields. But what was this?

As soon as Raza parked the car in a large, compound-like area fenced in by tall walls of wire mesh, and when her dizziness subsided, Sakina Bano glanced out of the window on her left. Her attention was snagged by what she thought was a naked woman. Certain that she was still a little dazed from the long drive, her vision subsequently befogged, Sakina Bano thought nothing of what she had seen. Then the naked figure moved closer. Disbelief gave way to the sudden, awful realization that the figure was indeed real and if not altogether naked, very nearly so.

A thin strip of colored cloth shaped like a flimsy brassiere loosely held the woman's breasts, or rather a part of her breasts; and below, beneath the level of her belly button, no, even lower than that, Sakina Bano observed in horror, was something that reminded her of the loincloths the men and youths in her village wore when they swam or worked on a construction site in the summer.

The girl was pretty, such fine features, hair that shone like a handful of gold thread, and she was young too, not much older than Hameeda perhaps. But the paleness of her skin was marred by irregular red blotches that seemed in dire need of a cooling balm. No one with such redness should be without a covering in the sun, Sakina Bano offered in silent rebuke.

The woman opened the door of her car, which was parked alongside Raza's, and as she leaned over to retrieve something from the interior of her car, Sakina Bano gasped. When the young female lowered her body, her breasts were not only nearly all bared, but stood in imminent danger of spilling out of their meager coverage. O God! Is there no shame here? Sakina Bano's cheeks burned. Hastily she glanced away. In the very next instant she stole a glimpse at her son from the corners of her eyes, anxiously wondering if he too were experiencing something of what she was going through; no, she noted with a mixture of surprise and relief, he and Jamil were taking things out from the trunk of their car. They did not show any signs of discomfort. Did she see a fleeting look of curiosity on Hameeda's face? There was something else, too, she couldn't quite decipher.

Relieved that her male companions were oblivious to the disturbing view of the woman's breasts, Sakina Bano sighed sadly. She shook her head, adjusted her white, chiffon *dupatta* over her head, and slowly eased her person out of her son's car.

The taste of the sea was upon her lips in an instant. Mingled with an occasional but strong whiff of Hameeda's perfume, the smell of fish filled her nostrils and quickly settled in her nose as if to stay there forever.

Milling around were countless groups of scantily clad people, men, women, and children, coming and going in all directions. Is all of *Amreeka* here? she asked herself uneasily. Feeling guilty for having judged Zeba's contrived imprudence on film a little too harshly, she tightened her *dupatta* about her and wondered why her son had chosen to bring her to this place. Did he not know his mother? She was an old woman, and the mother of a son, but she would not surrender to anger or derision and make her son uncomfortable. His poise and confidence were hers too, were they not? Certainly he had brought her to the sea for a purpose. She must not appear ungrateful or intolerant.

While Raza and Jamil walked on casually and without any show of awkwardness, laughing and talking as though they might be in their sitting room rather than a place crowded with people in a state of disconcerting undress, she and Hameeda followed closely behind. Her head swam as she turned her eyes from the glare of the sun and attempted to examine the perturbing nakedness around her.

Sakina Bano's memories of nakedness were short and limited, extending to the time when she bathed her younger brother and sister under the water pump in the courtyard of her father's house, followed by the period in which she bathed her own three children until they were old enough to do it themselves. Of her own nakedness she carried an incomplete image; she had always bathed sitting down, on a low wooden stool.

Once, and that too shortly before his stroke, she came upon her husband getting out of his *dhoti* in their bedroom. Standing absently near the foot of his bed as if waiting for something or someone, the *dhoti* a crumpled heap about his ankles, he lifted his face to look at her blankly when she entered, but made no attempt to move or cover himself. Not only did she have to hand him his pajamas, she also had to assist him as he struggled to pull up first one leg and then the other. A week later he suffered a stroke, in another week he was gone. It had been nearly ten years since he died. But for some reason the image of a naked disoriented man in the middle of a room clung to her mind like permanent discolorations on a well-worn copper pot.

And there was the unforgettable sharp and unsullied picture of her mother's body laid out on a rectangular slab of cracked, yellowed wood for a pre-burial bath, her skin, ash-brown, laced with a thousand wrinkles, soft, like wet, rained-on mud.

But nothing could have prepared her for this. Nakedness, like all things in nature, has a purpose, she firmly told herself as the four of them trudged toward the water.

The July sun on this day was not as hot as the July sun in Sialkot, but a certain oily humidity had begun to attach itself to her face and hands. Lifting a corner of her white *dupatta*, she wiped her face with it. Poor Hameeda, no doubt she too longed to divest herself of the *shalwar* and *qamis* she was wearing and don a swimming suit so she could join the rest of the women on the beach, be more like them. But could she swim?

They continued onward, and after some initial plodding through hot, moist sand, Sakina Bano became sure-footed; instead of having to drag her feet through the weighty volume of over-heated sand, she was now able to tread over it with relative ease. They were receiving stares already, a few vaguely curious, others unguardedly inquisitive.

Where the bodies ended she saw the ocean began, stretching to the horizon in the distance. The picture she had carried in her head of the boyish actor Waheed Murad running after Zeba on a sandy Karachi beach quickly diminished and faded away. The immensity of the sea on film was reduced to a mere blue splash of color, its place usurped by a vastness she could scarce hold within the frame of her vision; a window opened in her head, she drew in the wonder of the sea as it touched the hem of the heavens and, despite the heat, Sakina Bano shivered involuntarily. God's touch is upon the world, she silently whispered to herself.

Again and again, as she had made preparations for the journey across what she liked to refer to as the 'seven seas,' she had been told *Amreeka* was so large that many Pakistans could fit into it. The very idea of Pakistan fitting into anything else was cause for bewilderment, and the analogy left her at once befuddled and awed. But had she expected this?

The bodies sprawled before her on the sand and exposed to the sun's unyielding rays seemed unmindful of what the ocean might have to say about God's touch upon the world. Assuming supine positions, flat either on their backs or their bellies, the people on the beach reminded Sakina

Bano of whole red chilies spread on a rag discolored from overuse, and left in the sun to dry and crackle. As sweat began to form in tiny droplets across her forehead and around her mouth, the unhappy thought presented itself to her that she was among people who had indeed lost their sanity.

In summer, one's first thought is to put as much distance as possible between oneself and the sun. Every effort is made to stay indoors; curtains are drawn and jalousies unfurled in order to shut out the fire the sun exudes. In the uneasy silence of a torrid June or July afternoon, even stray dogs seek shade under a tree or behind a bush, curling up into fitful slumber as the sun beats its fervid path across the sky.

Sakina Bano couldn't understand why these men and women wished to scorch their bodies, and why, if they were here by the shore of an ocean which seemed to reach up to God, they didn't at least gaze wide-eyed at the wonder which lay at their feet. Why did they choose instead to shut their eyes and merely wallow in the heat. Their skins had rebelled, the red and darkly-pink blotches spoke for themselves. Perhaps this is a ritual they must, of necessity, follow, she mused. Perhaps they yearn to be brown as we yearn to be white.

She felt an ache insidiously putter behind her eyes. The sun always gave her a headache, even in winter, the only season when sunshine evoked pleasing sensations, when one could look forward to its briskness, its sharp touch. The heat from the sand under the *dari* on which she and Hameeda now sat seeped through the coarse fabric after a while and hugged her thighs; as people in varying shades of pink, white and red skin ran or walked past them, particles of sand flew in the air and landed on her clothes, her hands, her face. Soon she felt sand in her mouth, scraping between her teeth like the remains of *chalia*, heavy on her tongue.

Ignoring the sand in her mouth and the hot-water-bottle effect of the sand beneath her thighs, Sakina Bano shifted her attention first toward a woman on her left, and then to the man on her right whose stomach fell broadly in loose folds (like dough left out overnight); he lay supine and still, his face shielded by a straw hat. Puzzled by the glitter on their nakedness, she peered closely and with intense concentration—she had to observe if she were to learn anything. The truth came to her like a flash of sudden light in a dark room: both the man and the woman had smeared their bodies with some kind of oil! Just then she remembered the oversized cucumbers she had encountered on her first trip to the Stop and Shop; shiny and slippery, one fell from her hands as she handled them, and she exclaimed in disbelief, "They've been greased!" How amused Raza had been at her reaction.

It's really very simple, Sakina Bano finally decided, sighing again, these people wish to be fried in the sun. But why? Not wishing to appear ignorant, she kept her mouth shut, although if she had addressed the query to Hameeda, she was sure she would not have received a satisfactory reply. The girl was a newcomer like herself. In addition, she was too young to know the answers to questions which warranted profound thought preceded by profound scrutiny. She didn't look very comfortable either; perhaps the heat was getting to her, too.

Raza and Jamil, both in swimming trunks, appeared totally at ease as they ran to the water and back, occasionally wading in a wave that gently slapped the beach and sometimes disappearing altogether for a second or two under a high wave. Then Sakina Bano couldn't tell where they were. They certainly seemed to be having a good time.

She and Hameeda must be the only women on the beach fully clothed, she reflected, quite a ridiculous sight if one were being viewed from the vantage point of those who were stretched out on the sand. And while Sakina Bano grappled with this disturbing thought, she saw the other woman approaching.

Attired in a *sari* and accompanied by a short, dark man (who had to be her son for he undoubtedly had her nose and her forehead) and an equally short, dark woman, both of whom wore swimming suits (the girl's as brief as that of the woman Sakina Bano had seen earlier in the parking lot), she looked no older than herself. Clutching the front folds of her *sari* as if afraid a sudden wind from the ocean might pull them out unfurling the *sari*, leaving her exposed, she tread upon the sand with a fiercely precarious step, looking only ahead, her eyes shielded with one small, flat palm.

This is how I must appear to the others, Sakina Bano ruminated. Suddenly, she felt a great sadness clutching at her chest and rising into her throat like a sigh as she watched the woman in the *sari* begin to make herself comfortable on a large, multi-colored towel thrown on the sand by her son and his wife; those two hurriedly dashed off in the direction of the water. Why are they in such haste? Sakina Bano wondered.

Her knees drawn up, one arm tensely wrapped around them, the woman appeared to be watching her son and her daughter-in-law. But could Sakina Bano really be sure? The woman's hand against her forehead concealed her eyes. As she continued to observe the woman's slight figure around which the green and orange cotton *sari* had been carelessly draped, she wondered what part of India she might be from. Perhaps the south, which meant she spoke no Hindi, which also meant a conversation would not be at all possible.

Sakina Bano's attention returned to Hameeda who had not said a word all this time. Like a break-through during muddled thought, it suddenly occurred to Sakina Bano that there was a distinct possibility Hameeda would be swimming if it weren't for her. In deference to her older companion she was probably foregoing the chance to swim. Will Raza's wife also wear a scant swimming suit and bare her body in the presence of strange men? The question disturbed her; she tried to shrug it aside. But it wouldn't go away. Stubbornly it returned, not alone this time but accompanied by the picture of a young woman who vaguely resembled the actress Zeba and who was clothed, partially, in a swimming suit much like the ones Sakina Bano saw about her. Running behind her was a man, not Waheed Murad, but alas, her own son, her Raza. Was she dreaming, had the sun weakened her brain? Such foolishness. Sakina Bano saw that Hameeda was staring ahead, like the woman on the towel, her eyes squinted because of the glare. Frozen on her full, red lips was a hesitant smile.

Once again Sakina Bano sought her son's figure among the throng near the water's edge. At first the brightness of the sun blinded her and she couldn't see where he was. She strained her eyes, shielding them from the sun with a hand on her forehead. And finally she spotted him. He and Jamil were talking to some people. A dark man and a dark girl. The son and daughter-in-law of the woman in the *sari*. Were they acquaintances then, perhaps friends? The four of them laughed like old friends, the girl standing so close to Raza he must surely be able to see her half-naked breasts. The poor boy!

They had begun to walk toward where she and Hameeda were seated. Raza was going to introduce his friends to his mother. How was she to conceal her discomfort at the woman's mode of dress?

"*Ama,* I want you to meet Ajit and Kamla. Ajit works at Ethan Allen with me. Kamla wants you to come to their house for dinner next Sunday."

Both Ajit and Kamla lifted their hands and said *"Namaste,"* and she nodded and smiled. What does one say in answer to *namaste,* anyway?

Hameeda was also introduced. Kamla made a joke about "the shy new bride," Hameeda showed her pretty teeth in a smile, and then Kamla said, "You have to come, Auntie." Sakina Bano wondered why Raza appeared so comfortable in the presence of a woman who was nearly all naked. Even her loincloth was flimsy. Granted it wasn't as bad as some of the others she had been seeing around her, but it was flimsy nonetheless.

"Yes, it's very nice of you to invite us. It's up to Raza. He's usually so busy. But if he is free . . ."

"Of course I'm free next Sunday. We'd love to come, Kamla."

Kamla said, "Good! I'll introduce you and Auntie to my mother-in-law after a swim. Coming?" She laid a hand on Raza's arm and Sakina Bano glanced away, just in time to catch Hameeda's smile of surprise. Well, one's son can become a stranger too, even a good son like Raza.

"Sure. *Yar*, Ajit, are you and Kamla planning to go to the late show?"

"Yes we are. You? Do you have tickets?" Ajit wasn't a bad looking boy. But he didn't measure up to Raza. No, Raza's nose was straight and to the point, his forehead wide and his eyes well-illuminated. But he had changed somehow; she felt she was distanced from him. A son is always a son, she thought and smiled and nodded again as Ajit and Kamla uttered their *Namaste's* and returned to the water with Raza and Jamil.

"*Khalaji*, why don't we wet our feet before we go?" Hameeda suddenly asked her.

"Wet our feet?"

"Yes, *Khala*. Just dip our feet in sea water. Come on. You're not afraid of the water, are you?"

"No, child." She wasn't afraid. Her mind was playing tricks with her, filling her head with thoughts that had no place there. A change was welcome. "Yes, why not?" she said, as if speaking to herself. When she attempted to get up she found that her joints had stiffened painfully. "Here, girl, give me your hand." She extended an arm toward Hameeda. Why not, especially since they had come so far and she had suffered the heat for what had seemed like a very long time.

Hameeda had rolled up her *shalwar* almost to the level of her knees. How pretty her legs are, the skin hairless and shiny, like a baby's, and not skinny at all, Sakina Bano mused in surprise, and how quick she is to show them.

She must do the same, she realized. Otherwise Hameeda would think she was afraid. She pulled up one leg of her *shalwar* tentatively, tucked it at the waist with one swift movement of her right hand, then looked about her sheepishly. Hameeda was laughing.

"The other one too, *Khala!*"

Who would want to look at her aged and scrawny legs? And her husband was not around to glare at her in remonstration. Gingerly the other leg of the *shalwar* was also lifted and tucked in. How funny her legs looked, the hair on them all gray now and curly, the calves limp. Now both women giggled like schoolgirls. And Raza would be amused, he would think she was having a good time, Sakina Bano told herself.

Raza and Jamil burst into laughter when they saw the women approach. They waved. Sakina Bano waved back.

Holding the front folds of her *shalwar* protectively, Sakina Bano strode toward the water. As she went past the other woman in the *sari* she smiled at her. The woman gave her a startled look, and then, dropping the hand with which she had been shielding her eyes from the sun, she let her arm fall away from her knees, and following Sakina Bano with her gaze, she returned her smile.

"Wait for me," Sakina Bano called to Hameeda in a loud, happy voice, "wait, girl."

FOR DISCUSSION AND WRITING

1. The author presents the beach scene from the point of view of Raza's mother, Sakina. What details show how Sakina views the beach scene in which her son is comfortable? How would the beach scene be different if it were told from Raza's point of view?

2. What qualities can help a person adapt to a different culture? Do you have these qualities? What in your life indicates whether or not you are adaptable?

3. How open to change is Sakina Bano? Use the story to support your response.

NOTES FROM A FRAGMENTED DAUGHTER
Elena Tajima Creef

"Notes From A Fragmented Daughter," is an autobiographical memoir by the daughter of a Japanese mother and a white North Carolinan father. Elena Tajima Creef, a Ph.D. candidate in the History of Consciousness at the University of California, describes herself as "your basic half-Japanese gemini feminist, existentialist would-be writer of bad one-act comedy revues." In the following selection, her wry humor provides a balance for her explorations of World War II and Asian-American women's history and literature.

SOME PERSONAL SCENES

I. At an art gallery opening for local Asian American women artists, a tall white man in glasses, beard, and big hair bundled up into a ponytail hovers over a table full of sushi, chow mein, egg rolls, and teriyaki chicken. He looks at me awkwardly and attempts conversation. "Did you make any of the food? I notice you look kinda Asian."

2. Marion is half Chinese and half Japanese and I like the way his face looks. We sit and talk about what it means to have mixed backgrounds in a culture that can't tell Chinese apart from Japanese and where McDonald's still serves Shanghai Chicken McNuggets with teriyaki sauce.

3. I am fifteen and am sitting in the back seat of my best friend Doreen's Volkswagon Bug, when her uncle's new wife Clara climbs into the passenger seat and we are introduced. Clara speaks in tongues at the Ladies Prayer Meetings, and has seen angels in the sky through her Kodak Instamatic.
She turns to me and shouts in a thick New York accent,
"So what are you studying?"
I say, "English."
She says, "Gee, your English is very good.
How long have you been in this country?"
I say, "All of my life."
She shouts, "Are you Chinese?"
I say, "Japanese."
She says, "I admire your people very much!"
I smile and say, "Yes, and we are very good with our hands, too."

4. Katie Gonzales follows me around for one week at sixth grade summer camp, her left arm in a sling from a tetherball accident. "I'm gonna get you, you flat-faced chinaman." I want to tell her that I'm only half-Japanese, but the words stick in my mouth and instead, I call her a beaner and imagine I am twisting that left arm right off her brown skinny body.

5. Later, when I am thirteen, I bury my mother once and for all and decide to go Mexican. It makes a lot of sense. I am no longer Elena, I am now Elaina and I begin insisting I am Mexican wherever I go. With my long black hair, my sun-darkened skin, and my new name, I can pass and I am safe. For the next year, I obsessively hide my Japanese mother and deny my Japanese roots. No one is allowed to meet her. I do not let her answer the phone if I can help it, or go near the door if I can get there first. I sabotage the PTA's efforts to get her to come to their monthly meetings, and

I conveniently get dates mixed up for "Open House." I live in fear that someone will find out that my mother is Japanese and spread it around the classroom like a dirty rumor. I love it when people ask if I am Español, because it is safe, because it means I do not stand out.

6. My mother and I are getting out of the car at Builder's Emporium when a young, ugly, straw-haired man gets out of his truck and shouts that my mother has stolen his parking space. She says she doesn't know what he's talking about and he tells her to shut up her slant-eyed face. My heart is pounding as we shop for light fixtures and nails but we never say a thing.

7. It is a dark, wet, rainy Santa Cruz night, and I go to see "Tampopo"— your basic Japanese noodle western—by myself. I am in a very good mood and allow a balding middle-aged man with a burgundy plum scarf tied around his neck to make conversation with me in the lobby.

"I really love Japanese films, almost as much as I love Asian girls! I'm going to Taiwan next month to meet this woman I've been corresponding with. I really prefer Oriental women to American because (he whispers) there are so many 'feminists' in this town. You are Asian, aren't you? Don't tell me, let me guess. Japanese? Chinese? Hawaiian? Eurasian?" Idiot. I am the daughter of a World War II Japanese war bride who met and married my North Carolinan hillbilly father one fine day in 1949 while she was hanging up the laundry to dry. Nine months out of the year, I pose as a doctoral student—a historian of consciousness; the rest of the time, I am your basic half-Japanese postmodernist gemini feminist, existentialist would-be writer of bad one-act comedy revues, avid cat trainer, and closet reader of mademoiselle, cosmo, signs, diacritics, elle, tv guide, cultural critique, representations, people magazine, critical inquiry, national enquirer, feminist issues, house beautiful, architectural digest, country living, cat fancy, bird talk, mother jones, covert action, vogue, glamour, the new yorker, l.a. times, l.a. weekly, and sometimes penthouse forum.

So how do you like them apples, bub? If you come near me one more time with your touch-me-feel-you New Age Bagwan male sensitivity, I just may strangle you with the burgundy plum scarf you have tied around your neck.

The headlines blare: "They're Bringing Home Japanese Brides! Six thousand Americans in Japan have taken Japanese brides since 1945, and all the little Madam Butterflys are studying hamburgers, Hollywood and home on the range, before coming to live in the U.S.A."

Although she is not interviewed, my mother appears in one of the bright technicolor photographs in the January 19, 1952, issue of the *Saturday Evening Post.* She is the short one with the funny hairdo, hovering over an apple pie, smiling with her classmates in the American Red Cross "Brides' School" for Japanese Wives. While the article attempts to tell the postwar story of the Japanese war bride in general, it also tells the story of how my own American G.I. father met and married my Japanese mother in war-torn occupied Japan. It is, in essence, my own pictorial origin story.

There are over 45,000 Japanese women who married American servicemen after World War II and immigrated to the United States. I have been meeting and interviewing these women for the last few years for a collection of oral histories I hope to someday publish. I have been told over and over again by many of these women that they despise the name "war bride." There is something dirty and derogatory about this word, but rarely has anyone told me why. "Call us 'Shin Issei' (the New Immigrants)," they say. Or how about, "Japanese Wives of American Servicemen." Don't call us "war brides." They whisper, "It is not nice."

I am the daughter of a World War II Japanese war bride
who met and married my white North Carolinan hillbilly father
one fine day in 1949 while she was hanging up the laundry to dry.

There is no escaping this body made out of history,
war and peace,
two languages,
and two cultures.

My name is Elena June,
I am the youngest daughter of Chiyohi,
who is the only surviving daughter of Iso,
who was the daughter of the Mayor of Yokoze

and was the Village Beauty
born in the last century to a Japanese woman
whose name is now forgotten,
but who lived in the Meiji era
and loved to tell ghost stories.

FOR DISCUSSION AND WRITING

1. Creef presents a number of situations that anger or exasperate her. Which of these situations would bother you most?

2. What attitude does the author have toward Shanghai Chicken McNuggets with teriyaki sauce?

3. Why does the author choose the "note" form for this memoir? Do you feel that it is effective? Explain.

4. Creef presents situations in which she feels people acted ignorantly or disrespectfully toward her. Create an additional note in the author's style in which someone she meets for the first time acts appropriately.

5. Create a dialogue between Creef and her mother about one of the incidents in the selection.

DIFFERENT CULTURAL LEVELS EAT HERE
Peter De Vries

Peter De Vries, one of the most highly acclaimed comic novelists in the United States, is known for his intimate observations of social reality. In this story, he brings the reader into a coffee shop to witness a conflict between a customer and a counterman. De Vries uses the situation in the coffee shop to explore common difficulties among members of different cultural groups in understanding and communicating with one another.

WHEN THE COUNTERMAN GLANCED UP FROM THE GRILL on which he was frying himself a hamburger and saw the two couples come in the door, he sized them up as people who had spent the evening at the theatre or the Horse Show or something like that, from their clothes. They were all about the same age—in their early forties, he decided, as they sat down on stools at the counter. Except for them, the place was empty. At least, the front was. Al Spain, the proprietor, was sitting out in the kitchen working on a ledger.

The counterman drew four glasses of water, stopping once to adjust the limp handkerchief around his neck. He had been whistling softly and without continuity when they entered, and he kept it up as he set the water glasses down.

"Well, what's yours?" he asked, wiping his hands on his apron and beginning with the man on the end.

"Hamburger."

"Mit or mitout?"

The man paused in the act of fishing a cigarette out of a package and glanced up. He was a rather good-looking fellow with dark circles under his eyes that, together with the general aspect of his face, gave him a sort of charred look. "Mit," he said at length.

The counterman moved down. "And yours?" he asked the woman who was next.

"I'll have a hamburger, too."

"Mit or mitout?"

The second woman, who had a gardenia pinned in her hair, leaned to her escort and started to whisper something about "a character," audibly, it happened, for the counterman paused and turned to look at her. Her escort jogged her with the side of his knee, and then she noticed the counterman watching her and stopped, smiling uneasily. The counterman looked at her a moment longer, then turned back to the other woman. "I'm sorry I didn't get that," he said. "Was that mit or mitout?"

She coughed into her fist and moved her bag pointlessly on the counter. "Mit," she said.

"That's two mits," the counterman said, and moved on down to the next one, the woman with the gardenia. "And yours?"

She folded her fingers on the counter and leaned toward him. "And what would we come here for except a hamburger?" She smiled sociably, showing a set of long, brilliant teeth.

"Mit or mitout?" he asked flatly.

She wriggled forward on the stool and smiled again. "May I ask a question?"

"Sure."

"Why do you say 'mit or mitout'?" Her escort jogged her again with his knee, this time more sharply.

The counterman turned around and picked up a lighted cigarette he had left lying on the ledge of the pastry case.

He took a deep inhale, ground the butt out underfoot, and blew out the smoke. "To find out the customer's wish," he said. "And now, how did you want it?"

"I think mitout," she said. "I like onions, but they don't like me."

"And yours?" he asked the remaining man.

"I'll have a hamburger, too," the man said. He fixed his eyes on a box of matches in his hands, as though steeling himself.

"Mit or mitout?"

The man fished studiously in the matchbox. "Mitout."

The four watched the counterman in complete silence as he took the hamburger patties from a refrigerator and set them to frying on the grill. They all wanted coffee, and he served it now. After slicing open four buns, he returned to his own sandwich. He put the meat in a bun and folded it closed, the others watching him as though witnessing an act of legerdemain. Conscious of their collective gaze, he turned his head, and scattered their looks in various directions. Just then the phone rang. The counterman set his sandwich down and walked past the four customers to answer it. He paused with his hand on the receiver a moment, finished chewing, swallowed, and picked up the phone.

"Al's," he announced, his elbows on the cigarette counter. "Oh, hello, Charlie," he said brightening, and straightened up. "How many? . . . Well, that's a little steep right now. I can let you have half of that, is all. . . . O. K., shoot. . . . That's nine mits and three mitouts, right? . . . Check. . . . That'll be O.K." He consulted the clock overhead. "Send the kid over then. So long."

He hung up and was on his way back to the grill when he became aware that the woman with the gardenia was whispering to her escort again. He stopped, and stood in front of her with his hands on his hips. "I beg your pardon, but what was that remark, lady?"

"Nothing."

"You passed a remark about me, if I'm not mistaken. What was it?"

"I just said you were wonderful."

"I was what?"

"Wonderful."

"That's what I thought." He went back to the hamburgers, which needed attention.

As he turned them in silence, the woman regarded him doubtfully. "What's the matter?" she asked at last, ignoring the nudging from her friends on either side.

The counterman's attention remained stonily fixed on his work.

"Is something wrong?" the woman asked.

The counterman lowered the flame, stopping to check it, and straightened up. "Maybe," he said, not looking at her.

She looked at her friends with a gesture of appeal. "But what?"

"Maybe I'm sore."

"What are you sore about?" the woman's escort asked. "She only said you were wonderful."

"I know what that means in her book."

"What?"

The counterman turned around and faced them. "We have a woman comes in here," he said, "who everything's wonderful to, too. She's got a dog she clips. When she hits a cab driver without teeth who doesn't know any streets and you got to show him how to get to where you want to go, he's wonderful. Fellow with a cap with earlaps come in here with some kind of a bird in his pocket one night when she was here. He had a coat on but no shirt and he sung tunes. *He* was wonderful. Everything is wonderful, till I can't stand to hear her talk to whoever she's with any more. This lady reminds me a lot of her. I got a picture of *her* all right going home and telling somebody I'm wonderful."

"But by wonderful she means to pay you a———"

"I know what wonderful means. You don't have to tell me. Saloons full of old junk, they're wonderful, old guys that stick cigar butts in their pipe———"

"The lady didn't mean any harm."

"Well . . ."

There was a moment of silence, and the charred-looking man signaled the others to let well enough—or bad enough, whichever it was—alone, but the other man was impelled to complete the conciliation. "I see perfectly well what you mean," he said. "But she meant not all of us stand out with a sort of—well, trademark."

The counterman seemed to bristle. "Meaning what?"

"Why, the way you say 'mit or mitout,' I guess," the man said, looking for confirmation to the woman, who nodded brightly.

The counterman squinted at him. "What about it?"

"Nothing, nothing at all. I just say I suppose it's sort of your trademark."

"Now, cut it out," the counterman said, taking a step closer. "Or you'll have a trademark. And when you get up tomorrow morning, you'll look a darn side more wonderful than anybody *she* ever saw."

The charred-looking man brought his hand down on the counter. "Oh, for Pete's sake, let's cut this out! Let's eat if we're going to eat, and get out of here."

"That suits me, bud," said the counterman.

The commotion brought Al Spain from the kitchen. "What seems to be the trouble?" he asked, stepping around to the customers' side of the counter.

"She said I was wonderful," the counterman said, pointing. "And I don't see that I have to take it from people just because they're customers, Al."

"Maybe she didn't mean any harm by it," the proprietor said.

"It's the way she said it. The way that type says it. I know. You know. We get 'em in here. You know what they think's wonderful, don't you?"

"Well," Al said, scratching his head and looking at the floor.

"Hack drivers that recite poems they wrote while they cart fares around, saloons full of old———"

"Are we going through that again?" the charred-looking man broke in. He stood up. "Let's just go," he said to his friends.

"We'll go into this quietly," Al said, and removed a toothpick from his mouth and dropped it on the floor. "We're intelligent human beings," he continued, with an edge of interrogation, looking at the others, who gave little nods of agreement. He sat down on one of the stools. "Now, the thing is this. This man is fine." He waved at the counterman, who stood looking modestly down at the grill. "He's a great fellow. But he's sensitive. By that I mean he gets along fine with the public—people who come in here from day to day, you understand. Has a pleasant way of passing the time of day, and a nice line of gab, *but*—different cultural levels eat here, and he doesn't like people that he thinks they're coming in here with the idea they're slumming. Now don't get me wrong," he went on when the woman with the gardenia started to say something. "I like all types of people and I'm tickled to death to have them come in here, you understand. I'm just saying that's his attitude. Some things set his back up, because he's like I say, sensitive." He crossed his legs. "Let's go into this thing like intelligent human beings a little farther. What prompted you to pass the remark—namely, he's wonderful?"

The charred-looking man groaned. "Oh, for Pete's sake, let's get————"

"Shut up, Paul," the woman with the gardenia said. She returned her attention to the proprietor. "It was just—oh, it all starts to sound so silly. I mean it was a perfectly insignificant remark. It's the way he says 'mit or mitout.'"

Al was silent a moment. "That's all?" he asked, regarding her curiously. "Yes."

"It's just a habit of his. A way he's got." Al looked from her to the counterman and back again.

"You see," she said, "it's making something out of nothing. It's the way he says it. It's so—so offhand-like and—well, the offhand way he evidently keeps saying it. It's so—marvelous."

"I see. Well, it's just a sort of habit of his." Al was studying her with mounting interest.

"Of course, we're sorry if we've offended him," said the woman's escort.

"We'll let it go that way," the counterman said.

"Fine! We'll say no more about it," Al said, gesturing covertly to the counterman to serve up the sandwiches. "Come again any time," he added, and went back to the kitchen.

The two couples composed themselves and ate. The counterman went and leaned on the cigarette case, over a newspaper. The door opened and a small man in a tight gray suit came in and sat down, pushed his hat back, drew a newspaper out of his pocket, and spread it on the counter. The counterman dropped his, drew a glass of water, and set it before the customer.

"What'll it be?"

"Two hamburgers."

The two couples stopped eating and looked up, and there was a blank silence for a moment. Then they bent over their food, eating busily and stirring their coffee with an excessive clatter of spoons. Suddenly the clink of cutlery subsided and there was dead silence again. The counterman wiped his hands on his apron, turned, and walked to the refrigerator. He opened it, took out two patties, set them on the grill, and peeled off the paper on them. He sliced the buns and set them in readiness on a plate. Standing there waiting for the meat to fry, he cleared his throat and said, looking out the window at something in the street, "Onion with these?"

"No. Plain," the customer said, without raising his head from the paper and turning a page.

The two couples hurried through their sandwiches and coffee, crumpled their paper napkins, and rose together. One of the men paid, left a dollar tip on the counter, turned, and herded the others through the door, following them himself and closing the door rapidly and quietly. The counterman shoved the cash register shut and went back to the grill without looking at them or glancing through the window as they unlocked their car at the curb, got in, and drove off. He served the man his sandwiches. Then he came around the counter and sat on a stool with the paper.

The door flew open and a big fellow in a bright checked shirt came in, grinning. "Hello, paesan!"[1] the newcomer said. "Loafing as usual, eh?"

The counterman jumped off the stool and held out his hand. "Louie! When did you get back?"

"Yesterday."

"For heavens sake!" The counterman went back behind the counter. "Glad to see you."

"Glad to see you, too, you lazy son of a gun."

"How many, Louie?"

"I'm starved. Fry me up three."

"Mit or mitout?"

"Mit!"

FOR DISCUSSION AND WRITING

1. What does the woman wearing the gardenia mean when she calls the counterman "wonderful"? What characteristics of the counterman elicit the woman's remark? Mit mitout I don't know

---

1. *paesan* (pī⁻ zôn), countryman (Italian).

2. *Do you think the counterman has reason to be angry? Do you think he is paranoid? How do you characterize his reaction? Explain.* Yes paranoid. No. It was over aggressive

3. *If you were the counterman, what would you say or do to express your feelings to the woman?* I wouldn't have even gotten mad. I would have said thanks.

I'LL CRACK YOUR HEAD KOTSUN

FROM *ALL I ASKING FOR IS MY BODY*
Milton Murayama

Milton Murayama was raised in Hawaii, where a wide variety of ethnic and socioeconomic groups coexist. In this story of two friends from different socioeconomic backgrounds, Kiyoshi, the main charac-ter, is from a family of Japanese heritage. His friend Makot is also of Japanese heritage, but his is the only Japanese family in a Filipino neighborhood. Friction between Kiyoshi and his parents develops as his parents interfere with his friendship with Makot. In the middle of an argument about Kiyoshi's visits to Makot's house, Kiyoshi's father threatens, "I'll crack your head kotsun." Kotsun does not mean anything in Japanese. As the story explains, "it's just the sound of something hard hitting your head."

THERE WAS SOMETHING FUNNY ABOUT MAKOT. He always played with guys younger than he and the big guys his own age always made fun of him. His family was the only Japanese family in Filipino camp and his father didn't seem to do anything but ride around in his brand-new Ford Model T. But Makot always had money to spend and the young kids liked him.

During the summer in Pepelau, Hawaii, the whole town spends the whole day at the beach. We go there early in the morning, then walk home for lunch, often in our trunks, then go back for more spearing fish, surfing, or just plain swimming, depending on the tide, and stay there till sunset. At night there were the movies for those who had the money and the Buddhist Bon dances and dance practices. The only change in dress was that at night we wore Japanese *zori* and in the day bare feet. Nobody owned shoes in Pepelau.

In August Makot became our gang leader. We were all at the beach and it was on a Wednesday when there was a matinee, and Makot said, "Come on, I'll take you all to the movies," and Mit, Skats, and I became his gang in no time. Mit or Mitsunobu Kato and Skats or Nobuyuki Asakatsu and I were not exactly a gang. There were only three of us and we were all going to be in the fourth grade, so nobody was leader. But we were a kind of a poor gang. None of us were in the Boy Scouts or had bicycles, we played football with tennis balls, and during basketball season we hung around Baldwin Park till some gang showed up with a rubber ball or real basketball.

After that day we followed Makot at the beach, and in spearing fish Skats and I followed him across the breakers. We didn't want to go at first, since no fourth-grader went across the breakers, but he teased us and called us yellow, so Skats and I followed. Mit didn't care if he was called yellow. Then at lunchtime, instead of all of us going home for lunch, Makot invited us all to his home in Filipino Camp. Nobody was home and he cooked us rice and canned corned beef and onions. The following day there was the new kind of Campbell soup in cans, which we got at home only when we were sick. So I began to look forward to lunchtime, when we'd go to Makot's home to eat. At home Father was a fisherman and so we ate fish and rice three times a day, and as my older brother Tosh, who was a seventh-grader always said, "What! Fish and rice again! No wonder the Japanese get beriberi!" I was sick of fish and rice too.

Mother didn't seem too happy about my eating at Makot's. About the fourth day when I came home at sunset, she said in Japanese, "You must be famished, Kiyo-chan, shall I fix you something?"

"No, I had lunch at Makoto-san's home."

"Oh, again?"

Mother was sitting on a cushion on the floor, her legs hid under her, and she was bending over and sewing a kimono by hand. It was what she always did. I sat down cross-legged. "Uh-huh. Makoto-san invited me. I ate a bellyful. Makoto-san is a very good cook. He fixed some corned beef and onions and it was delicious."

"Oh, are you playing with Makoto-san now? He's too old for you, isn't he? He's Toshio's age. What about Mitsunobu-san and Nobuyuki-san?"

"Oh, they still with me. We all play with Makoto-san. He invited all of us."

"Makoto-san's mother or father wasn't home?"

"No, they're usually not home."

"You know, Kiyo-chan, you shouldn't eat at Makoto-san's home too often."

"Why? But he invites us."

"But his parents didn't invite you. Do you understand, Kiyo-chan?"

"But why? Nobuyuki-san and Mitsunobu-san go."

"Kiyo-chan is a good boy so he'll obey what his mother says, won't he?"

"But why, Mother! I eat at Nobuyuki's and Mitsunobu's homes when their parents aren't home. And I always thank their parents when I see them. I haven't thanked Makoto's parents yet, but I will when I see them."

"But don't you see, Kiyoshi, you will bring shame to your father and me if you go there to eat. People will say, 'Ah, look at the Oyama's number two boy. He's a *hoitobo*! He's a *chorimbo*! That's because his parents are *hoitobo* and *chorimbo*!'"

Hoitobo means beggar in Japanese and *chorimbo* is something like a bum, but they're ten times worse than beggar and bum because you always make your face real ugly when you say them and they sound horrible!

"But Makoto invites us, Mother! Once Mitsunobu didn't want to go and Makoto dragged him. We can always have Makoto-san over to our home and repay him the way we do Mitsunobu-san and Nobuyuki-san."

"But can't you see, Kiyo-chan, people will laugh at you. 'Look at that Kiyoshi Oyama,' they'll say, 'he always eats at the Sasakis'. It's because his parents are poor and he doesn't have enough to eat at home.' You understand, don't you, Kiyo-chan? You're a good filial boy so you'll obey what your parents say, won't you? Your father and I would cry if we had two unfilial sons like Toshio . . ."

"But what about Nobuyuki and Mitsunobu? Won't people talk about them and their parents like that too?"

"But Kiyoshi, you're not a monkey. You don't have to copy others. Whatever Nobuyuki and Mitsunobu do is up to them. Besides, we're poor and poor families have to be more careful."

"But Mitsunobu's home is poor too! They have lots of children and he's always charging things at the stores and his home looks poor like ours!"

"Nemmind! You'll catch a sickness if you go there too often." She made a real ugly face.

"What kind of sickness? Won't Mitsunobu-san and Nobuyuki-san catch it too?"

She dropped her sewing on her lap and looked straight at me. "Kiyoshi, you will obey your parents, won't you?"

I stood up and hitched up my pants. I didn't say yes or no. I just grunted like Father and walked out.

But the next time I went to eat at Makot's I felt guilty and the corned beef and onions didn't taste so good. And when I came home that night the first thing Mother asked was, "Oh, did you have lunch, Kiyo-chan?"

then, "At Makoto-san's home?" and her face looked as if she was going to cry.

But I figured that that was the end of that so I was surprised when Father turned to me at the supper table and said, "Kiyoshi . . ." Whenever he called me by my full name instead of Kiyo or Kiyo-chan, that meant he meant business. He never punched my head once, but I'd seen him slap and punch Tosh's head all over the place till Tosh was black and blue in the head.

"Yes, Father." I was scared.

"Kiyoshi, you're not to eat anymore at Makoto-san's home. You understand?"

"But why, Father? Nobuyuki-san and Mitsunobu-san eat with me too!"

"Nemmind!" he said in English. Then he said in Japanese, "You're not a monkey. You're Kiyoshi Oyama."

"But why?" I said again. I wasn't being smart-alecky like Tosh. I really wanted to know why.

Father grew angry. You could tell by the way his eyes bulged and the way he twisted his mouth. He flew off the handle real easily, like Tosh. He said, "If you keep on asking 'Why? Why?' I'll crack your head *kotsun!*"

Kotsun doesn't mean anything in Japanese. It's just the sound of something hard hitting your head.

"Yeah, slap his head, slap his head!" Tosh said in pidgin Japanese and laughed.

"Shut up! Don't say uncalled-for things!" Father said to Tosh and Tosh shut up and grinned.

Whenever Father talked about this younger generation talking too much and talking out of turn and having no respect for anything, he didn't mean me, he meant Tosh.

"Kiyoshi, you understand, you're not to eat anymore at Makoto's home," Father said evenly, his anger gone now.

I was going to ask "Why?" again but I was afraid. "Yes," I said.

Then Tosh said across the table in pidgin English, which the old folks couldn't understand, "You know why, Kyo?" I never liked the guy, he couldn't even pronounce my name right. "Because his father no work and his mother do all the work; thass why! Ha-ha-ha-ha!"

Father told him to shut up and not to joke at the table and he shut up and grinned.

Then Tosh said again in pidgin English, his mouth full of food; he always talked with his mouth full, "Go tell that *kodomo taisho* to go play with guys his own age, not small shrimps like you. You know why he doan play with us? Because he scared, thass why. He too *wahine*. We bust um up!"

Wahine was the Hawaiian word for woman. When we called anybody *wahine* it meant she was a girl or he was a sissy. When Father said *wahine* it meant the old lady or Mother.

Then I made another mistake. I bragged to Tosh about going across the breakers. "You *pupule* ass! You wanna die or what? You want shark to eat you up? Next time you go outside the breakers I goin' slap your head!" he said.

"Not dangerous. Makot been take me go."

"Shaddup! You tell that *kodomo taisho* if I catch um taking you outside the breakers again, I going bust um up! Tell um that! Tell um I said go play with guys his own age!"

"He never been force me. I asked um to take me."

"Shaddup! The next time you go out there, I goin' slap your head!"

Tosh was three years older than me and when he slapped my head, I couldn't slap him back because he would slap me right back, and I couldn't cry like my kid sister because I was too big to cry. All I could do was to walk away mad and think of all the things I was going to do to get even when I grew up. When I slapped my sister's head she would grumble or sometimes cry but she would always talk back, "No slap my head, you! Thass where my brains stay, you know!" Me, I couldn't even talk back. Most big brothers were too cocky anyway and mine was more cocky than most.

Then at supper Tosh brought it up again. He spoke in pidgin Japanese (we spoke four languages: good English in school, pidgin English among ourselves, good or pidgin Japanese to our parents and the other old folks). "Mama, you better tell Kyo not to go outside the breakers. By-'n'-by he drown. By-'n'-by by the shark eat um up."

"Oh, Kiyo-chan, did you go outside the breakers?" she said in Japanese.

"Yeah," Tosh answered for me, "Makoto Sasaki been take him go."

"Not dangerous," I said in pidgin Japanese; "Makoto-san was with me all the time."

"Why shouldn't Makoto-san play with people his own age, *ne*?" Mother said.

"He's a *kodomo taisho*, thass why!"

Kodomo taisho meant General of the kids.

"Well, you're not to go outside the breakers anymore. Do you understand, Kiyo-chan?" Mother said.

I turned to Father, who was eating silently. "Is that right, Father?"

"*So*," he grunted.

· · ·

"Boy, your father and mother real strict," Makot said. I couldn't go outside the breakers, I couldn't go eat at his place. But Makot always saved some corned beef and onions and Campbell soup for me. He told me to go home and eat fast and just a little bit and come over his place and eat with them and I kept on doing that without Mother catching on. And Makot was always buying us pie, ice cream, and chow fun, and he was always giving me the biggest share of the pie, ice cream, or chow fun. He also took us to the movies now and then and when he had money for only one treat or when he wanted to take only me and spend the rest of the money on candies, he would have me meet him in town at night, as he didn't want me to come to his place at night. "No tell Mit and Skats," he told me and I didn't tell them or the folks or Tosh anything about it, and when they asked where I was going on the movie nights, I told them I was going over to Mit's or Skats'.

Then near the end of summer the whole town got tired of going to the beach and we all took up slingshots and it got to be slingshot season. Everybody made slingshots and carried pocketsful of little rocks and shot linnets and myna birds and doves. We would even go to the old wharf and shoot the black crabs which crawled on the rocks. Makot made each of us a dandy slingshot out of a guava branch, as he'd made each of us a big barbed spear out of a bedspring coil during spearing-fish season. Nobody our age had slingshots or spears like ours, and of the three he made, mine was always the best. I knew he liked me the best.

Then one day Makot said, "Slingshot waste time. We go buy a rifle. We go buy .22."

"How?" we all said.

Makot said that he could get five dollars from his old folks and all we needed was five dollars more and we could go sell coconuts and mangoes to raise that.

"Sure!" we all said. A rifle was something we saw only in the movies and Sears Roebuck catalogues. Nobody in Pepelau owned a rifle.

So the next morning we got a barley bag, two picks, and a scooter wagon. We were going to try coconuts first because they were easier to sell. There were two bakeries in town and they needed them for coconut pies. The only trouble was that free coconut trees were hard to find. There were trees at the courthouse, the Catholic church, and in Reverend Hastings' yard, but the only free trees were those deep in the cane fields and they were too tall and dangerous. Makot said, "We go ask Reverend

Hastings." Reverend Hastings was a minister of some kind and he lived alone in a big old house in a big weedy yard next to the kindergarten. He had about a dozen trees in his yard and he always let you pick some coconuts if you asked him, but he always said, "Sure, boys, provided you don't sell them." "Aw, what he doan know won't hurt um," Makot said.

Makot said he was going to be the brains of the gang and Mit and Skats were going to climb the trees and I was going to ask Reverend Hastings. So we hid the wagon and picks and bags and I went up to the door of the big house and knocked.

Pretty soon there were footsteps and he opened the door. "Yes?" He smiled. He was a short, skinny man who looked very weak and who sort of wobbled when he walked, but he had a nice face and a small voice.

"Reverend Hastings, can we pick some coconuts?" I said.

Makot, Mit, and Skats were behind me and he looked at them and said, "Why, sure boys, provided you don't sell them."

"Thank you, Reverend Hastings," I said, and the others mumbled, "thank you."

"You're welcome," he said and went back into the house.

Mit and Skats climbed two trees and knocked them down as fast as they could and I stuck my pick in the ground and started peeling them as fast as I could. We were scared. What if he came out again? Maybe it was better if we all climbed and knocked down lots and took them somewhere else to peel them, we said. But Makot sat down on the wagon and laughed, "Naw, he not gonna come out no more. No be chicken!" As soon as he said that the door slammed and we all looked. Mit and Skats stayed on the trees but didn't knock down any more. Reverend Hastings jumped down the step and came walking across the yard in big angry strides! It was plain we were going to sell the coconuts because we had more than half a bagful and all the husks were piled up like a mountain! He came up, his face red, and he shouted, "I thought you said you weren't going to sell these! Get down from those trees!"

I looked at my feet and Makot put his face in the crook of his arm and began crying, "Wah-wah . . ." though I knew he wasn't crying.

Reverend Hastings grabbed a half-peeled coconut from my hand and, grabbing it by a loose husk, threw it with all his might over the fence and nearly fell down and shouted, "Get out! At once!" Then he turned right around and walked back and slammed the door after him.

"Ha-ha-ha!" Makot said as soon as he disappeared. "We got enough anyway."

We picked up the rest of the coconuts and took them to the kindergarten to peel them. We had three dozen and carted them to the two bakeries on Main Street. But they said they had enough coconuts and that ours were too green and six cents apiece was too much. We pulled the wagon all over town and tried the fish markets and grocery stores for five cents. Finally we went back to the first bakery and sold them for four cents. It tooks us the whole day and we made only $1.44. By that time, Mit, Skats, and I wanted to forget about the rifle, but Makot said, "Twenty-two or bust."

The next day we went to the tall trees in the cane fields. We had to crawl through tall cane to get to them, and once we climbed the trees and knocked down the coconuts we had to hunt for them in the tall cane again. After the first tree we wanted to quit but Makot wouldn't hear of it, and when we didn't move he put on his *habut*. *Habut* is short for *habuteru*, which means to pout the way girls and children do. Makot would blow up his cheeks like a balloon fish and not talk to us. "I not goin buy you no more chow fun, no more ice cream, no more pie," he'd sort of cry, and then we would do everything to please him and make him come out of his *habut*. When we finally agreed to do what he wanted he would protest and slap with his wrist like a girl, giggle with his hand over his mouth, talk in the kind of Japanese which only girls use, and in general make fun of the girls. And when he came out of his *habut* he usually bought us chow fun, ice cream, or pie.

So we crawled through more cane fields and climbed more coconut trees. I volunteered to climb too because Mit and Skats grumbled that I got all the easy jobs. By three o'clock we had only a half a bag, but we brought them to town and again went all over Main Street trying to sell them. The next day we went to pick mangoes, first at the kindergarten, then at Mango Gulch, but they were harder to sell so we spent more time carting them around town.

"You guys think you so hot, eh," Tosh said one day. "Go sell mangoes and coconuts. He only catching you head. You know why he pick on you guys for a gang? Because you guys the last. That *kodomo taisho* been leader of every shrimp gang and they all quit him one after another. You, Mit, and Skats stick with him because you too stupid!"

I shrugged and walked away. I didn't care. I liked Makot. Besides, all the guys his age were jealous because Makot had so much money to spend.

Then several days later Father called me. He was alone at the outside sink, cleaning some fish. He brought home the best fish for us to eat but it was always fish. He was still in his fisherman's clothes.

"Kiyoshi," he said and he was not angry, "you're not to play with Makoto Sasaki anymore. Do you understand?"

"But why, Father?"

"Because he is bad." He went on cleaning fish.

"But he's not bad. He treats us good! You mean about stealing mangoes from kindergarten! It's not really stealing. Everybody does it."

"But you never sold the mangoes you stole before?"

"No."

"There's a difference between a prank and a crime. Everybody in town is talking about you people. Not about stealing, but about your selling mangoes and coconuts you stole. It's all Makoto's fault. He's older and he should know better but he doesn't. That's why he plays with younger boys. He makes fools out of them. The whole town is talking about what fools he's making out of you and Nobuyuki and Mitsunobu."

"But he's not really making fools out of us, Father. We all agreed to make some money so that we could buy a rifle and own it together. As for the work, he doesn't really force us. He's always buying us things and making things for us and teaching us tricks he learns in Boy Scout, so it's one way we can repay him."

"But he's bad. You're not to play with him. Do you understand?"

"But he's not bad! He treats us real good and me better than Mitsunobu-san or Nobuyuki-san!"

"Kiyoshi, I'm telling you for the last time. Do not play with him."

"But why?"

"Because his home is bad. His father is bad. His mother is bad."

"Why are his father and mother bad?"

"Nemmind!" He was mad now.

"But what about Mitsunobu-san and Nobuyuki-san? I play with them too!"

"Shut up!" He turned to face me. His mouth was twisted. "You're not a monkey! Stop aping others! You are not to play with him. Do you understand! Or do I have to crack your head *kotsun!*"

"Yes," I said and walked away.

Then I went inside the house and asked Mother, "Why are they bad? Because he doesn't work?"

"You're too young to understand, Kiyo-chan. When you grow up you'll know that your parents were right."

"But whom am I going to play with then?"

"Can't you play with Toshi-chan?"

"Yeah, come play with me, Kyo. Any time you want me to bust up that *kodomo taisho* I'll bustum up for you," Tosh said.

That night I said I was going to see Mit and went over to Makot's home. On the way over I kept thinking about what Father and Mother said. There was something funny about Makot's folks. His father was a tall, skinny man and he didn't talk to us kids the way all the other old Japanese men did. He owned a Model T when only the *haoles*, or whites, had cars. His mother was funnier yet. She wore lipstick in broad daylight, which no other Japanese mother did.

I went into Filipino Camp and I was scared. It was a spooky place, not like Japanese Camp. The Filipinos were all men and there were no women or children and the same-looking houses were all bare, no curtains in the windows or potted plants on the porches. The only way you could tell them apart was by their numbers. But I knew where Makot's house was in the daytime, so I found it easily. It was the only one with curtains and ferns and flowers. There were five men standing in the dark to one side of the house. They wore shoes and bright aloha shirts and sharply pressed pants, and smelled of expensive pomade. They were talking in low voices and a couple of them were jiggling so hard you could hear the jingle of loose change.

I called from the front porch. "Makot! Makot!" I was scared he was going to give me hell for coming at night.

Pretty soon his mother came out. I had never spoken to her though I'd seen her around and knew who she was. She was a fat woman with a fat face, which made her eyes look very small.

"Oh, is Makoto-san home?" I asked in Japanese.

"Makotooooo!" she turned and yelled into the house. She was all dressed up in kimono. Mother made a lot of kimonos for other people but she never had one like hers. She had a lot of white powder on her face and two round red spots on her cheeks.

"Oh, Sasaki-san," I said, "I've had lunch at your home quite a few times. I wanted to thank you for it but I didn't have a chance to speak to you before. It was most delicious. Thank you very much."

She stared at me with her mouth open wide and suddenly burst out laughing, covering her mouth and shaking all over, her shoulders, her arms, her cheeks.

Makot came out. "Wha-at?" he pouted in Japanese. Then he saw me and his face lit up. "Hiya, Kiyo, old pal, old pal, what's cookin'?" he said in English.

His mother was still laughing and shaking and pointing at me.

"What happened?" Makot said angrily to his mother.

"That boy! That boy!" She still pointed at me. "Such a nice little boy! Do you know what he said? He said, 'Sasaki-san . . .'" And she started to shake and cough again.

"Aw, shut up, Mother!" Makot said. "Please go inside!" and he practically shoved her to the door.

She turned around again. "But you're such a courteous boy, aren't you? 'It was most delicious. Thank you very much.' A-hahahaha. A-hahahaha . . ."

"Shut up, Mother!" Makot shoved her into the doorway. I would never treat my mother like that but then my mother would never act like that. When somebody said, "Thank you for the feast," she always said, "But what was served you was really rubbish."

Makot turned to me. "Well, what you say, old Kiyo, old pal? Wanna go to the movies tonight?"

I shook my head and looked at my feet. "I no can play with you no more."

"Why?'"

"My folks said not to."

"But why? We never been do anything bad, eh?"

"No."

"Then why? Because I doan treat you right? I treat you okay?"

"Yeah. I told them you treat me real good."

"Why, then?"

"I doan know."

"Aw, hell, you can still play with me. They doan hafta know. What they doan know won't hurt them."

"Naw, I better not. This time it's my father and he means business."

"Aw, doan be chicken Kiyo. Maybe you doan like to play with me."

"I like to play with you."

"Come, let's go see a movie."

"Naw."

"How about some chow fun. Yum-yum."

"Naw."

"Maybe you doan like me, then?"

"I like you."

"You sure."

"I sure."

"Why, then?"

"I doan know. They said something about your father and mother."

"Oh," he said and his face fell and I thought he was going to cry.

"Well, so long, then, Kiyo," he said and went into the house.

"So long," I said and turned and ran out of the spooky camp.

FOR DISCUSSION AND WRITING

1. Do you think Kiyoshi's parents should allow him to play with Makot? If you do not agree with them, can you understand their point of view? Consider the reasons Kiyoshi's parents give him for not playing with Makot. Also consider who benefits and who is hurt by the parents' position. *no*

2. If you were Kiyoshi's mother or father, what stand would you take about his friendship with Makot? What criteria would you use to determine whether your son or daughter of Kiyoshi's age is allowed to play with someone? Explain. *Not bad /trouble-maker*
Tell him no

3. Why does Makot's mother laugh when Kiyoshi thanks her for the food he eats at her house? *Never happened before — maybe drunk*

4. Create a dialogue between a parent and child in which the parent intervenes in one of the child's friendships. The problem, according to the parent, is the economic, ethnic, or religious background of the friend. In the dialogue demonstrate how the backgrounds of the two friends differ and what the parent's issues are. For an extra challenge, take the side of the party with whom you disagree.

"MOMMY, WHAT DOES 'NIGGER' MEAN?"
Gloria Naylor

Gloria Naylor is an award-winning author of three novels that examine African-American life in a variety of settings. She injects her work with a sociological interest in cultural patterns and traditions. In this essay, Naylor provides a glimpse into her extended family to demonstrate how African Americans have responded to language that was originally meant to degrade them. Language can evoke strong emotions. Here, Naylor writes about how language derives its power.

LANGUAGE IS THE SUBJECT. It is the written form with which I've managed to keep the wolf away from the door and, in diaries, to keep my sanity. In spite of this, I consider the written word inferior to the spoken, and much of the frustration experienced by novelists is the awareness that whatever we manage to capture in even the most transcendent passages falls far short of the richness of life. Dialogue achieves its power in

Sargent Johnson,
Forever Free, *1933*

the dynamics of a fleeting moment of sight, sound, smell and touch.

I'm not going to enter the debate here about whether it is language that shapes reality or vice versa. That battle is doomed to be waged whenever we seek intermittent reprieve from the chicken and egg dispute. I will simply take the position that the spoken word, like the written word, amounts to a nonsensical arrangement of sounds or letters without a censensus that assigns "meaning." And building from the meanings of what we hear, we order reality. Words themselves are innocuous; it is the consensus that gives them true power.

. . .

I remember the first time I heard the word "nigger." In my third-grade class, our math tests were being passed down the rows, and as I handed the papers to a little boy in back of me, I remarked that once again he had received a much lower mark than I did. He snatched his test from me and spit out that word. Had he called me a nymphomaniac or a necrophiliac, I couldn't have been more puzzled. I didn't know what a nigger was, but I knew that whatever it meant, it was something he shouldn't have called me. This was verified when I raised my hand, and in a loud voice repeated what he had said and watched the teacher scold him for using a "bad" word. I was later to go home and ask the inevitable question that every black parent must face—"Mommy, what does 'nigger' mean?"

And what exactly did it mean? Thinking back, I realize that this could not have been the first time the word was used in my presence. I was part of a large extended family that had migrated from the rural South after World War II and formed a close-knit network that gravitated around my maternal grandparents. Their ground-floor apartment in one of the buildings they owned in Harlem was a weekend mecca for my immediate family, along with countless aunts, uncles and cousins who brought along assorted friends. It was a bustling and open house with assorted neighbors and tenants popping in and out to exchange bits of gossip, pick up an old quarrel or referee the ongoing checkers game in which my grandmother cheated shamelessly. They were all there to let down their hair and put up their feet after a week of labor in the factories, laundries and shipyards of New York.

Amid the clamor, which could reach deafening proportions—two or three conversations going on simultaneously, punctuated by the sound of a baby's crying somewhere in the back rooms or out on the street—there was still a rigid set of rules about what was said and how. Older children were sent out of the living room when it was time to get into the juicy details about "you-know-who" up on the third floor who had gone and gotten herself "p-r-e-g-n-a-n-t!" But my parents, knowing that I could spell well beyond my years, always demanded that I follow the others out to play. Beyond sexual misconduct and death, everything else was considered harmless for our young ears. And so among the anecdotes of the triumphs and disappointments in the various workings of their lives, the word "nigger" was used in my presence, but it was set within contexts and inflections that caused it to register in my mind as something else.

In the singular, the word was always applied to a man who had distinguished himself in some situation that brought their approval for his strength, intelligence or drive:

"Did Johnny really do that?"

"I'm telling you, that nigger pulled in $6,000 of overtime last year. Said he got enough for a down payment on a house."

When used with a possessive adjective by a woman—"my nigger"—it became a term of endearment for husband or boyfriend. But it could be more than just a term applied to a man. In their mouths it became the pure essence of manhood—a disembodied force that channeled their past history of struggle and present survival against the odds into a victorious statement of being: "Yeah, that old foreman found out quick enough—you don't mess with a nigger."

In the plural, it became a description of some group within the community that had overstepped the bounds of decency as my family defined it: Parents who neglected their children, a drunken couple who fought in public, people who simply refused to look for work, those with excessively dirty mouths or unkempt households were all "trifling niggers." This particular circle could forgive hard times, unemployment, the occasional bout of depression—they had gone through all of that themselves—but the unforgivable sin was lack of self-respect.

A woman could never be a "nigger" in the singular, with its connotation of confirming worth. The noun "girl" was its closest equivalent in that sense, but only when used in direct address and regardless of the gender doing the addressing. "Girl" was a token of respect for a woman. The one-syllable word was drawn out to sound like three in recognition of the extra ounce of wit, nerve or daring that the woman had shown in the situation under discussion.

"G-i-r-l, stop. You mean you said that to his face?"

But if the word was used in a third-person reference or shortened so that it almost snapped out of the mouth, it always involved some element of communal disapproval. And age became an important factor in these exchanges. It was only between individuals of the same generation, or from an older person to a younger (but never the other way around), that "girl" would be considered a compliment.

. . .

I don't agree with the argument that use of the word nigger at this social stratum of the black community was an internalization of racism. The dynamics were the exact opposite: the people in my grandmother's living room took a word that whites used to signify worthlessness or degradation and rendered it impotent. Gathering there together, they transformed "nigger" to signify the varied and complex human beings they knew themselves to be. If the word was to disappear totally from the mouths of even the most liberal of white society, no one in that room was naïve enough to believe it would disappear from white minds. Meeting the word head-on, they proved it had absolutely nothing to do with the way they were determined to live their lives.

So there must have been dozens of times that the word "nigger" was spoken in front of me before I reached the third grade. But I didn't "hear" it until it was said by a small pair of lips that had already learned it could be a way to humiliate me. That was the word I went home and asked my mother about. And since she knew that I had to grow up in America, she took me in her lap and explained.

FOR DISCUSSION AND WRITING

1. Gloria Naylor writes that language is the subject of her essay. What is her theory of how linguistic expressions get their meaning? How does her theory explain why she did not "hear" the word nigger until she was in the third grade?

2. What techniques does Naylor use to express, in writing, the oral subtleties of the speech she is analyzing? Do you think written language or speech is more expressive? Explain.

3. Does Gloria Naylor argue that it is all right to use the word nigger? What does she say are appropriate and inappropriate contexts for the word?

4. What should a person do when classmates, coworkers, or friends use racist expressions or tell racist jokes? What are some specific responses people may have? Do possible responses differ between people who are not specifically targeted by the derogatory language and people who are? How might the teacher have been more effective in handling the situation? How might the girl have responded, had she understood the word? Explain.

A SEAT IN THE GARDEN
Thomas King

Thomas King, a writer of Cherokee, Greek, and German descent, is a professor of American and Native-American studies at the University of Minnesota. In this satirical story, he brings stereotypes of Native Americans into the open and confronts the issue of how stereotypes are perpetuated. A reviewer's comment about Medicine River, *King's first novel, also applies to "A Seat in the Garden." The review in the* Toronto Star *states that King "with a skillful sleight of hand entertains, while slipping his serious messages into the reader's consciousness."*

JOE HOVAUGH SETTLED INTO THE GARDEN on his knees and began pulling at the wet, slippery weeds that had sprung up between the neat rows of beets. He trowled his way around the zucchini and up and down the lines of carrots, and he did not notice the big Indian at all until he stopped at the tomatoes, sat back, and tried to remember where he had set the ball of twine and the wooden stakes.

The big Indian was naked to the waist. His hair was braided and wrapped with white ermine and strips of red cloth. He wore a single feather held in place by a leather band stretched around his head, and, even though his arms were folded tightly across his chest, Joe could see the glitter and flash of silver and turquoise on each finger.

"If you build it, they will come," said the big Indian.

Joe rolled forward and shielded his eyes from the morning sun.

"If you build it, they will come," said the big Indian again.

"Christ sakes," Joe shouted. "Get the hell out of the corn, will ya!"

"If you build it . . ."

"Yeah, yeah. Hey! This is private property. You people ever hear of private property?"

". . . they will come."

Joe struggled to his feet and got his shovel from the shed. But when he got back to the garden, the big Indian was gone.

"All right!" Joe shouted, and drove the nose of the shovel into the ground. "Come out of that corn!"

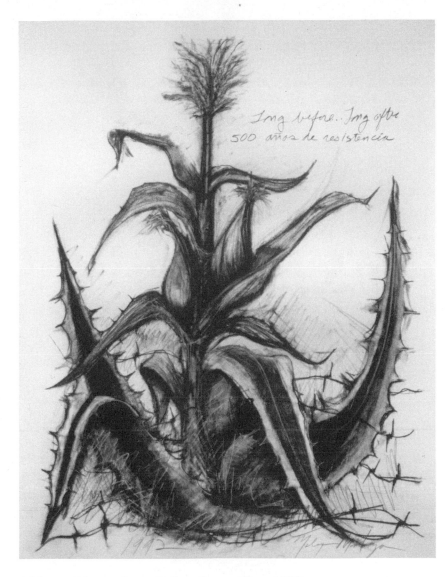

Malaquias Montoya, Long Before—Long After, *1992*

The cornstalks were only about a foot tall. Nevertheless, Joe walked each row, the shovel held at the ready, just in case the big Indian tried to take him by surprise.

. . .

When Red Mathews came by in the afternoon, Joe poured him a cup of coffee and told him about the big Indian and what he had said. Red told Joe that he had seen the movie.

"Wasn't a movie, Red, damn it. It was a real Indian. He was just standing there in the corn."

"You probably scared him away."

"You can't let them go standing in your garden whenever they feel like it."

"That's the truth."

.   .   .

The next day, when Joe came out to the garden to finish staking the tomatoes, the big Indian was waiting for him. The man looked as though he were asleep, but as soon as he saw Joe, he straightened up and crossed his arms on his chest.

"You again!"

"If you build it . . ."

"I'm going to call the police. You hear me. The police are going to come and haul you away."

". . . they will come."

Joe turned around and marched back into the house and phoned the RCMP, who said they would send someone over that very afternoon.

"Afternoon? What am I supposed to do with him until then? Feed him lunch?"

The RCMP officer told Joe that it might be best if he stayed in his house. There was the chance, the officer said, that the big Indian might be drunk or on drugs, and if that were the case, it was better if Joe didn't antagonize him.

"He's walking on my corn. Does that mean anything to you?"

The RCMP officer assured Joe that it meant a great deal to him, that his wife was a gardener, and he knew how she would feel if someone walked on her corn.

"Still," said the officer, "it's best if you don't do anything."

What Joe did do was to call Red, and when Red arrived, the big Indian was still in the garden, waiting.

"Wow, he's a big sucker, all right," said Red. "You know, he looks a little like Jeff Chandler."

"I called the police, and they said not to antagonize him."

"Hey, there are two of us, right?"

"That's right," said Joe.

"You bet it's right."

Joe got the shovel and a hoe from the shed, and he and Red wandered out into the garden, as if nothing were wrong.

"He's watching us," said Red.

"Don't step on the tomatoes," said Joe.

Joe walked around the zucchini, casually dragging the shovel behind him. Red ambled through the beets, the hoe slung over his shoulder.

"If you build it, they will come," the Indian said.

"Get him!" shouted Joe. And before Red could do anything, Joe was charging through the carrots, the shovel held out in front like a lance.

"Wait a minute, Joe," yelled Red, the hoe still on his shoulder. But Joe was already into the tomatoes. He was closing on the big Indian, who hadn't moved, when he stepped on the bundle of wooden stakes and went down in a heap.

"Hey," said Red. "You okay?"

Red helped Joe to his feet, and when the two men looked around, the big Indian was gone.

"Where'd he go?" said Joe.

"Beats me," said Red. "What'd you do to get him so angry?"

Red helped Joe to the house, wrapped an ice pack on his ankle, and told him to put his leg on the chair.

"I saw a movie a couple of years back about a housing development that was built on top of an ancient Indian burial mound," Red said.

"I would have got him, if I hadn't tripped."

"They finally had to get an authentic medicine man to come in and appease the spirits."

"Did you see the look on his face when he saw me coming?"

"And you should have seen some of those spirits."

. . .

When the RCMP arrived, Joe showed the officer where the Indian had stood, how he had run at him with the shovel, and how he had stumbled over the bundle of stakes.

After Joe got up and brushed himself off, the RCMP officer asked him if he recognized the big Indian.

"Not likely," said Joe. "There aren't any Indians around here."

"Yes, there are," said Red. "Remember those three guys who come around on weekends every so often."

"The old winos?" said Joe.

"They have that grocery cart, and they pick up cans."

"They don't count."

"They sit down there by the hydrangea and crush the cans and eat their lunch. Sometimes they get to singing."

"You mean drink their lunch."

"Well, they could have anything in that bottle."

"Most likely Lysol."

The RCMP officer walked through the garden with Joe and Red and made a great many notes. He shook hands with both men and told Joe to call him if there was any more trouble.

"Did you ever wonder," said Red, after the officer left, "just what he wants you to build or who 'they' are?"

"I suppose you saw a movie."

"Maybe we should ask the Indians."

"The drunks?"

"Maybe they could translate for us."

"The guy speaks English."

"That's right, Joe. God, this gets stranger all the time. Ed Ames, that's who he reminds me of."

.   .   .

On Saturday morning, when Joe and Red walked out on the porch, the big Indian was waiting patiently for them in the corn. They were too far away to hear him, but they could see his mouth moving.

"Okay," said Red. "All we got to do is wait for the Indians to show up."

They showed up around noon. One Indian had a green knapsack. The other two pushed a grocery cart in front of them. It was full of cans and bottles. They were old, Joe noticed, and even from the porch, he imagined he could smell them. They walked to a corner of the garden behind the hydrangea where the sprinklers didn't reach. It was a dry, scraggly wedge that Joe had never bothered to cultivate. As soon as the men stopped the cart and sat down on the ground, Red got to his feet and stretched.

"Come on. Can't hurt to talk with them. Grab a couple of beers, so they know we're friendly."

"A good whack with the shovel would be easier."

"Hey, this is kind of exciting. Don't you think this is kind of exciting?"

"I wouldn't trip this time."

When Joe and Red got to the corner, the three men were busy crushing the cans. One man would put a can on a flat stone and the second man would step on it. The third man picked up the crushed can and put it in a brown grocery bag. They were older than Joe had thought, and they didn't smell as bad as he had expected.

"Hi," said Red. "That's a nice collection of cans."

"Good morning," said the first Indian.

"Getting pretty hot," said the second Indian.

"You fellows like a drink," said the third Indian, and he took a large glass bottle out of the knapsack.

"No thanks," said Red. "You fellows like a beer?"

"Lemon water," said the third Indian. "My wife makes it without any sugar so it's not as sweet as most people like."

"How can you guys drink that stuff?" said Joe.

"You get used to it," said the second Indian. "And it's better for you than pop."

As the first Indian twisted the lid off the bottle and took a long drink, Joe looked around to make sure none of his neighbors were watching him.

"I'll bet you guys know just about everything there is to know about Indians," said Red.

"Well," said the first Indian, "Jimmy and Frank are Nootka and I'm Cree. You guys reporters or something?"

"Reporters? No."

"You never know," said the second Indian. "Last month, a couple of reporters did a story on us. Took pictures and everything."

"It's good that these kinds of problems are brought to the public's attention," said Red.

"You bet," said the third Indian. "Everyone's got to help. Otherwise there's going to be more garbage than people."

Joe was already bored with the conversation. He looked back to see if the big Indian was still there.

"This is all nice and friendly," said Joe. "But we've got a problem that we were hoping you might be able to help us with."

"Sure," said the first Indian. "What's the problem?"

Joe snapped the tab on one of the beers, took a long swig, and jerked his thumb in the direction of the garden. "I've got this big Indian who likes to stand in my garden."

"Where?" asked the second Indian.

"Right there," said Joe.

"Right where?" asked the third Indian.

"If you build it, they will come," shouted the big Indian.

"There, there," said Joe. "Did you hear that?"

"Hear what?" said the first Indian.

"They're embarrassed," said Red under his breath. "Let me handle this."

"This is beginning to piss me off," said Joe, and he took another pull on the beer.

"We were just wondering," Red began. "If you woke up one day and found a big Indian standing in your cornfield and all he would say was, 'if you build it, they will come,' what would you do?"

"I'd stop drinking," said the second Indian, and the other two Indians covered their faces with their hands.

"No, no," said Red. "That's not what I mean. Well . . . you see that big Indian over there in the cornfield, don't you?"

The Indians looked at each other, and then they looked at Joe and Red.

"Okay," said the first Indian. "Sure, I see him."

"Oh yeah," said the second Indian. "He's right there, all right. In the . . . beets?"

"Corn," said Joe.

"Right," said the third Indian. "In the corn. I can see him, too. Clear as day."

"That's our problem," said Red. "We think maybe he's a spirit or something."

"No, we don't," said Joe.

"Yes, we do," said Red, who was just getting going. "We figure he wants us to build something to appease him so he'll go away."

"Sort of like . . . a spirit?" said the first Indian.

"Hey," said the second Indian, "remember that movie we saw about that community that was built . . ."

"That's the one," said Red. "What we have to figure out is what he wants us to build. You guys got any ideas?"

The three Indians looked at each other. The first Indian looked at the corn field. Then he looked at Joe and Red.

"Tell you what," he said. "We'll go over there and talk to him and see what he wants. He looks . . . Cree. You guys stay here, okay?"

Joe and Red watched as the three Indians walked into the garden. They stood together, facing the beets.

"Hey," shouted Joe. "You guys blind? He's behind you."

The first Indian waved his hand and smiled, and the three men turned around. Red could see them talking, and he tried to watch their lips, but he couldn't figure out what they were saying. After a while, the Indians waved at the rows of carrots and came back over to where Joe and Red were waiting.

"Well," said Red. "Did you talk to him?"

"Yes," said the first Indian. "You were right. He is a spirit."

"I knew it!" shouted Red. "What does he want?"

The first Indian looked back to the cornfield. "He's tired of standing, he says. He wants a place to sit down. But he doesn't want to mess up the garden. He says he would like it if you would build him a . . . a . . . bench right about . . . here."

"A bench?" said Joe.

"That's what he said."

"So he can sit down?"

"He gets tired standing."

"The hell you say."

"Do you still see him?" asked the second Indian.

"You blind? Of course I still see him."

"Then I'd get started on the bench right away," said the third Indian.

"Come on, Red," said Joe, and he threw the empty beer can into the hydrangea and opened the other one. "We got to talk."

. . .

Joe put the pad of paper on the kitchen table and drew a square. "This is the garden," he said. "These are the carrots. These are the beets. These are the beans. And this is the corn. The big Indian is right about here."

"That's right," said Red. "But what does it mean?"

"Here's where those winos crush their cans and drink their Lysol," Joe continued, marking a spot on the pad and drawing a line to it.

"Lemon water."

"You listening?"

"Sure."

"If you draw lines from the house to where the big Indian stands and from there to where the winos crush their cans and back to the house . . . Now do you see it?"

"Hey, that's pretty good, Joe."

"What does it remind you of?"

"A bench?"

"No," said Joe. "A triangle."

"Okay, I can see that."

"And if you look at it like this, you can see clearly that the winos and the big Indian are there, and the house where you and I are is here."

"What if you looked at it this way, Joe," said Red, and he turned the paper a half turn to the right. "Now the house is there and the old guys and the big Indian are here."

"That's not the way you look at it. That's not the way it works."

"Does that mean we're not going to build the bench?"

"It's our battle plan."

"A bench might be simpler," said Red.

"I'll attack him from the house along this line. You take him from the street along that line. We'll catch him between us."

"I don't know that this is going to work."

"Just don't step on the tomatoes."

The next morning, Red waited behind the hydrangea. He was carrying the hoe and a camera. Joe crouched by the corner of the house with the shovel.

"Charge!" yelled Joe, and he broke from his hiding place and lumbered across the lawn and into the garden. Red leapt through the hydrangea and struggled up the slight incline to the cornfield.

"If you build it, they will come," shouted the Indian.

"Build it yourself," shouted Joe, and he swung the shovel at the big Indian's legs. Red, who was slower, stopped at the edge of the cornfield to watch Joe whack the Indian with his shovel and to take a picture, so he saw Joe and his shovel run right through the Indian and crash into the compost mound.

"Joe, Joe . . . you all right? God, you should have seen it. You ran right through that guy. Just like he wasn't there. I got a great picture. Wait till you see the picture. Just around the eyes, he looks a little like Sal Mineo."

Red helped Joe back to the house and cleaned the cuts on Joe's face. He wrapped another ice pack on Joe's ankle and then drove down to the one-hour photo store and turned the film in. By the time he got back to the house, Joe was standing on the porch, leaning on the railing.

"You won't believe it, Joe," said Red. "Look at this."

Red fished a photograph out of the pack. It showed Joe and the shovel in mid-swing plunging through the corn. The colors were brilliant.

Joe looked at the photograph for a minute and then be looked at the cornfield. "Where's the big Indian?"

"That's just it. He's not there."

"Christ!"

"Does that mean we're going to build the bench?"

. . .

The bench was a handsome affair with a concrete base and a wooden seat. The Indians came by the very next Saturday with their knapsack and grocery cart, and Red could tell that they were impressed.

"Boy," said the first Indian, "that's a good-looking bench."

"You think this will take care of the problem?" asked Red.

"That Indian still in the cornfield?" said the second Indian.

"Of course he's still there," said Joe. "Can't you hear him?"

"I don't know," said the third Indian, and he twisted the lid off the bottle and took a drink. "I don't think he's one of ours."

"What should we do?"

"Don't throw your cans in the hydrangea," said the first Indian. "It's hard to get them out. We're not as young as we used to be."

.   .   .

Joe and Red spent the rest of the day sitting on the porch, drinking beer, and watching the big Indian in the garden. He looked a little like Victor Mature, Red thought, now that he had time to think about it, or maybe Anthony Quinn, only he was taller. And there was an air about the man that made Red believe—believe with all his heart—that he had met this Indian before.

FOR DISCUSSION AND WRITING

1. What do you think is the author's attitude toward Joe and Red? What details show how much or little they know about Native Americans?

2. Does the story change the way you view Native Americans? If so, how has your perspective changed? If not, what in the story reinforces your views?

3. What role does humor play in this story? Would your response to this story be different if King had expressed his ideas without humor? If so, how would your response be different?

4. Can you think of ways society perpetuates false stereotypes of Native Americans? What suggestions do you think King would give to dispel inaccurate stereotypes of Native Americans and other people? What activities or programs would you propose to counteract stereotypes?

WE WEAR THE MASK
Paul Laurence Dunbar

Paul Laurence Dunbar, born in 1872 to former slaves, was the first African-American poet in the United States to be widely acclaimed. Although he was the only black student in his high school class, he became class president and class poet. After graduation, however, he was rejected from newspaper jobs because of racism. In "We Wear the Mask," Dunbar describes how and why people choose to hide their feelings.

WE WEAR THE MASK THAT GRINS AND LIES,
It hides our cheeks and shades our eyes—
This debt we pay to human guile;
With torn and bleeding hearts we smile,
And mouth with myriad subtleties.

Why should the world be overwise,
In counting all our tears and sighs?
Nay, let them only see us, while
        We wear the mask.

We smile, but, O great Christ, our cries
To thee from tortured souls arise.
We sing, but oh the clay is vile
Beneath our feet, and long the mile;
But let the world dream otherwise,
        We wear the mask!

FOR DISCUSSION AND WRITING

1. Using your knowledge of what life was like for many African Americans at the turn of the century, create a situation in which Dunbar might invoke his mask rather than express his true feelings. Describe his real feelings, then describe how he would hide them and what he would express instead.

2. *What are the benefits of wearing a mask for the speaker in the poem? What are alternative strategies? Are they worse or better? Explain.*

3. *What are other situations in which people might choose to disguise their real feelings? Describe cases in which you or people you know have chosen to hide genuine feelings.*

Naomi Savage, Mask, *1965*

SONRISAS
Pat Mora

Award-winning poet Pat Mora was born in El Paso, Texas, at the United States—Mexico border. Reflections on her Chicana background have been a focus of Mora's two books of poetry, Chants *and* Borders. Sonrisas *means "smiles" in Spanish.*

I LIVE IN A DOORWAY
between two rooms, I hear
quiet clicks, cups of black
coffee, *click, click* like facts
budgets, tenure, curriculum,
from careful women in crisp beige
suits, quick beige smiles
that seldom sneak into their eyes.

I peek
in the other room señoras
in faded dresses stir sweet
milk coffee, laughter whirls
with steam from fresh *tamales*
    sh, sh, mucho ruido,[1]
they scold one another,
press their lips, trap smiles
in their dark, Mexican eyes.

FOR DISCUSSION AND WRITING

1. What details does the author use to contrast the two rooms? Which ones strike you as most telling? Are there differences in what the author describes in the two rooms? Read the poem aloud. Are there differences in the sounds that convey the two worlds?

2. What do you imagine to be the difference in the day-to-day lives of the women in the two different rooms?

---

1. A lot of noise. (Spanish)

3. *Describe what you imagine the speaker's life to be like. Can you think of factors, both external and internal, that can make it difficult for a person to move out of the "doorway" into one or both rooms?*

4. *Describe a fictional or real situation in which a person lives between two social worlds.*

5. *Is there a situation in your own life where you are pulled between two contrasting worlds? Do you change when you step from one world to the next? Does your clothing, language, or body language change?*

Yreina Cervántez, La Offrenda (detail), 1989

A SONG IN THE FRONT YARD
Gwendolyn Brooks

Gwendolyn Brooks has always been deeply involved with Chicago's African-American community and has written extensively about the experience of being black in the United States. Her writing includes numerous books of poetry, a novelette titled Maud Martha, *and children's books. In this poem, a young girl peeks over a border into a way of life very different from her own.*

I'VE STAYED IN THE FRONT YARD ALL MY LIFE.
I want a peek at the back
Where it's rough and untended and hungry weed
    .grows.
A girl gets sick of a rose.

I want to go in the back yard now
And maybe down the alley,
To where the charity children play.
I want a good time today.

They do some wonderful things.
They have some wonderful fun.
My mother sneers, but I say it's fine
How they don't have to go in at quarter to nine.
My mother, she tells me that Johnnie Mae
Will grow up to be a bad woman.
That George'll be taken to jail soon or late.
(On account of last winter he sold our back gate.)

But I say it's fine. Honest, I do.
And I'd like to be a bad woman, too,
And wear the brave stockings of night-black lace
And strut down the streets with paint on my face.

1. Describe in detail what you imagine the speaker's life to be like.

2. What does "front yard" mean in this poem? What does "back yard" mean? Can you think of any places that would fit these descriptions of "front yard" and "back yard"?

3. Would you prefer to live in the "front yard" or the "back yard," or would you like to move freely between both? Explain.

DOORS
Chitra Divakaruni

When patterns of different cultures exist within one family, the situation can become dramatic. In this story, a conflict simmers between a husband and wife about the fundamental issue of how much privacy is appropriate in the home. Chitra Divakaruni, who came to the United States from India to attend the University of California, now lives in the United States and is a writer as well as a college teacher of English and Yoga.

I T ALL STARTED WHEN RAJ CAME TO LIVE WITH THEM.

Not that there hadn't been signs earlier. Asha's mother, for one, had warned of it right at the time of the wedding.

"It'll never work, I tell you. Here you are, living in the U.S. since you were twelve. And Deepak—he's straight out of India. Just because you took a few classes together at the University, and you liked how he talks, doesn't mean that you can live with him. What do you *really* know about how Indian men think? About what they expect from their women?"

"Now, Ma, don't start on that again. He's not like the others," Asha had protested. "And besides, I can adjust, too."

On the whole Asha had been right. She and Deepak had lived together happily enough for the last three years. In all matters, as their friends often commented envyingly, they were a well-adjusted couple. In all, that is, except the matter of doors.

Deepak liked to leave them open, and Asha liked them closed.

Deepak had laughed about it at first, early in the marriage.

"Are the pots and pans from the kitchen going to come and watch us making love?" he would joke when she meticulously locked the bedroom door at night, although there were just the two of them in the house. Or, "Do you think I'm going to come in and attack you?" when she locked the bathroom door behind her with an audible click. He himself always bathed with the door open, song and steam pouring out of the bathroom with equal abandon.

But soon he realized that it was not a laughing matter with her. Asha would shut the study door before settling down with her dissertation. When in the garden, she would make sure the gate was securely fastened as she weeded. If there had been a door to the kitchen, she would have closed it as she cooked.

Deepak was puzzled by all this door-shutting. He himself had grown up in a large family, and although they had been affluent enough to possess three bedrooms—one for Father, one for Mother and his two sisters, and the third for the three boys—they had never observed boundaries. They had constantly spilled into each others' rooms, doors always left open for the chance remark or joke.

He asked Asha about it one day. She wasn't able to give him an answer.

"I don't know. It's not like I'm shutting you out or anything. I've just always done it this way. I know it's not what you're used to. Does it bother you?"

She seemed so troubled by it that Deepak, feeling a pang of guilt, emphatically denied any feelings of unease. And really, he didn't mind. People were different. And he was more than ready to accept the unique needs of this exotic creature—Indian and yet not Indian—who had by some mysterious chance become his wife.

So things went on smoothly—until Raj descended on them.

II

"Tomorrow!" Asha was distraught, although she tried to hide it in the face of Deepak's obvious delight. Her mind raced over lists of things to be done—the guest bedroom dusted, the sheets washed, a special welcome dinner cooked (that entailed a trip to the grocery), perhaps some flowers. . . . And her advisor was pressuring her for the second chapter of the dissertation, which wasn't going well.

Joel Meyerowitz, Hartwig House, Truro, Cape Cod, *1976*

"Yes, tomorrow! His plane comes in at ten-thirty at night." Deepak waved the aerogram excitedly. "Imagine, it's been five years since I've seen him! We used to be inseparable back home, although he was so much younger. He was always in and out of our house, laughing and joking and playing pranks. I know you'll just love him—everyone does! And see, he calls you bhaviji—sister-in-law—already!"

At the airport, Raj was a lanky whirlwind, rushing from the gate to throw his arms around Deepak, kissing him soundly on both cheeks, oblivious to American stares. Asha found his strong Bombay accent hard to follow as he breathlessly regaled them with news of India that had Deepak throwing back his head in loud laughter.

But the trouble really started after dinner.

"What a marvelous meal, Bhaviji! I can see why Deepak is getting a pot-belly!" Raj belched in appreciation as he pushed back his chair. "I know I'll sleep soundly tonight—my eyes are closing already. If you tell me where the bedclothes are, I'll bring them over and start making my bed while you're clearing the table."

"Thanks, Raj, but I made the bed already, upstairs in the guest room."

"The guest room? I'm not a guest, Bhavi! I'm going to be with you for quite a while. You'd better save the guest bedroom for real guests. About six square feet of space—right here between the dining table and the sofa—is all I need. See, I'll just move the chairs a bit."

Seeing the look on Asha's face, Deepak tried to intervene.

"Come on Raju—why not use the guest bed for tonight since it's made already? We can work out the long-term arrangements later."

"Aare yaar, you know I don't like all this formal treatment. Don't you remember what fun it was to spread a big sheet on the floor of the living room and spend the night, all us boys together, telling stories? Have you become Americanized, or what? Come along and help me carry the bed-clothes down. . . ."

Asha stood frozen as his sing-song voice faded beyond the bend of the stairs; then she made her own way upstairs silently. When Deepak came to bed an hour later, she was waiting for him.

"What! Not asleep yet? Don't you have an early class to teach tomorrow?"

"You have to leave for work early, too."

"Well, as a matter of fact I was thinking of taking a day off tomorrow. You know—take Raju to San Francisco, maybe."

Asha tried to subdue the jealousy she felt.

"I really don't think you should be neglecting your work—but that's your own business." She tried to shake off the displeasure that colored her voice and speak reasonably. "What I do need to straighten out is this matter of sleeping downstairs. I need to use the dining area in the morning and I can't do it with him sleeping there." She shuddered silently as she pictured herself trying to enjoy her quiet morning tea with him sprawled on the floor nearby. "By the way, just what did he mean he's going to be here for a long time?"

"Well, he wants to stay here until he completes his Master's—maybe a year and a half—and I told him that was fine with us."

"You *what*? Isn't this my house, too? Don't I get a say in who stays here?"

"Fine, then. Go ahead and tell him that you don't want him to stay here. Go ahead, wake him up and tell him tonight." There was an edge to Deepak's voice that she hadn't heard before, and she suddenly realized, frightened, that they were having their first serious quarrel. Her mother's face, triumphant, rose in her mind.

"You know that's not what I want. I realize how much it means to you to have your old friend here, and I'll do my best to make him welcome.

I'm just not used to having a long-term houseguest around, and it makes things harder when he insists on sleeping on the living room floor." Asha offered her most charming smile to her husband, desperately willing the stranger in his eyes—cold, defensive—to disappear.

It worked. He smiled back and pulled her to him, her own dear Deepak again, promising to get Raj to use the guest room, kissing the back of her neck in that delicious way that always sent shivers up her spine. And as she snuggled against him with a deep sigh of pleasure, curving her body spoonlike to fit his warm hardness, Asha promised herself to do her best to accept Raj.

III

It was harder than she had expected.

For the concept of doors did not exist in Raj's universe, and he ignored their physical reality—so solid and reassuring to Asha—whenever he could. He would burst into her closed study to tell her of the latest events at school, leaving the door ajar when he left. He would throw open the door to the garage, where she did the laundry, to offer help, usually just as she was folding her underwear. Even when she retreated to her little garden in search of privacy there was no escape. From the porch, he would solicitously give her advice on the drooping fuschias, while behind him the swinging screen door afforded free entry to hordes of insects. Perhaps to set her an example, he left his own bedroom door wide open, so that the honest rumble of his snores assaulted Asha on her way to the bathroom every morning.

A couple of times she tried to explain to Deepak how she felt, but he responded with surprising testiness.

"What d'you mean he's driving you crazy? He's only trying to be friendly, poor chap. I should think you'd be able to open up a bit more to him. After all, we're the only family he has in this strange country."

What use was it to tell him that her own family had never intruded upon her like this? Instead, Asha took to locking herself up in the bedroom with her work in the evenings, while downstairs Deepak and Raj talked over the old days. Often, she fell asleep over her books and woke to the sound of Deepak's irritated knocks on the door.

"I just don't understand you nowadays!" he would exclaim with annoyance. "Why must you lock the bedroom door when you're reading? Isn't that being a bit paranoid? Maybe you should talk to someone about it."

Asha would turn away in silence, thinking, it can't be forever, he can't stay with us forever, I can put up with it until he leaves, and then everything will be as before.

And so things might have continued, had it not been for one fateful afternoon.

IV

It was the end of the semester, and Asha was lying on her bed, eyes closed. That morning her advisor had told her that her dissertation lacked originality and depth, and had suggested that she restructure the argument. His final comment kept resounding in her brain: "I don't know what's been wrong with you for the past few months—you've consistently produced second rate work; even your students have been complaining about you. Maybe you need a break—a semester away from school."

"Not from school—it's a semester away from home that I need," she whispered now as the door banged downstairs and Raj's eager voice floated up to her.

"Bhavi, Bhavi, where are you? Have I got great news for you!"

Asha put her pillow over her head, willing him away like the dull, throbbing headaches that came to her so often nowadays. But he was at the bedroom door, knocking.

"Open up, Bhavi! I have something to show you—I aced the Math final—I was the only one who did."

"Not now, Raj, please, I'm very tired."

"What's wrong? Do you have a headache? Wait a minute, I'll bring you some of my tigerbalm—excellent for headaches."

She heard his footsteps recede, then return.

"Thanks, Raj," she called out to forestall any more conversation. "Just leave it outside. I don't feel like getting up for it right now."

"Oh, you don't have to get up. I'll bring it in to you." And before she could refuse, Raj had opened the door—how could she have forgotten to lock it?—and had walked in.

Shocked, speechless, Asha watched Raj. He seemed to advance in slow motion across the suddenly enormous expanse of bedroom, holding a squat green bottle in his extended hand. His lips moved, but she could not hear him above the pounding in her skull. He had invaded her last sanctuary, her bedroom. He had violated her.

Through the red haze a piercing voice rose, screaming at him to get out, get out right now. A hand snatched the bottle and hurled it against the wall where it shattered and fell in emerald fragments. Dimly she recognized the voice, the hand. They were hers. And then she was alone in the sudden silence.

V

The bedroom was as neat and tranquil as ever when Deepak walked in; only a very keen eye would have noted the pale stain against the far wall.

"Are you O.K.? Raju mentioned something about you not being well." And then, as his glance fell on the packed suitcase, "What's going on?"

Very calm, she told him she was leaving. She felt a mild surprise when he swore softly and violently.

"You can't leave. You're my wife. This is your home. You belong here." She looked at him a long moment, eyes expressionless.

"It's Raju, isn't it? You just can't stand him, can you? Well, I guess I'll have to do something about the poor chap."

She listened silently to his footsteps fading down the stairs, listened to the long low murmur of voices from the living room, listened to sounds of packing from the guestroom. She listened as Raj said his goodbyes, listened as the front door banged behind the men.

Much later she listened as Deepak told her that Raj would be staying in a hotel till he found a room on campus, listened as he stated that he would sleep in the guestroom tonight, listened to his awkward bedmaking efforts. She listened as a part of herself cried out to her to go to him, to apologize and offer to have Raj back, to fashion her curves to his warm hardness, to let his lips soothe her into sleep.

Then for the first time she lay down alone in the big bed and let the night cover her slowly, layer by cold layer. And when the door finally clicked shut, she did not know whether it was in the guestroom or deep inside her being.

FOR DISCUSSION AND WRITING

1. The characters differ in how much privacy they feel is natural. What details does the author use to show that each character's preference is deeply ingrained? her homelife/growing up

2. How much privacy do you like to have in your home? Can you think of a time when you wanted more privacy than you were given? Can you think of a time when you intruded on someone else's privacy?
I like my door shut but other doors don't matter. Camp

3. *Was either Deepak or Asha right? If you were a marriage counselor, what would you say and do if the couple came to you in the weeks immediately after Raj arrived?*

4. *Explain what happens at the end of the story. Write an afterword about what the characters are doing one year after the end of the story.* Next day/sort of ignoring normal

---

NIKKI-ROSA
Nikki Giovanni

Since the 1960s, poet, essayist, and children's book author Nikki Giovanni has been an eloquent voice expressing the need for black awareness and unity. In this poem about her childhood, Giovanni alters the picture of black authors she feels is painted by white biographers. In addition, in "Nikki-Rosa," Giovanni questions the commonly perceived connection between financial comfort and happiness.

CHILDHOOD REMEMBRANCES ARE ALWAYS A DRAG
if you're Black
you always remember things like living in Woodlawn
with no inside toilet
and if you become famous or something
they never talk about how happy you were to have your
        mother
all to yourself and
how good the water felt when you got your bath from one of
        those
big tubs that folk in Chicago barbecue in
and somehow when you talk about home
it never gets across how much you
understood their feelings
as the whole family attended meetings about Hollydale
and even though you remember
your biographers never understand
your father's pain as he sells his stock
and another dream goes
and though you're poor it isn't poverty that

concerns you
and though they fought a lot
it isn't your father's drinking that makes any difference
but only that everybody is together and you
and your sister have happy birthdays and very good
        christmases
and I really hope no white person ever has cause to write
        about me
because they never understand Black love is Black wealth and
        they'll
probably talk about my hard childhood and never understand
        that
all the while I was quite happy

Elizabeth Catlett, Malcolm
X Speaks for Us, *1969*

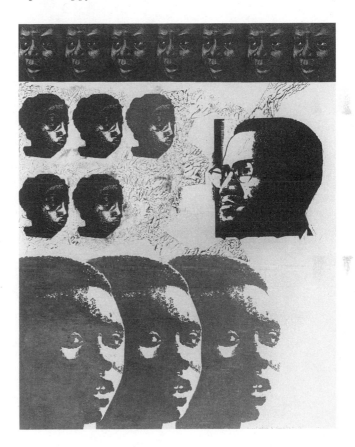

FOR DISCUSSION AND WRITING

1. How does the speaker in the poem feel about white biographers of black authors? Provide details from the poem that indicate these feelings. Do Giovanni's feelings make sense to you? Explain.

2. Is it important for you to be materially well off in order to be happy? For instance, how important is it for you to own name brand items? How important is it or will it be for you to own a new car or a spacious home in an affluent neighborhood?

3. What are three or four events or situations in your childhood that made you happy? Are any of these events tied to wealth? What conclusions do you draw from your examples?

L·O·V·E

FAMILY DINNER
Tina Koyama

Introducing that "special person" to one's family may cause embarrassment or self-consciousness on anyone's part. In this autobiographical story, Tina Koyama, a third-generation Japanese-American author, describes the Thanksgiving dinner at which she introduced Greg, the man who was to become her husband, to her parents. Through Koyama's eyes, the reader glimpses the romantic relationship as well as some aspects of her Japanese-American family and Greg's Scandinavian-American background.

*T*HANK YOU FOR THE TURKEY. Thanks for our health too, and we hope next year will be a good one." Seated before us at the head of the table, hands folded, my father fidgets like a child.

Startled, I glance at him through the side of my eye, then stare at my plate. For the benefit of the man I've brought to Thanksgiving dinner, my father has said grace for the first time in his life. For the moment, we let neither the 20-pound turkey in the table's center nor the wet-earth fragrance of matsutake divert our attention. Our faces, our hands, even steam from the rice are suspended. I am annoyed, embarrassed and moved by his awkward sincerity.

Suddenly the moment cracks open like an egg, and all arms are in motion: my mother fluffing the rice, my father pouring champagne, the candied yams, broccoli, soy sauce, rolls, corn, stuffing, matsutake gravy and butter criss-crossing from hand to hand.

My mother uncoils the cord on the electric knife and prepares to assign carving duty. Some years she announces that it's "American style" for the man of the house to have the honor and presents the knife to my father. Once she challenged my sister to try it because a woman should learn to do it too. And sometimes she does the task herself, efficiently separating the dark meat from the light on the platter, all the while apologizing that she should someday learn the correct way to carve.

Tonight she turns to the man beside me, her eyes neither asking for help nor bestowing an honor. She offers Greg the knife as she might fresh towels or a cup of coffee. In her shy English, she tells him how to work the switch on the electric knife.

What does she know of this blue-eyed man, a foot taller than herself, cheerfully slicing white meat, except what her last unmarried child tells her with flushed animation one moment, self-conscious lack of detail the next? What do I know of him except his soft grey voice, the passion with which he launches a balloon from the doorstep or touches the back of my neck?

Dinner is early enough tonight that Lake Washington still mimics the sky's ink-blue.

"Let's have a toast!" my father shouts. Everyone clinks someone else's glass. The only glass I can't reach is my father's, but he doesn't notice.

Or at least we both pretend not to. With my father, it's easy to pretend something doesn't matter, to let my mother be the buffer between the words we don't say. We argue freely and loudly about who should be president or the morality of killing animals for sport. But how often has my mother been the one to say he's proud of my poems even when he doesn't read them all the way through? Does it startle him to see me as a woman? Or am I still the child who screams for him to kill a spider on the wall?

Done with the polite nonsense of champagne, my father pours V.O. for the Men—himself and my sister's husband—and offers some to Greg. He accepts, passing my father's first test. In my father's home, this sturdy brick house where I grew up, a real man drinks hard liquor, doesn't help with dishes and plays pool in the basement to scratchy recordings of Japanese music.

This could be a long night.

"I betcha never had this stuff, huh, Greg?" my father says with his mouth full, passing him a plate of raw squid and a pair of chopsticks. The smooth white flesh shines like glass.

Greg crooks an eyebrow, says, "I'll try anything." As the V.O. pours and my father's laugh grows louder, he occasionally lets slip words in Japanese to him. For the first time I notice how much my parents' two languages interchange from listener to listener, word to word. How easily I've always understood both languages, answered in one, sometimes listened to neither.

My parents, my sister, her husband—they all try hard to be normal. So do I.

I poke around inside the turkey for the wishbone and, finding it, offer one end to Greg. I start to give him a flirtatious look when I feel the weight of my family's scrutiny. "I have a wish for both of you," my mother says with quiet mystery. Does he notice my wince? Like saplings too green and wet to burn, the oily bone tears apart rather than breaks.

On the sundeck, bonsai trees paint dark silhouettes against the sky.

. . .

In September I sat by a fireplace in Minnesota as Greg's father told childhood stories. The state park cabin smelled of cedar and burning birch. His sister worked a needlepoint of geese in flight; his mother and aunt paged through magazines. We all settled into the deep worn furniture, the warmth, the contentment that follows a big dinner and a day of hiking among Norway pines so old they wear scars from more than one forest fire.

"Dad, tell about when you made firecrackers for the Fourth of July." Like a child, Greg made requests. "What about the time your dog heard wild noises outside?"

Outside, a single loon call rose from Lake Itasca, pure and clear in the night. We all held our breath, but no others followed.

In the circle of his family, even as I felt warmth pass from the logs to hands, from words to words, I shifted back and forth inside myself, now lover and guest, now stranger and intruder. Simultaneously I looked in from a window and looked out from one. The way orange deepens to red and red to purple at dusk, what I know and love of him joined a spectrum of White Castles and trains and Minnesota farms, a past I have no part of, opened to me.

Wanting to hold his hand but feeling too self-conscious, wanting to give them all something in return, I started folding origami cranes. "If I fold the necks short, like this," I told them, "they become loons."

If I fold one thousand cranes I get one wish, I thought. Nine hundred ninety-five to go.

As we walked back to our cabin, the sky was full of more stars than I've ever seen. The flashlight picked out two startled animal eyes in the darkness. I never felt so small. So whole.

. . .

My sister and I clear the dishes, the turkey now missing two legs, most of its breast and all of its dignity. The pieces of the broken wishbone lie between two plates. My mother runs the dishwater and scrapes turkey skin, bits of rice and half a dinner roll into the dog's dish. A floor below, three billiard cues crack against the balls. I expect the usual bad recordings to vibrate the floor, but the music we hear surprises me. My father owns two tapes that are not Japanese: Crystal Gayle and Neil Diamond. Tonight Crystal's the lucky one.

I sneak downstairs. A little self-conscious, Greg takes billiard instructions from my father, who belches with glee. Full of turkey, whiskey and happiness, my father closes his cataractal eye, aims the cue stick. He misses and groans in mock agony.

It's Greg's turn. I watch his long fingers around the pool cue, the angle of his body leaning over the table. I imagine how his hands will feel tonight, his palms on my face, my back. In candle darkness, his eyes will look more grey than blue, at once tender and whimsical, grey as the horizon behind Lake Washington. Our skins will be bubbles, membranes so thin they collide without breaking, neither liquid nor solid nor gas, the spheres of our souls joined by one surface, nothing between them but heartbeat.

"Don't it make my brown eyes blue," croons Crystal. Making another tally-mark by his name, my father snickers, "Aw, whatsamatter, can't you beat a half-blind man?" He winks his good eye at Greg. The man his youngest daughter brought home smiles at me as I slip back upstairs.

. . .

Two shopping bags strain at the handles from the weight of sliced turkey wrapped in foil, jars of soup, pumpkin pie, cottage cheese cartons of candied yams and stuffing—one bag for each of us. My mother checks the jar lids once more as Greg and I pull on our jackets, say good-night, good-night. She makes sure I haven't forgotten my gloves. We all feel the sting of November air through the opened door.

When I lived here, she watched me walk out this door with boys-almost-men, then men, each a tiny hope as much for herself as for me. She'd sent us off with good-bye, good-bye, have a good time, drive carefully, what time will you be home—all wrapped in the package of her wave as she stood in the driveway, her face full of anticipation and anxiety.

Tonight she reminds the man I love how to heat the turkey broth with noodles, grasps his hand with both of hers and shyly thanks him for joining us.

As I pull away from the curb, I watch her in the rearview mirror, her hand waving high above her head.

The freeway to his house is dotted with headlights, cars full of people full of food. We both heave sighs, mine more of relief than contentment. The C-shaped moon tries to hide behind parting clouds. Streetlights throw white lines into Lake Union. I want to sigh again, but something still bumps against my heart. "What was it you wished for?" I ask him.

"Huh?"

"The wishbone. What did you wish for?"

Stars blink. The sky, the water, the freeway—wherever I look spots of light move in the darkness. "It doesn't matter," he says, squeezing my shoulder playfully. "It's probably the same wish."

FOR DISCUSSION AND WRITING

1. Which expressions in the story most clearly indicate the speaker's feelings toward Greg?

2. How important is it to the speaker that Greg and her family like and approve of each other? Support your response with evidence from the story. Would you feel the same way if you were in the speaker's place? Explain.

3. Do you think the difference between Greg and the speaker's cultural backgrounds will become a problem in the future? If so, can you think of specific problematic situations? If not, what qualities of their relationship may help prevent problems?

~ ~ ~ ~ ~ ~ ~ ~ ~ ~ ~ ~ ~

JUKE BOX LOVE SONG
Langston Hughes

Langston Hughes is one of the most beloved authors in United States literary history. His work consistently affirms the strength and beauty of the black community. He was first recognized in the 1920s during the Harlem Renaissance, a period of literary and artistic ferment centered in Harlem, New York. "Juke Box Love Song" is at once a love song to a woman and a tribute to the community of Harlem.

I COULD TAKE THE HARLEM NIGHT
and wrap around you,
Take the neon lights and make a crown,
Take the Lenox Avenue buses,
Taxis, subways,
And for your love song tone their rumble down.
Take Harlem's heartbeat,
Make a drumbeat,
Put it on a record, let it whirl,
And while we listen to it play,
Dance with you till day—
Dance with you, my sweet brown Harlem girl.

1. Find out about Harlem, New York, and the Harlem Renaissance. What is the history of the African-American community and other communities in that area? Research some of the artists and writers of the Harlem Renaissance. What were their major themes and concerns? Using the information you obtain about Harlem during the 1920s and 1930s and the Harlem Renaissance, write a letter home in the voice of a young man or woman who has recently arrived to Harlem from a rural area of the South.

2. Create a story about the man and woman in the poem. How old are they? What do they do for a living? Describe their everyday lives.

Miguel Covarrubias, Lindy Hop, *1936*

FROM *CHILDREN OF THE RIVER*
Linda Crew

The novel Children of the River *tells the story of a teenager, Sundara Sovann, who fled war-torn Cambodia with her aunt's family. Sundara wants to be accepted in her Oregon high school, yet she respects her own culture. In the chapter that follows, Sundara's conflict sharpens as she and her classmate Jonathan develop strong feelings for one another. Linda Crew, a farmer and author from Oregon, wrote the novel as she became friendly with a Cambodian family who worked on her farm. Crew hopes this book helps people understand Cambodian Americans who have recently immigrated to the United States.*

So—HOW ABOUT IT?" JONATHAN SAID. "We could go to the movies if you want. Whatever."

"Oh . . ." She looked away from him, across the patio, stalling for time. A date. He was actually asking her out on a date. A picture flashed in her mind: Jonathan on the doorstep, like in the TV commercials, Naro and Soka looking him over, making him promise to bring her home on time. . . . No, no, never in a thousand years . . . She turned back to Jonathan. "Thank you, but I cannot."

"Come on, don't you like me?"

Her cheeks burned. "You teasing." He knew very well she liked him.

"Sorry." He smiled, not sorry at all. "But what's the problem?"

She bit her lip. "I like to go with you, but—in my country, we don't go out on a date at all."

Still he smiled, refusing to take her seriously. "How do you figure out who you want to marry, then?"

"Our parents arrange. The boy's mother ask the girl's mother."

"But that's . . . *archaic.*"

She lifted her chin. "My family would choose well for me. And my mother and father, they very happy together, even they see each other for the first time on their wedding day."

"Yeah?" He sounded skeptical.

She shifted away from him. "If the family make a good match, two people can grow to love each other. Our system not so bad." She gave him a sidelong look. "In Cambodia we do not talk divorce every time somebody get mad."

"Hey, I didn't mean to sound critical. It's just that things are different here."

"Yes," she said, softening, "but not for me."

His smile had faded. He seemed bewildered. "So you really won't go out with me?"

"Jonatan, I shouldn't even have lunch with you. To go to the movie . . . I'm sorry. I just can't."

He blinked, at a loss. "Well . . . I guess if that's the way you feel . . ."

She thought about Cathy, about the other girls who gave him admiring glances. Perhaps no one had ever turned him down before. He looked so hurt.

But was she supposed to throw away the traditions of centuries to save the feelings of one American boy?

Of course not.

Still, imagine . . . to openly say to the world, *Yes, I want to be with him and he wants to be with me.* To venture into public, the two of them, alone together for all to see . . .

No, of course not.

But she couldn't pretend she hadn't felt it—a surprising little thrill of temptation.

. . .

After PE one day, Sundara and Kelly were dressing amid clouds of steam and deodorant spray when Cathy Gates started talking about Jonathan on the other side of the lockers.

"Leave it to me," she said, "I'll get him to do the rally skit."

"I wouldn't count on it, Cath. Craig says Jonathan's acting kind of weird lately."

"Well, he's *my* boyfriend," Cathy said. "I ought to know him better than Craig Keltner does."

My boyfriend. Something welled up in Sundara. How easily those words slipped off this girl's tongue.

"What's the matter?" Kelly said.

Sundara had stopped dressing and was standing still, her head tilted. She laid a finger across her lips and glanced toward the lockers.

"I've *told* you," Cathy's voice came again. "He's just working on a class project with her. And the only reason he's doing it at lunch is because he didn't get lunch period with us. Believe me, it's nothing."

Nothing. Had Jonathan actually said that?

Kelly leaned close to Sundara. "Are they talking about you?"

Sundara nodded grimly. Perhaps it was as Soka said. There was an order to things. Family must come first. Blood lines must not be broken. Destroy the order and it will destroy you. She'd opened her heart just the tiniest bit to an American boy, and already this had given Cathy's words the power to tear her apart. She resumed buttoning her blouse.

Cathy's friend said something Sundara couldn't catch. Then Cathy laughed in that easy, confident way she had. Sundara flushed. Maybe she *was* just a class project to Jonathan. She hadn't thought so, especially when he asked her out. But what did she understand about American boys? As Cathy said, he was her boyfriend. She was the one who really knew him.

Cathy and her friend slammed their lockers and left.

"What's going on?" Kelly asked.

Sundara clicked the padlock on her gym basket. "Jonatan McKinnon. Her boyfriend, but he ask me to have lunch with him every day."

"So that's where you've been!" Kelly stared in awe. Then she bounced up from the bench. "Well, does he like you, or what? This is really incredible!"

Sundara raised her eyebrows. "This is such a shock, that he can like me?"

"No, no, I didn't mean it that way. It's just that . . . Jonathan McKinnon! If he ever even looked at me I'd probably melt into a helpless little puddle. And he *likes* you?" She peered at Sundara, trying to push her glasses up by wrinkling her nose. "I don't get it. You just do not look the way a normal, sane girl ought to look if Jonathan McKinnon likes her!"

"Oh, Kelly, not so simple for me. Better he doesn't like me. I'm so scared. My family hear about this, they gonna be mad."

"Who cares?" Kelly said. "For a boy like him I'd let my parents completely disown me."

Sundara had to smile. Kelly was so funny. But she could afford to talk this way; for her, being thrown out wasn't a real possibility.

"So what's he really like?" Kelly wiggled her eyebrows. "Up close and personal? I mean, what do you guys talk about?"

"Well, he want to know about my life in Cambodia—"

"Sure, sure, but what about Cathy? Is he going to break up with her?"

"Oh, we never talk about that. . . . Sometime he talk about football. He such a big star, but I don't think he so happy about it."

"Really? That's weird."

Sundara closed her locker and leaned back on it. "Kelly? Will your parents let you go on a date?"

"*Let* me? Are you kidding? My mother would *die* for me to have a date.

She's always bugging me about boys, and believe me, I don't appreciate being reminded I don't have anything to hide."

Sundara sighed. "I have something to hide—and it scare me to death!"

· · ·

In spite of her fears, Sundara found herself letting Jonathan fall in step beside her every day after international relations. Then she would follow him with her lunch tray to their special place on the patio. She watched herself doing this, day after day, almost as if she were watching someone else. So daring! Yet somehow the risk made her moments with Jonathan all the sweeter.

Then one day, when she had almost grown complacent, her luck ran out.

"I never understand why the American student so noisy in class," she was telling Jonathan as they finished their lunches. "Don't they want a good education?"

"Sure, I guess, but—"

"In my country, you get goofy like that—whap, whap —you gonna get it with a stick on your back!"

"They *beat* you?"

"Oh, yes. Or one teacher I have, he pinch your ear like this." She demonstrated, pretending to yank her gold earring.

"Sounds pretty rough."

"Well, they don't have to do that too much, because most of the student have good behavior. They know they must learn; they gonna be in big trouble at home if their parent find out they not respecting the teacher. But here . . ." She shook her head. "Even you! I'm shock when you get so sassy, ask so many question. Like yesterday in international relations when everybody argue? That make me kind of nervous."

"That was just a good discussion. Lanegren *wants* everyone to get involved."

"He like it when the student argue with him? In my country, you don't even dare ask the teacher to repeat if you don't understand. That like saying he doing a bad job of explaining. Same thing if somebody your boss."

"But if everybody's always pretending they understand when they don't, doesn't that lead to lots of misunderstandings?"

She frowned. "Sometime. But we don't like to argue about that face-to-face. We rather smooth it over, keep everything nice, try to understand without having a . . . what you call it?"

"A confrontation?"

"Yes! That the word. I'm shock when the American argue so much. Why you do this?"

"Beats me. I didn't know we did. Maybe we're just used to saying what we think."

"But sometime that so rude!"

He laughed. "Hey, Sundara, guess what?"

"What?"

"You're arguing!"

"Oh, you! You always make fun of—"

She stopped dead. Across the patio—Pok Simo with his Chinese friend. She held her breath, willing herself invisible. He hadn't seen her yet. But then his friend spotted her. He nudged Pok Simo.

Pok Simo took in their little scene—the lunch trays on the bench, the notebooks unopened. His eyes narrowed to a hard glare. She turned away, trembling. What fate! Of all people to walk by and find her alone with a white skin. For Pok Simo would love nothing better than to get her in trouble.

"You know him?" Jonathan asked.

She nodded, feeling sick. "He is Khmer also." Pok Simo resented the fact that her uncle had risen to the position of accountant while his father, once a high military attaché, now worked as a janitor. He resented even more Sundara's proud way of walking through the halls, her refusal to give him the deferential nod due one of high rank. Sundara shivered. He would savor his revenge in spreading this story.

"Is he gone yet?"

"Yeah, he took off. But what's his problem?"

She shook her head distractedly. Better if she had humbly bowed to Pok Simo each time they'd passed in the school halls, declaring herself lower than the dust beneath his feet. Now, for holding her head high, she would pay. Because what would Soka do if word of a white skin reached her ears?

News traveled fast among the Cambodians; Sundara did not expect to be kept in suspense long.

. . . .

The following morning, her aunt's voice, harsher than usual, rudely ended Sundara's dream, a dream that somehow combined the warmth of Jonathan's smile with the softness of a night in Phnom Penh. Which was worse, the shattering nightmares, or waking from such loveliness at the snap of Soka's voice? Cold fear rushed through her as she remembered the previous day. Was it possible her aunt had already heard Pok Simo's story?

Sundara took her quick turn in the bathroom, washing her face, touching on some makeup, staring at her reflection. Did she look like a wicked girl? A girl who ate lunch alone with a boy? She would miss talking with him. Never before had anyone seemed so interested in her life, her feelings. What a relief it had been to speak of things so long held inside.

When she came into breakfast wearing jeans and a jade green blouse, Soka gave her one of those accusing looks. "You spend a lot of time on yourself lately."

Sundara swallowed. She *had* taken extra care in winding the ends of her hair around the curling iron, but her clothes were nothing special, except in comparison to Soka's. Soka refused to buy clothes for herself, and wished Sundara would also refrain. But Sundara didn't want to dress out of charity boxes as she'd had to at first. What fate! All those horrible pants suits of stretchy material . . . They were nothing like what the other girls were wearing. Not that she ever missed looking *exactly* like everyone else as she had at home, skipping to school each day in a blue skirt and white blouse. It was just that now she wanted to fit in with the Americans. She wanted jeans and tops like everyone else.

"Little ones! Come eat!" Soka had set their places to eat around the table western style. Now she poured the sugary cereal the boys had seen advertised on television.

Pon punched off his cartoons and carried in the jar of strawflowers he'd been wiring for Mr. Bonner's wife. He earned two cents for each stem he attached.

"Wonderful!" Soka said. "At least three dollars' worth. What a clever son." She gave his cheek a quick nuzzle. "Ravy, here is your note for the school."

"What's this?" Naro wanted to know as Ravy stuffed the paper in the back pocket of his jeans and sat down.

"The school called," Soka said. "They wanted me to write my permission so he can play football after school."

"Football? Ravy, why do you want to smash into other people?"

"It's flag football, Papa, not tackle. You just yank the flag out of the other guy's pocket."

Sundara and Ravy exchanged glances. She knew very well he could hardly wait to play tackle.

"Talking to those people at his school is like pouring water on a duck's back," Soka complained. "No matter how many times I tell them, I cannot make them understand that I am not Mrs. Tep, there *is* no Mrs. Tep. I am Kem Soka, I tell them on the phone yesterday, but it does no good."

"You should give up trying to put *Kem* first," Naro said. "It only confuses them."

She took a seat. "Well, I can understand that. But why is it so difficult for them to understand a married woman keeping the name she is born with? *They* invented this women's lib, not us."

"Haven't you learned yet?" Naro said. "This is their country. They don't care about our ways. We are expected to imitate *them.*"

"And some of their ways I don't mind. But I'll tell you one thing, these children of ours must not become too American." She took each of them in with her eyes. "We don't want those bad things happening to the children of *this* family. Drinking, drugs, getting pregnant . . ."

Sundara's face got hot. She couldn't help it—Soka's black eyes boring into her like that. If her aunt's vague suspicions were this hard to endure, imagine how terrifying to face her wrath at the truth!

Her cousins had gobbled their cereal and excused themselves. They went back down the hall to collect Ravy's homework papers and Pon's toy motorcycle for first grade show-and-tell.

"The best American idea, as far as I'm concerned," Soka went on, "is a man being allowed only one wife at a time." She gave Naro a pointed look, then turned back to Sundara. "At home, Niece, if you get a good husband who makes a lot of money, there will always be younger women coming around, wanting to be wife number two. A terrible nuisance."

Sundara kept her eyes on her noodles, unable to enjoy the rare hint of intimacy in Soka's voice. Even if this old quarrel had lost its heat for Soka and Naro, it still served as an ominous reminder of her aunt's temper. To this day Sundara recalled overhearing her own parents discussing it—something about a younger woman, and Soka taking an ax to Naro's prized motorcycle. Sundara shuddered. Soka was not a good person to cross.

And how treacherously close Sundara always felt to Soka's anger. It was do this, don't do that, every minute of the day. Now that Soka had her food service job at the university, she seemed to have completely forgotten how much she had depended on Sundara that first year, how much Sundara had helped her, answering the phone, going to the door while Soka cowered in the bedroom as if expecting to be dragged away. . . . For a while Sundara had hoped all this might win Soka's forgiveness for the baby's death, but when Soka became strong again and unafraid, she also turned meaner than ever, as if blaming Sundara for her own period of helplessness.

Now her aunt spoke to Naro with excessive sweetness. "You're better off here, I think, where you can't talk to other women so much."

"You mean *you're* better off," he teased. "You know, you ought to watch how much you become American, Little Sister. You've put yourself high up enough in this family as it is."

"Too bad!" Soka replied, suppressing a smile, jutting her chin out at him.

"Oh Niece," Naro said with mock weariness, "why did my parents match me with such a sassy woman?"

Soka smiled broadly at this. She had good, even teeth, and a very nice look about her, Sundara thought, when she was joking with someone she liked. And they all knew Naro was only teasing, for Soka had proven a good wife to him. Especially after the first year in America, when he sank into depression. He, who had supported so many relatives at home, shamed by having to send his wife to work! But while he brooded in silence those long months, waiting for time to heal his spirit, Soka had been the most loyal and loving of wives.

Now he grinned at her. "At least she is better than the wife of Pok Sary." He jerked up his arms as if to ward off her blow.

"Ha! You *better* think so."

"I saw the two of them yesterday," he said. "Let me tell you, this is what *I* like about America: Here I don't have to bow down to *them*. You should have heard them, boasting about that son of theirs. It makes me tired."

Sundara's pulse raced at the mere mention of Pok Simo. Nervously she rose to fill her bowl again, hoping they wouldn't notice her hands shaking.

"You would think," Soka said, "that if they were so high-class they would have the good manners not to brag."

Naro nodded. "I've often thought that myself. I don't know how many times I've heard about their big brick house in Phnom Penh, their car, how everybody wanted to be their friend."

"I suppose we should try to be understanding," Soka said. "Perhaps we would feel the same way if we fell so low from so high up. But still . . ."

"Where's Grandmother?" Sundara said. "Not well again?"

Soka turned in her chair and gave Sundara one of those measuring looks. Had her attempt to change the subject been too obvious?

But to Sundara's relief, Soka merely sighed. "She doesn't want to eat. She doesn't even want to get out of bed today. Sometimes it seems hopeless. I finally persuade her to come to the supermarket with me, and then the checker is so rude Grandmother says she won't ever go back."

"They just don't have any respect for the elderly, do they?" Naro said. "And sometimes, Little Sister, I don't think you show her the respect she deserves, either."

"Me!" Soka was indignant. "What about you? You're not exactly humbling yourself for her advice all the time."

This stopped him. "Well, it's different here."

"Yes," she snapped, "I've noticed that." Then her voice softened. "I'm sorry, Naro. I do the best I can with your mother, but as you say, it's different here, and what can she tell us about coping with life in America when all she does is stay in the house, dreaming of home?"

"Ah, so understanding America is the way to be respected, then? If that's so, perhaps we should all fall on our knees before young Ravy!"

"Ha! Or Sundara here."

Oh, no. How American Sundara Has Become. A topic Soka relished and Sundara loathed. So unfair, to be criticized for everything right down to what Soka claimed was her overly bold way of walking. If only her aunt could see what an outsider she was at school. What did Soka think? That she could go to an American school and squat in the cafeteria to eat as if she were still half a world away? Would that have satisfied her? At home Sundara was too American; at school she felt painfully aware of not being American enough. She didn't fit in anywhere. *Please don't start on this,* she thought.

Fortunately, Soka seemed more inclined, at the moment, to analyze Grandmother's problems. "She has nothing like school or a job to force her out of the house. If only we could find something . . ." She considered this for a moment, then jumped up. "As for me, I have more than enough to do. That's the answer, you see. Work. Keep busy. Then there's less time to brood. Niece, you will start the dinner tonight so we can eat as soon as I get home. I promised to take that new family shopping for warm clothes tonight."

"They're having a sale at Valu-Time," Sundara offered, trying to be helpful. Unable to bargain here, Soka liked to at least find the best sales.

But Soka waved away that suggestion. "Last time I bought a jacket there the threads unraveled after one washing. I thought everything here would be good quality, but you really have to be careful."

Sundara nodded. The jacket she'd put on layaway for herself was at one of the nice stores downtown. But Soka would consider that an extravagance, and would like it even less if she knew Sundara hadn't waited to walk in with cash. But after one more payday she'd have enough, and what if the beautiful plum-colored jacket were gone by then?

She scooped out the last of the noodles from the pot into her bowl, causing her aunt to cluck.

"That's your third bowl! I don't know why you're not fat, all the food you eat and nothing but sitting in school all day."

"I'm sorry," Sundara said meekly. "I should have asked if either of you would like the rest. Would you?"

Naro shook his head and Soka said she'd had enough—she was getting a bit plump herself lately—so Sundara ate the noodles. But Soka had spoiled her appetite.

Once out the door, Sundara began to breathe easier. Nothing said about Pok Simo. She sank into her bus seat thinking maybe she'd be lucky this time. Maybe they wouldn't find out. If she stayed away from Jonathan from now on, there was still a chance she might save herself.

And after all, was he really worth the risk? Maybe Cathy was right. Maybe she *was* just a curiosity to him. Maybe she was making a fool of herself, letting herself care about him as if there were the slightest chance they could ever belong to the same world.

Besides, she already had one failure on her conscience: the death of Soka's baby. There was no more room in her life for mistakes, large or small.

Yes, what she must do was quite clear. She would not think of him. She would not waste any more time looking for him in the halls. She would study hard during lunch hour the way she used to, and when her parents came they would be proud. She would not talk to him. She would not look at him. She would forget it ever happened.

And then the school bus pulled up to the patio. Through the tinted window, she saw him standing by the flagpole. What was he doing there all by himself? Usually she didn't see him until international relations. He looked so nice. She loved those faded jeans and that flannel shirt of his. The morning sun shone on his blond hair as he tapped his notebook against his thigh and looked around.

Her heart pounded, her knees felt weak as she stood up in the bus aisle. She must pretend she hadn't seen him and walk past to the building. With so many students milling around, maybe she'd escape his notice.

But when she stepped off the bus, he hurried right toward her. He had been waiting especially for her. He knew which bus she rode.

"Sundara! I've got to talk to you." He led her away from the others. His hand on her arm felt nice, nicer than it should have. "How about explaining that little scene yesterday. Is that guy your boyfriend or something?"

She glanced up at him in surprise. "Oh, no! He be mad to hear you say this. We not the same class."

"So? Lots of girls go out with older guys. I thought—"

"Not class in school! *Social class*, don't you know? Oh, too hard to explain now." She looked over her shoulder. Were they being watched?

"But why'd you run off, then?"

"Because he *see* us. With my people everyone watch everyone else. He will talk."

"We were just sitting there."

"But I am a girl and you are a boy!"

"You noticed that too, huh?"

"Oh, you make fun!" Her voice wavered between a giggle and a wail; her cheeks were warm. "I could get in trouble. How many times do I have to tell you? In Cambodia a girl doesn't go with a boy alone."

"You're in America now."

"Oh, is that so?" She made a face. "Sometime I forget!"

He grinned. "Meet me for lunch?"

"*Jonatan.*" So persistent! Was it possible he really didn't understand? How blunt you sometimes had to be with Americans! But the longer she stayed there with him in the fresh morning air, the easier it was to let herself be persuaded, the harder it was to tell him they must not see each other. Soka had a strong power over her, but so did Jonathan.

And right now, as he stood looking at her with those strange and lovely blue eyes, she just *liked* him, liked the way he made her feel, liked the way he was banishing her nightmares by stealing into her dreams. Was that so terrible? After all, it was not as if staying away from him would bring the baby back to life. . . .

"Okay," she said. "I meet you." And her heart beat with the most extraordinary mixture of joy and fear.

FOR DISCUSSION AND WRITING

1. What would you do in Sundara's situation? Would you agree to see Jonathan or would you end the relationship? Explain.

2. Sundara explains to Jonathan how arranged marriages work. Which do you think works better, a marriage based on arrangement or on prior love and attraction? Why?

3. Are relationships at the high school portrayed realistically? Explain. Do students relate to one another in much the same way as they would at your school? Explain.

SHE IS BEAUTIFUL IN HER WHOLE BEING

FROM *THE ANCIENT CHILD*
N. Scott Momaday

Through his work, Pulitzer Prize-winning author, artist, and professor of English N. Scott Momaday explores and recreates for the public his Kiowa heritage. He shares information about his background because he feels that everyone can benefit from the Native-American belief that human beings are an intrinsic part of nature. The setting of "She Is Beautiful In Her Whole Being" is the homeland of the Navahos—the canyons and plateaus of northeast Arizona and northwest New Mexico. This love story suggests that for the Navaho and Kiowa, marriage is not just a private act between two people, but is part of a larger vision involving the elements of nature, the entire community, the past, and the future.

A REMARKABLE CHANGE CAME UPON GREY, ALMOST AT ONCE. She stood and moved and talked differently. Here, in her mother's home, she assumed an attitude of deep propriety, dignity. With Set she could still tease and joke and whisper words in her old diction, but now she spoke quietly, in a plain and simple way, and her language was made of rhythms and silences that he had not heard before. She put on the bright blouses and long pleated skirts of her mother's people. She combed out her long black hair and fashioned it in the old way, in a queue wrapped with white twine at the back of her head, and she adorned herself with silver and turquoise, old, simple pieces. She wore no makeup, except a pollen on her forehead and cheeks, which after days shone faintly, as from within, an orange-copper glow. Set observed her with wonder. She had been a beautiful girl—he held on to the vision of her in the buckskin dress, with feathers in her braided hair, her face painted—with a free and original and irrepressible spirit. And now, in a wholly different context, she was a beautiful woman, endowed with experience and purpose and grace. She ripened before his eyes. He felt almost boyish in her presence, and indeed, in keeping with the story, he must play out his part as Set-talee, Tsoai-talee, boy bear, rock-tree boy. But Grey had evolved from a girl into a woman, and he had been witness to it. And, fittingly, he began to attend her. One day, while looking at her as she played with Nanibah, it became clear to him that she belonged to him, and he to her. And he felt a happiness beyond anything he had ever known.

That summer they lived in the hogan beyond her mother's house. Little by little Set fitted himself into the rhythm of life at Lukachukai. In the night he went out to see, as for the first time, the innumerable brilliant points of light in the sky. Looking at them he thought he had never seen the night, and he wept and laughed and at last kept the silence of the stars. In the early morning he walked into the dawn's light, slowly at first, stiff with cold, but warming as the flood of light fell from the east, and he saw with wonder and fear and thanksgiving the land become radiant, defined by light and long, color-bearing distances. And when enough of his strength returned he began to run.

The boy ran. In the days he drew and painted, watching the light change and the colors turn and shift upon the earth, the shadows extend and deepen. His paintings were strong and simple, primary, like those of a child. He listened to the wind and the birds and thunder rolling on the cliffs; in the darkness there was the yip-yip-yipping of coyotes, and at first light the coyotes set up a din that was otherworldly, that was like an electronic music descending from every point on the horizon to the center of creation, to this place, this hogan. And he listened to the voices of Grey and her mother, of Antonia and Nanibah, of old men and women passing by. He listened to the turning of their voices in the element of *diné bizaad*, to the exotic words with their innumerable edges and hollows and inclines—*chizh, dlǫǫ́, tł'izí, todiłhił.* And he began to understand and use very simple words and constructions in Navajo—*aoo', dooda, daats'í hágoónee', Set yinishyé, haash yinilyé?*

At first he did not know how to behave with Lela and Antonia, nor did they with him. But Grey was a good intermediary, and by and large all was well. Nanibah made a great difference, too. She was, like Grey, mischievous and undaunted in her spirit. She took a liking to Set, and she taught him very quickly how to get along with her. He had no experience of children to speak of, and so he walked on eggs. Nanibah adopted him.

One day, when Grey was working at the loom and Antonia had taken Nanibah to Chinle to buy hay and grain, Lela approached close to Set. He was drawing.

"She weaves well," Lela said, under an obligation to speak offhand.

"I think so too," Set said.

"She talks like a Navajo."

"I am glad," Set said.

There was a long pause, which to Set was uncomfortable, to Lela not. He made heavy strokes on the paper with a piece of charcoal.

"She has told us that you are Kiowa."

Set considered. Lela knew from the first that he was Kiowa. She, having been married to one, knew better than he what it was to be Kiowa. This oblique conversation would have frustrated him at one time; it did not frustrate him now. It was the proper way to proceed.

"I am Kiowa," he said.

"You have strong medicine," Lela said, as a matter of fact.

"Yes."

"Grey knows of this medicine." Again, not a question.

"She gave it to me," he said.

"Yes, so I have heard," Lela said. She was a large woman. She looked him in the eye for a long moment. Wisps of hair turned on the air at her temples. Her hands were at her sides. He could read nothing in her eyes. After a long time she said, "It is a hard thing to be what you must be, *daats'i.*"

"*Daats'i,*" he said. Perhaps.

There was another long pause.

"Do you think you will marry my daughter?" Lela asked. She spoke in a considered way, with measured breath. Anachronism forwards, he thought. Her face was shining, especially her forehead and cheeks, and was almost the color of copper. Her face was wonderfully round. She held hands with herself; it was a habit with her. She held them clasped lightly together and low on her abdomen. Her hands were brown and shapely; on three of her fingers were silver rings with bright turquoise stones. She stood with her feet apart. Her stance, and the lines of her body suggested a fine and firm balance.

Puppies were romping and yelping in the shadow of the house. Butterflies were flitting and floating on the shine of the air. The walls of red rock in the distance appeared to vibrate in the rising heat. The spring had taken hold of the long valley. In looking out across the wide, warming land, Set could conceive of the summer—it was a conception like memory, the remembered summertime of his boyhood at the Peter and Paul Home or at the house on Scott Street; and he marveled to feel his senses awakening—as Lela had conceived of it days and weeks ago, in advance of the final snowfall, when the skies above the Lukachukai Mountains were still curdled and dark. He drew his gaze back upon the closer ground to see Dog standing beyond the hogan, his ears pricked, appearing to search the horizon, standing like some old granitic cairn on the plain, and closer, before the hogan, Grey, at three quarters, sitting, her fine brown fingers picking at the loom.

"I don't know," he said. He looked into her eyes and could see nothing devious there, nothing, unless it was the faintest glint of mischief, a humor so tentative that he dare not count on it. "But it is a thing I have in mind."

"You *want* to marry my daughter, *daats'i?*"

Then he heard himself say, "Yes. Yes, I do. I want to marry your daughter. There is nothing I want more than that."

Then he thought of her asking, You have told her this? And he was ashamed; he searched desperately for some plausible answer: No—not yet . . . I did not know. . . . I have not been clear in my mind. I am going to tell her now. But it did not come to that. Instead, Lela said, "My daughter is a beautiful woman, like me."

"Yes, she is."

"She is beautiful in her whole being, like me."

"Yes."

"She will bear beautiful children, like me."

"Yes."

Pause.

"But you, if I may speak in a clear way, you are sick. This I have heard. This I have seen. The bear stands against you."

"Yes."

"Yes?"

"Yes. I am sick. I have been sick for a long time, but I hope to be well and strong. I can be well and strong with Grey's help—she knows how to help me. I have become stronger since I have been here, because of Grey."

"*Aoo'.* Yes."

"*Aoo',* I have been afflicted. The bear stands against me."

"*Aoo'.*"

"*Aoo'.* I am the bear."

"*Aoo'.*"

· · ·

In the early mornings, when he inhaled the cold air that ran down from the mountains, and when he touched the earth through the soles of the moccasins Lela and Grey had made for him, he knew how glad he was to be alive. His skin grew darker, and his body began to grow hard, and his hair grew over his ears and shaggy at the nape of his neck. It seemed to him that he could see a little farther into the distance each day and that his legs were hardening and becoming more flexible at the ankles and knees, his stride longer and more regular and persistent. He ran until the sweat streamed on his body, and he tasted the salty exertion at the corners of his mouth, and he ran on until his breathing came in time with his stride and his whole body was fitted into the most delicate and precise rhythm. He entered into the current of the wind, of water running, of shadows extending, of sounds rising up and falling away. His life was in motion; in motion was his life. He ran until running became the best expression of his spirit, until it seemed he could not stop, that if he stopped he would lose his place in the design of creation—and beyond that, until his lungs burned and his breath came hard and fast and loud, and his legs and feet were almost too heavy to lift—and beyond that, deeper into the rhythm, into a state of motion, mindless and inexorable, without end. And when he returned to the hogan Grey bathed him while he stood naked, allowing his body to settle down. Then she gave him water to drink and a kind of gruel, made of crushed corn and goat's milk, piñons and dried fruit, and in the manner of old Najavo men a hundred years ago, he wrapped his loins in white cloth and lay down on a pallet in the shade of a juniper, near the loom, and Grey slowly kneaded the muscles in his shoulders and back and legs. She made a mild abrasive out of sand and oil and massaged his feet, and she sat beside him, singing softly, stirring the air over him with a grass broom, and he sank into deep relaxation. And in the afternoon he drew and painted and dreamed and set his mind upon marriage. He spoke Navajo to Lela as far as he could, and he was not offended when she laughed at him. He played games with Nanibah and put notions of the wide world in her head. He instructed her in painting, and in turn she gave him words, the words of a child, which are at the center of language. And he observed with deep appreciation, wonder, and respect Grey's return to the Navajo world.

In the late afternoon they convened at Lela's table. There was usually lamb or mutton, and dried corn and tinned tomatoes and beans, and dried fruit. There were wonderful breads: fried bread, corn bread, oven bread. Set liked best the dense, sweet oven bread, baked in a *horno* of adobe bricks and mud plaster, it was the bread of the pueblos; Lela had learned to make it when she was a girl attending the fiestas in the ancient towns on the Rio Grande.

At dusk Grey prepared a sweat lodge for him, a small conical hogan with an opening on the west. When the stones in the pit were hot and the flames had died down, Grey and Set entered the sweat lodge in breechcloths and sat next to each other. Grey poured water on the stones, and

Edward Curtis, Prayer to the
Stars, *n.d.*

they hissed and let off steam. In the bare light of the embers, before they
were extinguished, Set looked at Grey discreetly, saw her smooth skin
shining and glistening, as bright beads of water appeared on her forehead,
her throat, her shoulders and thighs. The tips of her breasts were nearly as
dark as her hair. He watched as she leaned to pour the water, her long side
and flank shining, her toes flexing into the sand. Discreetly he watched,
the heat of the steam and of his desire coming upon him. And for a time
he became dull and heavy, as on the verge of sleep, dreaming of the
woman beside him, dreaming longingly of her body, which was so anom-
alously soft and firm, which was so exciting in its curves and lines and

hollows and folds, of the smell of her when she came fresh from sleep, of her casual gestures, of her voice in the day and night when she spoke of this and that with interest or excitement, or with anger or frustration or sorrow, of the breathy cooing of her ecstasy, of her singing softly, of her gentle breathing in the night. And then the drowsiness and the dreaming dissolved, and he felt suddenly refreshed and invigorated and clean and hot, and he began to laugh, and Grey too, and they touched, and their hands slipped over their bodies, describing desire, but yet discreetly, for Lela and perhaps Antonia and Nanibah might be close by. All things in their places. In this little house was peace and purification. Outside the evening air bit them with cold and was sharply delicious. And they walked away from the house and hogan and lay down on a dune, observing the night sky. And later, when the moon was high, they rode horses into the arroyos, among shadows that were like pools of time and eternity.

. . .

At the end of April a man came down from the Chuskas, bringing mountain earth. In the center of the hogan he constructed an altar and performed a ceremony through most of the night. Set and Grey sat side by side to the left of the priest. Coals were laid upon the altar, and a firestick was placed in the coals just so, on the east side, so that the pointed end smoldered and shone like a brand. Crystals were placed here and there on the altar's rim. The priest arranged his paraphernalia before him. There were herbs and pollens, a gourd rattle, pots of liquors and teas, peyote pastes, feather fans, a bowl of water, and an eagle-bone whistle. Nanibah slept on a pallet at the wall of the hogan. Lela and Antonia assisted the priest, keeping the coals alive, sprinkling sage and cedar, crushed with tobacco in their fingers, bringing water and coals as needed. Set and Grey glanced at each other occasionally, and sometimes they touched hands, but they were concentrated upon the ceremony. Smoke was fanned upon them, and when it was proper to do so they spoke of their visions. Their visions were very beautiful, and their words were the best that were in their hearts, and their voices were joined in the smoke to other voices, ancient and original. Their voices were soft and everlasting, and in them were laughter and wailing and reverence and awe, and they made stories and songs and prayers. And in the dark early morning, after they had gone out of the hogan to say themselves to the night sky and returned, they stood before the altar, holding each other close. In their honor the priest gave the firestick to the fire, and they knew, though it was not an explicit knowledge, that they were married. In ceremony, in tradition out of time, in a sacred manner, in beauty they were married forever.

1. The natural setting plays an important role in the story. Which descriptions of objects, large or small, are most vivid? Explain.

2. Contrast Grey and Set's courtship and marriage ceremony with others with which you are familiar.

3. Would you like to be married in a ceremony like the one described? Why or why not? Describe your ideal marriage ceremony.

~ ~ ~ ~ ~ ~ ~ ~ ~ ~ ~ ~ ~ ~ ~ ~

A CERTAIN BEGINNING
Kim Chi-wŏn   translated by Bruce and Ju-Chan Fulton

Kim Chi-wŏn was born in Korea and has lived in the New York City area since the 1970s. She often writes about the problems of Korean immigrant women in American cities. In "A Certain Beginning," a young man, Chŏng-il, needs to get married in order to obtain a green card. He pays Yun-ja, a middle-aged woman who works in a factory, to marry him for this reason. The arrangement between the two lurches self-consciously into a friendship with romantic undertones. The story examines how barriers people build around themselves may be overcome by the desire for intimacy.

YUN-JA FLOATED ON THE BLUE SWELLS, her face toward the dazzling sun. At first the water had chilled her, but now it felt agreeable, almost responding to her touch. Ripples slapped about her ears, and a breeze brushed the wet tip of her nose. Sailboats eased out of the corner of her eye and into the distance. She heard the drone of powerboats, the laughter of children, and the babble of English, Spanish, and other tongues blending indistinguishably like faraway sounds in a dream. Her only reaction to all this was an occasional blink. She felt drugged by the sun.

Yun-ja straightened herself in the water and looked for Chŏng-il. There he was, sitting under the beach umbrella with his head tilted back, drinking something. From her distant vantage point, twenty-seven-year-old Chŏng-il looked as small as a Boy Scout. He reminded her of a houseboy she had seen in a photo of some American soldiers during the Korean War.

"Life begins all over after today," Yun-ja thought. She had read in a women's magazine that it was natural for a woman who was alone after a divorce, even a long-awaited one, to be lonely, to feel she had failed, because in any society a happy marriage is considered a sign of a success-ful life. And so a divorced woman ought to make radical changes in her life-style. The magazine article had suggested getting out of the daily routine—sleeping as late as you want, eating what you want, throwing a party in the middle of the week, getting involved in new activities. "My case is a bit different, but like the writer says, I've got to start over again. But how? How is my life going to be different?" Yun-ja hadn't the slight-est idea how to start a completely new life. Even if she were to begin sleeping all day and staying up all night, what difference would it make if she hadn't changed inwardly? Without a real change the days ahead would be boring and just blend together, she thought. Day would drift into night; she would find herself hardly able to sleep and another empty day would dawn. And how tasteless the food eaten alone; how unbearable to hear only the sound of her own chewing. These thoughts hadn't occurred to her before. "He won't be coming anymore starting tomorrow," she thought. The approaching days began to look meaningless.

Several days earlier, Chŏng-il had brought some soybean sprouts and tofu to Yun-ja's apartment and had begun making soybean-paste soup. Yun-ja was sitting on the old sofa, knitting.

"Mrs. Lee, how about a trip to the beach to celebrate our 'marriage'? A honeymoon, you know?"

Yun-ja laughed. She and Chŏng-il found nothing as funny as the word *marriage*. Chŏng-il also laughed, to show that his joke was innocent.

"Marriage" to Chŏng-il meant the permanent resident card he was obtaining. He and Yun-ja were already formally married, but it was the day he was to receive the green card he had been waiting for that Chŏng-il called his "wedding day."

Chŏng-il had paid Yun-ja fifteen hundred dollars to marry him so that he could apply for permanent residency in the U.S. Until his marriage he had been pursued by the American immigration authorities for working without the proper visa.

"Americans talk about things like inflation, but they're still a super-power. Don't they have anything better to do than track down foreign stu-dents?" Chŏng-il had said the day he met Yun-ja. His eyes had been moist with tears.

Now, almost two months later, Chŏng-il had his permanent resident card and Yun-ja the fifteen hundred dollars. And today their relationship would come to an end.

Chŏng-il ambled down the beach toward the water, his smooth bronze skin gleaming in the sun. He shouted to Yun-ja and smiled, but she couldn't make out the words. Perhaps he was challenging her to a race, or asking how the water was.

Yun-ja had been delighted when Ki-yŏng's mother, who had been working with her at a clothing factory in Chinatown, sounded her out about a contract marriage with Chŏng-il. "He came here on a student visa," the woman had explained. "My husband tells me his older brother makes a decent living in Seoul. . . . The boy's been told to leave the country, so his bags are packed and he's about to move to a different state. . . . It's been only seven months since he came to America. . . . Just his luck— other Korean students work here without getting caught. . . ."

"Why not?" Yun-ja had thought. If only she could get out of that sunless, roach-infested Manhattan basement apartment that she had been sharing with a young Chinese woman. And her lower back had become stiff as a board from too many hours of piecework at the sewing machine. All day long she was engulfed by Chinese speaking in strange tones and sewing machines whirring at full tilt. Yun-ja had trod the pedals of her sewing machine in the dusty air of the factory, the pieces of cloth she handled feeling unbearably heavy. Yes, life in America had not been easy for Yun-ja, and so she decided to give herself a vacation. With the fifteen hundred dollars from a contract marriage she could get a sunny room where she could open the window and look out on the street.

And now her wish had come true. She had gotten a studio apartment on the West Side, twenty minutes by foot from the end of a subway line, and received Chŏng-il as a "customer," as Ki-yŏng's mother had put it.

After quitting her job Yun-ja stayed in bed in the morning, listening to the traffic on the street below. In the evening, Chŏng-il would return from his temporary accounting job. Yun-ja would greet him like a boardinghouse mistress, and they would share the meal she had prepared. Her day was divided between the time before he arrived and the time after.

Thankful for his meals, Chŏng-il would sometimes go grocery shopping and occasionally he would do the cooking, not wishing to feel obligated to Yun-ja.

Chŏng-il swam near. "Going to stay in forever?" he joked. His lips had turned blue.

"Anything left to drink?" she asked.

"There's some Coke, and I got some water just now."

Chŏng-il had bought everything for this outing—Korean-style grilled beef, some Korean delicacies, even paper napkins.

"Mrs. Lee, this is a good place for clams—big ones too. A couple of them will fill you up—or so they say. Let's go dig a few. Then we can go home, steam them up, and have them with rice. A simple meal, just right for a couple of tired bodies. What do you think?"

Instead of answering, Yun-ja watched Chŏng-il's head bobbing like a watermelon. "So he's thinking about dropping by my place. . . . Will he leave at eleven-thirty again, on our last day? Well, he has to go there anyway to pick up his things." While eating lunch, she had mentally rehearsed some possible farewells at her apartment: "I guess you'll be busy with school again pretty soon," or "Are you moving into a dorm?"

Yun-ja was worried about giving Chŏng-il the impression that she was making a play for him. At times she had wanted to hand Chŏng-il a fresh towel or some lotion when he returned sopping wet from the shower down the hall, but she would end up simply ignoring him.

Yun-ja thought about the past two months. Each night after dinner at her apartment Chŏng-il would remain at the table and read a book or newspaper. At eleven-thirty he would leave to spend the night with a friend who lived two blocks away. Chŏng-il had been told by his lawyer that a person ordered out of the country who then got married and applied for a permanent resident card could expect to be investigated by the Immigration and Naturalization Service. And so he and Yun-ja had tried to look like a married couple. This meant that Chŏng-il had to be seen with Yun-ja. He would stay as late as he could at her apartment, and he kept a pair of pajamas, some old shoes, and other belongings there.

Tick, tick, tick. . . . Yun-ja would sit knitting or listening to a record, while Chŏng-il read a book or wrote a letter. Pretending to be absorbed in whatever they were doing, both would keep stealing glances at their watches. . . . Tick, tick, tick. . . .

At eleven-thirty Chŏng-il would strap on his watch and get up. Jingling his keys, he would mumble "Good night" or "I'm going." Yun-ja would remain where she was and pretend to be preoccupied until his lanky, boyish figure had disappeared out the door.

. . .

It hadn't always been that way. During the first few days after their marriage they would exchange news of Korea or talk about life in America—U.S. immigration policy, the high prices, the unemployment, or whatever. And when Chŏng-il left, Yun-ja would see him to the door. The silent evenings had begun the night she had suggested they live together. That night Chŏng-il had brought some beer and they had sung some children's ditties, popular tunes, and other songs they both knew. The people in the next apartment had pounded on the wall in protest.

Chŏng-il and Yun-ja had lowered their voices, but only temporarily. It was while Chŏng-il was bringing tears of laughter to Yun-ja, as he sang and clowned around, that she had broached the subject: Why did Chŏng-il want to leave right at eleven-thirty every night only to sleep at a friend's apartment where he wasn't really welcome? He could just as easily curl up in a corner of her apartment at night and the two of them could live together like a big sister and her little brother—now wouldn't that be great? Immediately Chŏng-il's face had hardened and Yun-ja had realized her blunder. That was the last time Chŏng-il had brought beer to the apartment. The lengthy conversations had stopped and Chŏng-il no longer entertained Yun-ja with songs.

Yun-ja had begun to feel resentful as Chŏng-il rose and left like clock-work each night. "Afraid I'm going to bite, you little stinker!" she would think, pouting at the sound of the key turning in the door. "It's a tug-of-war. You want to keep on my good side, so you sneak looks at me to see how I'm feeling. You're scared I might call off the marriage. It's true, isn't it—if I said I didn't want to go through with it, what would you do? Where would you find another unmarried woman with a green card? Would you run off to another state? Fat chance!"

The evening following her ill-advised proposal to live together, Yun-ja had left her apartment around the time Chŏng-il was to arrive. She didn't want him to think she was sitting around the apartment waiting for him. She walked to a nearby playground that she had never visited before and watched a couple of Asian children playing with some other children. She wondered if being gone when Chŏng-il arrived would make things even more awkward between them. She wanted to return and tell him that her suggestion the previous evening had had no hidden meaning. Yun-ja had no desire to become emotionally involved with Chŏng-il. This was not so much because of their thirteen-year age difference (though Yun-ja still wasn't used to the idea that she was forty), but because Yun-ja had no illusions about marriage.

The man Yun-ja had married upon graduating from college had done well in business, and around the time of their divorce seven years later he had become a wealthy man, with a car and the finest house in Seoul's Hwagok neighborhood.

"Let's get a divorce; you can have the house," he had said one day.

Yun-ja was terribly shocked.

"But why?. . . Is there another woman?"

"No, it's not that. I just don't think I'm cut out for marriage.

In desperation Yun-ja had suggested a trial separation. But her husband had insisted on the divorce, and one day he left, taking only a toiletry kit and some clothes. Yun-ja had wept for days afterward. She was convinced that another woman had come on the scene, and sometimes she secretly kept an eye on her husband's office on T'oegye Avenue to try to confirm this.

"Was there really no other woman?" she asked herself at the playground. "Did he want the divorce because he was tired of living with me?" Their only baby had been placed in an incubator at birth, but the sickly child had died. Being a first-time mother had overwhelmed Yun-ja. "Maybe he just got sick and tired of everything. Or maybe he just wanted to stop living with me and go somewhere far away—that's how I felt toward him when he stayed out late." She had heard recently that he had remarried.

"Are you Korean?"

Yun-ja looked up to see a withered old Korean woman whose hair was drawn into a bun the size of a walnut. Yun-ja was delighted to see another Korean, though she couldn't help feeling conspicuous because of the older woman's traditional Korean clothing, which was made of fine nylon gauze.

Before Yun-ja could answer, the woman plopped herself down and drew a crimson pack of cigarettes from the pocket of her bloomers.

"Care for one, miss?"

"No, thank you."

The old woman lit a cigarette and began talking as if she were ripe for a quarrel: "Ah me, this city isn't fit for people to live in. It's a place for animals, that's what. In Korea I had a nice warm room with a laminated floor, but here no one takes their shoes off and the floors are all messy."

"Can't you go back to Korea?"

"Are you kidding? Those darn sons of mine won't let me. I have to babysit their kids all day long. Whenever I see a plane I start crying—I tell you! To think that I flew over here on one of those damned things!"

The old woman's eyes were inflamed, as if she cried every day, and now fresh tears gathered. Yun-ja looked up and watched the plane they had spotted. It had taken off from the nearby airport and seemed to float just above them as it climbed into the sky. Its crimson and emerald green landing lights winked.

"I don't miss my hometown the way this grandmother does. And I don't feel like crying at the sight of that plane," thought Yun-ja. Her homeland was the source of her shame. She had had to get away from it—there was no other way.

It was around seven when Yun-ja returned from the playground.

Chŏng-il opened the door. "Did you go somewhere?" he asked politely, like a schoolboy addressing his teacher.

Yun-ja was relieved to have been spoken to first.

"I was talking with an elderly Korean woman."

"The one who goes around in Korean clothes? Was she telling you how
bad it is here in America?"

"You know her?"

"Oh, she's notorious—latches on to every Korean she sees."

This ordinary beginning to the evening would eventually yield to a
silent standoff, taut like the rope in a tug-of-war.

. . .

Chŏng-il's joking reference to "marriage" the evening he had offered
to take Yun-ja to the beach had come easily because his immigration
papers had finally been processed. All he had to do was see his lawyer and
sign them, and he would get his permanent resident card.

Though it was six o'clock, it was still bright as midday. It was a muggy
August evening, and the small fan in the wall next to the window stut-
tered, as if it were panting in the heat of Yun-ja's top-floor apartment.

Realizing that Chŏng-il was only joking, Yun-ja stopped knitting. She
got up and put a record on. The reedy sound of a man's mellow voice
unwound from the cheap stereo:

> Now that we're about to part
> Take my hand once again. . . .

Yun-ja abruptly turned off the stereo. "Listening to songs makes me
feel even hotter," she said.

Several days later, after Chŏng-il had obtained his permanent resident
card, he borrowed a car and took Yun-ja to the beach, as promised. Yun-
ja had thought it a kind of token of his gratitude, like the flowers or wine
you give to the doctor who delivered your baby, or a memento you give to
your teacher at graduation.

. . .

They stayed late at the beach to avoid the Friday afternoon rush hour.
As the day turned to evening, the breeze became chilly and the two of
them stayed out of the water, sitting together on the cool sand. Whether
it was because they were outside or because this was their last day together, Yun-ja somehow felt that the tug-of-war between them had eased. But
the parting words a couple might have said to each other were missing:

"Give me a call or drop me a line and let me know how things are going." Chŏng-il did most of the talking, and Yun-ja found his small talk refreshing. He told her about getting measles at age nine, practicing martial arts in college, and going around Seoul in the dog days of summer just to get a driver's license so he could work while going to school in America. And he talked about a book he'd read, entitled *Papillon*.

"If you have Papillon's will, the sky's the limit on what you can do in America. You've heard Koreans when they get together here. They're always talking about the Chinese. The first-generation Chinese saved a few pennies doing unskilled labor when the subways were built. The second generation opened up small laundries or noodle stands. Buying houses and educating the kids didn't happen until the third generation. Whenever I hear that, I realize that Koreans want to do everything in a hurry—I'm the same way. They sound like they want to accomplish in a couple of years what it took the Chinese three generations to do. . . . When I left Korea I told my friends and my big brother not to feel bad if I didn't write, because I might not be able to afford the postage. My brother bought me an expensive fountain pen and told me that if I went hungry in the States I should sell it and buy myself a meal. And then my older sister had a gold ring made for me. I put the damned thing on my finger, got myself decked out in a suit for the plane ride, and then on the way over I was so excited I couldn't eat a thing—not a thing. The stewardess was probably saying to herself, 'Here's a guy who's never been on a plane before.' That damned ring—I must have looked like a jerk!"

Yun-ja related a few details about the elderly Korean woman she had met in the park. (Why did her thoughts return so often to this grandmother?) Then she told Chŏng-il a little about herself, realizing he had probably already learned through Ki-yŏng's mother that she was just another divorcee with no one to turn to.

The cool wind picked up as the sunlight faded, and they put their clothes on over their swimsuits. Chŏng-il's shirt was inside out, and Yunja could read the brand name on the neck tag.

"Your shirt's inside out."

Chŏng-il roughly pulled the shirt off and put it on right side out. Her steady gaze seemed to annoy him.

The beach was deserted except for a few small groups and some young couples lying on the sand nearby, exchanging affections. Hundreds of sea gulls began to gather. The birds frightened Yun-ja. Their wings looked ragged; their sharp, ceaselessly moving eyes seemed treacherous. Yun-ja felt as if their pointed beaks were about to bore into her eyes, maybe even her heart. She folded the towel she had been sitting on and stood up.

"Let's get going."

More gulls had alighted on the nearly empty parking lot, which stretched out as big as a football field.

"Want to get a closer look?" Chŏng-il asked as he started the car.

"They'll fly away."

"Not if we go slow. God, there must be thousands of them."

The car glided in a slow circle around the sea gulls. Just as Chŏng-il had said, the birds stayed where they were. Yun-ja watched them through the window, her fear now gone.

They pulled out onto the highway and the beach grew distant. A grand sunset flared up in the dark blue sky. The outline of distant hills and trees swung behind the car and gradually disappeared. Yun-ja noticed that Chŏng-il had turned on the headlights.

"You must be beat," Chŏng-il said. "Why don't you lean back and make yourself comfortable."

Perhaps because he was silent for a time, Yun-ja somehow felt his firm, quiet manner in the smooth, steady motion of the car. She wondered what to do when they arrived at her apartment. Invite him in? Arrange to meet him somewhere the following day to give him his things? But the second idea would involve seeing him again. . . . The tide hadn't been low, so they hadn't been able to dig clams. . . . "I'll bet I've looked like a nobody to him, a woman who's hungry for love and money." Yun-ja recalled something Chŏng-il had once told her: "After I get my degree here, write a couple of books, and make a name for myself, I'd like to go back to Korea. Right now there are too many Ph.D.'s over there. I know I wouldn't find a job if I went back with just a degree."

"And for the rest of your life," Yun-ja now thought, "I'll be a cheap object for you to gossip about. You'll say, 'I was helpless when they told me to leave the country—so I bought myself a wife who was practically old enough to be my mother. What a pain in the neck—especially when she came up with the idea of living together.' And at some point in the future when you propose to your sweetheart, maybe you'll blabber something like 'I have a confession to make—I've been married before. . . .'"

Chŏng-il drove on silently. His hand on the steering wheel was fine and delicate—a student's hand. Yun-ja felt like yanking that hand, biting it, anything to make him see things her way, to make him always speak respectfully of her in the future. Chŏng-il felt Yun-ja's gaze and stole a glance at her. The small face that had been angled toward his was now looking straight ahead. "She's no beauty—maybe it's that thin body of hers that makes her look kind of shriveled up—but sometimes she's really pretty. Especially when it's hot. Then that honey-colored skin of hers gets a nice shine to it and her eyelashes look even darker." But Chŏng-il had rarely felt comfortable enough to examine Yun-ja's face.

"Mrs. Lee, did you ever have any children?"

"One—it died."

Chŏng-il lit a cigarette. Her toneless voice rang in his ears. "She doesn't seem to have any feelings. No expression, no interest in others, it even sounds as if her baby's death means nothing to her. True—time has a way of easing the pain. I don't show any emotion either when I tell people that my father died when I was young and my mother passed away when I was in college. Probably it's the same with her. But her own baby? How can she say 'It died' just like that?"

He had known from the beginning, through Ki-yŏng's mother, that Yun-ja was a single woman with no money. It had never occurred to him when he paid Ki-yŏng's mother the first installment of the fifteen hundred dollars that a woman with such a common name as Yun-ja might have special qualities. What had he expected her to be like, this woman who was to become his wife in name only? Well, a woman who had led a hard life, but who would vaguely resemble Ki-yŏng's mother—short permed hair, a calf-length sack dress, white sandals—a woman in her forties who didn't look completely at ease in Western-style clothing. But the woman Ki-yŏng's father had taken him to meet at the bus stop was thin and petite with short, straight hair and a sleeveless dress. Her eyelids had a deep double fold, and her skin had a dusky sheen that reminded Chŏng-il of Southeast Asian women. She was holding a pair of sunglasses, and a large handbag hung from her long, slender arm.

As they walked the short distance to Ki-yŏng's mother's for dinner that first night, Chŏng-il had felt pity for this woman who didn't even come up to his shoulders. He had also felt guilty and ill at ease. But Yun-ja had spoken nonchalantly: "So you're a student? Well, I just found an apartment yesterday. I'll be moving in three days from now. We can go over a little later and I'll show you around. It's really small—kitchen, bathroom, living room, and bedroom all in one." To Chŏng-il this breezy woman of forty or so acted like an eighteen-year-old girl. "This woman's marrying me for money." He felt regretful, as if he were buying an aging prostitute.

"Why don't you two forget about the business part of it and get married for real?" Ki-yŏng's mother had said at dinner. And when she sang a playful rendition of the wedding march, Chŏng-il had felt like crawling under the table. Yun-ja had merely laughed.

The traffic between the beach and the city was heavy, occasionally coming to a standstill. Among the procession of vehicles Yun-ja and Chŏng-il noticed cars towing boats, cars carrying bicycles, cars with tents and shovels strapped to their roof racks.

As Chŏng-il drove by shops that had closed for the day, he thought of all the time he had spent on the phone with his older brother in Korea, of all the hard-earned money he had managed to scrounge from him (did his sister-in-law know about that?)—all because of this permanent resident card. And now he couldn't even afford tuition for next semester. These thoughts depressed him. But then he bucked up: Now that he had his green card (his chest swelled at the idea), there was no reason he couldn't work. "I'll take next semester off, put my nose to the grindstone, and by the following semester I'll have my tuition." And now that he was a permanent resident, his tuition would be cut in half. He made some mental calculations: How much could he save by cutting his rent and food to the bone? "But you can't cut down on the food too much," Chŏng-il reminded himself. There were students who had ended up sick and run-down, who couldn't study or do other things as a result. "This woman Yun-ja really has it easy—doesn't have to study. All she has to do is eat and sleep, day after day." Chŏng-il felt it was disgraceful that a young, intelligent Korean such as himself was living unproductively in America, as if he had no responsibilities to his family or country. "Why am I busting my butt to be here? Is the education really that wonderful?" In English class back in Korea he had vaguely dreamed of studying in America. Or rather he had liked the idea of hearing people say he had studied there. More shameful than this was the impulse he had to stay on in America. "What about the other people from abroad who live in the States—do they feel guilty about their feelings for their country, too?" He had read diatribes about America's corrupt material civilization. But he couldn't figure out what was so corrupt about it, and that bothered him. He wanted to see just what a young Korean man could accomplish in the world, and he wanted to experience the anger of frustration rather than the calm of complacency. He wanted knowledge, and recognition from others. But this woman Yun-ja didn't even seem to realize she was Korean.

The car pulled up on a street of six-story apartment buildings whose bricks were fading. Children were running and bicycling on the cement sidewalk; elderly couples strolled hand in hand, taking in the evening. Chŏng-il got out, unpacked the cooler and the towels, and loaded them on his shoulder. He and Yun-ja had the elevator to themselves. Yun-ja felt anxious and lonely, as if she had entered an unfamiliar neighborhood at dusk. She braced herself against the side of the elevator as it accelerated and slowed. When she was young it seemed the world belonged to her, but as time went on these "belongings" had disappeared; now she felt as if she had nothing. When it came time to part from someone, her heart ached as if she were separating from a lover. "Am I so dependent on people that I drove my husband away? Nobody wants to be burdened with me, so they all leave—even my baby. . . . I wonder if that old woman at the playground went back to Korea. Maybe she's still smoking American cigarettes and bending the ear of every Korean she sees here. Maybe I'll end up like her when I'm old. Already my body feels like a dead weight because of my neuralgia—God forbid that I latch on to just anybody and start telling a sob story."

Yun-ja unlocked the door to the apartment and turned on the light.

Today the small, perfectly square room looked cozy and intimate to them. They smelled the familiar odors, which had been intensified by the summer heat.

But Chŏng-il felt awkward when he saw that Yun-ja had packed his trunk and set it on the sofa. If only he could unpack it and return the belongings to their places.

"You must feel pretty sticky—why don't you take a shower?" Yun-ja said.

Chŏng-il returned from washing his salt-encrusted body to find Yun-ja cleaning the sand from the doorway. She had changed to a familiar, well-worn yellow dress. The cooler had been emptied and cleaned, the towels put away. Yun-ja had shampooed, and comb marks were still visible in her wet hair. Chŏng-il tried to think of something to say, gave up, and tiptoed to the sofa to sit down. "She's already washed her hair, changed, and started sweeping up," he thought. As Yun-ja bustled about, she looked to Chŏng-il as if she had just blossomed.

"Shouldn't I offer him some dinner?" Yun-ja thought as she swept up the sand. "He went to the trouble of borrowing a car and taking me out—the least I can do is give him a nice meal. And where would he eat if he left now? He'd probably fill up on junk food. . . . But if I offer to feed him, he might think I had something in mind. And when I've paid people for something, they never offered me dinner, did they?"

"How about some music?" Chŏng-il mumbled. He got up, walked stiffly to the stereo, and placed the needle on the record that happened to be on the turntable. The rhythm of a Flamenco guitar filled the room. Although Chŏng-il didn't pay much attention to the music Yun-ja played, it seemed that this was a new record. "Why have I been afraid of this woman? You'd think she was a witch or something."

"If that woman sinks her hooks into you, you've had it." Chŏng-il had heard this from his roommate, Ki-yŏng's father, and goodness knows how many others. "Nothing happened again today?" the roommate would joke when Chŏng-il returned in the evening from Yun-ja's apartment. "When it comes to you-know-what, nothing beats a middle-aged woman. I hope you're offering good service in return for those tasty meals you're getting."

The shrill voices of the children and the noise of airplanes and traffic were drowned out by the guitar music. The odor of something rotten outside wafted in with the heat of the summer night.

Chŏng-il began to feel ashamed. Here he was about to run out on this woman he'd used in return for a measly sum of money—a woman whose life he had touched. He had visited this room for almost two months, and now he wished he could spend that time over again. "Why didn't I try to make it more enjoyable?" he asked himself. He and Yun-ja had rarely listened to music, and when they had gone strolling in the nearby park after dinner he had felt uneasy, knowing that they did this only so that others would see the two of them together.

Yun-ja finished sweeping the sand up and sat down at the round dinner table. "If you're hungry, why don't you help yourself to some leftovers from yesterday's dinner? There's some lettuce and soybean paste and a little rice too."

Yun-ja's hair had dried, and a couple of strands of it drooped over her forehead. She looked pretty to Chŏng-il.

"And some marinated peppers," she continued.

Chŏng-il's body stiffened. This offer of dinner was a signal that it was time for him to leave. He rose and fumbled for something appropriate to say about the past two months. The blood rushed to his head and his face burned. Finally he blurted out, "What would you say if I . . . proposed to you?" Then he flung open the door as if he were being chased out. In his haste to leave he sent one of Yun-ja's sandals flying from the doorway toward the gas range. The door slammed shut behind him.

Yun-ja sprang up from the table. "What did he say?" Her body prickled, as if she were yielding to a long-suppressed urge to urinate. "I don't believe in marriage," she told herself. "Not after what I went through."

She rushed to the door and looked through the peephole into the hall. She saw Chŏng-il jab futilely at the elevator button and then run toward the stairway.

"The boy proposed to me—I should be thankful," Yun-ja thought. Like water reviving a dying tree, hot blood began to buzz through her sleepy veins. This long-forgotten sensation of warmth made her think that maybe their relationship had been pointing in this direction all along. "It was fun prettying myself up the day I met him. And before that, didn't I expect some good times with him even though we weren't really married?"

Yun-ja turned and looked around the room. There was Chŏng-il's trunk on the sofa. "But he'd end up leaving me too." Suddenly she felt very vulnerable. Everything about her, starting with her age and the divorce, and then all the little imperfections—the wrinkles around the eyes, the occasional drooling in her sleep—reared up in her mind. "But I'm not going to let my shortcomings get me down," she reassured herself. "It's time to make a stand."

FOR DISCUSSION AND WRITING

1. Do you think Yun-ja has romantic feelings for Chŏng-il? Does Chŏng-il have romantic feelings for Yun-ja? Use the story to support your response.

2. Why are Chŏng-il and Yun-ja indirect with each other? Why do they not talk honestly to each other about their feelings at the beginning of the story?

3. Yun-ja is many years older than Chŏng-il. In what ways, if any, can such an age difference affect a relationship?

ANNIVERSARY

FOR JOHN
Judith Ortiz Cofer

Judith Ortiz Cofer, a poet and novelist, was born in Hormigueros, Puerto Rico, and moved to Patterson, New Jersey, when her father was transferred with the Army. Family is an important focus of her work. In "Anniversary," a woman reflects on her marriage and how she and her husband fell in love. She remembers how they participated together in turbulent antiwar demonstrations during the Vietnam War. While thinking about their relationship, she finds threads that hold their marriage together.

LYING IN BED LATE, YOU READ TO ME
about a past war, about young men who each year
become more like our sons, who died the year we met,
or the year we got married, or the year our child was born.
  You read to me about how they dragged their feet
through a green maze, how they fell,
again and again, victims to an enemy
wily enough to be the critter-villain of some nightmare
tale with his booby-traps in the shape of children
and his cities under the earth; and about how,
even when they survived, these boys left something behind

in the thick brush or muddy swamp
where no one can get it back—caught like a baseball cap
on a low-hanging branch.

And I think about you and me, nineteen, and angry,
and in love, in that same year when America, erupting

like a late-blooming adolescent, broke into violence,
caught in a turmoil it could neither understand nor control;
how we walked through the rough parade
wearing the insignias of our rebellion: peace symbols
and scenes of Eden embroidered our faded jeans,
necks heavy with beads we did not count on
for patience, singing *Revolution*: a song we misunderstood
for years. Death was a slogan to shout about with raised fists,
or hang on banners.

Now here we are, listening more closely than ever to old songs,
sung for new reasons by new voices; survivors
of an undeclared war someone might decide to remake
like a popular tune. Sometimes, in the dark, alarmed by silence,
I lay my hand on your chest, for the familiar, steady beat
to which I have attuned my breathing for so many years.

FOR DISCUSSION AND WRITING

1. About how long has this couple been married?

2. How do you imagine it would feel to fall in love in the midst of a political and social upheaval such as the antiwar movement of the 1960s?

3. Do you think the couple's relationship is happy and close? Use the story to support your response.

FINDING A WIFE
Gary Soto

Poet and prose writer Gary Soto is also a professor of English and Chicano studies at the University of California, where he is helping to educate a new generation of writers. Soto was raised in Fresno, California, the center of the agricultural San Joaquin Valley, and his work often reflects his working-class Chicano background. Whether he is writing about painful social issues or the pleasures of life, he sheds light on the seemingly "ordinary" facts of life.

*I*T'S EASY TO FIND A WIFE, I TOLD MY STUDENTS. Pick anybody, I said, and they chuckled and fidgeted in their chairs. I laughed a delayed laugh, feeling hearty and foolish as a pup among these young men who were in my house to talk poetry and books. We talked, occasionally making sense, and drank cup after cup of coffee until we were so wired we had to stand up and walk around the block to shake out our nerves.

When they left I tried to write a letter, grade papers, and finally nap on the couch. My mind kept turning to how simple it is to find a wife; that we can easily say after a brief two- or three-week courtship, "I want to marry you."

When I was twenty, in college and living on a street that was a row of broken apartment buildings, my brother and I returned to our apartment from a game of racquetball to sit in the living room and argue whether we should buy a quart of beer. We were college poor, living off the cheap blessings of rice, raisins, and eggs that I took from our mom's refrigerator when Rick called her into the back yard about a missing sock from his laundry—a ploy from the start.

"Rick, I only got a dollar," I told him. He slapped his thigh and told me to wake up. It was almost the end of the month. And he was right. In two days our paychecks from Zak's Car Wash would burn like good report cards in our pockets. So I gave in. I took the fifteen cents—a dime and five pennies—he had plucked from the ashtray of loose change in his bedroom, and went downstairs, across the street and the two blocks to Scott's Liquor. While I was returning home, swinging the quart of beer like a lantern, I saw the Japanese woman who was my neighbor, cracking walnuts on her front porch. I walked slowly so that she looked up, smiling. I smiled, said hello, and continued walking to the rhythm of her hammer rising and falling.

In the apartment I opened the beer and raised it like a chalice before we measured it in glasses, each of us suspicious that the other would get more. I rattled sunflower seeds onto a plate, and we pinched fingersful, the beer in our hands cutting loose a curtain of bubbles. We were at a party with no music, no host, no girls. Our cat, Mensa, dawdled in, blinking from the dull smoke of a sleepy afternoon. She looked at us, and we looked at her. Rick flicked a seed at her and said, "That's what we need— a woman!"

I didn't say anything. I closed my eyes, legs shot out in a V from the couch, and thought of that girl on the porch, the rise and fall of her hammer, and the walnuts cracking open like hearts.

I got up and peeked from our two-story window that looked out onto a lawn and her apartment. No one. A wicker chair, potted plants, and a pile of old newspapers. I looked until she came out with a broom to clean up the shells. "Ah, my little witch," I thought, and raced my heart downstairs, but stopped short of her house because I didn't know what to say or do. I stayed behind the hedge that separated our yards and listened to her broom swish across the porch, then start up the walk to the curb. It was then that I started to walk casually from behind the hedge and, when she looked at me with a quick grin, I said a hearty hello and walked past her without stopping to talk. I made my way to the end of the block where I stood behind another hedge, feeling foolish. I should have said something. "Do you like walnuts," I could have said, or maybe, "Nice day to sweep, isn't it?"—anything that would have my mouth going.

I waited behind that hedge, troubled by my indecision. I started back up the street and found her bending over a potted geranium, a jar of cloudy water in her hand. Lucky guy, I thought, to be fed by her.

I smiled as I passed, and she smiled back. I returned to the apartment and my bedroom where I stared at my homework and occasionally looked out the window to see if she was busy on the porch. But she wasn't there. Only the wicker chair, the plants, the pile of newspapers.

The days passed, white as clouds. I passed her house so often that we began to talk, sit together on the porch, and eventually snack on sandwiches that were thick as Bibles, with tumblers of milk to wash down her baked sweet bread flecked with tiny crushed walnuts.

After the first time I ate at her house, I hurried to the apartment to brag about my lunch to my brother who was in the kitchen sprinkling raisins on his rice. Sandwiches, I screamed, milk, cold cuts, chocolate ice cream! I spoke about her cupboards, creaking like ships weighed down with a cargo of rich food, and about her, that woman who came up to my shoulder. I was in love and didn't know where to go from there.

As the weeks passed, still white as clouds, we saw more of each other. Then it happened. On another Saturday, after browsing at a thrift shop among gooseneck lamps and couches as jolly as fat men, we went to the west side of Fresno for Mexican food—menudo for me and burritos for her, with two beers clunked down on our table. When we finished eating and were ready to go, I wiped my mouth and plucked my sole five-dollar bill from my wallet as I walked to the cashier. It was all the big money I had. I paid and left the restaurant as if it were nothing, as if I spent such money every day. But inside I was thinking, "What am I going to do?"

Scared as I was, I took Carolyn's hand into mine as we walked to the car. I released it to open the door for her. We drove and drove, past thrift shops she longed to browse through, but I didn't want to stop because I was scared I would want to hold her hand again. After turning corners aimlessly, I drove back to her house where we sat together on the front porch, not touching. I was shivering, almost noticeably. But after a while, I did take her hand into mine and that space between us closed. We held hands, little tents opening and closing, and soon I nuzzled my face into her neck to find a place to kiss.

I married this one Carolyn Oda, a woman I found cracking walnuts on an afternoon. It was a chance meeting: I was walking past when she looked up to smile. It could have been somebody else, a girl drying persimmons on a line, or one hosing down her car, and I might have married another and been unhappy. But it was Carolyn, daughter of hard workers, whom I found cracking walnuts. She stirred them into dough that she shaped into loaves, baked in the oven, and set before me so that my mouth would keep talking in its search of the words to make me stay.

FOR DISCUSSION AND WRITING

1. What does the couple know about each other before they fall in love? Use the story to support your response.

2. Explain what the speaker in the story means when he says to his students, "It's easy to find a wife. Pick anybody."

3. Ask your parents, relatives, and friends how they met their spouses. Ask them how long they knew their spouse and what they knew about him or her before they felt they were in love.

4. How long do you feel you should know someone before getting married? What would you want to know about them?

NEVER OFFER YOUR HEART
TO SOMEONE WHO EATS HEARTS
Alice Walker

Alice Walker received the Pulitzer Prize in 1983 for her popular book The Color Purple. *Much of her writing, as well as her work in voter registration and Head Start education programs, reflects her desire for a world without racism and sexism. Most of Walker's writing addresses the struggles of black women in the United States. She portrays the strength of women who have remained open to the joys of life despite the problems they have faced. The poem "Never Offer Your Heart To Someone Who Eats Hearts" affirms the power of African women and offers advice to careless lovers of all cultures and both genders.*

NEVER OFFER YOUR HEART
to someone who eats hearts
who finds heartmeat
delicious
but not rare
who sucks the juices
drop by drop
and bloody-chinned
grins
like a God.

Never offer your heart
to a heart gravy lover.
Your stewed, overseasoned
heart consumed
he will sop up your grief
with bread
and send it shuttling
from side to side
in his mouth
like bubblegum.

Sara Alexander, Collage, *1990*

If you find yourself
in love
with a person
who eats hearts
these things
you must do:

Freeze your heart
immediately.
Let him—next time
he examines your chest—
find your heart cold
flinty and unappetizing.

Refrain from kissing
lest he in revenge
dampen the spark
in your soul.

Now,
sail away to Africa
where holy women
await you
on the shore—
long having practiced the art
of replacing hearts
with God
and Song.

FOR DISCUSSION AND WRITING

1. Describe in detail what you imagine someone who "eats hearts" to be like. What do they do to gain this description? How do they get away with it?

2. What does the speaker mean by the third piece of advice? What do you think of the speaker's overall advice? Do you have any additions?

3. Do you believe that some people are more susceptible to those who "eat hearts" than others? Explain. Are you vulnerable to such people?

THE PIECES *and*
WHEN YOUR EYES SPEAK

Angela De Hoyos

Angela De Hoyos is a Chicana writer who was born in Mexico and was raised in San Antonio, Texas. She often writes her poetry in a blend of Spanish and English to preserve, as she says, "a vestige of her Mexican-Indian-Spanish heritage."

THE PIECES

SOMEWHERE
      in the clashing
        of sharp words
the bright ribbon of love was torn
—the mizpah[1] of our faith
          broken.

I am looking for the pieces.
I have drawn the curtains
to let in the light.

But the shadows remain:
    the sly image of doubt
that lurks in corners
and appears unexpectedly
in a leering face.
        . . . Can the heart
once broken
      be mended?

FRAGMENTOS

En algún lugar, en el estallido
de agudas palabras
quedó rasgado el lazo de amor
—roto el Mispa de nuestra fe.

Busco los fragmentos.
Abro las cortinas
para que entre la luz.

Pero aún quedan las sombras:
la fingida imagen de la duda
acechando en los rincones
asoma de pronto
su taimado rostro.

. . . Puede sanar
el corazón herido?

FOR DISCUSSION AND WRITING

1. How would you answer the question the speaker asks in the poem?

2. Is there a comment or a manner of arguing that you would neither forgive nor forget?

---

1. Hebrew word meaning a marker to remember a promise.

Minor White, Windowsill
Daydreaming, *1958*

WHEN YOUR EYES SPEAK

WHEN YOUR EYES SPEAK TO ME
　　of love
my old wounds slide
from my flesh:

I am that care-free lizard
basking in the sun
happy once again
　　beneath your glance.

CUANDO HABLAN TUS OJOS

Cuando tus ojos me hablan
　　de amor
mis viejas heridas se deslizan
de mi carne:

Soy entonces ese despreocupado lagarto
que se baña al sol
feliz
bajo tu mirada.

FOR DISCUSSION AND WRITING

1. Do you think the metaphor of the lizard in the sun effectively expresses the meaning of the poem? Explain.

2. To what extent do you think a person's happiness is based on being loved by a special person? Does this change with age? Explain.

F·A·M·I·L·Y A·N·D
G·E·N·E·R·A·T·I·O·N·S

✳ ✳ ✳ ✳ ✳ ✳ ✳ ✳ ✳ ✳ ✳ ✳ ✳ ✳ ✳ ✳ ✳ ✳ ✳

IN SEARCH OF OUR MOTHERS' GARDENS
Alice Walker

In this autobiographical essay, Pulitzer Prize-winning author Alice Walker describes her mother's garden as a colorful, lush work of art. The garden also functions as a metaphor for the creativity of African-American women of previous generations. In her own garden Walker grows onions, corn, tomatoes, beans, eggplant, artichokes, and more.

WHEN THE POET JEAN TOOMER WALKED THROUGH THE SOUTH in the early twenties, he discovered a curious thing: Black women whose spirituality was so intense, so deep, so *unconscious*, that they were themselves unaware of the richness they held. They stumbled blindly through their lives: creatures so abused and mutilated in body, so dimmed and confused by pain, that they considered themselves unworthy even of hope. . . .

In the still heat of the Post-Reconstruction South,[1] this is how they seemed to Jean Toomer: exquisite butterflies trapped in an evil honey, toiling away their lives in an era, a century, that did not acknowledge them, except as "the *mule* of the world." They dreamed dreams that no one knew—not even themselves, in any coherent fashion—and saw visions no one could understand. They wandered or sat about the countryside crooning lullabies to ghosts, and drawing the mother of Christ in charcoal on courthouse walls. . . .

Our mothers and grandmothers, some of them: moving to music not yet written. And they waited.

They waited for a day when the unknown thing that was in them would be made known; but guessed, somehow in their darkness, that on the day of their revelation they would be long dead. Therefore to Toomer they walked, and even ran, in slow motion. For they were going nowhere immediate, and the future was not yet within their grasp. . . .

How was the creativity of the Black woman kept alive, year after year and century after century, when for most of the years Black people have

---

1. During Reconstruction (1865-1877), the South was governed by pro-Union blacks and whites, backed by Federal troops. After this era, resentful former Confederate supporters regained power, and oppression of blacks resumed.

been in America, it was a punishable crime for a Black person to read or write? And the freedom to paint, to sculpt, to expand the mind with action, did not exist. Consider, if you can bear to imagine it, what might have been the result if singing, too, had been forbidden by law. Listen to the voices of Bessie Smith, Billie Holiday, Nina Simone, Roberta Flack, and Aretha Franklin, among others, and imagine those voices muzzled for life. Then you may begin to comprehend the lives of our "crazy," "Sainted" mothers and grandmothers. The agony of the lives of women who might have been Poets, Novelists, Essayists, and Short Story Writers (over a period of centuries), who died with their real gifts stifled within them.

And, if this were the end of the story, we would have cause to cry out in my paraphrase of Okot p'Bitek's[2] great poem:

O, my clanswomen
Let us all cry together!
Come,
Let us mourn the death of our mother,
The death of a Queen
The ash that was produced
By a great fire!
O this homestead is utterly dead
Close the gates
With *lacari* thorns,[3]
For our mother
The creator of the Stool is lost!
And all the young women
Have perished in the wilderness!

But this is not the end of the story, for all the young women—our mothers and grandmothers, *ourselves*—have not perished in the wilderness. And if we ask ourselves why, and search for and find the answer, we will know beyond all efforts to erase it from our minds, just exactly who, and of what, we Black American women are.

One example, perhaps the most pathetic, most misunderstood one, can provide a backdrop for our mothers' work: Phillis Wheatley, a slave in the 1700s.

---

2. [o' koɛ pə bətek'], a poet, novelist, essayist, and anthropologist (1931–) from Uganda in Africa.
3. Probably a kind of dense thorn bush used to block African village gates at night.

Virginia Woolf, in her book, *A Room of One's Own,* wrote that in order for a woman to write fiction she must have two things, certainly: a room of her own (with key and lock) and enough money to support herself.

What then are we to make of Phillis Wheatley, a slave, who owned not even herself? This sickly, frail, Black girl who required a servant of her own at times—her health was so precarious—and who, had she been white, would have been easily considered the intellectual superior of all the women and most of the men in the society of her day. . . .

When we read the poetry of Phillis Wheatley—as when we read the novels of Nella Larsen or the oddly false-sounding autobiography of that freest of all Black women writers, Zora Hurston—evidence of "contrary instincts" is everywhere. Her loyalties were completely divided, as was, without question, her mind.

But how could this be otherwise? Captured at seven, a slave of wealthy, doting whites who instilled in her the "savagery" of the Africa they "rescued" her from . . . one wonders if she was even able to remember her homeland as she had known it, or as it really was. . . .

In the last years of her brief life, burdened not only with the need to express her gift but also with a penniless, friendless "freedom" and several small children for whom she was forced to do strenuous work to feed, she lost her health, certainly. Suffering from malnutrition and neglect and who knows what mental agonies, Phillis Wheatley died.

So torn by "contrary instincts" was Black, kidnapped, enslaved Phillis that her description of "the Goddess"—as she poetically called the Liberty she did not have—is ironically, cruelly humorous. And, in fact, has held Phillis up to ridicule for more than a century. It is usually read prior to hanging Phillis's memory as that of a fool. She wrote:

The Goddess comes, she moves divinely fair,
Olive and laurel binds her *golden* hair:
Wherever shines this native of the skies,
Unnumber'd charms and recent graces rise.
(Emphasis mine)

It is obvious that Phillis, the slave, combed the "Goddess's" hair every morning; prior, perhaps, to bringing in the milk, or fixing her mistress's lunch. She took her imagery from the one thing she saw elevated above all others.

With the benefit of hindsight we ask, "How could she?"

But at last, Phillis, we understand. No more snickering when your stiff, struggling, ambivalent lines are forced on us. We know now that you were not an idiot nor a traitor; only a sickly little Black girl, snatched from your home and country and made a slave; a woman who still struggled to sing the song that was your gift, although in a land of barbarians who praised you for your bewildered tongue. It is not so much what you sang, as that you kept alive, in so many of our ancestors, *the notion of song.* . . .

We must fearlessly pull out of ourselves and look at and identify with our lives the living creativity some of our great-grandmothers were not allowed to know. I stress *some* of them because it is well known that the majority of our great-grandmothers knew, even without "knowing" it, the reality of their spirituality, even if they didn't recognize it beyond what happened in the singing at church—and they never had any intention of giving it up.

How they did it: those millions of Black women who were not Phillis Wheatley, or Lucy Terry or Frances Harper or Zora Hurston or Nella Larsen or Bessie Smith—nor Elizabeth Catlett, nor Katherine Dunham, either—bring me to the title of this essay, "In Search of Our Mothers' Gardens," which is a personal account that is yet shared, in its theme and its meaning, by all of us. I found, while thinking about the far-reaching world of the creative Black woman, that often the truest answer to a question that really matters can be found very close. So I was not surprised when my own mother popped into my mind.

In the late 1920s my mother ran away from home to marry my father. Marriage, if not running away, was expected of seventeen-year-old girls. By the time she was twenty, she had two children and was pregnant with a third. Five children later, I was born. And this is how I came to know my mother: she seemed a large, soft, loving-eyed woman who was rarely impatient in our home. Her quick, violent temper was on view only a few times a year, when she battled with the white landlord who had the misfortune to suggest to her that her children did not need to go to school.

She made all the clothes we wore, even my brothers' overalls. She made all the towels and sheets we used. She spent the summers canning vegetables and fruits. She spent the winter evenings making quilts enough to cover all our beds.

During the "working" day, she labored beside—not behind—my father in the fields. Her day began before sunup, and did not end until late at night. There was never a moment for her to sit down, undisturbed, to unravel her own private thoughts; never a time free from interruption—

Faith Ringgold, Sunflowers Quilting Bee at Arles, *1991. This piece is a story quilt. The people pictured left to right, respectively, are Madame Walker, Sojourner Truth, Ida Wells, Fannie Lou Hamer, Harriet Tubman, Rosa Parks, Mary McLeod Bethune, Ella Baker, Vincent van Gogh. In addition to the story that runs along the top and bottom edges of the quilt, the following statement is included: "An international symbol of our dedication to change the world."*

by work or the noisy inquiries of her many children. And yet, it is to my mother—and all our mothers who were not famous—that I went in search of the secret of what has fed that muzzled and often mutilated, but vibrant, creative spirit that the Black woman has inherited, and that pops out in wild and unlikely places to this day.

But when, you will ask, did my overworked mother have time to know or care about feeding the creative spirit?

The answer is so simple that many of us have spent years discovering it. We have constantly looked high, when we should have looked high—and low.

For example: in the Smithsonian Institution in Washington, D.C., there hangs a quilt unlike any other in the world. In fanciful, inspired, and yet simple and identifiable figures, it portrays the story of the Crucifixion. It is considered rare, beyond price. Though it follows no known pattern of quilt-making, and though it is made of bits and pieces of worthless rags, it is obviously the work of a person of powerful imagination and deep spiritual feeling. Below this quilt I saw a note that says it was made by "an anonymous Black woman in Alabama, a hundred years ago."

If we could locate this "anonymous" Black woman from Alabama, she would turn out to be one of our grandmothers—an artist who left her mark in the only materials she could afford, and in the only medium her position in society allowed her to use. . . .

And so our mothers and grandmothers have, more often than not anonymously, handed on the creative spark, the seed of the flower they themselves never hoped to see: or like a sealed letter they could not plainly read.

And so it is, certainly, with my own mother. Unlike "Ma" Rainey's songs, which retained their creator's name even while blasting forth from Bessie Smith's mouth, no song or poem will bear my mother's name. Yet so many of the stories that I write, that we all write, are my mother's stories. Only recently did I fully realize this: that through years of listening to my mother's stories of her life, I have absorbed not only the stories themselves, but something of the manner in which she spoke, something of the urgency that involves the knowledge that her stories—like her life—must be recorded. It is probably for this reason that so much of what I have written is about characters whose counterparts in real life are so much older than I am.

But the telling of these stories, which came from my mother's lips as naturally as breathing, was not the only way my mother showed herself as an artist. For stories, too, were subject to being distracted, to dying without conclusion. Dinners must be started, and cotton must be gathered before the big rains. The artist that was and is my mother showed itself to me only after many years. This is what I finally noticed:

Like Mem, a character in *The Third Life of Grange Copeland*,[4] my mother adorned with flowers whatever shabby house we were forced to live in. And not just your typical straggly country stand of zinnias, either. She planted ambitious gardens—and still does—with over fifty different varieties of plants that bloom profusely from early March until late November. Before she left home for the fields, she watered her flowers,

---

4. Walker's first novel (1970), it is about a family of sharecroppers.

chopped up the grass, and laid out new beds. When she returned from the fields she might divide clumps of bulbs, dig a cold pit, uproot and replant roses, or prune branches from her taller bushes or trees—until night came and it was too dark to see.

Whatever she planted grew as if by magic, and her fame as a grower of flowers spread over three counties. Because of her creativity with her flowers, even my memories of poverty are seen through a screen of blooms—sunflowers, petunias, roses, dahlias, forsythia, spirea, delphiniums, verbena . . . and on and on.

And I remember people coming to my mother's yard to be given cuttings from her flowers; I hear again the praise showered on her because whatever rocky soil she landed on, she turned into a garden. A garden so brilliant with colors, so original in its design, so magnificent with life and creativity, that to this day people drive by our house in Georgia—perfect strangers and imperfect strangers—and ask to stand or walk among my mother's art.

I notice that it is only when my mother is working in her flowers that she is radiant, almost to the point of being invisible—except as Creator: hand and eye. She is involved in work her soul must have. Ordering the universe in the image of her personal conception of Beauty.

Her face, as she prepares the Art that is her gift, is a legacy of respect she leaves to me, for all that illuminates and cherishes life. She has handed down respect for the possibilities—and the will to grasp them.

For her, so hindered and intruded upon in so many ways, being an artist has still been a daily part of her life. This ability to hold on, even in very simple ways, is work Black women have done for a very long time.

This poem is not enough, but it is something, for the woman who literally covered the holes in our walls with sunflowers:

They were women then
My mama's generation
Husky of voice—Stout of
Step
With fists as well as
Hands
How they battered down
Doors
And ironed
Starched white
Shirts

How they led
Armies
Headragged Generals
Across mined
Fields
Booby-trapped
Ditches
To discover books
Desks
A place for us
How they knew what we
Must know
Without knowing a page
Of it
Themselves.

Guided by my heritage of a love of beauty and a respect for strength—
in search of my mother's garden, I found my own.

And perhaps in Africa over two hundred years ago, there was just such
a mother; perhaps she painted vivid and daring decorations in oranges
and yellows and greens on the walls of her hut; perhaps she sang—in a
voice like Roberta Flack's—*sweetly* over the compounds of her village;
perhaps she wove the most stunning mats or told the most ingenious stories of all the village storytellers. Perhaps she was herself a poet—though
only her daughter's name is signed to the poems that we know.

Perhaps Phillis Wheatley's mother was also an artist.

Perhaps in more than Phillis Wheatley's biological life is her mother's
signature made clear.

FOR DISCUSSION AND WRITING

1. What main question does the author explore in this essay?

2. What tribute does the author make to the poet Phillis Wheatley?

3. Which section best helps you understand the tribute the author makes to her mother?

4. Why do you think that slaves in the United States were not allowed to read or write?

*5. In what ways do your family and community members create their art in "the only materials they can
afford"? Do you enjoy creative pursuits such as music, dance, visual arts, drama, gardening, woodwork-
ing, photography, writing, or others? Who in your background may have influenced you to try these arts?*

6. *Research and describe the accomplishments of the following authors, musicians, and artists Walker mentions in her essay: Jean Toomer, Bessie Smith, Billie Holiday, Nina Simone, Roberta Flack, Aretha Franklin, Phillis Wheatley, Virginia Woolf, Lucy Terry, Frances Harper, Zora Neale Hurston, Nella Larsen, Elizabeth Catlett, Katherine Dunham, and "Ma" Rainey.*

✳ ✳ ✳ ✳ ✳ ✳ ✳ ✳ ✳ ✳ ✳ ✳ ✳ ✳ ✳ ✳ ✳ ✳ ✳ ✳

A MOVING DAY
Susan Nunes

Moving away from one's home can be a traumatic event—especially if one has lived in a place for many years. In her story, "A Moving Day," Susan Nunes examines some of the emotional issues many people face when they move. These issues include decisions about which objects to shed and questions about what the next stage of life will bring. The author shows how family members may answer these questions differently, possibly causing strain or conflict. Nunes is a writer of short stories and children's books. She was raised in Hilo, Hawaii, and now lives in Honolulu, Hawaii.

ACROSS THE STREET, THE BULLDOZER ROARS TO LIFE. Distracted, my mother looks up from the pile of embroidered linen that she has been sorting. She is seventy, tiny and fragile, the flesh burned off her shrinking frame. Her hair is grey now—she has never dyed it—and she wears it cut close to her head with the nape shaved. Her natural hairline would have been better suited to the kimono worn by women of her mother's generation. She still has a beautiful neck. In recent years she has taken a liking to jeans, cotton smocks, baggy sweaters, and running shoes. When I was a child she wouldn't have been caught dead without her nylons.

Her hands, now large-jointed with arthritis, return to the pile of linen. Her movements always had a no-nonsense quality and ever since I was a child, I have been wary of her energy because it was so often driven by suppressed anger. Now she is making two stacks, the larger one for us, the smaller for her to keep. There is a finality in the way she places things in the larger pile, as if to say that's *it*. For her, it's all over, all over but this last accounting. She does not look forward to what is coming. Strangers. Schedules. The regulated activities of those considered too old to regulate themselves. But at least, at the *very* least, she'll not be a burden. She sorts through the possessions of a lifetime, she and her three daughters. It's time she passed most of this on. Dreams are lumber. She can't *wait* to be rid of them.

My two sisters and I present a contrast. There is nothing purposeful or systematic about the way we move. In fact, we don't know where we're going. We know there is a message in all this activity, but we don't know what it is. Still, we search for it in the odd carton, between layers of tissue paper and silk. We open drawers, peer into the recesses of cupboards, rummage through the depths of closets. What a lot of stuff! We lift, untuck, unwrap, and set aside. The message is there, we know. But what is it? Perhaps if we knew, then we wouldn't have to puzzle out our mother's righteous determination to shed the past.

There is a photograph of my mother taken on the porch of my grandparents' house when she was in her twenties. She is wearing a floral print dress with a square, lace-edged collar and a graceful skirt that shows off her slim body. Her shoulder length hair has been permed. It is dark and thick and worn parted on the side to fall over her right cheek. She is very fair; "one pound powder," her friends called her. She is smiling almost reluctantly, as if she meant to appear serious but the photographer has said something amusing. One arm rests lightly on the railing, the other, which is at her side, holds a handkerchief. They were her special pleasures, handkerchiefs of hand-embroidered linen as fine as ricepaper. Most were gifts (she used to say that when she was a girl, people gave one another little things—a handkerchief, a pincushion, pencils, hair ribbons), and she washed and starched them by hand, ironed them, taking care with the rolled hems, and stored them in a silk bag from Japan.

There is something expectant in her stance, as if she were waiting for something to happen. She says, your father took this photograph in 1940, before we were married. She lowers her voice confidentially and adds, now he cannot remember taking it. My father sits on the balcony, an open book on his lap, peacefully smoking his pipe. The bulldozer tears into the foundations of the Kitamura house.

. . .

What about this? My youngest sister has found a fishing boat carved of tortoise shell.

Hold it in your hand and look at it. Every plank on the hull is visible. Run your fingers along the sides, you can feel the joints. The two masts, about six inches high, are from the darkest part of the shell. I broke one of the sails many years ago. The remaining one is quite remarkable, so thin that the light comes through it in places. It is delicately ribbed to give the effect of canvas pushed gently by the wind.

My mother reaches for a sheet of tissue paper and takes the boat from my sister. She says, it was a gift from Mr. Oizumi. He bought it from an artisan in Kamakura.

Stories cling to the thing, haunt it like unrestful spirits. They are part of the object. They have been there since we were children, fascinated with her possessions. In 1932, Mr. Oizumi visits Japan. He crosses the Pacific by steamer, and when he arrives he is hosted by relatives eager to hear of his good fortune. But Mr. Oizumi soon tires of their questions. He wants to see what has become of the country. It will be arranged, he is told. Mr. Oizumi is a meticulous man. Maps are his passion. A trail of neat X's marks the steps of his journey. On his map of China, he notes each military outpost in Manchuria and appends a brief description of what he sees. Notes invade the margins, march over the blank spaces. The characters are written in a beautiful hand, precise, disciplined, orderly. Eventually, their trail leads to the back of the map. After Pearl Harbor, however, Mr. Oizumi is forced to burn his entire collection. The U.S. Army has decreed that enemy aliens caught with seditious materials will be arrested. He does it secretly in the shed behind his home, his wife standing guard. They scatter the ashes in the garden among the pumpkin vines.

My grandfather's library does not escape the flames either. After the Army requisitions the Japanese school for wartime headquarters, they give my mother's parents twenty-four hours to vacate the premises, including the boarding house where they lived with about twenty students from the plantation camps outside Hilo. There is no time to save the books. Her father decides to nail wooden planks over the shelves that line the classrooms. After the Army moves in, they rip open the planks, confiscate the books, and store them in the basement of the post office. Later, the authorities burn everything. Histories, children's stories, primers, biographies, language texts, everything, even a set of Encyclopaedia Brittanica. My grandfather is shipped to Oahu and imprisoned on Sand Island. A few months later, he is released after the prominent Caucasians vouch for his character. It is a humiliation he doesn't speak of, ever.

All of this was part of the boat. After I broke the sail, she gathered the pieces and said, I'm not sure we can fix this. It was not a toy. Why can't you leave my things alone?

For years the broken boat sat on our bookshelf, a reminder of the brutality of the next generation.

Now she wants to give everything away. We have to beg her to keep things. Dishes from Japan, lacquerware, photographs, embroidery, letters. She says, I have no room. You take them, here, *take* them. Take them or I'll get rid of them.

They're piled around her, they fill storage chests, they fall out of open drawers and cupboards. She only wants to keep a few things—her books, some photographs, three carved wooden figures from Korea that belonged to her father, a few of her mother's dishes, perhaps one futon.

My sister holds a porcelain teapot by its bamboo handle. Four white cranes edged in black and gold fly around it. She asks, Mama, can't you hang on to this? If you keep it, I can borrow it later.

My mother shakes her head. She is adamant. And what would I do with it? I don't want any of this. Really.

My sister turns to me. She sighs. The situation is hopeless. You take it, she says. It'll only get broken at my place. The kids.

. . .

It had begun slowly, this shedding of the past, a plate here, a dish there, a handkerchief, a doily, a teacup, a few photographs, one of my grandfather's block prints. Nothing big. But then the odd gesture became a pattern; it got so we never left the house empty-handed. At first we were amused. After all, when we were children she had to fend us off her things. Threaten. We were always *at* them. She had made each one so ripe with memories that we found them impossible to resist. We snuck them outside, showed them to our friends, told and retold the stories. They bear the scars of all this handling, even her most personal possessions. A chip here, a crack there. Casualties. Like the music box her brother brought home from Italy after the war. It played a Brahms lullaby. First we broke the spring, then we lost the winding key, and for years it sat mutely on her dresser.

She would say again and again, it's impossible to keep anything nice with you children. And we'd retreat, wounded, for a while. The problem with children is they can wipe out your history. It's a miracle that anything survives this onslaught.

There's a photograph of my mother standing on the pier in Honolulu in 1932, the year she left Hawaii to attend the University of California. She's loaded to the ears with leis. She's wearing a fedora pulled smartly to the side. She's not smiling. Of my mother's two years there, my grandmother recalled that she received good grades and never wore kimono again. My second cousin, with whom my mother stayed when she first arrived, said she was surprisingly sophisticated—she liked hats. My mother said that she was homesick. Her favorite class was biology and she entertained ambitions of becoming a scientist. Her father, however, wanted her to become a teacher, and his wishes prevailed, even though he would not have forced them upon her. She was a dutiful daughter.

During her second year, she lived near campus with a mathematics professor and his wife. In exchange for room and board she cleaned house, ironed, and helped prepare meals. One of the things that survives from this period is a black composition book entitled, *Recipes of California*. As a child, I read it like a book of mysteries for clues to a life which seemed both alien and familiar. Some entries she had copied by hand; others she cut out of magazines and pasted on the page, sometimes with a picture or drawing. The margins contained her cryptic comments: "Saturday bridge club," "From Mary G. Do not give away," underlined, "chopped suet by hand, wretched task, bed at 2 a.m., exhausted." I remember looking up "artichoke" in the dictionary and asking Mr. Okinaga, the vegetable vendor, if he had any edible thistles. I never ate one until I was sixteen.

That book holds part of the answer to why our family rituals didn't fit the recognized norm of either our relatives or the larger community in which we grew up. At home, we ate in fear of the glass of spilled milk, the stray elbow on the table, the boarding house reach. At my grandparents', we slurped our chasuke. We wore tailored dresses, white cotton pinafores, and Buster Brown shoes with white socks; however, what we longed for were the lacy, ornate dresses in the National Dollar Store that the Puerto Rican girls wore to church on Sunday. For six years, I marched to Japanese language school after my regular classes; however, we only spoke English at home. We talked too loudly and all at once, which mortified my mother, but she was always complaining about Japanese indirectness. I know that she smarted under a system in which the older son is the center of the familial universe, but at thirteen I had a fit of jealous rage over her fawning attention to our only male cousin.

My sister has found a photograph of my mother, a round faced and serious twelve or thirteen, dressed in kimono and seated, on her knees, on the tatami floor. She is playing the koto. According to my mother, girls were expected to learn this difficult stringed instrument because it was thought to teach discipline. Of course, everything Japanese was a lesson in discipline—flower arranging, caligraphy, judo, brush painting, embroidery, everything. One summer my sister and I had to take ikebana, the art of flower arrangement, at Grandfather's school. The course was taught by Mrs. Oshima, a diminutive, softspoken, terrifying woman, and my supplies were provided by my grandmother, whose tastes ran to the oversized. I remember little of that class and its principles. What I remember most clearly is having to walk home carrying, in a delicate balancing act, one of our creations, which, more often than not, towered above our heads.

How do we choose among what we experience, what we are taught, what we run into by chance, or what is forced upon us? What is the principle of selection? My sisters and I are not bound by any of our mother's obligations, nor do we follow the rituals that seemed so important. My sister once asked, do you realize that when she's gone that's *it*? She was talking about how to make sushi, but it was a profound question nonetheless.

I remember, after we moved to Honolulu and my mother stopped teaching and began working long hours in administration, she was less vigilent about the many little things that once consumed her attention. While we didn't exactly slide into savagery, we economized in more ways than one. She would often say, there's simply no time anymore to do things right.

I didn't understand then why she looked so sad when she said it, but somehow I knew the comment applied to us. It would be terrible if centuries of culture are lost simply because there is not time.

.   .   .

Still, I don't understand why we carry out this fruitless search. Whatever it is we are looking for, we're not going to find it. My sister tries to lift a box filled with record albums, old seventy-eights, gives up, and sets it down again. My mother says, there are people who collect these things. Imagine.

Right, just imagine.

I think about my mother bathing me and singing, "The snow is snowing, the wind is blowing, but I will weather the storm." And I think of her story of the village boy carried by the Tengu on a fantastic flight over the cities of Japan, but who returns to a disbelieving and resistant family. So much for questions which have no answers, why we look among objects for meanings which have somehow escaped us in the growing up and growing old.

However, my mother is a determined woman. She will take nothing with her if she can help it. It is all ours. And on the balcony my father knocks the ashes of his pipe into a porcelain ashtray, and the bulldozer is finally silent.

1. What is the mother's mood on moving day? Use the story to support your response. Explain what may account for her mood.

2. What message do the three daughters search for in their mother's possessions?

3. Describe objects of yours or your family's that have significant stories associated with them. What are the stories? Are these objects treated with great care and respect?

4. Have you ever moved away from your home? What were your feelings? Were there objects that you wanted to leave behind? Were there items that you insisted on taking with you? Explain.

❋ ❋ ❋ ❋ ❋ ❋ ❋ ❋ ❋ ❋ ❋ ❋ ❋ ❋ ❋ ❋ ❋ ❋ ❋

ANCESTOR
Jimmy Santiago Baca

Jimmy Santiago Baca, a poet of Chicano and Apache descent, taught himself to read and began to publish poetry in prison. He now lives with his family in New Mexico, has published five volumes of poetry, and won the prestigious American Book Award in 1988. Baca had an exceptionally difficult youth: his parents divorced, his father died of alcoholism, and his mother was murdered. After living in an orphanage, he spent many years on the streets. He wrote his first volume of poems, Immigrants in Our Own Land, *from which "Ancestor" was selected, while he was in prison, and earned great critical acclaim. The poetry in this collection, as in his others, passionately celebrates the human spirit. The speaker in "Ancestor" affirms the positive qualities of a father who does not fit the accepted ideal.*

*I*T WAS A TIME WHEN THEY WERE AFRAID OF HIM.
My father, a bare man, a gypsy, a horse
with broken knees no one would shoot.
Then again, he was like the orange tree,
and young women plucked from him sweet fruit.
To meet him, you must be in the right place,
even his sons and daughter, we wondered
where was papa now and what was he doing.
He held the mystique of travelers
that pass your backyard and disappear into the trees.

Then, when you follow, you find nothing,
not a stir, not a twig displaced from its bough.
And then he would appear one night.
Half covered in shadows and half in light,
his voice quiet, absorbing our unspoken thoughts.
When his hands lay on the table at breakfast,
they were hands that had not fixed our crumbling home,
hands that had not taken us into them
and the fingers did not gently rub along our lips.
They were hands of a gypsy that filled our home
with love and safety, for a moment;
with all the shambles of boards and empty stomachs,
they filled us because of the love in them.
Beyond the ordinary love, beyond the coordinated life,
beyond the sponging of broken hearts,
came the untimely word, the fallen smile, the quiet tear,
that made us grow up quick and romantic.
Papa gave us something: when we paused from work,
my sister fourteen years old working the cotton fields,
my brother and I running like deer,
we would pause, because we had a papa no one could catch,
who spoke when he spoke and bragged and drank,
he bragged about us: he did not say we were smart,
nor did he say we were strong and were going to be rich someday.
He said we were good. He held us up to the world for it to see,
three children that were good, who understood love in a quiet way,
who owned nothing but calloused hands and true freedom,
and that is how he made us: he offered us to the wind,
to the mountains, to the skies of autumn and spring.
He said, "Here are my children! Care for them!"
And he left again, going somewhere like a child
with a warrior's heart, nothing could stop him.
My grandmother would look at him for a long time,
and then she would say nothing.
She chose to remain silent, praying each night,
guiding down like a root in the heart of earth,
clutching sunlight and rains to her ancient breast.
And I am the blossom of many nights.
A threefold blossom: my sister is as she is,
my brother is as he is, and I am as I am.

Through sacred ceremony of living, daily living,
arose three distinct hopes, three loves,
out of the long felt nights and days of yesterday.

FOR DISCUSSION AND WRITING

1. What is the speaker's attitude toward his father? What does he learn from his father?

2. Do you believe that the man portrayed in the poem can be considered a good father?

✳ ✳ ✳ ✳ ✳ ✳ ✳ ✳ ✳ ✳ ✳ ✳ ✳ ✳ ✳ ✳ ✳ ✳

THOSE WINTER SUNDAYS
Robert Hayden

Robert Hayden was a poet, a consultant to the Library of Congress, and a professor of English. He wrote about a broad range of topics; many of his poems are about the history of African Americans, while others are about nature, childhood, parents, or religion. "Those Winter Sundays" provides a unique perspective on fathers.

SUNDAYS TOO MY FATHER GOT UP EARLY
and put his clothes on in the blueblack cold,
then with cracked hands that ached
from labor in the weekday weather made
banked fires blaze. No one ever thanked him.

I'd wake and hear the cold splintering, breaking.
When the rooms were warm, he'd call,
and slowly I would rise and dress,
fearing the chronic angers of that house,

Speaking indifferently to him,
who had driven out the cold
and polished my good shoes as well.
What did I know, what did I know
of love's austere and lonely offices?

1. Why do you think the poet describes his father on winter Sundays?

2. How did the speaker treat his father when he was a boy? As a grown man, how does he feel about his father?

3. Who in your household plays a role most similar to the father in this poem? Explain.

* *

THE MORNING MY FATHER DIED, APRIL 7, 1963
James Masao Mitsui

How can one adequately convey in words how it feels when one's father dies? How is it possible to explain the change that a parent's death makes in one's life? In this nineteen line poem, James Masao Mitsui, poet and high school English teacher, uses his own experience to shed light on universal feelings of loss.

THE YOUNGEST SON, I LEFT THE FAMILY INSIDE AND STOOD
alone in the unplanted garden by a cherry tree
we had grown ourselves, next to a trash barrel
smoldering what we couldn't give away or move
to Seattle. Looking over the rusty edge I could see
colors of volcano. Feathers of ash floated
up to a sky that was changing. I stared at the sound
of meadowlarks below the water tank
on the pumice-colored hill where the sun would come.
I couldn't stop smelling sagebrush, the creosote
bottoms of posts, the dew that was like a thunderstorm
had passed an hour before. Thoughts were trees
under a lake; that moment was sunflower, killdeer
and cheatgrass. Volunteer wheat grew strong
on the far side of our place along the old highway.
Undeberg's rooster gave the day its sharper edge,

the top of the sun. Turning to go back inside,
twenty years of Big Bend Country
took off like sparrows from a startled fence.

FOR DISCUSSION AND WRITING

1. How do you make sense of the details the author noticed the morning his father died? Do you think you would have noticed these things? Explain.

2. What do the last three lines mean?

3. The author combines surprising elements in his statements. Which combinations stand out? What do they mean?

* *

THE BENDING OF A TWIG
Alfred Otero y Herrera

In the short story "The Bending of a Twig," Alfred Otero y Herrera portrays a family in which verbal and physical violence is routine. Today the serious issue of the emotional and physical abuse of children receives much media attention. "The Bending of a Twig," first published in 1969, was ahead of its time in depicting the silent suffering of many young people.

RALPH SHOOED THE FLIES away from the screen door before he hurried into the back porch. He set the groceries down on the rickety table covered with a worn, red-checked oilcloth. As he did, the bag split, sending apples bouncing off the table onto a heap of dirty clothes that lay on the floor.

"I'm home, mother," he cried.

Ralph's mother, wearing a faded cotton print dress, came out of the kitchen. She was a tall, gaunt woman in her early forties with dark circles under her eyes and an enormous pile of disheveled gray hair. Her husband, a happy-go-lucky bartender, had died of pneumonia the previous winter. Unable to find work in Roswell because of his reputation for drinking more than he served, he had gone to Portales to tend bar in the

Elks Club. He had written to her several times, telling her that he would send for her and the boys as soon as he had the money. But he had died suddenly, leaving her penniless. Not knowing how to do anything else, she began washing the clothes for the bachelors of Roswell and those families who could afford to have their laundry done for them. She worked from dawn far into the night every day, washing, ironing, and mending in order to support herself and her two sons, Leo, twelve, and Ralph, ten. She complained constantly of headaches, telling her sons that she would probably die soon too.

As she reached under her dress to adjust the strap of her undergarments that were always slipping from her shoulders, she inspected the contents of the grocery bag.

"My god, Ralphie, did you have to go and bust the bag?"

"It wasn't my fault. The apples was wet and made it bust," he pleaded.

"Did you get the starch?" she asked, taking the groceries from the ripped bag.

"Jeez, mom. I plum forgot."

"My god, can't you do nothing right? Where's the change?"

"What change?" he replied, with his eyes directed to the floor.

"What change?" she screamed as she pulled the yellow-gray hair from about her face. "I gave you a five-dollar bill, and I know that it came to only $4.80. Where's the receipt?"

She crossed to him, forced his head back, and grabbed him by the shoulders. Ralph's face puckered, straining, trying not to cry.

"Did you stop by the Chocolate Shop and spend it?"

Ralph tried to lower his head again, but she snapped it back up.

"I met Lalo Garcia," he said, trying to control the quivering of his chin.

"That dirty Mexican. I told you to stay away from that cheap trash, didn't I?"

She jerked his ear severely, causing him to burst into tears.

"By god, you're going to get a beating for this."

"But mother, the groceries cost $4.95, and I thought you wouldn't care."

"Wouldn't care about what?" she hissed, giving his ear another sharp pull.

"Wouldn't care if I spent the nickel for a Coke. I was thirsty," he sobbed.

"Why didn't you get a drink from the fountain in front of the courthouse if you was thirsty?"

"It's broke," he choked. "Ol' man Gardner is fixing it and said we couldn't have no water."

"You're lying to me, Ralph, just like your dad did, 'cause I seen Gardner drive past the house on his way to the slaughterhouse about an hour ago."

"Honest, mother, I did talk with him."

"You're going to get a beating for this. First you steal from your own mother, run around with dirty Mexican trash, and now you go and lie to me."

Ralph's face turned white; then he ran into the tiny bedroom adjoining the back porch screaming, "I'm not lying. Honest, mother, I'm not lying."

His mother pulled a worn slipper from her right foot and went after him.

Ralph gave a sharp cry as he bumped his head on the iron railing in his effort to crawl under the bed and to temporary safety. He huddled in the corner under the bed, pressing close to the wall. His head hurt him. He pressed his face to the green-and-yellow flowered linoleum. The lint and dust that had gathered there made him sneeze. It frightened him. He felt helpless waiting.

His mother strode into the room and stood at the foot of the bed, shouting, "Come out from under that bed, Ralph, or you're going to get a worse beating."

"No," he muttered weakly.

"Ralph! Do as I say!" she screamed again.

He could see the lower parts of her bare legs streaked with the angry blue varicose veins. He thought them ugly and wondered why they were there, what he had done, why she was going to beat him. The prospect of the beating caused him to burst into tears anew. He saw her feet shift and heard her call out to his elder brother who had just entered the back porch.

"Leo, go get me the razor strop. I'm really going to teach him a lesson.

At the mentioning of the razor strop he stopped crying in fear and called timidly, "I'm sorry, mother. I won't do it again."

In reply he heard his brother's footsteps retreating to the far side of the porch where the strop hung on the wall next to the fly swatter. He seemed to return so quickly.

"Help me move the bed," she commanded his brother.

The bed was rolled back, squeaking on its rusty casters.

Ralph, realizing he couldn't escape, rose slowly and stood before her submissively, trying to smile in hopes that she wouldn't beat him. She grabbed his arm and dragged him onto the porch. He looked at his brother, as if for help, but Leo only winced and swallowed hard.

"Now, are you ever going to lie to me again? Or steal?" she hissed as she brought the strop down hard against the back of his legs. "Are you? Huh? Are you?"

Ralph let out a piercing scream. He threw his right hand in front of his face in protection as he hopped wildly in his efforts to escape the blows that fell on his skinny body. He seemed to be dancing around his mother as if she were a Maypole. His head was thrown back; his mouth was opened as widely as it could. The lips, drawn tightly over his teeth, had turned a pale blue. He wasn't screaming any more. So great was his crying that he only made guttural sounds as he tried to get his breath. He threw himself upon the floor, falling on the cat's saucer full of milk, kicking his feet frantically, as she hit him for the last time.

Leo, witnessing the beating, let out an embarrassed giggle. She turned on him and spat, "Do you want some too? Get in there and do those dishes!"

"But I didn't do nothing, mother," he whined.

She motioned as if to strike him.

"Get in there and do those dishes!"

He ran into the kitchen, slamming the door after him.

She walked over to where Ralph lay.

"Get up!" she ordered him.

He got up crying loudly, his back hunched over—cowering from her.

"Are you going to lie to me again?" she asked, advancing towards him. She paused momentarily to get her breath.

"And if I ever hear of you with that dirty Mexican again, you're going to get another beating. Do you hear?"

Sobbing uncontrollably, he scrambled over the pile of dirty clothes and rushed out of the porch into the hot afternoon sun to the woodshed with its rotting boards and rusty tin roof. The bright sun blinded him, adding to his misery. The rain of the night before had made the air so humid and heavy that when he entered the shed, he caught his breath. But he welcomed its darkness. Susie, his cat, lay asleep on a mound of dirt made damp by the rain that had seeped through the numerous holes in the roof. Leaving the door partly open, he went to the coal bin and sat on its edge. He hoisted his pant leg. The red welts glared at him. He rubbed saliva over the welts, hoping to soothe them. They were painful. He let his pant leg drop, and holding out his hand, called to his cat.

"Here, Susie. Here, Susie. Nice kitty-kitty. Nice kitty."

The cat stretched luxuriously and came to him slowly. Gently the cat sniffed his fingertips. He reached out to pick her up, but she drew back quickly.

"Here, Susie. Nice, nice Susie," he pleaded.

Once again she sniffed his fingertips. This time he snatched her up before she could get away and pressed her tightly to his chest.

"You love me, don't you, Susie? I won't hurt you, will I?" he asked, stroking the back of her head.

Whipping her tail furiously and yowling unhappily, she dug her claws into his shoulder. Letting out a surprised cry, he leaped up and flung the cat away from him. She darted toward the door, stopping at the threshold, her tail still whipping back and forth.

"You don't love me either, you dirty cat!" he said as he picked up a small piece of coal and threw it at her. The coal smashed against the door, frightening Susie out of the shed and out of sight.

"Nobody loves me. Nobody."

With a weary sigh he sat on the dirt floor and leaned against the bin. He wiped his nose on his shirt sleeve, and resting his head against the dirty black boards, closed his eyes. Soon he was sound asleep.

"What you doing in here?" his brother asked, awakening him.

"Nothing. "

"I've been looking all over for you for the past half hour," he said, staring at his brother. "Jeez, Ralphie, you're going to sweat yourself to death. Besides, mother has been calling you."

"What does she want?"

"You're supposed to go to confession this afternoon. Jeez, Ralphie, you've done spoiled your shirt. You put it on clean only this morning."

"It was dirty anyhow. I got Susie's milk all over it. Is mother still mad?"

"I don't know. She went over to see Mrs. Collins so as she could use her phone." He dug his feet into the soft dirt, then added, "You had better get inside the house and take a bath before she comes back."

"O.K."

He stood up and brushed the dirt off the back of his trousers. The perspiration ran down the sides of his face into the hollow of his neck, leaving streaks where it had washed away the dirt and coal dust.

"If you hurry, I'll let you wear my tee shirt."

"I don't want to wear it."

"Why not? You were mad 'cause I wouldn't let you wear it yesterday."

"So what?"

"Come on, Ralphie! I'll race you to the house," he yelled, pulling him out of the woodshed.

Ralph jerked away from him violently.

"Quit pushing me, damn you, and leave me alone!"

Frightened by his own outburst, he ran into the house and locked himself in the bathroom. He washed his face and hands, dried them on a washrag, then left the house and walked to the church. When he reached it, he sat on the stone wall and looked up at the white statue of the Virgin Mary set above the doorway. He had always liked the smile on her face. He wondered what she was doing now. He climbed down from the fence and entered the church. He genuflected, crossed himself with holy water, and half-kneeled and half-sat in a back pew. He recited the Act of Contrition mechanically, then tried to number the sins he had committed as the sisters had told him to do. But the memory of the beating brought him close to tears. His chin started to quiver. He looked around quickly, embarrassed as if someone might have seen him; but no one had. He left the pew for the confessional. There was only one other in line—Mrs. Soltero. She was dressed in black, as were most of the old Mexican women in town. Her black shawl that covered her head almost reached the wooden floor. Her back was bent with age, making her no taller than Ralph. He watched her wipe the perspiration from her face and finger the bright blue beads of her rosary rapidly. She paid no attention to him. He remembered seeing her boiling clothes in a blackened tub in her back yard when he and Leo had gone to look for Coke bottles in the town dump. She entered the booth after Mrs. McDevitt, the fat lady who always sang the loudest during Benediction. His heart began to beat rapidly at the thought of being next. He stared hard at the floor and prayed that Mrs. Soltero would stay in a long time. He looked up and saw her come out.

.   .   .

His heart pounded as he entered the hot, dark confessional booth. He kneeled on the hard wood floor, crossing himself hurriedly as he did so. The booth, smelling strongly of garlic and human sweat, nearly suffocated him. He looked at the cheap plastic crucifix nailed on the wall and at the priest's profile outlined on the white cloth that was draped before the screen. He closed his eyes tightly.

"Forgive me, Father, for I have sinned."

"When was your last confession?"

"Two weeks ago."

He faltered, not knowing what to say next.

"Well, son, come on. Do you want me to confess for you?"

Now his temples throbbed with the beating of his heart.

"No, Father."

He squeezed his hands together tightly and leaned against the wall.

"I hate my mother," he said breathlessly.

"What did you say?" whispered the priest.

"I hate my mother," he repeated weakly.

"You don't mean that, son. You're just upset. What did she do? Spank you?"

"Yes." The tears started to come. He fought them. "She spanks me all the time."

"Well, you must do something to make her spank you. Now don't you?"

"She said that I lied and stole from her, but I didn't and she knew it."

He began to cry softly.

"Come now, you must have done something. She wouldn't spank you for no reason at all."

"She did. She wouldn't believe me. She said that I stole her grocery change today."

"Did you?"

"No, I only spent it on a Coke," he said between sobs.

"Why did you do that? Did you have her permission?"

Ralph tried to answer but couldn't.

The priest asked again, "Did you have her permission?"

"No. I was thirsty. I didn't steal from her."

"It was her money, wasn't it? You didn't have permission to spend her money, did you?"

"No."

"How old are you, son?"

"Ten."

"You're old enough to know that you have to have permission. Now you don't want to be a bad boy and do things like that, do you? Jesus doesn't like for us to do things like that."

"I'm not a bad boy!"

"Calm down, son. Don't raise your voice. Remember there are others outside."

"No. I hate her. She doesn't love me," he said, crying uncontrollably, "and you don't believe me either."

"Shh. Please."

"I hate her! I hate you!" he sobbed, his voice rising steadily in pitch. "Nobody believes me!"

He scrambled to his feet and pushed wildly at the door, causing it to bang loudly against the back pew. He rushed hysterically out of the church toward the railroad tracks that would eventually lead to his house.

Upon reaching home he stood near the clump of hollyhocks which grew by the side of the house. His mother had recently poured water on them. The water had hit an anthill nearby. He watched the ants swarm frantically over the hole. He wondered why they were so silent. He heard his mother singing "Ramona" to herself as she scrubbed clothes on the washboard. He stood listening intently until she had ceased the scrubbing, wrung out the clothes, and gone into the back yard to hang them to dry. He slipped unnoticed into the house and into the bathroom. He washed his face and combed his thick black hair carefully. He heard his mother enter the back porch and shout at his brother to not let the beans burn. When he entered the back porch, his mother was sorting a new bundle of laundry. She looked at him as she searched the pockets of a pair of khaki trousers and asked, "Well, did you go to confession?"

Ralph leaned over a rinsing tub and plunged his hands into the water. Avoiding his mother's gaze, he contemplated his hands through the water tinted with bluing and answered, "Yes, mother; he made me say ten Our Fathers and ten Hail Marys for my penance."

FOR DISCUSSION AND WRITING

1. Is the title of the story appropriate? Explain.

2. How would you describe the relationship between the brothers? Use the story to support your response.

3. How do you think Ralph's experiences will affect his life as an adult?

4. Can you think of someone close to you who you feel does not trust or respect you? Do you find yourself living up to their low expectations?

✳ ✳ ✳ ✳ ✳ ✳ ✳ ✳ ✳ ✳ ✳ ✳ ✳ ✳ ✳ ✳ ✳ ✳ ✳

SCRIBBLES
Pedro Juan Soto

Pedro Juan Soto is a highly regarded Puerto Rican author whose writing reflects the human trauma caused by the exploitation of Puerto Rico. Since the early 1900s large sugar companies and other industries have taken over small farmers' land on the island. As a result, tens of thousands of Puerto Ricans have moved to the mainland United States to find other means of earning a living. On the mainland they have faced cultural differences and difficult economic conditions. Soto is known for his ability to capture the colloquial language of Puerto Rican immigrants with great precision.

THE CLOCK SAID SEVEN AND HE WOKE UP FOR A MOMENT. His wife wasn't in bed and the children weren't on their cot. He buried his head under the pillow to close out the racket coming from the kitchen. He didn't open his eyes again until ten, forced to by Graciela's shaking.

He rubbed his small eyes and wiped away the bleariness, only to see his wife's broad body standing firmly in front of the bed in that defiant attitude. He heard her loud voice and it seemed to be coming directly from her navel.

"So? You figured you'd spend your whole life in bed? Looks like you're the one with a bad belly, but I'm carryin the kid."

He still didn't look at her face. He fixed his eyes on the swollen stomach, on the ball of flesh that daily grew and threatened to burst the robe's belt.

"Hurry and get up, you damned good-for-nothin! Or do you want me to throw water on you?"

He shouted at the open legs and the arms akimbo, the menacing stomach, the angry face: "I get up when I want to and not when you tell me. Hell! Who do you think you are?"

He turned his face back into the sheets and smelled the Brilliantine stains on the pillow and the stale sweat on the bedspread.

She felt overpowered by the man's inert mass: the silent threat of those still arms, the enormous lizard his body was.

Biting her lips, she drowned her reproaches and went back to the kitchen, leaving the room with the sputtering candle for Saint Lazarus on the dresser, the Holy Palm from last Palm Sunday and the religious prints hanging on the wall.

They lived in the basement. But even though they lived miserably, it was a roof over them. Even though overhead the other tenants stamped and swept, even though garbage rained through the cracks, she thanked her saints for having someplace to live. But Rosendo still didn't have a job. Not even the saints could find him one. Always in the clouds, more concerned with his own madness than with his family.

She felt she was going to cry. Nowadays she cried so easily. Thinking: *Holy God all I do is have kid after kid like a bitch and that man doesn't bother to look for work because he likes the government to support us by mail while he spends his time out there watching the four winds like Crazy John and saying he wants to be an artist.*

She stopped her sobs by gritting her teeth, closing off the complaints which struggled to become cries, returning sobs and complaints to the well of her nerves, where they would remain until hysteria opened them a path and transformed them into insults for her husband, or a spanking for the children, or a supplication to the Virgin of Succour.

She sat down at the table, watching her children run through the kitchen. Thinking of the Christmas tree they wouldn't have and the other children's toys that tomorrow hers would envy. Because tonight is Christmas Eve and tomorrow is Christmas.

"Now I shoot you and you fall down dead!"

The children were playing under the table.

"Children, don' make so much noise, *bendito!*"

"I'm Gene Autry!" said the oldest one.

"An I'm Palong Cassidy!"

"Children, I gotta headache, for God's sake . . ."

"You ain Palong Nobody! You the bad guy and I kill you!"

"No! Maaaaaaaa!"

Graciela twisted her body and put her head under the table to see them fighting.

"Boys, geddup from under there! *Maldita sea mi vida.* What a life. ROSENDO, HURRY AND GET UP!"

The kids were running through the room again, one of them shouting and laughing, the other crying.

"ROSENDO!"

.   .   .

Rosendo drank his coffee and ignored his wife's insults.

"Waddaya figure on doin today, lookin for work or goin from store to store and from bar to bar drawin all those bums?"

He drank his breakfast coffee, biting his lips distractedly, smoking his last cigarette between sips. She circled the table, rubbing her hand over her belly to calm the movement of the fetus.

"I guess you'll go with those good-for-nothin friends of yours and gamble with some borrowed money, thinkin that manna's gonna fall from the sky today."

"Lemme alone, woman . . ."

"Yeah, its always the same: lemme alone. Tomorrow's Christmas and those kids ain gonna have no presents."

"Kings Day's in January . . ."

"Kings don' come to New York. Santa Claus comes to New York!"

"Well, anyhow, whoever comes, we'll see . . ."

"Holy Mother of God! What a father, my God! You only care about your scribbles. The artist! A grown man like you."

He left the table and went to the bedroom, tired of hearing the woman. He looked out the only window. All the snow that had fallen day after day was filthy. The cars had flattened and blackened it on the pavement. On the sidewalks it had been trampled and pissed on by men and dogs. The days were colder now that the snow was there, hostile, ugly, at home with misery. Denuded of all the innocence it had had the first day.

It was a murky street, under heavy air, on a grandiosely opaque day.

Rosendo went to the bureau and took a bundle of papers from the drawer. Sitting on the window sill, he began to examine them. There were all the paper bags he had collected to tear up and draw on. He drew at night, while the woman and children slept. From memory he drew the drunken faces, the anguished faces of the people of Harlem: everything seen and shared during his daytime wanderings.

Graciela said he was in his second childhood. If he spent time away from the grumbling woman and the crying children, exploring absent-mindedly in his penciled sketches, the woman muttered and sneered.

Tomorrow was Christmas and she was worried because the children wouldn't have presents. She didn't know that this afternoon he would collect ten dollars for the sign he painted yesterday at the corner bar. He was saving that surprise for Graciela. Like he was saving the surprise about her present.

For Graciela he would paint a picture. A picture that would summarize their life together, in the midst of deprivation and frustration. A painting with a melancholy similarity to those photographs taken at saints' day parties in Bayamon. The photographs from the days of their engagement, part of the family's album of memories: they were both leaning against a high stool, on the front of which were the words "Our Love" or "Forever

Together." Behind was the backdrop with palm trees and the sea and a golden paper moon.

Graciela would certainly be pleased to know that in his memory nothing had died. Maybe afterward she wouldn't sneer at his efforts anymore.

Lacking materials, he would have to do the picture on a wall, and with charcoal. But it would be his, from his hands, made for her.

· · ·

Into the building's boiler went all the old and useless wood the super collected. From there Rosendo took the charcoal he needed. Then he went through the basement looking for a wall. It couldn't be in the bedroom. Graciela wouldn't let him take down her prints and palms.

The kitchen wall was too cracked and grimy.

He had no choice but to use the bathroom. It was the only room left.

"If you need to go to the bathroom," he said to his wife, "wait or use the pot. I have to fix some pipes."

He closed the door and cleaned the wall of nails and spiders' webs. He sketched out his idea: a man on horseback, naked and muscled, leaning down to embrace a woman, also naked, wrapped in a mane of black hair from which the night bloomed.

Meticulously, patiently, he repeatedly retouched the parts that didn't satisfy him. After a few hours he decided to go out and get the ten dollars he was owed and buy a tree and toys for his children. On the way he'd get colored chalks at the candy store. This picture would have the sea, and palm trees, and the moon. Tomorrow was Christmas.

Graciela was coming and going in the basement, scolding the children, putting away the laundry, watching the lighted burners on the stove.

He put on his patched coat.

"I'm gonna get a tree for the kids. Don Pedro owes me ten bucks."

She smiled, thanking the saints for the miracle of the ten dollars.

· · ·

That night he returned to the basement smelling of whiskey and beer. The children had already gone to sleep. He put up the tree in a corner of the kitchen and surrounded the trunk with presents.

He ate rice and fritters, without hunger, absorbed in what he would do later. From time to time he glanced at Graciela, looking for a smile that did not appear.

He moved the chipped coffee cup, put the chalk on the table, and looked in his pocket for the cigarette he didn't have.

"I erased all those drawins."

He forgot all about the cigarette.

"So now you're paintin filth?"

He dropped his smile into the abyss of reality.

"You don' have no more shame . . ."

His blood became cold water.

". . . makin yer children look at that filth, that indecency . . . I erased them and that's that and I don' want it to happen again."

He wanted to strike her but the desire was paralyzed in some part of his being, without reaching his arms, without becoming uncontrolled fury in his fists.

When he rose from the chair he felt all of him emptying out through his feet. All of him had been wiped out by a wet rag and her hands had squeezed him out of the world.

He went to the bathroom. Nothing of his remained. Only the nails, bent and rusted, returned to their holes. Only the spiders, returned to their spinning.

The wall was no more than the wide and clear gravestone of his dreams.

FOR DISCUSSION AND WRITING

1. If Graciela tried to communicate her feelings and perspective to Rosendo, what might she have said when she saw the drawings? Similarly, if Rosendo tried to communicate his feelings and perspective to Graciela, what might he have said when he saw that the drawings had been removed?

2. Do you feel that the responsibility for the conflict is primarily Graciela's or Rosendo's, or does the responsibility lie with both people? What other factors contribute to the family's problems? Explain.

* * * * * * * * * * * * * * * * * * * *

I STAND HERE IRONING
Tillie Olsen

Tillie Olsen is a popular, prizewinning short-story writer of Jewish heritage. She has been a role model for women authors who face the challenge of simultaneously working at jobs, caring for family, and perfecting their writing. While raising her four children, Olsen worked in industry, delaying her writing during much of that time. She often writes about people who, because of their class, gender, or ethnicity, have been denied the opportunity to express their full potential. In "I Stand Here Ironing," a mother reflects on raising a daughter, Emily, during the worst years of the Great Depression. The story encourages readers to think about the extent to which our lives are the products of circumstances beyond our control.

I STAND HERE IRONING, and what you asked me moves tormented back and forth with the iron.

"I wish you would manage the time to come in and talk with me about your daughter. I'm sure you can help me understand her. She's a youngster who needs help and whom I'm deeply interested in helping."

"Who needs help." Even if I came, what good would it do? You think because I am her mother I have a key, or that in some way you could use me as a key? She has lived for nineteen years. There is all that life that has happened outside of me, beyond me.

And when is there time to remember, to sift, to weigh, to estimate, to total? I will start and there will be an interruption and I will have to gather it all together again. Or I will become engulfed with all I did or did not do, with what should have been and what cannot be helped.

She was a beautiful baby. The first and only one of our five that was beautiful at birth. You do not guess how new and uneasy her tenancy in her now-loveliness. You did not know her all those years she was thought homely, or see her poring over her baby pictures, making me tell her over and over how beautiful she had been—and would be, I would tell her—and was now, to the seeing eye. But the seeing eyes were few or nonexistent. Including mine.

I nursed her. They feel that's important nowadays. I nursed all the children, but with her, with all the fierce rigidity of first motherhood, I did like the books then said. Though her cries battered me to trembling and my breasts ached with swollenness, I waited till the clock decreed.

Why do I put that first? I do not even know if it matters, or if it explains anything.

She was a beautiful baby. She blew shining bubbles of sound. She loved motion, loved light, loved color and music and textures. She would lie on the floor in her blue overalls patting the surface so hard in ecstasy her hands and feet would blur. She was a miracle to me, but when she was eight months old I had to leave her daytimes with the woman downstairs to whom she was no miracle at all, for I worked or looked for work and for Emily's father, who "could no longer endure" (he wrote in his good-bye note) "sharing want with us."

I was nineteen. It was the pre-relief, pre-WPA world of the depression. I would start running as soon as I got off the streetcar, running up the stairs, the place smelling sour, and awake or asleep to startle awake, when she saw me she would break into a clogged weeping that could not be comforted, a weeping I can hear yet.

After a while I found a job hashing at night so I could be with her days, and it was better. But it came to where I had to bring her to his family and leave her.

It took a long time to raise the money for her fare back. Then she got chicken pox and I had to wait longer. When she finally came, I hardly knew her, walking quick and nervous like her father, looking like her father, thin, and dressed in a shoddy red that yellowed her skin and glared at the pockmarks. All the baby loveliness gone.

She was two. Old enough for nursery school, they said and I did not know then what I know now—the fatigue of the long day, and the lacerations of group life in nurseries that are only parking places for children.

Except that it would have made no difference if I had known. It was the only place there was. It was the only way we could be together, the only way I could hold a job.

And even without knowing, I knew. I knew the teacher that was evil because all these years it has curdled into my memory, the little boy hunched in the corner, her rasp, "why aren't you outside, because Alvin hits you? that's no reason, go out, scaredy." I knew Emily hated it even if she did not clutch and implore "don't go Mommy" like the other children, mornings.

She always had a reason why we should stay home. Momma, you look sick, Momma. I feel sick. Momma, the teachers aren't there today, they're sick. Momma, we can't go, there was a fire there last night. Momma, it's a holiday today, no school, they told me.

But never a direct protest, never rebellion. I think of our others in their three-, four-year-oldness—the explosions, the tempers, the denunciations, the demands—and I feel suddenly ill. I put the iron down. What in me demanded that goodness in her? And what was the cost, the cost to her of such goodness?

The old man living in the back once said in his gentle way: "You should smile at Emily more when you look at her." What *was* in my face when I looked at her? I loved her. There were all the acts of love.

It was only with the others I remembered what he said, and it was the face of joy, and not of care or tightness or worry I turned to them—too late for Emily. She does not smile easily, let alone almost always as her brothers and sisters do. Her face is closed and sombre, but when she wants, how fluid. You must have seen it in her pantomimes, you spoke of her rare gift for comedy on the stage that rouses a laughter out of the audience so dear they applaud and applaud and do not want to let her go.

Where does it come from, that comedy? There was none of it in her when she came back to me that second time, after I had had to send her away again. She had a new daddy now to learn to love, and I think perhaps it was a better time.

Except when we left her alone nights, telling ourselves she was old enough.

"Can't you go some other time, Mommy, like tomorrow?" she would ask. "Will it be just a little while you'll be gone? Do you promise?"

The time we came back, the front door open, the clock on the floor in the hall. She rigid awake. "It wasn't just a little while. I didn't cry. Three times I called you, just three times, and then I ran downstairs to open the door so you could come faster. The clock talked loud. I threw it away, it scared me what it talked."

She said the clock talked loud again that night I went to the hospital to have Susan. She was delirious with the fever that comes before red measles, but she was fully conscious all the week I was gone and the week after we were home when she could not come near the new baby or me.

She did not get well. She stayed skeleton thin, not wanting to eat, and night after night she had nightmares. She would call for me, and I would rouse from exhaustion to sleepily call back: "You're all right, darling, go to sleep, it's just a dream," and if she still called, in a sterner voice, "now go to sleep, Emily, there's nothing to hurt you." Twice, only twice, when I had to get up for Susan anyhow, I went in to sit with her.

Now when it is too late (as if she would let me hold and comfort her like I do the others) I get up and go to her at once at her moan or restless stirring. "Are you awake, Emily? Can I get you something?" And the answer is always the same: "No, I'm all right, go back to sleep, Mother."

They persuaded me at the clinic to send her away to a convalescent home in the country where "she can have the kind of food and care you can't manage for her, and you'll be free to concentrate on the new baby." They still send children to that place. I see pictures on the society page of sleek young women planning affairs to raise money for it, or dancing at the affairs, or decorating Easter eggs or filling Christmas stockings for the children.

They never have a picture of the children so I do not know if the girls still wear those gigantic red bows and the ravaged looks on the every other Sunday when parents can come to visit "unless otherwise notified"—as we were notified the first six weeks.

Oh it is a handsome place, green lawns and tall trees and fluted flower beds. High up on the balconies of each cottage the children stand, the girls in their red bows and white dresses, the boys in white suits and giant red ties. The parents stand below shrieking up to be heard and the children shriek down to be heard, and between them the invisible wall "Not To Be Contaminated by Parental Germs or Physical Affection."

There was a tiny girl who always stood hand in hand with Emily. Her parents never came. One visit she was gone. "They moved her to Rose Cottage" Emily shouted in explanation. "They don't like you to love anybody here."

She wrote once a week, the labored writing of a seven-year-old. "I am fine. How is the baby. If I write my letter nicly I will have a star. Love." There never was a star. We wrote every other day, letters she could never hold or keep but only hear read—once. "We simply do not have room for children to keep any personal possessions," they patiently explained when we pieced one Sunday's shrieking together to plead how much it would mean to Emily, who loved so to keep things, to be allowed to keep her letters and cards.

Each visit she looked frailer. "She isn't eating," they told us.

(They had runny eggs for breakfast or mush with lumps, Emily said later, I'd hold it in my mouth and not swallow. Nothing ever tasted good, just when they had chicken.)

It took us eight months to get her released home, and only the fact that she gained back so little of her seven lost pounds convinced the social worker.

I used to try to hold and love her after she came back, but her body would stay stiff, and after a while she'd push away. She ate little. Food sickened her, and I think much of life too. Oh she had physical lightness and brightness, twinkling by on skates, bouncing like a ball up and down up and down over the jump rope, skimming over the hill; but these were momentary.

She fretted about her appearance, thin and dark and foreign-looking at a time when every little girl was supposed to look or thought she should look a chubby blonde replica of Shirley Temple. The doorbell sometimes rang for her, but no one seemed to come and play in the house or be a best friend. Maybe because we moved so much.

There was a boy she loved painfully through two school semesters. Months later she told me how she had taken pennies from my purse to buy him candy. "Licorice was his favorite and I brought him some every day, but he still liked Jennifer better'n me. Why, Mommy?" The kind of question for which there is no answer.

School was a worry to her. She was not glib or quick in a world where glibness and quickness were easily confused with ability to learn. To her overworked and exasperated teachers she was an overconscientious "slow learner" who kept trying to catch up and was absent entirely too often.

I let her be absent, though sometimes the illness was imaginary. How different from my now-strictness about attendance with the others. I wasn't working. We had a new baby, I was home anyhow. Sometimes, after Susan grew old enough, I would keep her home from school, too, to have them all together.

Mostly Emily had asthma, and her breathing, harsh and labored, would fill the house with a curiously tranquil sound. I would bring the two old dresser mirrors and her boxes of collections to her bed. She would select beads and single earrings, bottle tops and shells, dried flowers and pebbles, old postcards and scraps, all sorts of oddments; then she and Susan would play Kingdom, setting up landscapes and furniture, peopling them with action.

Those were the only times of peaceful companionship between her and Susan. I have edged away from it, that poisonous feeling between them, that terrible balancing of hurts and needs I had to do between the two, and did so badly, those earlier years.

Oh there are conflicts between the others too, each one human, needing, demanding, hurting, taking—but only between Emily and Susan, no, Emily toward Susan that corroding resentment. It seems so obvious on the surface, yet it is not obvious. Susan, the second child, Susan, golden-

and curly-haired and chubby, quick and articulate and assured, everything in appearance and manner Emily was not; Susan, not able to resist Emily's precious things, losing or sometimes clumsily breaking them; Susan telling jokes and riddles to company for applause while Emily sat silent (to say to me later: that was *my* riddle, Mother, I told it to Susan); Susan, who for all the five years' difference in age was just a year behind Emily in developing physically.

I am glad for that slow physical development that widened the difference between her and her contemporaries, though she suffered over it. She was too vulnerable for that terrible world of youthful competition, of preening and parading, of constant measuring of yourself against every other, of envy, "If I had that copper hair," "If I had that skin. . . ." She tormented herself enough about not looking like the others, there was enough of the unsureness, the having to be conscious of words before you speak, the constant caring—what are they thinking of me? without having it all magnified by the merciless physical drives.

Ronnie is calling. He is wet and I change him. It is rare there is such a cry now. That time of motherhood is almost behind me when the ear is not one's own but must always be racked and listening for the child cry, the child call. We sit for a while and I hold him, looking out over the city spread in charcoal with its soft aisles of light. "*Shoogily*," he breathes and curls closer. I carry him back to bed, asleep. *Shoogily*. A funny word, a family word, inherited from Emily, invented by her to say: *comfort*.

In this and other ways she leaves her seal, I say aloud. And startle at my saying it. What do I mean? What did I start to gather together, to try and make coherent? I was at the terrible, growing years. War years. I do not remember them well. I was working, there were four smaller ones now, there was not time for her. She had to help be a mother, and housekeeper, and shopper. She had to set her seal. Mornings of crisis and near hysteria trying to get lunches packed, hair combed, coats and shoes found, everyone to school or Child Care on time, the baby ready for transportation. And always the paper scribbled on by a smaller one, the book looked at by Susan then mislaid, the homework not done. Running out to that huge school where she was one, she was lost, she was a drop; suffering over the unpreparedness, stammering and unsure in her classes.

There was so little time left at night after the kids were bedded down. She would struggle over books, always eating (it was in those years she developed her enormous appetite that is legendary in our family) and I would be ironing, or preparing food for the next day, or writing V-mail to Bill, or tending the baby. Sometimes, to make me laugh, or out of her despair, she would imitate happenings or types at school.

I think I said once: "Why don't you do something like this in the school amateur show?" One morning she phoned me at work, hardly understandable through the weeping: "Mother, I did it. I won, I won; they gave me first prize; they clapped and clapped and wouldn't let me go.'

Now suddenly she was Somebody, and as imprisoned in her difference as she had been in anonymity.

She began to be asked to perform at other high schools, even in colleges, then at city and statewide affairs. The first one we went to, I only recognized her that first moment when thin, shy, she almost drowned herself into the curtains. Then: Was this Emily? The control, the command, the convulsing and deadly clowning, the spell, then the roaring, stamping audience, unwilling to let this rare and precious laughter out of their lives.

Afterwards: You ought to do something about her with a gift like that—but without money or knowing how, what does one do? We have left it all to her, and the gift has as often eddied inside, clogged and clotted, as been used and growing.

She is coming. She runs up the stairs two at a time with her light graceful step, and I know she is happy tonight. Whatever it was that occasioned your call did not happen today.

"Aren't you ever going to finish the ironing, Mother? Whistler painted his mother in a rocker. I'd have to paint mine standing over an ironing board." This is one of her communicative nights and she tells me everything and nothing as she fixes herself a plate of food out of the icebox.

She is so lovely. Why did you want me to come in at all? Why were you concerned? She will find her way.

She starts up the stairs to bed. "Don't get me up with the rest in the morning." "But I thought you were having midterms." "Oh, those," she comes back in, kisses me, and says quite lightly, "in a couple of years when we'll all be atom-dead they won't matter a bit."

She has said it before. She *believes* it. But because I have been dredging the past, and all that compounds a human being is so heavy and meaningful in me, I cannot endure it tonight.

I will never total it all. I will never come in to say: She was a child seldom smiled at. Her father left me before she was a year old. I had to work her first six years when there was work, or I sent her home and to his relatives. There were years she had care she hated. She was dark and thin and foreign-looking in a world where the prestige went to blondeness and curly hair and dimples, she was slow where glibness was prized. She was a child of anxious, not proud, love. We were poor and could not afford for her the soil of easy growth. I was a young mother, I was a distracted mother. There were the other children pushing up, demanding. Her younger sister seemed all that she was not. There were years she did not want me to touch her. She kept too much in herself, her life was such she had to keep too much in herself. My wisdom came too late. She has much to her and probably nothing will come of it. She is a child of her age, of depression, of war, of fear.

Let her be. So all that is in her will not bloom—but in how many does it? There is still enough left to live by. Only help her to know—help make it so there is cause for her to know—that she is more than this dress on the ironing board, helpless before the iron.

FOR DISCUSSION AND WRITING

1. If you were Emily's high school teacher, what behaviors in Emily would you identify that indicate a need for help?

2. How does Emily's mother feel as she tells the story? Use the selection to support your response.

3. As Emily was growing up, what, if anything, could her mother have done to prevent or lessen her daughter's problems? Explain.

4. Can you think of any existing or potential social and economic options for single mothers that might help prevent situations like the one depicted in this selection?

✳ ✳

INDIAN BOARDING SCHOOL: THE RUNAWAYS
Louise Erdrich

The characters of Chippewa, Cree, German, English, and French descent who populate the stories and poems of Louise Erdrich are based on the people with whom she grew up. She was raised in Minnesota in the region of the Turtle Mountain Chippewa Reservation and is of Chippewa and German heritage. The poem "Indian Boarding School" is about the forced assimilation of Native Americans by the United States government. Government programs forced Native-American children to attend boarding schools great distances from their families to teach them "American" ways. In "Indian Boarding School," as well as in her other works, Erdrich makes unexpected connections between events occurring at different times.

HOME'S THE PLACE WE HEAD FOR IN OUR SLEEP.
Boxcars stumbling north in dreams
don't wait for us. We catch them on the run.
The rails, old lacerations that we love,
shoot parallel across the face and break
just under Turtle Mountains. Riding scars
you can't get lost. Home is the place they cross.

The lame guard strikes a match and makes the dark
less tolerant. We watch through cracks in boards
as the land starts rolling, rolling till it hurts
to be here, cold in regulation clothes.
We know the sheriff's waiting at midrun
to take us back. His car is dumb and warm.
The highway doesn't rock, it only hums
like a wing of long insults. The worn-down welts
of ancient punishment lead back and forth.

All runaways wear dresses, long green ones,
the color you would think shame was. We scrub
the sidewalks down because it's shameful work.
Our brushes cut the stone in watered arcs
and in the soak frail outlines shiver clear

a moment, things us kids pressed on the dark
face before it hardened, pale, remembering
delicate old injuries, the spines of names and leaves.

FOR DISCUSSION AND WRITING

1. *Why do the students run away? How has the school attempted to change them? Where are they going?*

2. *Describe the students' daily life in the boarding school.*

3. *Why do so many words and phrases in the poem refer to pain? What is the author describing in each of these cases?*

4. *Although the poem includes many references to pain, do you find anything hopeful in the poem? Explain.*

* * * * * * * * * * * * * * * * * *

THE POET IMAGINES HIS GRANDFATHER'S THOUGHTS ON THE DAY HE DIED
Wing Tek Lum

Can you imagine the everyday scenes and the important events your grandparents witnessed when they were young? "The Poet Imagines His Grandfather's Thoughts on the Day He Died" sweeps through time, allowing the reader to see through the eyes of both grandfather and grandson. In addition to writing, Hawaiian poet Wing Tek Lum has practiced social work in Hong Kong and New York City's China-town. He is immersed in Chinese and American history and popular culture.

THIS IS THE FIRST YEAR
the Dragon Eyes tree has ever borne fruit:
let us see what this omen brings.
Atop one of its exposed roots
a small frog squats, not moving, not even blinking.
I remember when my children were young
and this whole front yard was a taro patch:
we would take them out at night with a lantern
blinding the frogs just long enough

to sneak a hook up under the belly.
In those days we grew taro
as far as the eye could see;
I even invented a new kind of trough
lined inside with a wire mesh
so we could peel the skins with ease.
The King bought our poi,
and gave me a pounder one day.
It is made of stone,

and looks like the clapper of a bell, smooth and heavy.
I keep it in my bedroom now—there—on the dresser.
The fish we call Big Eyes
lies on an oval plate beside it.
I have not been hungry today.
The full bowl of rice attracts a fly
buzzing in anticipation.
I hear the laughter of one of my grandchildren
from the next room: which one is it?
Maybe someday one of them will think of me
and see the rainbows that I have seen,
the opium den in Annam that frightened me so,
my mother's tears when I left home.

Dear ancestors, all this is still one in mind.

FOR DISCUSSION AND WRITING

1. Who is speaking in the poem? Does the title help you to understand the poem?

2. What scenes do you imagine your grandparents saw as part of their everyday lives?

3. How might you be able to know or guess what your ancestors saw?

FROM *A BINTEL BRIEF:*
LETTERS FROM THE WORLD OF OUR FATHERS
Isaac Metzker

"A Bintel Brief," letters to the editor, was a regular feature of the Yiddish language Jewish Daily For-ward newspaper from 1906 to 1967. The column was similar to the current "Dear Abby" column. As editor, Isaac Metzker said about the Jewish Daily Forward "newcomers, who were lonely here, clung to the Forward . . . as to a new found friend. It became their teacher and guide." "A Bintel Brief" provided a significant way for the Forward to speak to the hearts of lonely Jewish immigrants. The two letters and responses included here are about the problems of assimilation and moving up the social ladder that many families face.

1941

DEAR EDITOR,

My husband and I came from Galicia to America thirty-three years ago right after we were married. At home I had received a secular educa-tion, and my husband had been ordained as a rabbi. However, he did not want to be a rabbi here, and since we had brought along a little money from home, we bought a small business and made a good living. My hus-band is religious but not a fanatic. I am more liberal, but I go to *shul* with him on *Rosh Hashanah* and *Yom Kippur.*

We have five children—two boys and three girls. The boys went to a *Talmud Torah,* and the girls, too, received a Jewish education. We always kept a Jewish home and a *kosher* kitchen.

Our eldest son is now a college teacher, tutors students privately, and earns a good deal of money. He is married, has two children, four and seven years old. They live in a fine neighborhood, and we visit them often.

It happened that on Christmas Eve we were invited to have dinner with friends who live near our son and daughter-in-law, so we decided to drop in to see them after the meal. I called up, my daughter-in-law answered the telephone and warmly invited us to come over.

Roman Vishniac, Granddaughter and Grandfather, Warsaw, *1938*

When we opened the door and went into the living room we saw a large Christmas tree which my son was busy trimming with the help of his two children. When my husband saw this he turned white. The two grandchildren greeted us with a "Merry Christmas" and were delighted to see us. I wanted to take off my coat, but my husband gave me a signal that we were leaving immediately.

Well, I had to leave at once. Our son's and daughter-in-law's pleading and talking didn't help, because my husband didn't want to stay there another minute. He is so angry at our son over the Christmas tree that he doesn't want to cross the threshold of their home again. My son justifies himself by saying he takes the tree in for the sake of his children, so they won't feel any different than their non-Jewish friends in the neighborhood. He assures us that it has nothing to do with religion. He doesn't consider it wrong, and he feels his father has no right to be angry over it.

My husband is a *kohen* and, besides having a temper, he is stubborn, too.

But I don't want him to be angry at our son. Therefore I would like to hear your opinion on this matter.

> With great respect,
> A Reader from the Bronx

ANSWER:

The national American holidays are celebrated here with love and joy, by Jews and Gentiles alike. But Christmas is the most religious Christian holiday and Jews have nothing to do with it. Jews, religious or not, should respect the Christmas holiday, but to celebrate it would be like dancing at a stranger's wedding. It is natural that a Jew who observes all the Jewish traditions should be opposed to seeing his son and grandchildren trimming a Christmas tree.

But he must not quarrel with his son. It is actually your husband's fault because he probably did not instill the Jewish traditions in his son. Instead of being angry with him, he should talk to his son and explain the meaning of Christmas to him.

FOR DISCUSSION AND WRITING

1. What specific thoughts and feelings do you think the father had when he saw his son trimming the Christmas tree?

2. Do you agree with the editor that it is wrong for a Jew to celebrate Christmas? What is the editor's reasoning behind his answer? Explain your views about celebrating religious holidays that are not part of a person's original heritage.

1966

DEAR EDITOR,

I am writing you, with my dear husband's permission, about the resentment we feel over our daughter-in-law, and I ask your advice.

We have two daughters and a son. They and our grandchildren are very dear to us, and it is our greatest pleasure to visit with them. Lately, however, we have been very upset by our daughter-in-law and our son. We used to go to them, as to our daughters and sons-in-law, quite often, and used to spend a lot of time with their children, who are five and three years old.

Our daughter-in-law was never too friendly toward us, but we overlooked a great deal. A short time ago, when my husband and I went there, she suddenly announced that she wanted us to visit our grandchildren only once in two weeks, and that we should avoid coming to them on weekends when they have guests.

I didn't know at first what my daughter-in-law meant, but she explained that, as her children were growing up, she didn't want them to learn from us to speak English with a Jewish accent. Our dear daughter-in-law wasn't even ashamed to tell us that we didn't fit in with her group of friends who were real Americans, while we were foreigners.

It's true we're not American-born (we came to this country over forty years ago) and our English is not "perfect," but we are very hurt by our daughter-in-law's remark. I answered her then that in our youth we had no time to learn the English that was spoken in high society because we had to work hard to raise a college-educated husband for her. I told her my husband often had to work overtime in order to be able to send our son to college, to make him a professional man.

My husband didn't let me continue arguing with our daughter-in-law, who is a young, foolish girl, and we went home angry. The next day my son called up. I thought he would tell us his wife had been wrong, but he said that he agreed with her that we should visit them every other week on a definite day. Very distressed, I hung up in the middle of the conversation and my husband and I haven't visited them at all for the past few weeks.

We ask you, is this right? Should children act this way? What can we do, dear Editor, since we miss our grandchildren so? We are hurt and want to know whether we must obey these rules laid down by our daughter-in-law. Please answer soon.

With heartfelt thanks,
Grandma and Grandpa

ANSWER:
You are rightfully bitter. Your son should be blamed even more than your daughter-in-law. He should never have permitted her to make such an arrangement. It is also natural that you should feel offended by your daughter-in-law's statement. The behavior of your daughter-in-law is ridiculous and contrary to the American tradition. Many great men, active in American government, education and business, were brought up

by immigrant parents who didn't speak English correctly, but this did not keep them from having successful careers. And these successful children of immigrants are not ashamed of their fathers and mothers who came to America from across the ocean. Just the opposite, they take every opportunity to mention their parents and grandparents with pride, and they stress the fact that these immigrants who speak English with a Jewish accent have enriched their lives.

We feel that someone in your family should explain this to your son and daughter-in-law, and they may see that they are wrong. We also feel that at present you should visit your grandchildren, your son and daughter-in-law, not as often as before, since a prolonged estrangement will do you more harm than them.

FOR DISCUSSION AND WRITING

1. What do the son and daughter-in-law value in life?

2. Do you sympathize with the parents or the grandparents? Explain.

* * * * * * * * * * * * * * * * * * * *

IN THE AMERICAN SOCIETY
Gish Jen

Novelist and short-story writer Gish Jen, the child of Chinese immigrants, was born and raised in New York City. Her name was originally Lillian Jen, but she was nicknamed "Gish" by her friends after the silent-screen actress, Lillian Gish. "In the American Society" is about a Chinese immigrant couple and their American-born children. The story shows how individual family members react differently to the pressures and challenges of fitting into the dominant culture and raises the issue of how families deal with these differences.

I. HIS OWN SOCIETY

WHEN MY FATHER TOOK OVER THE PANCAKE HOUSE, it was to send my little sister Mona and me to college. We were only in junior high at the time, but my father believed in getting a jump on things. "Those Americans always saying it," he told us. "Smart guys thinking in advance." My mother elaborated, explaining that businesses took bringing up, like children. They could take years to get going, she said, years.

In this case, though, we got rich right away. At two months we were breaking even, and at four, those same hotcakes that could barely withstand the weight of butter and syrup were supporting our family with ease. My mother bought a station wagon with air conditioning, my father an oversized, red vinyl recliner for the back room; and as time went on and the business continued to thrive, my father started to talk about his grandfather and the village he had reigned over in China—things my father had never talked about when he worked for other people. He told us about the bags of rice his family would give out to the poor at New Year's, and about the people who came to beg, on their hands and knees, for his grandfather to intercede for the more wayward of their relatives. "Like that Godfather in the movie," he would tell us as, his feet up, he distributed paychecks. Sometimes an employee would get two green envelopes instead of one, which meant that Jimmy needed a tooth pulled, say, or that Tiffany's husband was in the clinker again.

"It's nothing, nothing," he would ·insist, sinking back into his chair.

"Who else is going to take care of you people?"

My mother would mostly just sigh about it. "Your father thinks this is China," she would say, and then she would go back to her mending. Once in a while, though, when my father had given away a particularly large sum, she would exclaim, outraged, "But this here is the U-S-of-A!"—this apparently having been what she used to tell immigrant stock boys when they came in late.

She didn't work at the supermarket anymore; but she had made it to the rank of manager before she left, and this had given her not only new words and phrases, but new ideas about herself, and about America, and about what was what in general. She had opinions, now, on how downtown should be zoned; she could pump her own gas and check her own oil; and for all she used to chide Mona and me for being "copycats," she herself was now interested in espadrilles, and wallpaper, and most recently, the town country club.

"So join already," said Mona, flicking a fly off her knee.

My mother enumerated the problems as she sliced up a quarter round of watermelon: there was the cost. There was the waiting list. There was the fact that no one in our family played either tennis or golf.

"So what?" said Mona.

"It would be waste," said my mother.

"Me and Callie can swim in the pool."

"Plus you need that recommendation letter from a member."

"Come *on*," said Mona. "Annie's mom'd write you a letter in a *sec*."

My mother's knife glinted in the early summer sun. I spread some more newspaper on the picnic table.

"*Plus* you have to eat there twice a month. You know what that means." My mother cut another, enormous slice of fruit.

"No, I *don't* know what that means," said Mona.

"It means Dad would have to wear a jacket, dummy," I said.

"Oh! Oh! Oh!" said Mona, clasping her hand to her breast. "Oh! Oh! Oh! Oh! Oh!"

We all laughed: my father had no use for nice clothes, and would wear only ten-year-old shirts, with grease-spotted pants, to show how little he cared what anyone thought.

"Your father doesn't believe in joining the American society," said my mother. "He wants to have his own society."

"So go to dinner without him." Mona shot her seeds out in long arcs over the lawn. "Who cares what he thinks?"

But of course we all did care, and knew my mother could not simply up and do as she pleased. For in my father's mind, a family owed its head a degree of loyalty that left no room for dissent. To embrace what he embraced was to love; and to embrace something else was to betray him.

He demanded a similar sort of loyalty of his workers, whom he treated more like servants than employees. Not in the beginning, of course. In the beginning all he wanted was for them to keep on doing what they used to do, and to that end he concentrated mostly on leaving them alone. As the months passed, though, he expected more and more of them, with the result that for all his largesse, he began to have trouble keeping help. The cooks and busboys complained that he asked them to fix radiators and trim hedges, not only at the restaurant, but at our house; the waitresses that he sent them on errands and made them chauffeur him around. Our head waitress, Gertrude, claimed that he once even asked her to scratch his back.

"It's not just the blacks don't believe in slavery," she said when she quit.

My father never quite registered her complaint, though, nor those of the others who left. Even after Eleanor quit, then Tiffany, then Gerald, and Jimmy, and even his best cook, Eureka Andy, for whom he had bought new glasses, he remained mostly convinced that the fault lay with them.

"All they understand is that assembly line," he lamented. "Robots, they are. They want to be robots."

There *were* occasions when the clear running truth seemed to eddy, when he would pinch the vinyl of his chair up into little peaks and wonder if he were doing things right. But with time he would always smooth the peaks back down; and when business started to slide in the spring, he kept on like a horse in his ways.

By the summer our dishboy was overwhelmed with scraping. It was no longer just the hashbrowns that people were leaving for trash, and the service was as bad as the food. The waitresses served up French pancakes instead of German, apple juice instead of orange, spilt things on laps, on coats. On the Fourth of July some greenhorn sent an entire side of fries slaloming down a lady's *massif centrale.* Meanwhile in the back room, my father labored through articles on the economy.

"What is housing starts?" he puzzled. "What is GNP?"

Mona and I did what we could, filling in as busgirls and bookkeepers and, one afternoon, stuffing the comments box that hung by the cashier's desk. That was Mona's idea. We rustled up a variety of pens and pencils, checked boxes for an hour, smeared the cards up with coffee and grease, and waited. It took a few days for my father to notice that the box was full, and he didn't say anything about it for a few days more. Finally, though, he started to complain of fatigue; and then he began to complain that the staff was not what it could be. We encouraged him in this—pointing out, for instance, how many dishes got chipped—but in the end all that happened was that, for the first time since we took over the restaurant, my father got it into his head to fire someone. Skip, a skinny busboy who was saving up for a sports car, said nothing as my father mumbled on about the price of dishes. My father's hands shook as he wrote out the severance check; and he spent the rest of the day napping in his chair once it was over.

As it was going on midsummer, Skip wasn't easy to replace. We hung a sign in the window and advertised in the paper, but no one called the first week, and the person who called the second didn't show up for his interview. The third week, my father phoned Skip to see if he would come back, but a friend of his had already sold him a Corvette for cheap.

Finally a Chinese guy named Booker turned up. He couldn't have been more than thirty, and was wearing a lighthearted seersucker suit, but he looked as though life had him pinned: his eyes were bloodshot and his chest sunken, and the muscles of his neck seemed to strain with the effort of holding his head up. In a single dry breath he told us that he had never bussed tables but was willing to learn, and that he was on the lam from the deportation authorities.

"I do not want to lie to you," he kept saying. He had come to the United States on a student visa, had run out of money, and was now in a bind. He was loath to go back to Taiwan, as it happened—he looked up at this point, to be sure my father wasn't pro-KMT—but all he had was a phony social security card and a willingness to absorb all blame, should anything untoward come to pass.

"I do not think, anyway, that it is against law to hire me, only to be me," he said, smiling faintly.

Anyone else would have examined him on this, but my father conceived of laws as speed bumps rather than curbs. He wiped the counter with his sleeve, and told Booker to report the next morning.

"I will be good worker," said Booker.

"Good," said my father.

"Anything you want me to do, I will do."

My father nodded.

Booker seemed to sink into himself for a moment. "Thank you," he said finally. "I am appreciate your help. I am very very appreciate for everything." He reached out to shake my father's hand.

My father looked at him. "Did you eat today?" he asked in Mandarin.

Booker pulled at the hem of his jacket.

"Sit down," said my father. "Please, have a seat."

My father didn't tell my mother about Booker, and my mother didn't tell my father about the country club. She would never have applied, except that Mona, while over at Annie's, had let it drop that our mother wanted to join. Mrs. Lardner came by the very next day.

"Why, I'd be honored and delighted to write you people a letter," she said. Her skirt billowed around her.

"Thank you so much," said my mother. "But it's too much trouble for you, and also my husband is . . ."

"Oh, it's no trouble at all, no trouble at all. I tell you." She leaned forward so that her chest freckles showed. "I know just how it is. It's a secret of course, but you know, my natural father was Jewish. Can you see it? Just look at my skin."

"My husband," said my mother.

"I'd be honored and delighted," said Mrs. Lardner with a little wave of her hands. "Just honored and delighted."

Mona was triumphant. "See, Mom," she said, waltzing around the kitchen when Mrs. Lardner left. "What did I tell you? 'I'm just honored and delighted, just honored and delighted.'" She waved her hands in the air.

"You know, the Chinese have a saying," said my mother. "To do nothing is better than to overdo. You mean well, but you tell me now what will happen."

"I'll talk Dad into it," said Mona, still waltzing. "Or I bet Callie can. He'll do anything Callie says."

"I can try, anyway," I said.

"Did you hear what I said?" said my mother. Mona bumped into the broom closet door. "You're not going to talk anything; you've already made enough trouble." She started on the dishes with a clatter.

Mona poked diffidently at a mop.

I sponged off the counter. "Anyway," I ventured. "I bet our name'll never even come up."

"That's if we're lucky," said my mother.

"There's all these people waiting," I said.

"Good," she said. She started on a pot.

I looked over at Mona, who was still cowering in the broom closet. "In fact, there's some black family's been waiting so long, they're going to sue," I said.

My mother turned off the water. "Where'd you hear that?"

"Patty told me."

She turned the water back on, started to wash a dish, then put it back down and shut the faucet.

"I'm sorry," said Mona.

"Forget it," said my mother. "Just forget it."

.   .   .

Booker turned out to be a model worker, whose boundless gratitude translated into a willingness to do anything. As he also learned quickly, he soon knew not only how to bus, but how to cook, and how to wait table, and how to keep the books. He fixed the walk-in door so that it stayed shut, reupholstered the torn seats in the dining room, and devised a system for tracking inventory. The only stone in the rice was that he tended to be sickly; but, reliable even in illness, he would always send a friend to take his place. In this way we got to know Ronald, Lynn, Dirk, and Cedric, all of whom, like Booker, had problems with their legal status and were anxious to please. They weren't all as capable as Booker, though, with the exception of Cedric, whom my father often hired even when Booker was well. A round wag of a man who called Mona and me *shou hou*—skinny monkeys—he was a professed nonsmoker who was nevertheless always begging drags off of other people's cigarettes. This last habit drove our head cook, Fernando, crazy, especially since, when refused a hit, Cedric would occasionally snitch one. Winking impishly at Mona and me, he would steal up to an ashtray, take a quick puff, and then break out laughing so that the smoke came rolling out of his mouth in a great incriminatory cloud. Fernando accused him of stealing fresh cigarettes too, even whole packs.

"Why else do you think he's weaseling around in the back of the store all the time," he said. His face was blotchy with anger. "The man is a frigging thief."

Other members of the staff supported him in this contention and joined in on an "Operation Identification," which involved numbering and initialing their cigarettes—even though what they seemed to fear for wasn't so much their cigarettes as their jobs. Then one of the cooks quit; and rather than promote someone, my father hired Cedric for the position. Rumors flew that he was taking only half the normal salary, that Alex had been pressured to resign, and that my father was looking for a position with which to placate Booker, who had been bypassed because of his health.

The result was that Fernando categorically refused to work with Cedric.

"The only way I'll cook with that piece of slime," he said, shaking his huge tattooed fist, "is if it's his ass frying on the grill."

My father cajoled and cajoled, to no avail, and in the end was simply forced to put them on different schedules.

The next week Fernando got caught stealing a carton of minute steaks. My father would not tell even Mona and me how he knew to be standing by the back door when Fernando was on his way out, but everyone suspected Booker. Everyone but Fernando, that is, who was sure Cedric had been the tip-off. My father held a staff meeting in which he tried to reassure everyone that Alex had left on his own, and that he had no intention of firing anyone. But though he was careful not to mention Fernando, everyone was so amazed that he was being allowed to stay that Fernando was incensed nonetheless.

"Don't you all be putting your bug eyes on me," he said. *"He's* the frigging crook." He grabbed Cedric by the collar.

Cedric raised an eyebrow. "Cook, you mean," he said.

At this Fernando punched Cedric in the mouth; and the words he had just uttered notwithstanding, my father fired him on the spot.

. . .

With everything that was happening, Mona and I were ready to be getting out of the restaurant. It was almost time: the days were still stuffy with summer, but our window shade had started flapping in the evening as if gearing up to go out. That year the breezes were full of salt, as they sometimes were when they came in from the East, and they blew anchors and docks through my mind like so many tumbleweeds, filling my dreams with wherries and lobsters and grainy-faced men who squinted, day in and day out, at the sky.

It was time for a change, you could feel it; and yet the pancake house was the same as ever. The day before school started my father came home with bad news.

"Fernando called police," he said, wiping his hand on his pant leg.

My mother naturally wanted to know what police; and so with much coughing and hawing, the long story began, the latest installment of which had the police calling immigration, and immigration sending an investigator. My mother sat stiff as whalebone as my father described how the man summarily refused lunch on the house and how my father had admitted, under pressure, that he knew there were "things" about his workers.

"So now what happens?"

My father didn't know. "Booker and Cedric went with him to the jail," he said. "But me, here I am." He laughed uncomfortably.

The next day my father posted bail for "his boys" and waited apprehensively for something to happen. The day after that he waited again, and the day after that he called our neighbor's law student son, who suggested my father call the immigration department under an alias. My father took his advice; and it was thus that he discovered that Booker was right: it was illegal for aliens to work, but it wasn't to hire them.

In the happy interval that ensued, my father apologized to my mother, who in turn confessed about the country club, for which my father had no choice but to forgive her. Then he turned his attention back to "his boys."

My mother didn't see that there was anything to do.

"I like to talking to the judge," said my father.

"This is not China," said my mother.

"I'm only talking to him. I'm not give him money unless he wants it."

"You're going to land up in jail."

"So what else I should do?" My father threw up his hands. "Those are my boys."

"Your boys!" exploded my mother. "What about your family? What about your wife?"

My father took a long sip of tea. "You know," he said finally. "In the war my father sent our cook to the soldiers to use. He always said it—the province comes before the town, the town comes before the family."

"A restaurant is not a town," said my mother.

My father sipped at his tea again. "You know, when I first come to the United States, I also had to hide-and-seek with those deportation guys. If people did not helping me, I'm not here today."

My mother scrutinized her hem.

After a minute I volunteered that before seeing a judge, he might try a lawyer.

He turned. "Since when did you become so afraid like your mother?"

I started to say that it wasn't a matter of fear, but he cut me off.

"What I need today," he said, "is a son."

My father and I spent the better part of the next day standing in lines at the immigration office. He did not get to speak to a judge, but with much persistence he managed to speak to a judge's clerk, who tried to persuade him that it was not her place to extend him advice. My father, though, shamelessly plied her with compliments and offers of free pancakes until she finally conceded that she personally doubted anything would happen to either Cedric or Booker.

"Especially if they're 'needed workers,'" she said, rubbing at the red marks her glasses left on her nose. She yawned. "Have you thought about sponsoring them to become permanent residents?"

Could he do that? My father was overjoyed. And what if he saw to it right away? Would she perhaps put in a good word with the judge?

She yawned again, her nostrils flaring. "Don't worry," she said. "They'll get a fair hearing."

My father returned jubilant. Booker and Cedric hailed him as their savior, their Buddha incarnate. He was like a father to them, they said; and laughing and clapping, they made him tell the story over and over, sorting over the details like jewels. And how old was the assistant judge? And what did she say?

That evening my father tipped the paperboy a dollar and bought a pot of mums for my mother, who suffered them to be placed on the dining room table. The next night he took us all out to dinner. Then on Saturday, Mona found a letter on my father's chair at the restaurant.

DEAR MR. CHANG,

You are the grat boss. But, we do not like to trial, so will runing away now. Plese to excus us. People saying the law in America is fears like dragon. Here is only $140. We hope some day we can pay back the rest bale. You will getting interest, as you diserving, so grat a boss you are. Thank you for every thing. In next life you will be burn in rich family, with no more pancaks.

Yours truley,
Booker + Cedric

In the weeks that followed my father went to the pancake house for crises, but otherwise hung around our house, fiddling idly with the sump pump and boiler in an effort, he said, to get ready for winter. It was as though he had gone into retirement, except that instead of moving South, he had moved to the basement. He even took to showering my mother with little attentions, and to calling her "old girl," and when we finally heard that the club had entertained all the applications it could for the year, he was so sympathetic that he seemed more disappointed than my mother.

Mrs. Lardner tempered the bad news with an invitation to a bon voyage "bash" she was throwing for a friend of hers who was going to Greece for six months.

"Do come," she urged. "You'll meet everyone, and then, you know, if things open up in the spring . . ." She waved her hands.

My mother wondered if it would be appropriate to show up at a party for someone they didn't know, but "the honest truth" was that this was an annual affair. "If it's not Greece, it's Antibes," sighed Mrs. Lardner. "We really just do it because his wife left him and his daughter doesn't speak to him, and poor Jeremy just feels so *unloved.*"

She also invited Mona and me to the going on, as "*demi*-guests" to keep Annie out of the champagne. I wasn't too keen on the idea, but before I could say anything, she had already thanked us for so generously agreeing to honor her with our presence.

"A pair of little princesses, you are!" she told us. "A pair of princesses!" The party was that Sunday. On Saturday, my mother took my father out shopping for a suit. As it was the end of September, she insisted that he buy a worsted rather than a seersucker, even though it was only ten, rather than fifty percent off. My father protested that it was as hot out as ever, which was true—a thick Indian summer had cozied murderously up to us—but to no avail. Summer clothes, said my mother, were not properly worn after Labor Day.

The suit was unfortunately as extravagant in length as it was in price, which posed an additional quandary, since the tailor wouldn't be in until Monday. The salesgirl, though, found a way of tacking it up temporarily.

"Maybe this suit not fit me," fretted my father.

"Just don't take your jacket off," said the salesgirl.

He gave her a tip before they left, but when he got home refused to remove the price tag.

"I like to asking the tailor about the size," he insisted.

"You mean you're going to *wear* it and then return it?" Mona rolled her eyes.

"I didn't say I'm return it," said my father stiffly. "I like to asking the tailor, that's all."

.   .   .

The party started off swimmingly, except that most people were wearing bermudas or wrap skirts. Still, my parents carried on, sharing with great feeling the complaints about the heat. Of course my father tried to eat a cracker full of shallots and burnt himself in an attempt to help Mr. Lardner turn the coals of the barbeque; but on the whole he seemed to be doing all right. Not nearly so well as my mother, though, who had accepted an entire cupful of Mrs. Lardner's magic punch, and seemed indeed to be under some spell. As Mona and Annie skirmished over whether some boy in their class inhaled when he smoked, I watched my mother take off her shoes, laughing and laughing as a man with a beard regaled her with Navy stories by the pool. Apparently he had been stationed in the Orient and remembered a few words of Chinese, which made my mother laugh still more. My father excused himself to go to the men's room then drifted back and weighed anchor at the hors d'oeuvres table, while my mother sailed on to a group of women, who tinkled at length over the clarity of her complexion. I dug out a book I had brought.

Just when I'd cracked the spine, though, Mrs. Lardner came by to bewail her shortage of servers. Her caterers were criminals, I agreed; and the next thing I knew I was handing out bits of marine life, making the rounds as amiably as I could.

"Here you go, Dad," I said when I got to the hors d'oeuvres table.

"Everything is fine," he said.

I hesitated to leave him alone; but then the man with the beard zeroed in on him, and though he talked of nothing but my mother, I thought it would be okay to get back to work. Just that moment, though, Jeremy Brothers lurched our way, an empty, albeit corked, wine bottle in hand. He was a slim, well-proportioned man, with a Roman nose and small eyes and a nice manly jaw that he allowed to hang agape.

"Hello," he said drunkenly. "Pleased to meet you."

"Pleased to meeting you," said my father.

"Right," said Jeremy. "Right. Listen. I have this bottle here, this most recalcitrant bottle. You see that it refuses to do my bidding. I bid it open sesame, please, and it does nothing." He pulled the cork out with his teeth, then turned the bottle upside down.

My father nodded.

"Would you have a word with it, please?" said Jeremy. The man with the beard excused himself. "Would you please have a goddamned word with it?"

My father laughed uncomfortably.

"Ah!" Jeremy bowed a little. "Excuse me, excuse me, excuse me. You are not my man, not my man at all." He bowed again and started to leave, but then circled back. "Viticulture is not your forte, yes I can see that, see that plainly. But may I trouble you on another matter? Forget the damned bottle." He threw it into the pool, and winked at the people he splashed. "I have another matter. Do you speak Chinese?"

My father said he did not, but Jeremy pulled out a handkerchief with some characters on it anyway, saying that his daughter had sent it from Hong Kong and that he thought the characters might be some secret message.

"Long life," said my father.

"But you haven't looked at it yet."

"I know what it says without looking." My father winked at me.

"You do?"

"Yes, I do."

"You're making fun of me, aren't you?"

"No, no, no," said my father, winking again.

"Who are you anyway?" said Jeremy.

His smile fading, my father shrugged.

"Who are you?"

My father shrugged again.

Jeremy began to roar. "This is my party, *my party*, and I've never seen you before in my life." My father backed up as Jeremy came toward him. *"Who are you? WHO ARE YOU?"*

Just as my father was going to step back into the pool, Mrs. Lardner came running up. Jeremy informed her that there was a man crashing his party.

"Nonsense," said Mrs. Lardner. "This is Ralph Chang, who I invited extra especially so he could meet you." She straightened the collar of Jeremy's peach-colored polo shirt for him.

"Yes, well we've had a chance to chat," said Jeremy.

She whispered in his ear; he mumbled something; she whispered something more.

"I do apologize," he said finally.

My father didn't say anything.

"I do." Jeremy seemed genuinely contrite. "Doubtless you've seen drunks before, haven't you? You must have them in China."

"Okay," said my father.

As Mrs. Lardner glided off, Jeremy clapped his arm over my father's shoulders. "You know, I really am quite sorry, quite sorry."

My father nodded.

"What can I do, how can I make it up to you?"

"No thank you."

"No, tell me, tell me," wheedled Jeremy. "Tickets to casino night?" My father shook his head. "You don't gamble. Dinner at Bartholomew's?" My father shook his head again. "You don't eat." Jeremy scratched his chin. "You know, my wife was like you. Old Annabelle could never let me make things up—never, never, never, never, never."

My father wriggled out from under his arm.

"How about sport clothes? You are rather overdressed, you know, excuse me for saying so. But here." He took off his polo shirt and folded it up. "You can have this with my most profound apologies." He ruffled his chest hairs with his free hand.

"No thank you," said my father.

"No, take it, take it. Accept my apologies." He thrust the shirt into my father's arms. "I'm so very sorry, so very sorry. Please, try it on."

Helplessly holding the shirt, my father searched the crowd for my mother. "Here, I'll help you off with your coat."

My father froze.

Jeremy reached over and took his jacket off. "Milton's one hundred twenty-five dollars reduced to one hundred twelve-fifty," he read. "What a bargain, what a bargain!"

"Please give it back," pleaded my father. "Please."

"Now for your shirt," ordered Jeremy.

Heads began to turn.

"Take off your shirt."

"I do not take orders like a servant," announced my father.

"Take off your shirt, or I'm going to throw this jacket right into the pool, just right into this little pool here." Jeremy held it over the water.

"Go ahead."

"One hundred twelve-fifty," taunted Jeremy. "One hundred twelve . . ."

.   .   .

My father flung the polo shirt into the water with such force that part of it bounced back up into the air like a fluorescent fountain. Then it settled into a soft heap on top of the water. My mother hurried up.

"You're a sport!" said Jeremy, suddenly breaking into a smile and slapping my father on the back. "You're a sport! I like that. A man with spirit, that's what you are. A man with panache. Allow me to return to you your jacket." He handed it back to my father. "Good value you got on that, good value."

My father hurled the coat into the pool too. "We're leaving," he said grimly. "Leaving!"

"Now, Ralphie," said Mrs. Lardner, bustling up; but my father was already stomping off.

"Get your sister," he told me. To my mother: "Get your shoes."

"That was *great*, Dad," said Mona as we walked down to the car. "You were *stupendous*."

"Way to show 'em," I said.

"What?" said my father offhandedly.

Although it was only just dusk, we were in a gulch, which made it hard to see anything except the gleam of his white shirt moving up the hill ahead of us.

"It was all my fault," began my mother.

"Forget it," said my father grandly. Then he said, "The only trouble is I left those keys in my jacket pocket."

"Oh *no*," said Mona.

"Oh no is right," said my mother.

"So we'll walk home," I said.

"But how're we going to get into the *house*," said Mona.

The noise of the party churned through the silence.

"Someone has to going back," said my father.

"Let's go to the pancake house first," suggested my mother. "We can wait there until the party is finished, and then call Mrs. Lardner."

Having all agreed that that was a good plan, we started walking again.

"God, just think," said Mona. "We're going to have to *dive* for them."

My father stopped a moment. We waited.

"You girls are good swimmers," he said finally. "Not like me."

Then his shirt started moving again, and we trooped up the hill after it, into the dark.

FOR DISCUSSION AND WRITING

1. What is Mrs. Lardner's attitude toward Callie and her family? Use the story to support your response.

2. What details show that the father "didn't believe in joining the American society?"

3. How well does the family handle the trip to the party? Explain. How do the family members feel toward each other when they leave the party?

4. Relate an experience in which you were not dressed "properly." Were you dressed for the wrong season or activity? Were you dressed too expensively or not expensively enough? How did you deal with the situation? How and why does clothing acquire such significance?

* *

POEM NEAR MIDWAY TRUCK STOP
Lance Henson

Virtually all people of the United States of every heritage and locale share experiences of the highway and the truck stop. The setting of this poem by Oklahoma author Lance Henson is a rest stop along the Turner Turnpike between Oklahoma City and Tulsa. The speaker in the poem wakes up at a rest stop and vividly imagines home. Henson is a Cheyenne Indian whose home is the Oklahoma farm where he was raised.

*A*LONG THE TURNER TURNPIKE AT A REST STOP BETWEEN
oklahoma city and tulsa
    i feel the morning sun inch over the leaves of a small elm
    rising to the scent of sage and wildflowers i lean on one
    elbow

    beyond the field the sound of cars and a lone water tower
    mark a small town

    i remove the knife from under the sleeping bag
    and place it in the sheath on my hip.

    ho hatama hestoz na no me[1]
    it is july
    i imagine coffee in a pale cup on a wooden table
    far from here
    and look west toward home

FOR DISCUSSION AND WRITING

1. What words and images does the speaker use to convey his or her attitude toward home? How is the rest stop contrasted with home?

2. What is the function of the sentence in the Cheyenne language?

---

1. There is a powerful trembling around me. (Cheyenne)

✳ ✳ ✳ ✳ ✳ ✳ ✳ ✳ ✳ ✳ ✳ ✳ ✳ ✳ ✳ ✳ ✳ ✳ ✳ ✳

MY MOTHER'S STORIES
Tony Ardizzone

Italian- and German-American author Tony Ardizzone, a teacher and award-winning writer, com-
memorates his mother's life in the story "My Mother's Stories." Besides being a portrait of his mother,
probably written near the time of her death, this story is a tribute to her storytelling art. Ardizzone cap-
tures his mother's life in large measure through her own stories about her childhood, her romance with her
husband, and the near calamities of family life. In the final analysis, though, Ardizzone crafts his moth-
er's stories into a story very much his own.

THEY WERE GOING TO THROW HER AWAY WHEN SHE WAS A BABY. The
doctors said she was too tiny, too frail, that she wouldn't live. They performed the baptism right there in the sink between their pots of boiling
water and their rows of shining instruments, chose who would be her
godparents, used water straight from the tap. Her father, however,
wouldn't hear one word of it. He didn't listen to their *she'll only die anyway*
and *please give her to us* and *maybe we can experiment*. No, the child's father stood
silently in the corner of the room, the back of one hand wiping his mouth
and thick mustache, his blue eyes fixed on the black mud which caked his
pants and boots.

Nein,[1] he said, finally. *Nein*, die anyvay.

With this, my mother smiles. She enjoys imitating the man's thick
accent. She enjoys the sounds, the images, the memory. Her brown eyes
look past me into the past. She draws a quick breath, then continues.

You can well imagine the rest. How the farmer took his wife and poor
sickly child back to his farm. How the child was nursed, coddled, fed
cow's milk, straight from the tops of the buckets—the rich, frothy cream.
How the child lived. If she hadn't, I wouldn't be here now in the corner of
this room, my eyes fixed on her, my mother and her stories. For now the
sounds and pictures are *my* sounds and pictures. Her memory, my memory.

I stand here, remembering. The family moved to Chicago. The city by
the Great Lake, the city of jobs, money, opportunity. Away from north-
western Ohio's flat fields. The child grew. She is a young girl now, enrolled

---

1. No. (German)

in school, Saint Theresa's, virgin. Chicago's Near North Side. The 1930s. And she is out walking with her girlfriend, a dark Sicilian. Spring, late afternoon. My mother wears a small pink bow in her brown hair.

Then from across the black pavement of the school playground comes a lilting stream of foreign sound, language melodic, of the kind sung solemnly at High Mass. The Sicilian girl turns quickly, smiling. The voice is her older brother's, and he too is smiling as he stands inside the playground fence. My mother turns but does not smile. She is modest. Has been properly, strictly raised. Is the last of seven children and, therefore, the object of many scolding eyes and tongues. Her name is Mary.

Perhaps our Mary, being young, is somewhat frightened. The boy behind the high fence is older than she, is in high school, is finely muscled, dark, deeply tanned. Around his neck hang golden things glistening on a thin chain. He wears a sleeveless shirt—his undershirt. Mary doesn't know whether to stay with her young friend or to continue walking. She stays, but she looks away from the boy's dark eyes and gazes instead at the worn belt around his thin waist.

That was my parents' first meeting. His name is Tony, as is mine. This is not a story she tells willingly, for she sees nothing special in it. All of the embellishments are mine. I've had to drag the story out of her, nag her from room to room. Ma? Ask your father, she tells me. I ask my father. He looks up from his newspaper, then starts to smile. He's in a playful mood. He laughs, then says: I met your mother in Heaven.

She, in the hallway, overhears. Bull, she says, looking again past me. He didn't even know I was alive. My father laughs behind his newspaper. I was Eva's friend, she says, and we were walking home from school—I watch him, listening as he lowers the paper to look at her. She tells the story.

She knows how to tell a pretty good story, I think. She's a natural. She knows how to use her voice, when to pause, how to pace, what expressions to mask her face with. Her hand slices out the high fence. She's not in the same room with you when she really gets at it; her stories take her elsewhere, somewhere back. She's there again, back on a 1937 North Side sidestreet. My father and I are only witnesses.

Picture her, then. A young girl, frightened, though of course for no good reason—my father wouldn't have harmed her. I'll vouch for him. I'm his first son. But she didn't know that as the afternoon light turned low and golden from between distant buildings. Later she'd think him strange and rather arrogant, flexing his tanned muscles before her inside the fence, like a bull before a heifer. And for years (wasted ones, I think) she didn't give him a second thought, or so she claims—the years that she dated boys who were closer to her kind. These are her words.

Imagine those years, years of *ja Fraulein, ja, bitte, entschuldigen Sie,*[2] years of pale Johnnys and freckled Fritzes and hairy Hermans, towheads all, who take pretty Mary dancing and roller-skating and sometimes downtown on the El to the movie theaters on State Street to see Clark Cable, and who buy popcorn and ice cream for her and, later, cups of coffee which she then drank with cream, and who hold her small hand and look up at the Chicago sky as they walk with her along the dark city streets to her father's flat on Fremont. Not *one* second thought? I cannot believe it. And whenever I interrupt to ask, she waves me away like I'm an insect flying between her eyes and what she really sees. I fold my arms, but I listen.

She was sweeping. This story always begins with that detail. With broom in hand. Nineteen years old and employed as a milliner and home one Saturday and she was sweeping. By now both her parents were old. Her mother had grown round, ripe like a fruit, like she would. Her father now fashioned wood. A mound of fluff and sawdust grows in the center of the room and she is humming, perhaps something from Glenn Miller, or she might have sung, as I've heard her do while ironing on the back porch, when from behind the locked back screen door there was suddenly a knock and it was my father, smiling.

She never tells the rest of the details. But this was the afternoon he proposed. Why he chose that afternoon, or even afternoon at all, are secrets not known to me. I ask her and she evades me. *Ask your father.* I ask him and he says he doesn't know. Then he looks at her and laughs, his eyes smiling, and I can see that he is making up some lie to tell me. I watch her. Because I loved her so much I couldn't wait until that night, he says. My mother laughs and shakes her head. No, he says, I'll tell you the truth this time. Now you really know he's lying. I was just walking down the street and the idea came to me. See, it was awful hot. His hand on his forehead, he pretends he had sunstroke. My mother laughs less.

There were problems. Another of her stories. They follow one after the next like cars out on the street—memories, there is just no stopping them. Their marriage would be mixed. Not in the religious sense—that would have been unthinkable—but in terms of language, origin, tradition. Like mixing your clubs with your hearts, mixing this girl from Liechtenstein with this boy from Sicily. Her family thought she was, per-

---

2. Yes miss, yes, please, excuse me. (German)

haps, lowering herself. An Italian? Why not your kind? And his family, likewise, felt that he would be less than happy with a non-Sicilian girl. She's so skinny, they told him. *Misca!*[3] Mary's skin and bones. When she has the first baby she'll bleed to death. And what will she feed you? Cabbages? *Marry your own kind.*

At their Mass someone failed to play "Ave Maria." Since that was the cue for my mother to stand and then to place a bouquet of flowers on Mary's side altar, she remained at the center altar, still kneeling, waiting patiently for the organist to begin. He was playing some other song, not "Ave Maria." The priest gestured to her. My mother shook her head.

She was a beautiful bride, and she wore a velvet dress. You should see the wedding photograph that hangs in the hallway of their house in Chicago.

Imagine a slender brown-haired bride in white velvet shaking her head at the priest who's just married her. No, the time is not yet for the young woman to stand, for her to kneel in prayer before the altar of the Virgin. This is her wedding day, remember. She is waiting for "Ave Maria."

She is waiting to this day, for the organist never did play the song, and the priest again motioned to her, then bent and whispered in her ear, and then, indignant, crushed, the young bride finally stood and angrily, solemnly, sadly waited for her maid of honor to gather the long train of her flowing velvet dress, and together the two marched to the Virgin's side altar.

She tells this story frequently, whenever there is a wedding. I think that each time she begins the story she is tempted to change the outcome, to make the stupid organist suddenly stop and slap his head. To make the organist begin the chords of "Ave Maria." That kind of power isn't possible in life. The organist didn't stop or slap his head.

I wonder if the best man tipped him. If my father was angry enough to complain. If the muscles in his jaws tightened, if his hands turned to fists if anyone waited for the organist out in the parking lot. I am carried, away.

Details *are* significant. Literally they can be matters of life and death. An organist makes an innocent mistake in 1946 and for the rest of her life a woman is compelled to repeat a story, as if for her the moment has not yet been fixed, as if by remembering and then speaking she could still influence the pattern of events since passed.

---

3. Gracious! (German)

I was hoping the counterpart wouldn't be able to work its way into this story. But it's difficult to keep death out. The final detail. Always coming along unexpectedly, the uninvited guest at the banquet, acting like you were supposed to have known all along that he'd get there, expecting to be seated and for you to offer him a drink.

My father called yesterday. He said he was just leaving work to take my mother again to the hospital. Tests. I shouldn't call her yet. No need to alarm her, my father said. Just tests. We'll keep you posted. My mother is in the hospital. I am not Meursault[4].

I must describe the counterpart, return, begin again. With 1947, with my mother, delirious, in labor. Brought to the hospital by my father early on a Saturday, and on Monday laboring still. The doctors didn't believe in using drugs. She lay three days, terrified, sweating. On Monday morning they brought my father into the room, clad in an antiseptic gown, his face covered by a mask. She mistook him for one of the doctors. When he bent to kiss her cheek she grabbed his arm and begged him. Doctor, doctor, can you give me something for the pain?

That Monday was Labor Day. Ironies exist. Each September now, on my older sister Diana's birthday, my mother smiles and tells that story.

Each of us was a difficult birth. Did my father's family know something after all? The fourth, my brother Bob, nearly killed her. He was big, over ten pounds. The doctors boasted, proudly, that Bob set their personal record. The fifth child, Jim, weighed almost ten-and-a-half pounds, and after Jim the doctors fixed my mother so that there wouldn't be a sixth child. I dislike the word fixed, but it's an appropriate word, I think.

When I was a child my mother once took Diana and me shopping, to one of those mom-and-pop stores in the middle of the block. I remember a blind man who always sat on a wooden milk crate outside the store with his large dog. I was afraid of the dog. Inside the store we shopped, and my mother told us stories, and the three of us were laughing. She lifted a carton of soda as she spoke. Then the rotted cardboard bottom of the carton gave way and the soda bottles fell. The bottles burst. The sharp glass bounced. She shouted and we screamed, and as she tells this story she makes a point of remembering how worried she was that the glass had reached our eyes. But then some woman in the store told her she was bleeding. My mother looked down. Her foot was cut so badly that blood gushed from her shoe. I remember the picture, but then the face of the

---

4. Narrator of Albert Camus's *The Stranger* (1942).

blind man's dog covers up the image and I see the wooden milk crate, the scratched white cane.

The middle child, Linda, is the special one. It was on a Christmas morning when they first feared she was deaf. Either Diana or I knocked over a pile of toy pans and dishes—a pretend kitchen—directly behind the one-year-old child playing on the floor, and Linda, bright and beautiful, did not move. She played innocently, unaffected, removed from the sound that had come to life behind her. Frantic, my mother then banged two of the metal dinner plates behind Linda's head. Linda continued playing, in a world by herself, softly cooing.

What I can imagine now from my mother's stories is a long procession of doctors, specialists, long trips on the bus. Snow-covered streets. Waiting in sterile waiting rooms. Questions. Answers. More questions. Tests. Hope. Then, no hope. Then guilt came. Tony and Mary blamed themselves.

Forgive the generalities. She is a friendly woman; she likes to make others laugh. Big-hearted, perhaps to a fault, my mother has a compulsion to please. I suspect she learned that trait as a child, being the youngest of so many children. Her parents were quite old, and as I piece her life together I imagine them strict, resolute, humorless. My mother would disagree were she to hear me. But I suspect that she's been bullied and made to feel inferior, by whom or what I don't exactly know, and, to compensate, she works very hard at pleasing.

She tells a story about how she would wash and wax her oldest brother's car and how he'd pay her one penny. How each day, regardless of the weather, she'd walk to a distant newsstand and buy for her father the *Abendpost*.[5] How she'd be sent on especially scorching summer days by another of her brothers for an ice cream cone, and how as she would gingerly carry it home she'd take not one lick. How could she resist? In my mother's stories she's always the one who's pleasing.

Her brown eyes light up, and like a young girl she laughs. She says she used to cheat sometimes and take a lick. Then, if her brother complained, she'd claim the ice cream had been melted by the sun. Delighted with herself, she smiles. Her eyes again twinkle with light.

I am carried away again. If it were me in that story I'd throw the cone to the ground and tell my brother to get his own damn ice cream.

· · ·

5. *Evening Post*, a German-language newspaper.

You've seen her. You're familiar with the kind of house she lives in, the red brick two-flat. You've walked the tree-lined city street. She hangs the family's wash up in the small backyard, the next clothespin in her mouth. She picks up the squashed paper cups and the mustard-stained foot-long hot dog wrappers out in the front that the kids from the public school leave behind as they walk back from the Tastee-Freeze on the corner. During the winter she sweeps the snow. Wearing a discarded pair of my father's earmuffs. During the fall she sweeps leaves. She gets angry when the kids cut through the backyard, leaving the chain-link gates open, for the dog barks then and the barking bothers her. The dog, a female schnauzer mutt, is called Alfie. No ferocious beast—the plastic BEWARE OF DOG signs on the gates have the harsher bite. My mother doesn't like it when the kids leave the alley gate open. She talks to both her neighbors across both her fences. Wearing one of Bob's old sweaters, green and torn at one elbow, she bends to pick up a fallen autumn twig. She stretches to hang the wash up—the rows of whites, then the coloreds. She lets Alfie out and checks the alley gate.

Summer visit. Over a mug of morning coffee I sit in the kitchen reading the *Sun-Times*. Alfie in the backyard barks and barks. My mother goes outside to quiet her. I turn the page, reading of rape or robbery, something distant. Then I hear the dog growl, then again bark. I go outside.

My mother is returning to the house, her face red, angry. Son of a B, she says. I just caught some punk standing outside the alley gate teasing Alfie. She points. He was daring her to jump at him, and the damn kid was holding one of the garbage can lids over his head, just waiting to hit her. My mother demonstrates with her hands.

I run to the alley, ready to fight, to defend. But there is no one in the alley.

My mother stands there on the narrow strip of sidewalk, her hands now at her sides. She looks tired. Behind her in the yard is an old table covered with potted plants. Coleus, philodendron, wandering Jew. One of the planters, a statue of the Sacred Heart of Jesus. Another, Mary with her white ceramic hands folded in prayer. Mother's Day presents of years ago. Standing in the bright morning sun.

And when I came out, my mother continues, the punk just looked at me, real snotty-like, like he was *daring* me, and then he said come on and hit me, lady, you just come right on and hit me. I'll show you, lady, come on.

And then he used the *F* word. She shakes her head and looks at me. Later, inside, as she irons one of my father's shirts, she tells me another story. It happened last week, at night. The ten o'clock news was on. Time to walk Alfie. She'd been feeling lousy all day so Jim took the dog out front instead.

So he was standing out there waiting for Alfie to finish up her business when all of a sudden he hears this engine and he looks up, and you know what it was, Tony? Can you guess, of all things? It was this car, this *car*, driving right down along the sidewalk with its lights out. Jim said he dove straight for the curb, pulling poor Alfie in the middle of number two right with him. And when they went past him they swore at him and threw an empty beer can at him. She laughs and looks at me, then stops ironing and sips her coffee. Her laughter is from fear. Well, you should have heard your little brother when he came back in. Boy was he steaming! They could have killed him they were driving so fast. The cops caught the kids up at Tastee-Freeze corner. We saw the squad car lights from the front windows. It was a good thing Jim took the dog out that night instead of me. She sprinkles the shirt with water from a Pepsi bottle. Can you picture your old mother diving then for the curb?

She makes a tugging gesture with her hands. Pulling the leash. Saving herself and Alfie. Again she laughs. She tells the story again when Jim comes home.

. . .

At first the doctors thought she had disseminated lupus erythematosus. Lupus means wolf. It is primarily a disease of the skin. As lupus advances the victim's face becomes ulcerated by what are called butterfly eruptions. The face comes to resemble a wolf's. Disseminated lupus attacks the joints as well as the internal organs. There isn't a known cure.

And at first they made her hang. My mother. They made her buy a sling into which she placed her head, five times each day. Pulling her head from the other side was a heavy water bag. My father put the equipment up on the door of my bedroom. For years when I went to sleep I stared at that water bag. She had to hang for two-and-a-half hours each day. Those were the years that she read every book she could get her hands on.

And those were the years that she received the weekly shots, the cortisone, the steroids, that made her puff up, made her put on the weight the doctors are now telling her to get rid of.

Then one of the doctors died, and then she had to find new doctors, and then again she had to undergo their battery of tests. These new doctors told her that she probably didn't have lupus, that instead they thought she had severe rheumatoid arthritis, that the ten years of traction and corticosteroids had been a mistake. They gave her a drugstore full of pills then. They told her to lose weight, to exercise each night.

A small blackboard hangs over the kitchen sink. The markings put there each day appear to be Chinese. Long lines for these pills, dots for those, the letter *A* for yet another. A squiggly line for something else.

The new doctors taught her the system. When you take over thirty pills a day you can't rely on memory.

. . .

My father called again. He said there was nothing new. Mary is in the hospital again, and she'd been joking that she's somewhat of a celebrity. So many doctors come in each day to see her. Interns. Residents. They hold conferences around her bed. They smile and read her chart. They question her. They thump her abdomen. They move her joints. They point. One intern asked her when she had her last menstrual cycle. My mother looked at the young man, then at the other doctors around her bed, then smiled and said twenty-some years ago but I couldn't for the life of me tell you which month. The intern's face quickly reddened. My mother's hysterectomy is written there in plain view on her chart.

They ask her questions and she recites her history like a litany.

Were the Ohio doctors right? Were they prophets? *Please give her to us. Maybe we can experiment.*

. . .

My father and I walk along the street. We've just eaten, then gone to Osco for the evening paper—an excuse, really, just to take a walk. And he is next to me suddenly bringing up the subject of my mother's health, just as suddenly as the wind from the lake shakes the thin branches of the trees. The moment is serious, I realize. My father is not a man given to unnecessary talk.

I don't know what I'd do without her, he says. I say nothing, for I can think of nothing to say. We've been together for over thirty years, he says. He pauses. For nearly thirty-four years. Thirty-four years this October. And, you know, you wouldn't think it, but I love her so much more now. He hesitates, and I look at him. He shakes his head and smiles. You know what I mean? he says. I say yes and we walk for a while in silence, and I think of what it must be like to live with someone for thirty-four years, but I cannot imagine it, and then I hear my father begin to talk about that afternoon's ball game—he describes at length and in comic detail a misjudged fly ball lost in apathy or ineptitude or simply in the sun—and for the rest of our walk home we discuss what's right and wrong with our favorite baseball team, our thorn-in-the-side Chicago Cubs.

· · ·

I stand here, not used to speaking about things that are so close to me. I am used to veiling things in my stories, to making things wear masks, to telling my stories through masks. But my mother tells her stories openly, as she has done so all of her life—since she lived on her father's farm in Ohio, as she walked along the crowded 1930 Chicago streets, to my father overseas in her letters, to the five of us children, as we sat on her lap, as we played in the next room while she tended to our supper in the kitchen. She tells them to everyone, to anyone who will listen. She taught Linda to read her lips.

I learn now to read her lips.

And I imagine one last story.

Diana and I are children. Our mother is still young. Diana and I are outside on the sidewalk playing and it's summer. And we are young and full of play and happy, and we see a dog, and it comes toward us on the street. My sister takes my hand. She senses something, I think. The dog weaves from side to side. It's sick, I think. Some kind of lather is on its mouth. The dog growls. I feel Diana's hand shake.

Now we are inside the house, safe, telling our mother. Linda, Bob, and Jim are there. We are all the same age, all children. Our mother looks outside, then walks to the telephone. She returns to the front windows. We try to look out the windows too, but she pushes the five of us away.

No, she says. I don't want any of you to see this.

We watch her watching. Then we hear the siren of a police car. We watch our mother make the sign of the Cross. Then we hear a shot. Another. I look at my sisters and brothers. They are crying. Worried, frightened, I begin to cry too.

Did it come near you? our mother asks us. Did it touch you? Any of you? Linda reads her lips. She means the funny dog. Or does she mean the speeding automobile with its lights off? The Ohio doctors? The boy behind the alley gate? The shards of broken glass? The wolf surrounded by butterflies? The ten-and-a-half-pound baby?

Diana, the oldest, speaks for us. She says that it did not.

Our mother smiles. She sits with us. Then our father is with us. Bob cracks a smile, and everybody laughs. Alfie gives a bark. The seven of us sit closely on the sofa. Safe.

That actually happened, but not exactly in the way that I described it. I've heard my mother tell that story from time to time, at times when she's most uneasy, but she has never said what it was that she saw from the front windows. A good storyteller, she leaves what she has all too clearly seen to our imaginations.

I stand in the corner of this room, thinking of her lying now in the hospital.

. . .

I pray none of us looks at that animal's face.

FOR DISCUSSION AND WRITING

1. What is the atmosphere of the author's family life? How are the parents different from each other?

2. What hints do the different passages about storytelling offer to readers? Where does the author use these hints? Which hints do you feel are most effective? Explain.

3. What purposes do you think family and community have? Use the story to support your response.

4. Do you have relatives who tell you stories about when they were young, how they met their spouses, etc.? Do they tell you stories without encouragement or must you coax the stories from them? How do the stories affect you? What do you learn from them?

✳ ✳ ✳ ✳ ✳ ✳ ✳ ✳ ✳ ✳ ✳ ✳ ✳ ✳ ✳ ✳ ✳ ✳ ✳

GIRL
Jamaica Kincaid

"Girl" is selected from Jamaica Kincaid's first volume of short stories, At The Bottom of the River. *This book and* Annie John, *her second book of short stories, are about growing up on the island of Antigua in the West Indies. The stories in these books celebrate life by presenting the small details in bright clarity. Kincaid grew up in the West Indies and immigrated to the United States, where she writes for* New Yorker *magazine. "Girl" is a detailed list of rules given to a young woman by her mother or elder of the community that instructs her how to act now that she is no longer a child.*

WASH THE WHITE CLOTHES ON MONDAY and put them on the stone heap; wash the color clothes on Tuesday and put them on the clothesline to dry; don't walk barehead in the hot sun; cook pumpkin fritters in very hot sweet oil; soak your little cloths right after you take them off; when buying cotton to make yourself a nice blouse, be sure that it doesn't have gum on it, because that way it won't hold up well after a wash; soak salt fish overnight before you cook it; is it true that you sing benna in Sunday school?; always eat your food in such a way that it won't turn someone else's stomach; on Sundays try to walk like a lady and not like the slut you are so bent on becoming; don't sing benna in Sunday school; you mustn't speak to wharf-rat boys, not even to give directions; don't eat fruits on the street—flies will follow you; *but I don't sing benna on Sundays at all and never in Sunday school;* this is how to sew on a button; this is how to make a buttonhole for the button you have just sewed on; this is how to hem a dress when you see the hem coming down and so to prevent yourself from looking like the slut I know you are so bent on becoming; this is how you iron your father's khaki shirt so that it doesn't have a crease; this is how you iron your father's khaki pants so that they don't have a crease; this is how you grow okra—far from the house, because okra tree harbors red ants; when you are growing dasheen, make sure it gets plenty of water or else it makes your throat itch when you are eating it; this is how you sweep a corner; this is how you sweep a whole house; this is how you sweep a yard; this is how you smile to someone you don't like too much; this is how you smile to someone you don't like at all; this is how you smile to someone you like completely; this is how you set a table for tea; this is how you set a table for dinner; this is how you set a table for dinner with an important guest; this is how you set a table for lunch; this is how you set a table for breakfast; this is how to behave in the presence of men who don't know you very well, and this way they won't recognize immediately the slut I have warned you against becoming; be sure to wash every day, even if it is with your own spit; don't squat down to play marbles—you are not a boy, you know; don't pick people's flowers—you might catch something; don't throw stones at blackbirds, because it might not be a blackbird at all; this is how to make a bread pudding; this is how to make doukona; this is how to make pepper pot; this is how to make a good medicine for a cold; this is how to make a good medicine to throw away a child before it even becomes a child; this is how to catch a fish; this is how to throw back a fish you don't like, and that way something bad won't fall on you; this is how to bully a man; this is how a man bullies you; this is how to love a man, and if this doesn't work there are other ways, and if they don't work don't feel too bad about giving up; this is how to spit up in the air if you feel like it, and this is how to move quick so that it doesn't fall on you; this is how to make ends meet; always squeeze bread to make sure it's fresh; *but what if the baker won't let me feel the bread?*; you mean to say that after all you are really going to be the kind of woman who the baker won't let near the bread?

FOR DISCUSSION AND WRITING

1. What do you think is the overall purpose of this advice? What kind of person does the parent or elder want the young woman to be?

2. If you were a parent or an older relative of a young woman or young man, what advice would you give her or him for coping today in your area of the United States? In your advice for today's teenager, be as specific as Jamaica Kincaid is in her list of rules.

S·O·C·I·E·T·Y

Conflict, Struggle, and Change

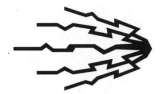

WASICHUS IN THE HILLS
from Black Elk Speaks
Black Elk as told through John G. Neihardt

"Wasichus in the Hills" (White Men in the Hills) is a chapter from the book Black Elk Speaks, *which is the life story of Black Elk, a holy man of the Oglala Sioux. In 1930 John G. Neihardt went to the Pine Ridge Indian Reservation in South Dakota to find a medicine man who could tell the world about the wars between the Indians and the United States government that ended with the massacre at Wounded Knee, South Dakota, on December 29, 1890. He met Black Elk, a Sioux spiritual leader and cousin of Chief Crazy Horse. Black Elk, who was very old by 1930, trusted Neihardt and told him the story of his life.*

*I*T WAS THE NEXT SUMMER, WHEN I WAS 11 YEARS OLD (1874), that the first sign of a new trouble came to us. Our band had been camping on Split-Toe Creek in the Black Hills, and from there we moved to Spring Creek, then to Rapid Creek where it comes out into the prairie. That evening just before sunset, a big thunder cloud came up from the west, and just before the wind struck, there were clouds of split-tail swallows flying all around above us. It was like a part of my vision, and it made me feel queer. The boys tried to hit the swallows with stones and it hurt me to see them doing this, but I could not tell them. I got a stone and acted as though I were going to throw, but I did not. The swallows seemed holy. Nobody hit one, and when I thought about this I knew that of course they could not.

The next day some of the people were building a sweat tepee for a medicine man by the name of Chips, who was going to perform a ceremony and had to be purified first. They say he was the first man who made a sacred ornament for our great chief, Crazy Horse. While they were heating the stones for the sweat tepee, some boys asked me to go with them to shoot squirrels. We went out, and when I was about to shoot at one, I felt very uneasy all at once. So I sat down, feeling queer, and wondered about it. While I sat there I heard a voice that said: "Go at once! Go home!" I told the boys we must go home at once, and we all hurried. When we got back, everybody was excited, breaking camp, catching the ponies and loading the drags; and I heard that while Chips was in the sweat tepee a voice had told him that the band must flee at once because something was going to happen there.

It was nearly sundown when we started, and we fled all that night on the back trail toward Spring Creek, then down that creek to the south fork of the Good River. I rode most of the night in a pony drag because I got too sleepy to stay on a horse. We camped at Good River in the morning, but we stayed only long enough to eat. Then we fled again, upstream, all day long until we reached the mouth of Horse Creek. We were going to stay there, but scouts came to us and said that many soldiers had come into the Black Hills; and that was what Chips saw while he was in the sweat tepee. So we hurried on in the night towards Smoky Earth River (the White), and when we got there, I woke up and it was daybreak. We camped a while to eat, and then went up the Smoky Earth, two camps, to Robinson, for we were afraid of the soldiers up there.

Afterward I learned that it was Pahuska[1] who had led his soldiers into the Black Hills that summer to see what he could find. He had no right to go in there, because all that country was ours. Also the Wasichus had made a treaty with Red Cloud (1868) that said it would be ours as long as grass should grow and water flow. Later I learned too that Pahuska had found there much of the yellow metal that makes the Wasichus crazy; and that is what made the bad trouble, just as it did before, when the hundred were rubbed out.

Our people knew there was yellow metal in little chunks up there; but they did not bother with it, because it was not good for anything.

We stayed all winter at the Soldiers' Town, and all the while the bad trouble was coming fast; for in the fall we heard that some Wasichus had come from the Missouri River to dig in the Black Hills for the yellow metal, because Pahuska had told about it with a voice that went everywhere. Later he got rubbed out for doing that.

The people talked about this all winter. Crazy Horse was in the Powder River country and Sitting Bull was somewhere north of the Hills. Our people at the Soldiers' Town thought we ought to get together and do something. Red Cloud's people said that the soldiers had gone in there to keep the diggers out, but we, who were only visiting, did not believe it. We called Red Cloud's people "Hangs-Around-The-Fort," and our peo-

---

1. Long Hair, General Custer.

ple said they were standing up for the Wasichus, and if we did not do something we should lose the Black Hills.

In the spring when I was twelve years old (1875), more soldiers with many wagons came up from the Soldiers' Town at the mouth of the Laramie River[2] and went into the Hills.

There was much talk all summer, and in the Moon of Making Fat (June) there was a sun dance there at the Soldiers' Town to give the people strength, but not many took part; maybe because everybody was so excited talking about the Black Hills. I remember two men who danced together. One had lost a leg in the Battle of the Hundred Slain and one had lost an eye in the Attacking of the Wagons, so they had only three eyes and three legs between them to dance with. We boys went down to the creek while they were sun dancing and got some elm leaves that we chewed up and threw on the dancers while they were all dressed up and trying to look their best. We even did this to some of the older people, and nobody got angry, because everybody was supposed to be in a good humor and to show their endurance in every kind of way; so they had to stand teasing too. I will tell about a big sun dance later when we come to it.

In the Moon When the Calves Grow Hair (September) there was a big council with the Wasichus on the Smoky Earth River at the mouth of White Clay Creek. I can remember the council, but I did not understand much of it then. Many of the Lakotas were there, also Shyelas and Blue Clouds[3]; but Crazy Horse and Sitting Bull stayed away. In the middle of the circle there was a shade made of canvas. Under this the councilors sat and talked, and all around them there was a crowd of people on foot and horseback. They talked and talked for days, but it was just like wind blowing in the end. I asked my father what they were talking about in there, and he told me that the Grandfather at Washington wanted to lease the Black Hills so that the Wasichus could dig yellow metal, and that the chief of the soldiers had said if we did not do this, the Black Hills would be just like melting snow held in our hands, because the Wasichus would take that country anyway.

It made me sad to hear this. It was such a good place to play and the people were always happy in that country. Also I thought of my vision, and of how the spirits took me there to the center of the world.

After the council we heard that creeks of Wasichus were flowing into the Hills and becoming rivers, and that they were already making towns

---

2. Colonel Dodge with 400 men and 75 wagons from Fort Laramie escorted a geological expedition into the hills that spring and remained until October.
3. Cheyennes and Arapahoes.

up there. It looked like bad trouble coming, so our band broke camp and started out to join Crazy Horse on Powder River. We camped on Horse head Creek, then on the War Bonnet after we crossed the old Wasichu's road[4] that made the trouble that time when the hundred were rubbed out. Grass was growing on it. Then we camped at Sage Creek, then on the Beaver, then on Driftwood Creek, and came again to the Plain of Pine Trees at the edge of the Hills.

The nights were sharp now, but the days were clear and still; and while we were camping there I went up into the Hills alone and sat a long while under a tree. I thought maybe my vision would come back and tell me how I could save that country for my people, but I could not see anything clear.

This made me sad, but something happened a few days later that made me feel good. We had gone over to Taking-The-Crow-Horses Creek, where we found many bison and made plenty of meat and tanned many hides for winter. In our band there was a man by the name of Fat, who was always talking about how fast his horse could run. One day while we were camping there I told Fat my pony could run faster than his could, and he laughed at me and said that only crows and coyotes would think my pony was any good. I asked him what he would give me if my pony could beat his, and he said he would give me some black medicine (coffee). So we ran, and I got the black medicine. All the while we were running I thought about the white wing of the wind that the Second Grandfather of my vision gave me; and maybe that power went into my pony's legs.

On Kills-Himself Creek we made more meat and hides and were ready to join Crazy Horse's camp on the Powder. There were some Hang-Around-The-Fort people with us, and when they saw that we were going to join Crazy Horse, they left us and started back to the Soldiers' Town. They were afraid there might be trouble, and they knew Crazy Horse would fight, so they wanted to be safe with the Wasichus. We did not like them very much.

We had no advisers, because we were just a little band, and when we were moving, the boys could ride anywhere. One day while we were heading for Powder River I was riding ahead with Steals Horses, another boy my age, and we saw some footprints of somebody going somewhere. We followed the footprints and there was a knoll beside a creek where a Lakota was lying. We got off and looked at him, and he was dead. His name was Root-of-the-Tail, and he was going over to Tongue River to see his relatives when he died. He was very old and ready to die, so he just lay down and died right there before he saw his relatives again.

---

4. The Bozeman Trail.

Afterwhile we came to the village on Powder River and went into camp at the downstream end. I was anxious to see my cousin, Crazy Horse, again, for now that it began to look like bad trouble coming, everybody talked about him more than ever and he seemed greater than before. Also I was getting older.

Of course I had seen him now and then ever since I could remember, and had heard stories of the brave things he did. I remember the story of how he and his brother were out alone on horseback, and a big band of Crows attacked them, so that they had to run. And while they were riding hard, with all those Crows after them, Crazy Horse heard his brother call out; and when he looked back, his brother's horse was down and the Crows were almost on him. And they told how Crazy Horse charged back right into the Crows and fought them back with only a bow and arrows, then took his brother up behind him and got away. It was his sacred power that made the Crows afraid of him when he charged. And the people told stories of when he was a boy and used to be around with the older Hump all the time. Hump was not young any more at the time, and he was a very great warrior, maybe the greatest we ever had until then. They say people used to wonder at the boy and the old man always being together; but I think Hump knew Crazy Horse would be a great man and wanted to teach him everything.

Crazy Horse's father was my father's cousin, and there were no chiefs in our family before Crazy Horse; but there were holy men; and he became a chief because of the power he got in a vision when he was a boy. When I was a man, my father told me something about that vision. Of course he did not know all of it; but he said that Crazy Horse dreamed and went into the world where there is nothing but the spirits of all things. That is the real world that is behind this one, and everything we see here is something like a shadow from that world. He was on his horse in that world, and the horse and himself on it and the trees and the grass and the stones and everything were made of spirit, and nothing was hard, and everything seemed to float. His horse was standing still there, and yet it danced around like a horse made only of shadow, and that is how he got his name, which does not mean that his horse was crazy or wild, but that in his vision it danced around in that queer way.

It was this vision that gave him his great power, for when he went into a fight, he had only to think of that world to be in it again, so that he could go through anything and not be hurt. Until he was murdered by the Wasichus at the Soldiers' Town on White River, he was wounded only twice, once by accident and both times by some one of his own people when he was not expecting trouble and was not thinking; never by an enemy. He was fifteen years old when he was wounded by accident; and the other time was when he was a young man and another man was jealous of him because the man's wife liked Crazy Horse.

They used to say too that he carried a sacred stone with him, like one he had seen in some vision, and that when he was in danger, the stone always got very heavy and protected him somehow. That, they used to say, was the reason no horse he ever rode lasted very long. I do not know about this; maybe people only thought it; but it is a fact that he never kept one horse long. They wore out. I think it was only the power of his great vision that made him great.

Now and then he would notice me and speak to me before this; and sometimes he would have the crier call me into his tepee to eat with him. Then he would say things to tease me, but I would not say anything back, because I think I was a little afraid of him. I was not afraid that he would hurt me; I was just afraid. Everybody felt that way about him, for he was a queer man and would go about the village without noticing people or saying anything. In his own tepee he would joke, and when he was on the warpath with a small party, he would joke to make his warriors feel good. But around the village he hardly ever noticed anybody, except little children. All the Lakotas like to dance and sing; but he never joined a dance, and they say nobody ever heard him sing. But everybody liked him, and they would do anything he wanted or go anywhere he said. He was a small man among the Lakotas and he was slender and had a thin face and his eyes looked through things and he always seemed to be thinking hard about something. He never wanted to have many things for himself, and did not have many ponies like a chief. They say that when game was scarce and the people were hungry, he would not eat at all. He was a queer man. Maybe he was always part way into that world of his vision. He was a very great man, and I think if the Wasichus had not murdered him down there, maybe we should still have the Black Hills and be happy. They could not have killed him in battle. They had to lie to him and murder him. And he was only about thirty years old when he died.

One day after we had camped there on Powder River, I went upstream to see him again, but his tepee was empty and he was gone somewhere, maybe with a war-party against the Crows, for we were close to them now and had to look out for them all the time. Later I did see him. He put his arm across my shoulder and took me into his tepee and we sat down together. I do not remember what he said, but I know he did not say much, and he did not tease me. Maybe he was thinking about the trouble coming.

We did not stay together there very long, but scattered out and camped in different places so that the people and the ponies would all have plenty. Crazy Horse kept his village on Powder River with about a hundred tepees, and our band made camp on the Tongue. We built a corral of poles for the horses at night and herded them all day, because the Crows were great horse-thieves and we had to be careful. The women chopped and stripped cottonwood trees during the day and gave the bark to the horses at night. The horses liked it and it made them sleek and fat.

Beside the mouth of the corral there was a tepee for the horse guard, and one night Crow Nose was staying there and his wife was with him. He had a hole in the tepee so that he could look through. Afterwhile he got very sleepy, so he woke his wife and told her to get up and watch while he had a little rest. By and by she saw something dark moving slowly on the snow out there, so she woke her husband and whispered, "Old man, you'd better get up, for I think I see something." So Crow Nose got up and peeped out and saw a man moving around the corral in the starlight looking for the best horse. Crow Nose told his wife to keep her eye at the hole and let him know when the man was coming out with a horse, and he lay down at the opening of the tepee with the muzzle of his gun sticking out of the flap. By and by they could hear the bar lifted at the mouth of the corral. When his wife touched him, Crow Nose thrust his head outside and saw the man just getting on a horse to ride away. He was black against the sky, so Crow Nose shot him, and the shot woke the whole camp so that many came running with guns and coup sticks. Yellow Shirt was the first to count coup[5] on the dead Crow, but many followed. A man who has killed an enemy must not touch him, for he has already had the honor of killing. He must let another count coup. When I got there to see, a pile of coup sticks was lying beside the Crow and the women had cut him up with axes and scattered him around. It was horrible. Then the people built a fire right there beside the Crow and we had a kill dance. Men, women, and children danced right in the middle of the night, and they sang songs about Crow Nose who had killed and Yellow Shirt who had counted the first coup.

Then it was daylight, and the crier told us we would move camp to the place where Root-of-the-Tail died. Crow Nose dressed up for war, painted his face black and rode the horse the enemy had tried to steal. When the men paint their faces black, the women all rejoice and make the

---

5. The act of striking an enemy, dead or alive, with a stick conferred distinction, the first coup naturally counting most.

tremolo, because it means their men are going to kill enemies.

When we camped again, one of Red Cloud's loafers who had started back for the Soldiers' Town because they were afraid there might be trouble, came in and said the Crows had killed all his party but himself, while they were sleeping, and he had escaped because he was out scouting.

During the winter, runners came from the Wasichus and told us we must come into the Soldiers' Town right away or there would be bad trouble. But it was foolish to say that, because it was very cold and many of our people and ponies would have died in the snow. Also, we were in our own country and were doing no harm.

Late in the Moon of the Dark Red Calves (February) there was a big thaw, and our little band started for the Soldiers' Town, but it was very cold again before we got there. Crazy Horse stayed with about a hundred tepees on Powder, and in the middle of the Moon of the Snowblind (March) something bad happened there. It was just daybreak. There was a blizzard and it was very cold. The people were sleeping. Suddenly there were many shots and horses galloping through the village. It was the cavalry of the Wasichus, and they were yelling and shooting and riding their horses against the tepees. All the people rushed out and ran, because they were not awake yet and they were frightened. The soldiers killed as many women and children and men as they could while the people were running toward a bluff. Then they set fire to some of the tepees and knocked the others down. But when the people were on the side of the bluff, Crazy Horse said something, and all the warriors began singing the death song and charged back upon the soldiers; and the soldiers ran, driving many of the people's ponies ahead of them. Crazy Horse followed them all that day with a band of warriors, and that night he took all the stolen ponies away from them, and some of their own horses, and brought them all back to the village.[6]

These people were in their own country and were doing no harm. They only wanted to be let alone. We did not hear of this until quite awhile afterward; but at the Soldiers' Town we heard enough to make us paint our faces black.

---

6. Colonel Reynolds with six companies of cavalry attacked Crazy Horse's village as stated in the early morning of March 16, 1876.

1. Which passages indicate that Black Elk is a religious or spiritual person?

2. Black Elk mentions a number of geographical places where the Sioux lived and interacted with white settlers. Locate the following places on a map: the Black Hills, Fort Laramie, the Laramie River, the Missouri River, the Powder River, Spring Creek, Rapid Creek, and the White River. In addition, locate Pine Ridge Indian Reservation, Wounded Knee, and Crazy Horse Monument.

3. Black Elk describes the Wasichu's interest in the yellow metal in the hills. He says, "Our people knew there was yellow metal in little chunks up there; but they did not bother with it, because it was not good for anything." Can you think of similar things today which are of little importance to the inhabitants of the areas where they are found, but are of great value to outsiders? How do these things acquire such importance? How should ownership of natural resources be regulated?

4. Do you think the wars between the Native Americans and the United States government could have been avoided? If so, how?

CONCENTRATION CONSTELLATION
Lawson Fusao Inada

Lawson Fusao Inada, a Sansei or third-generation Japanese American, is an acclaimed poet and professor of English. His book Before the War: Poems As They Happened, *published in 1971, was the first book of poetry by an Asian American published by a major publishing company. In addition to writing poems, Inada reads his work in festivals, at colleges, and on the radio. He has been listed as one of America's "Heavy 100" by* Rolling Stone *magazine. A young boy during World War II, Inada was interned in detention camps for Japanese Americans in Arkansas and Colorado.*

*I*N THIS EARTHLY CONFIGURATION,
we have, not points of light,
but prominent barbs of dark.

It's all right there on the map.
It's all right there in the mind.
Find it. If you care to look.

Begin between the Golden State's
highest and lowest elevations
and name that location
Manzanar. Rattlesnake a line
southward to the zone
of Arizona, to the home
of natives on the reservation,
and call those *Gila, Poston.*

Then just take you time
winding your way across
the Southwest expanse, the Lone
Star State of Texas, gathering
up a mess of blues as you
meander around the banks
of the humid Mississippi; yes,
just make yourself at home

in the swamps of Arkansas,
for this is *Rohwer* and *Jerome.*

By now, you weary of the way.
It's a big country, you say.
It's a big history, hardly
halfway through—with *Amache*
looming in the Colorado desert,
Heart Mountain high in wide
Wyoming, *Minidoka* on the moon
of Idaho, then down to Utah's
jewel of *Topaz* before finding
yourself at northern California's
frozen shore of *Tule Lake* . . .

Now regard what sort of shape
this constellation takes.
It sits there like a jagged scar,
massive, on the massive landscape.
It lies there like the rusted wire
of a twisted and remembered fence.

1. Locate the detention centers mentioned in the poem on a map of the United States. What are the environmental conditions of these areas? Why were the camps located in such places?

2. What is the tone of the poem? Cite examples from the poem to support your response.

Miné Okubo, Moving In *(Topaz, Utah), 1942*

THE LESSON
Toni Cade Bambara

Toni Cade Bambara is a writer and a professor of English and African-American Studies. She won the prestigious American Book Award for her novel The Salt Eaters *in 1980. In the 1960s she was a writer, dancer, and community activist. She continues to work in black communities, organizing, filming, and reading at rallies, museums, and prisons. Her stories often depict people who, like herself, care deeply about their communities. Writing primarily about black neighborhoods in large cities, Bambara uses language that highlights street styles as the characters engage in rapid conversations rich with wit, wisdom, and affection.*

BACK IN THE DAYS WHEN EVERYONE WAS OLD AND STUPID or young and foolish and me and Sugar were the only ones just right, this lady moved on our block with nappy hair and proper speech and no makeup. And quite naturally we laughed at her, laughed the way we did at the junk man who went about his business like he was some big-time president and his sorry-ass horse his secretary. And we kinda hated her too, hated the way we did the winos who cluttered up our parks and pissed on our handball walls and stank up our hallways and stairs so you couldn't halfway play hide-and-seek without a goddamn gas mask. Miss Moore was her name. The only woman on the block with no first name. And she was black as hell, cept for her feet, which were fish-white and spooky. And she was always planning these boring-ass things for us to do, us being my cousin, mostly, who lived on the block cause we all moved North the same time and to the same apartment then spread out gradual to breathe. And our parents would yank our heads into some kinda shape and crisp up our clothes so we'd be presentable for travel with Miss Moore, who always looked like she was going to church, though she never did. Which is just one of things the grown-ups talked about when they talked behind her back like a dog. But when she came calling with some sachet she'd sewed up or some gingerbread she'd made or some book, why then they'd all be too embarrassed to turn her down and we'd get handed over all spruced up. She'd been to college and said it was only right that she should take responsibility for the young ones' education, and she not even related by

Morgan Paul (age 10), Legs, *1989*

marriage or blood. So they'd go for it. Specially Aunt Gretchen. She was
the main gofer in the family. You got some ole dumb shit foolishness you
want somebody to go for, you send for Aunt Gretchen. She been screwed
into the go-along for so long, it's a blood-deep natural thing with her.
Which is how she got saddled with me and Sugar and Junior in the first
place while our mothers were in a la-de-da apartment up the block having
a good ole time.

So this one day Miss Moore rounds us all up at the mailbox and it's
puredee hot and she's knockin herself out about arithmetic. And school
suppose to let up in summer I heard, but she don't never let up. And the
starch in my pinafore scratching the shit outta me and I'm really hating
this nappy-head bitch and her goddamn college degree. I'd much rather
go to the pool or to the show where it's cool. So me and Sugar leaning on
the mailbox being surly, which is a Miss Moore word. And Flyboy check-
ing out what everbody brought for lunch. And Fat Butt already wasting
his peanut-butter-and-jelly sandwich like the pig he is. And Junebug
punchin on Q.T.'s arm for potato chips. And Rosie Giraffe shifting from
one hip to the other waiting for somebody to step on her foot or ask her if
she from Georgia so she can kick ass, perferably Mercedes'. And Miss

Moore asking us do we know what money is, like we a bunch of retards. I mean real money, she say, like it's only poker chips or monopoly papers we lay on the grocer. So right away I'm tired of this and say so. And would much rather snatch Sugar and go to the Sunset and terrorize the West Indian kids and take their hair ribbons and their money too. And Miss Moore files that remark away for next week's lesson on brotherhood, I can tell. And finally I say we oughta get to the subway cause it's cooler and besides we might meet some cute boys. Sugar done swiped her mama's lipstick, so we ready.

So we heading down the street and she's boring us silly about what things cost and what our parents make and how much goes for rent and how money ain't divided up right in this country. And then she gets to the part about we all poor and live in the slums, which I don't feature. And I'm ready to speak on that, but she steps out in the street and hails two cabs just like that. Then she hustles half the crew in with her and hands me a five-dollar bill and tells me to calculate 10 percent tip for the driver. And we're off. Me and Sugar and Junebug and Flyboy hangin out the window and hollering to everybody, putting lipstick on each other cause Flyboy a faggot anyway, and making farts with our sweaty armpits. But I'm mostly trying to figure how to spend this money. But they all fascinated with the meter ticking and Junebug starts laying bets as to how much it'll read when Flyboy can't hold his breath no more. Then Sugar lays bets as to how much it'll be when we get there. So I'm stuck. Don't nobody want to go for my plan, which is to jump out at the next light and run off to the first bar-b-que we can find. Then the driver tells us to get the hell out cause we there already. And the meter reads eighty-five cents. And I'm stalling to figure out the tip and Sugar say give him a dime. And I decide he don't need it bad as I do, so later for him. But then he tries to take off with Junebug foot still in the door so we talk about his mama something ferocious. Then we check out that we on Fifth Avenue and everybody dressed up in stockings. One lady in a fur coat, hot as it is. White folks crazy.

"This is the place," Miss Moore say, presenting it to us in the voice she uses at the museum. "Let's look in the windows before we go in."

"Can we steal?" Sugar asks very serious like she's getting the ground rules squared away before she plays. "I beg your pardon," say Miss Moore, and we fall out. So she leads us around the windows of the toy store and me and Sugar screamin, "This is mine, that's mine, I gotta have that, that was made for me, I was born for that," till Big Butt drowns us out.

"Hey, I'm goin to buy that there."

"That there? You don't even know what it is, stupid."

"I do so," he say punchin on Rosie Giraffe. "It's a microscope."

"Whatcha gonna do with a microscope, fool?"

"Look at things."

"Like what, Ronald?" ask Miss Moore. And Big Butt ain't got the first notion. So here go Miss Moore gabbing about the thousands of bacteria in a drop of water and the somethinorother in a speck of blood and the million and one living things in the air around us is invisible to the naked eye. And what she say that for? Junebug go to town on that "naked" and we rolling. Then Miss Moore ask what it cost. So we all jam into the window smudgin it up and the price tag say $300. So then she ask how long'd take for Big Butt and Junebug to save up their allowances. "Too long," I say. "Yeh," adds Sugar, "outgrown it by that time." And Miss Moore say no, you never outgrow learning instruments. "Why, even medical students and interns and," blah, blah, blah. And we ready to choke Big Butt for bringing it up in the first damn place.

"This here costs four hundred eighty dollars," say Rosie Giraffe. So we pile up all over her to see what she pointin out. My eyes tell me it's a chunk of glass cracked with something heavy, and different-color inks dripped into the splits, then the whole thing put into a oven or something. But the $480 it don't make sense.

"That's a paperweight made of semi-precious stones fused together under tremendous pressure," she explains slowly, with her hands doing the mining and all the factory work.

"So what's a paperweight?" asks Rosie Giraffe.

"To weigh paper with, dumbbell," say Flyboy, the wise man from the East.

"Not exactly," say Miss Moore, which is what she say when you warm or way off too. "It's to weigh paper down so it won't scatter and make your desk untidy." So right away me and Sugar curtsy to each other and then to Mercedes who is more the tidy type.

"We don't keep paper on top of the desk in my class," say Junebug, figuring Miss Moore crazy or lyin one.

"At home, then," she say. "Don't you have a calendar and a pencil case and a blotter and a letter-opener on your desk at home where you do your homework?" And she know damn well what our homes look like cause she nosys around in them every chance she gets.

"I don't even have a desk," say Junebug. "Do we?"

"No. And I don't get no homework neither," say Big Butt.

"And I don't even have a home," say Flyboy like he do at school to keep the white folks off his back and sorry for him. Send this poor kid to camp posters, is his specialty.

"I do," says Mercedes. "I have a box of stationery on my desk and a picture of my cat. My godmother bought the stationery and the desk. There's a big rose on each sheet and the envelopes smell like roses."

"Who wants to know about your smelly-ass stationery," say Rosie Giraffe fore I can get my two cents in.

"It's important to have a work area all your own so that . . ."

"Will you look at this sailboat, please," say Flyboy, cuttin her off and pointin to the thing like it was his. So once again we tumble all over each other to gaze at this magnificent thing in the toy store which is just big enough to maybe sail two kittens across the pond if you strap them to the posts tight. We all start reciting the price tag like we in assembly. "Handcrafted sailboat of fiberglass at one thousand one hundred ninety-five dollars."

"Unbelievable," I hear myself say and am really stunned. I read it again for myself just in case the group recitation put me in a trance. Same thing. For some reason this pisses me off. We look at Miss Moore and she lookin at us, waiting for I dunno what.

Who'd pay all that when you can buy a sailboat set for a quarter at Pop's, a tube of glue for a dime, and a ball of string for eight cents? "It must have a motor and a whole lot else besides," I say. "My sailboat cost me about fifty cents."

"But will it take water?" say Mercedes with her smart ass.

"Took mine to Alley Pond Park once," say Flyboy. "String broke. Lost it. Pity."

"Sailed mine in Central Park and it keeled over and sank. Had to ask my father for another dollar."

"And you got the strap," laugh Big Butt. "The jerk didn't even have a string on it. My old man wailed on his behind."

Little Q.T. was staring hard at the sailboat and you could see he wanted it bad. But he too little and somebody'd just take it from him. So what the hell. "This boat for kids, Miss Moore?"

"Parents silly to buy something like that just to get all broke up," say Rosie Giraffe.

"That much money it should last forever," I figure.

"My father'd buy it for me if I wanted it."

"Your father, my ass," say Rosie Giraffe getting a chance to finally push Mercedes.

"Must be rich people shop here," say Q.T.

"You are a very bright boy," say Flyboy. "What was your first clue?" And he rap him on the head with the back of his knuckles, since Q.T. the only one he could get away with. Though Q.T. liable to come up behind you years later and get his licks in when you half expect it.

"What I want to know," I says to Miss Moore though I never talk to her, I wouldn't give the bitch that satisfaction, "is how much a real boat costs? I figure a thousand'd get you a yacht any day."

"Why don't you check that out," she says, "and report back to the group?" Which really pains my ass. If you gonna mess up a perfectly good swim day least you could do is have some answers. "Let's go in," she say like she got something up her sleeve. Only she don't lead the way. So me and Sugar turn the corner to where the entrance is, but when we get there I kinda hang back. Not that I'm scared, what's there to be afraid of, just a toy store. But I feel funny, shame. But what I got to be shamed about? Got as much right to go in as anybody. But somehow I can't seem to get hold of the door, so I step away for Sugar to lead. But she hangs back too. And I look at her and she looks at me and this is ridiculous. I mean, damn, I have never ever been shy about doing nothing or going nowhere. But then Mercedes steps up and then Rosie Giraffe and Big Butt crowd in behind and shove, and next thing we all stuffed into the doorway with only Mercedes squeezing past us, smoothing out her jumper and walking right down the aisle. Then the rest of us tumble in like a glued-together jigsaw done all wrong. And people lookin at us. And it's like the time me and Sugar crashed into the Catholic church on a dare. But once we got in there and everything so hushed and holy and the candles and the bowin and the handkerchiefs on all the drooping heads, I just couldn't go through with the plan. Which was for me to run up to the altar and do a tap dance while Sugar played the nose flute and messed around in the holy water. And Sugar kept givin me the elbow. Then later teased me so bad I tied her up in the shower and turned it on and locked her in. And she'd be there till this day if Aunt Gretchen hadn't finally figured I was lyin about the boarder takin a shower.

Same thing in the store. We all walkin on tiptoe and hardly touchin the games and puzzles and things. And I watched Miss Moore who is steady watchin us like she waitin for a sign. Like Mama Drewery watches the sky and sniffs the air and takes note of just how much slant is in the bird formation. Then me and Sugar bump smack into each other, so busy gazing at the toys, 'specially the sailboat. But we don't laugh and go into our fat-lady bump-stomach routine. We just stare at that price tag. Then Sugar run a finger over the whole boat. And I'm jealous and want to hit her. Maybe not her, but I sure want to punch somebody in the mouth.

"Watcha bring us here for, Miss Moore?"

"You sound angry, Sylvia. Are you mad about something?" Givin me one of them grins like she tellin a grown-up joke that never turns out to be funny. And she's lookin very closely at me like maybe she plannin to do my portrait from memory. I'm mad, but I won't give her that satisfaction. So I slouch around the store bein very bored and say, "Let's go."

Me and Sugar at the back of the train watchin the tracks whizzin by large then small then gettin gobbled up in the dark. I'm thinkin about this tricky toy I saw in the store. A clown that somersaults on a bar then does chin-ups just cause you yank lightly at his leg. Cost $35. I could see me askin my mother for a $35 birthday clown. "You wanna who that costs what?" she'd say, cocking her head to the side to get a better view of the hole in my head. Thirty-five dollars could buy new bunk beds for Junior and Gretchen's boy. Thirty-five dollars and the whole household could visit Grandaddy Nelson in the country. Thirty-five dollars would pay for the rent and the piano bill too. Who are these people that spend that much for performing clowns and $1,000 for toy sailboats? What kinda work they do and how they live and how come we ain't in on it? Where we are is who we are, Miss Moore always pointin out. But it don't necessarily have to be that way, she always adds then waits for somebody to say that poor people have to wake up and demand their share of the pie and don't none of us know what kind of pie she talkin about in the first damn place. But she ain't so smart cause I still got her four dollars from the taxi and she sure ain't gettin it. Messin up my day with this shit. Sugar nudges me in my pocket and winks.

Miss Moore lines us up in front of the mailbox where we started from, seem like years ago, and I got a headache for thinkin so hard. And we lean all over each other so we can hold up under the draggy-ass lecture she always finishes us off with at the end before we thank her for borin us to tears. But she just looks at us like she readin tea leaves. Finally she say, "Well, what did you think of F.A.O. Schwarz?"

Rosie Giraffe mumbles, "White folks crazy."

"I'd like to go there again when I get my birthday money," says Mercedes, and we shove her out the pack so she has to lean on the mailbox by herself.

"I'd like a shower. Tiring day," say Flyboy.

Then Sugar surprises me by sayin, "You know, Miss Moore, I don't think all of us here put together eat in a year what that sailboat costs."

And Miss Moore lights up like somebody goosed her. "And?" she say, urging Sugar on. Only I'm standin on her foot so she don't continue.

"Imagine for a minute what kind of society it is in which some people can spend on a toy what it would cost to feed a family of six or seven. What do you think?"

"I think," say Sugar pushing me off her feet like she never done before, cause I whip her ass in a minute, "that this is not much of a democracy if you ask me. Equal chance to pursue happiness means an equal crack at the dough, don't it?" Miss Moore is besides herself and I am disgusted with Sugar's treachery. So I stand on her foot one more time to see if she'll shove me. She shuts up, and Miss Moore looks at me, sorrowfully I'm thinkin. And somethin weird is goin on, I can feel it in my chest.

"Anybody else learn anything today?" lookin dead at me. I walk away and Sugar has to run to catch up and don't even seem to notice when I shrug her arm off my shoulder.

"Well, we got four dollars anyway," she says.

"Uh hunh."

"We could go to Hascombs and get half a chocolate layer and then go to the Sunset and still have plenty money for potato chips and ice-cream sodas."

"Uh hunh."

"Race you to Hascombs," she say.

We start down the block and she gets ahead which is O.K. by me cause I'm going to the West End and then over to the Drive to think this day through. She can run if she want to and even run faster. But ain't nobody gonna beat me at nuthin.

FOR DISCUSSION AND WRITING

1. Who is the speaker? About how old is she when the event she narrates takes place? How old do you think she is now? In whose voice is the story told? Is this an effective choice? Explain.

2. What kind of person is the speaker? Would you want to be her friend when she is that age? Use the story to explain your response.

3. Does the speaker learn anything from the day? Use the story to support your response. Why is there such a difference between what the speaker thinks and what she shows by her actions and speech?

4. What is the lesson? Why does Miss Moore teach it? Is Miss Moore a good teacher? How would you feel on Miss Moore's field trip?

5. Is Tony Cade Bambara a good teacher? What does she try to show? What teaching techniques does she use?

LETTER FROM A BIRMINGHAM JAIL
Martin Luther King, Jr.

Martin Luther King, Jr. was one of the most respected social and moral leaders in United States history. He received numerous awards, including Time Man of the Year *for 1963 and the Nobel Prize for Peace in 1964, for his central leadership in the struggle for justice and civil rights for African Americans.*

The goal of King and other civil rights leaders in 1962 and 1963 was to desegregate Birmingham, Alabama, which, in King's words, was "the most segregated city in America." King was arrested for disobeying a court injunction prohibiting him from leading demonstrations in Birmingham. While in prison in the Spring of 1963, he wrote "Letter from a Birmingham Jail," to explain his strategy of nonviolent civil disobedience. In this letter King also responds to church leaders who disagreed with the strategy of civil disobedience. These moderate leaders called on King to take the battle of segregation off the streets and back into the courts. Although he did not know this when he wrote the letter, the struggle to desegregate Birmingham would end in triumph. Birmingham's leaders were finally pressured into eliminating laws that upheld the segregation of public facilities.

MY DEAR FELLOW CLERGYMEN,

While confined here in the Birmingham city jail, I came across your recent statement calling our present activities "unwise and untimely." Seldom, if ever, do I pause to answer criticism of my work and ideas. If I sought to answer all of the criticisms that cross my desk, my secretaries would be engaged in little else in the course of the day, and I would have no time for constructive work. But since I feel that you are men of genuine good will and your criticisms are sincerely set forth, I would like to answer your statement in what I hope will be patient and reasonable terms.

I think I should give the reason for my being in Birmingham, since you have been influenced by the argument of "outsiders coming in." I have the honor of serving as president of the Southern Christian Leadership Conference, an organization operating in every southern state, with headquarters in Atlanta, Georgia. We have some eighty-five affiliate organizations all across the South—one being the Alabama Christian Movement for Human Rights. Whenever necessary and possible we share staff, educational and financial resources with our affiliates. Several months ago our local affiliate here in Birmingham invited us to be on call to engage in a nonviolent direct-action program if such were deemed necessary. We readily consented and when the hour came we lived up to our promises. So I am here, along with several members of my staff, because we were invited here. I am here because I have basic organizational ties here.

Beyond this, I am in Birmingham because injustice is here. Just as the eighth-century prophets left their little villages and carried their "thus saith the Lord" far beyond the boundaries of their hometowns; and just as the Apostle Paul left his little village of Tarsus and carried the gospel of Jesus Christ to practically every hamlet and city of the Graeco-Roman world, I too am compelled to carry the gospel of freedom beyond my particular hometown. Like Paul, I must constantly respond to the Macedonian call for aid.

Moreover, I am cognizant of the interrelatedness of all communities and states. I cannot sit idly by in Atlanta and not be concerned about what happens in Birmingham. Injustice anywhere is a threat to justice everywhere. We are caught in an inescapable network of mutuality, tied in a single garment of destiny. Whatever affects one directly affects all indirectly. Never again can we afford to live with the narrow, provincial "outside agitator" idea. Anyone who lives in the United States can never be considered an outsider anywhere in this country.

You deplore the demonstrations that are presently taking place in Birmingham. But I am sorry that your statement did not express a similar concern for the conditions that brought the demonstrations into being. I am sure that each of you would want to go beyond the superficial social analyst who looks merely at effects, and does not grapple with underlying causes. I would not hesitate to say that it is unfortunate that so-called demonstrations are taking place in Birmingham at this time, but I would say in more emphatic terms that it is even more unfortunate that the white power structure of this city left the Negro community with no other alternative.

In any nonviolent campaign there are four basic steps: (1) collection of the facts to determine whether injustices are alive, (2) negotiation, (3) self-purification, and (4) direct action. We have gone through all of these steps in Birmingham. There can be no gainsaying of the fact that racial injustice engulfs this community.

Birmingham is probably the most thoroughly segregated city in the United States. Its ugly record of police brutality is known in every section of this country. Its unjust treatment of Negroes in the courts is a notorious reality. There have been more unsolved bombings of Negro homes and churches in Birmingham than any city in this nation. These are the hard, brutal and unbelievable facts. On the basis of these conditions Negro leaders sought to negotiate with the city fathers. But the political leaders consistently refused to engage in good faith negotiation.

Then came the opportunity last September to talk with some of the leaders of the economic community. In these negotiating sessions certain promises were made by the merchants—such as the promise to remove the humiliating racial signs from the stores. On the basis of these promises Rev. Shuttlesworth and the leaders of the Alabama Christian Movement for Human Rights agreed to call a moratorium on any type of demonstrations. As the weeks and months unfolded we realized that we were the victims of a broken promise. The signs remained. Like so many experiences of the past we were confronted with blasted hopes, and the dark shadow of a deep disappointment settled upon us. So we had no alternative except that of preparing for direct action, whereby we would present our very bodies as a means of laying our case before the conscience of the local and national community. We were not unmindful of the difficulties involved. So we decided to go through a process of self-purification. We started having workshops on nonviolence and repeatedly asked ourselves the questions, "Are you able to accept blows without retaliating?" "Are you able to endure the ordeals of jail?" We decided to set our direct-action program around the Easter season, realizing that with the exception of Christmas, this was the largest shopping period of the year. Knowing that a strong economic withdrawal program would be the by-product of direct action, we felt that this was the best time to bring pressure on the merchants for the needed changes. Then it occurred to us that the March election was ahead and so we speedily decided to postpone action until after election day. When we discovered that Mr. Connor was in the run-off, we decided again to postpone action so that the demonstrations could not be used to cloud the issues. At this time we agreed to begin our nonviolent witness the day after the run-off.

This reveals that we did not move irresponsibly into direct action. We too wanted to see Mr. Connor defeated; so we went through postponement after postponement to aid in this community need. After this we felt that direct action could be delayed no longer.

You may well ask, "Why direct action? Why sit-ins, marches, etc.? Isn't negotiation a better path?" You are exactly right in your call for negotia-

Martin Luther King, Jr. in a Jefferson County Courthouse Jail Cell, Birmingham, Alabama, 1967

tion. Indeed, this is the purpose of direct action. Nonviolent direct action seeks to create such a crisis and establish such creative tension that a community that has constantly refused to negotiate is forced to confront the issue. It seeks so to dramatize the issue that it can no longer be ignored. I just referred to the creation of tension as a part of the work of the nonviolent resister. This may sound rather shocking. But I must confess that I am not afraid of the word *tension.* I have earnestly worked and preached against violent tension, but there is a type of constructive nonviolent tension that is necessary for growth. Just as Socrates felt that it was necessary to create a tension in the mind so that individuals could rise from the bondage of myths and half-truths to the unfettered realm of creative analysis and objective appraisal, we must see the need of having nonviolent gadflies to create the kind of tension in society that will help men to rise from the dark depths of prejudice and racism to the majestic heights of understanding and brotherhood. So the purpose of the direct action is to create a situation so crisis-packed that it will inevitably open the door to negotiation. We, therefore, concur with you in your call for negotiation. Too long has our beloved Southland been bogged down in the tragic attempt to live in monologue rather than dialogue.

One of the basic points in your statement is that our acts are untimely. Some have asked, "Why didn't you give the new administration time to act?" The only answer that I can give to this inquiry is that the new administration must be prodded about as much as the outgoing one before it acts. We will be sadly mistaken if we feel that the election of Mr. Boutwell will bring the millennium to Birmingham. While Mr. Boutwell is much more articulate and gentle than Mr. Connor, they are both segregationists, dedicated to the task of maintaining the status quo. The hope I see in Mr. Boutwell is that he will be reasonable enough to see the futility of massive resistance to desegregation. But he will not see this without pressure from the devotees of civil rights. My friends, I must say to you that we have not made a single gain in civil rights without determined legal and nonviolent pressure. History is the long and tragic story of the fact that privileged groups seldom give up their privileges voluntarily. Individuals may see the moral light and voluntarily give up their unjust posture; but as Reinhold Niebuhr has reminded us, groups are more immoral than individuals.

We know through painful experience that freedom is never voluntarily given by the oppressor; it must be demanded by the oppressed. Frankly, I have never yet engaged in a direct action movement that was "well-timed," according to the timetable of those who have not suffered unduly from the disease of segregation. For years now I have heard the word "Wait!" It rings in the ear of every Negro with a piercing familiarity. This "Wait" has almost always meant "Never." It has been a tranquilizing thalidomide, relieving the emotional stress for a moment, only to give birth to an ill-formed infant of frustration. We must come to see with the distinguished jurist of yesterday that "justice too long delayed is justice denied." We have waited for more than 340 years for our constitutional and God-given rights. The nations of Asia and Africa are moving with jet-like speed toward the goal of political independence, and we still creep at horse and buggy pace toward the gaining of a cup of coffee at a lunch counter. I guess it is easy for those who have never felt the stinging darts of segregation to say, "Wait." But when you have seen vicious mobs lynch your mothers and fathers at will and drown your sisters and brothers at whim; when you have seen hate-filled policemen curse, kick, brutalize and even kill your black brothers and sisters with impunity; when you see the vast majority of your twenty million Negro brothers smothering in an airtight cage of poverty in the midst of an affluent society; when you suddenly find your tongue twisted and your speech stammering as you seek to explain to your six-year-old daughter why she can't go to the public amusement park that has just been advertised on television, and see tears welling up in her little eyes when she is told that Funtown is closed to colored children, and see the depressing clouds of inferiority begin to form in her little mental sky, and see her begin to distort her little personality by unconsciously developing a bitterness toward white people; when you have to concoct an answer for a five-year-old son asking in agonizing pathos: "Daddy, why do white people treat colored people so mean?"; when you take a cross-country drive and find it necessary to sleep night after night in the uncomfortable corners of your automobile because no motel will accept you; when you are humiliated day in and day out by nagging signs reading "white" and "colored"; when your first name becomes "nigger" and your middle name becomes "boy" (however old you are) and your last name becomes "John," and when your wife and mother are never given the respected title "Mrs."; when you are harried by day and haunted by night by the fact that you are a Negro, living constantly at tiptoe stance never quite knowing what to expect next, and plagued with inner fears and outer resentments; when you are forever fighting a degenerating sense of "nobodiness"; then you will understand why we find it difficult to wait. There comes a time when the cup of endurance runs over, and men are no longer willing to be plunged into an abyss of injustice where they experience the blackness of corroding despair. I hope, sirs, you can understand our legitimate and unavoidable impatience.

You express a great deal of anxiety over our willingness to break laws. This is certainly a legitimate concern. Since we so diligently urge people to obey the Supreme Court's decision of 1954 outlawing segregation in the public schools, it is rather strange and paradoxical to find us consciously breaking laws. One may well ask, "How can you advocate breaking some laws and obeying others?" The answer is found in the fact that there are two types of laws: there are *just* and there are *unjust* laws. I would agree with Saint Augustine that "An unjust law is no law at all."

Now what is the difference between the two? How does one determine when a law is just or unjust? A just law is a man-made code that squares with the moral law or the law of God. An unjust law is a code that is out of harmony with the moral law. To put it in the terms of Saint Thomas Aquinas, an unjust law is a human law that is not rooted in eternal and natural law. Any law that uplifts human personality is just. Any law that degrades human personality is unjust. All segregation statutes are unjust because segregation distorts the soul and damages the personality. It gives the segregator a false sense of superiority, and the segregated a false sense of inferiority. To use the words of Martin Buber, the great Jewish philosopher, segregation substitutes an "I-it" relationship for the "I-thou" relationship, and ends up relegating persons to the status of things. So segregation is not only politically, economically and sociologically unsound, but it is morally wrong and sinful. Paul Tillich has said that sin is separation. Isn't segregation an existential expression of man's tragic separation, an expression of his awful estrangement, his terrible sinfulness? So I can urge men to disobey segregation ordinances because they are morally wrong.

Let us turn to a more concrete example of just and unjust laws. An unjust law is a code that a majority inflicts on a minority that is not binding on itself. This is difference made legal. On the other hand a just law is a code that a majority compels a minority to follow that it is willing to follow itself. This is sameness made legal.

Let me give another explanation. An unjust law is a code inflicted upon a minority which that minority had no part in enacting or creating because they did not have the unhampered right to vote. Who can say that the legislature of Alabama which set up the segregation laws was democratically elected? Throughout the state of Alabama all types of conniving methods are used to prevent Negroes from becoming registered voters and there are some counties without a single Negro registered to vote despite the fact that the Negro constitutes a majority of the population. Can any law set up in such a state be considered democratically structured?

These are just a few examples of unjust and just laws. There are some instances when a law is just on its face and unjust in its application. For instance, I was arrested Friday on a charge of parading without a permit. Now there is nothing wrong with an ordinance which requires a permit for a parade, but when the ordinance is used to preserve segregation and to deny citizens the First Amendment privilege of peaceful assembly and peaceful protest, then it becomes unjust.

I hope you can see the distinction I am trying to point out. In no sense do I advocate evading or defying the law as the rabid segregationist would do. This would lead to anarchy. One who breaks an unjust law must do it *openly, lovingly* (not hatefully as the white mothers did in New Orleans when they were seen on television screaming, "nigger, nigger, nigger"), and with a willingness to accept the penalty. I submit that an individual who breaks a law that conscience tells him is unjust, and willingly accepts the penalty by staying in jail to arouse the conscience of the community over its injustice, is in reality expressing the very highest respect for law.

Of course, there is nothing new about this kind of civil disobedience. It was seen sublimely in the refusal of Shadrach, Meshach and Abednego to obey the laws of Nebuchadnezzar because a higher moral law was involved. It was practiced superbly by the early Christians who were willing to face hungry lions and the excruciating pain of chopping blocks, before submitting to certain unjust laws of the Roman Empire. To a degree academic freedom is a reality today because Socrates practiced civil disobedience.

We can never forget that everything Hitler did in Germany was "legal" and everything the Hungarian freedom fighters did in Hungary was "illegal." It was "illegal" to aid and comfort a Jew in Hitler's Germany. But I am sure that if I had lived in Germany during that time I would have aided and comforted my Jewish brothers even though it was illegal. If I lived in a Communist country today where certain principles dear to the Christian faith are suppressed, I believe I would openly advocate disobeying these anti-religious laws. I must make two honest confessions to you, my Christian and Jewish brothers. First, I must confess that over the last few years I have been gravely disappointed with the white moderate. I have almost reached the regrettable conclusion that the Negro's great stumbling block in the stride toward freedom is not the White Citizens Counciler or the Ku Klux Klanner, but the white moderate who is more devoted to "order" than to justice; who prefers a negative peace which is the absence of tension to a positive peace which is the presence of justice; who constantly says, "I agree with you in the goal you seek, but I can't agree with your methods of direct action"; who paternalistically feels that he can set the timetable for another man's freedom, who lives by the myth of time and who constantly advised the Negro to wait until a "more convenient season." Shallow understanding from people of good will is more frustrating than absolute misunderstanding from people of ill will. Lukewarm acceptance is much more bewildering than outright rejection.

I had hoped that the white moderate would understand that law and order exist for the purpose of establishing justice, and that when they fail to do this they become dangerously structured dams that block the flow of social progress. I had hoped that the white moderate would understand that the present tension of the South is merely a necessary phase of the transition from an obnoxious negative peace, where the Negro passively accepted his unjust plight, to a substance-filled positive peace, where all men will respect the dignity and worth of human personality. Actually, we who engage in nonviolent direct action are not the creators of tension. We merely bring to the surface the hidden tension that is already alive. We bring it out in the open where it can be seen and dealt with. Like a boil that can never be cured as long as it is covered up but must be opened with all its pus-flowing ugliness to the natural medicines of air and light, injustice must likewise be exposed, with all of the tension its exposing creates, to the light of human conscience and the air of national opinion before it can be cured.

In your statement you asserted that our actions, even though peaceful, must be condemned because they precipitate violence. But can this assertion be logically made? Isn't this like condemning the robbed man because his possession of money precipitated the evil act of robbery? Isn't this like condemning Socrates because his unswerving commitment to truth and his philosophical delvings precipitated the misguided popular mind to make him drink the hemlock? Isn't this like condemning Jesus because His unique God-consciousness and never-ceasing devotion to his will precipitated the evil act of crucifixion? We must come to see, as federal courts have consistently affirmed, that it is immoral to urge an individual to withdraw his efforts to gain his basic constitutional rights because the quest precipitates violence. Society must protect the robbed and punish the robber.

I had also hoped that the white moderate would reject the myth of time. I received a letter this morning from a white brother in Texas which said: "All Christians know that the colored people will receive equal rights eventually, but it is possible that you are in too great of a religious hurry. It has taken Christianity almost two thousand years to accomplish what it has. The teachings of Christ take time to come to earth." All that is said here grows out of a tragic misconception of time. It is the strangely irrational notion that there is something in the very flow of time that will inevitably cure all ills. Actually time is neutral. It can be used either destructively or constructively. I am coming to feel that the people of ill will have used time much more effectively than the people of good will. We will have to repent in this generation not merely for the vitriolic words and actions of the bad people, but for the appalling silence of the good people. We must come to see that human progress never rolls in on wheels of inevitability. It comes through the tireless efforts and persistent work of men willing to be co-workers with God, and without this hard work time itself becomes an ally of the forces of social stagnation. We must use time creatively, and forever realize that the time is always ripe to do right. Now is the time to make real the promise of democracy, and transform our pending national elegy into a creative psalm of brotherhood. Now is the time to lift our national policy from the quicksand of racial injustice to the solid rock of human dignity.

You spoke of our activity in Birmingham as extreme. At first I was rather disappointed that fellow clergymen would see my nonviolent efforts as those of the extremist. I started thinking about the fact that I stand in the middle of two opposing forces in the Negro community. One is a force of complacency made up of Negroes who, as a result of long years of oppression, have been so completely drained of self-respect and a sense of "somebodiness" that they have adjusted to segregation, and, of a few Negroes in the middle class who, because of a degree of academic and economic security, and because at points they profit by segregation, have unconsciously become insensitive to the problems of the masses. The other force is one of bitterness and hatred, and comes perilously close to advocating violence. It is expressed in the various black nationalist groups that are springing up over the nation, the largest and best known being Elijah Muhammad's Muslim movement. This movement is nourished by the contemporary frustration over the continued existence of racial discrimination. It is made up of people who have lost faith in America, who have absolutely repudiated Christianity, and who have concluded that the white man is an incurable "devil." I have tried to stand between these two forces, saying that we need not follow the "donothingism" of the complacent or the hatred and despair of the black nationalist. There is the more excellent way of love and nonviolent protest. I'm grateful to God that, through the Negro church, the dimension of nonviolence entered our struggle. If this philosophy had not emerged, I am convinced that by now many streets of the South would be flowing with floods of blood. And I am further convinced that if our white brothers dismiss as "rabble-rousers" and "outside agitators" those of us who are working through the channels of nonviolent direct action and refuse to support our nonviolent efforts, millions of Negroes, out of frustration and despair, will seek solace and security in black nationalist ideologies, a development that will lead inevitably to a frightening racial nightmare.

Oppressed people cannot remain oppressed forever. The urge for freedom will eventually come. This is what happened to the American Negro. Something within has reminded him of his birthright of freedom; something without has reminded him that he can gain it. Consciously and unconsciously, he has been swept in by what the Germans call the

Zeitgeist, and with his black brothers of Africa, and his brown and yellow brothers of Asia, South America and the Caribbean, he is moving with a sense of cosmic urgency toward the promised land of racial justice. Recognizing this vital urge that has engulfed the Negro community, one should readily understand public demonstrations. The Negro has many pent-up resentments and latent frustrations. He has to get them out. So let him march sometime; let him have his prayer pilgrimages to the city hall; understand why he must have sit-ins and freedom rides. If his repressed emotions do not come out in these nonviolent ways, they will come out in ominous expressions of violence. This is not a threat; it is a fact of history. So I have not said to my people "get rid of your discontent." But I have tried to say that this normal and healthy discontent can be channelized through the creative outlet of nonviolent direct action. Now this approach is being dismissed as extremist. I must admit that I was initially disappointed in being so categorized.

But as I continued to think about the matter I gradually gained a bit of satisfaction from being considered an extremist. Was not Jesus an extremist in love—"Love your enemies, bless them that curse you, pray for them that despitefully use you." Was not Amos an extremist for justice—"Let justice roll down like waters and righteousness like a mighty stream." Was not Paul an extremist for the gospel of Jesus Christ—"I bear in my body the marks of the Lord Jesus." Was not Martin Luther an extremist—"Here I stand; I can do none other so help me God." Was not John Bunyan an extremist—"I will stay in jail to the end of my days before I make a butchery of my conscience." Was not Abraham Lincoln an extremist—"This nation cannot survive half slave and half free." Was not Thomas Jefferson an extremist—"We hold these truths to be self-evident, that all men are created equal." So the question is not whether we will be extremist but what kind of extremist will we be. Will we be extremists for hate or will we be extremists for love? Will we be extremists for the preservation of injustice—or will we be extremists for the cause of justice? In that dramatic scene on Calvary's hill, three men were crucified. We must not forget that all three were crucified for the same crime—the crime of extremism. Two were extremists for immorality, and thusly fell below their environment. The other, Jesus Christ, was an extremist for love, truth and goodness, and thereby rose above his environment. So, after all, maybe the South, the nation and the world are in dire need of creative extremists.

I had hoped that the white moderate would see this. Maybe I was too optimistic. Maybe I expected too much. I guess I should have realized that few members of a race that has oppressed another race can understand or appreciate the deep groans and passionate yearnings of those that have been oppressed and still fewer have the vision to see that injustice must be rooted out by strong, persistent and determined action. I am thankful, however, that some of our white brothers have grasped the meaning of this social revolution and committed themselves to it. They are still all too small in quantity, but they are big in quality. Some like Ralph McGill, Lillian Smith, Harry Golden and James Dabbs have written about our struggle in eloquent, prophetic and understanding terms. Others have marched with us down nameless streets of the South. They have languished in filthy roach-infested jails, suffering the abuse and brutality of angry policemen who see them as "dirty nigger-lovers." They, unlike so many of their moderate brothers and sisters, have recognized the urgency of the moment and sensed the need for powerful "action" antidotes to combat the disease of segregation.

Let me rush on to mention my other disappointment. I have been so greatly disappointed with the white church and its leadership. Of course, there are some notable exceptions. I am not unmindful of the fact that each of you has taken some significant stands on this issue. I commend you, Rev. Stallings, for your Christian stance on this past Sunday, in welcoming Negroes to your worship service on a nonsegregated basis. I commend the Catholic leaders of this state for integrating Springhill College several years ago.

But despite these notable exceptions I must honestly reiterate that I have been disappointed with the church. I do not say that as one of the negative critics who can always find something wrong with the church. I say it as a minister of the gospel, who loves the church; who was nurtured in its bosom; who has been sustained by its spiritual blessings and who will remain true to it as long as the cord of life shall lengthen.

I had the strange feeling when I was suddenly catapulted into the leadership of the bus protest in Montgomery several years ago that we would have the support of the white church. I felt that the white ministers, priests and rabbis of the South would be some of our strongest allies. Instead, some have been outright opponents, refusing to understand the freedom movement and misrepresenting its leaders; all too many others have been more cautious than courageous and have remained silent behind the anesthetizing security of the stained-glass windows.

In spite of my shattered dreams of the past, I came to Birmingham with the hope that the white religious leadership of this community would see the justice of our cause, and with deep moral concern, serve as the channel through which our just grievances would get to the power structure. I had hoped that each of you would understand. But again I have been disappointed. I have heard numerous religious leaders of the South call upon their worshippers to comply with a desegregation decision because it is the *law*, but I have longed to hear white ministers say, "Follow this decree because integration is morally *right* and the Negro is your brother." In the midst of blatant injustices inflicted upon the Negro, I have watched white churches stand on the sideline and merely mouth pious irrelevancies and sanctimonious trivialities. In the midst of a mighty struggle to rid our nation of racial and economic injustice, I have heard so many ministers say, "Those are social issues with which the gospel has no real concern," and I have watched so many churches commit themselves to a completely otherworldly religion which made a strange distinction between body and soul, the sacred and the secular.

So here we are moving toward the exit of the twentieth century with a religious community largely adjusted to the status quo, standing as a taillight behind other community agencies rather than a headlight leading men to higher levels of justice.

I have traveled the length and breadth of Alabama, Mississippi and all the other southern states. On sweltering summer days and crisp autumn mornings I have looked at her beautiful churches with their lofty spires pointing heavenward. I have beheld the impressive outlay of her massive religious education buildings. Over and over again I have found myself asking: "What kind of people worship here? Who is their God? Where were their voices when the lips of Governor Barnett dripped with words of interposition and nullification? Where were they when Governor Wallace gave the clarion call for defiance and hatred? Where were their voices of support when tired, bruised and weary Negro men and women decided to rise from the dark dungeons of complacency to the bright hills of creative protest?"

Yes, these questions are still in my mind. In deep disappointment I have wept over the laxity of the church. But be assured that my tears have been tears of love. There can be no deep disappointment where there is not deep love. Yes, I love the church; I love her sacred walls. How could I do otherwise? I am in the rather unique position of being the son, the grandson and the great-grandson of preachers. Yes, I see the church as the body of Christ. But, oh! How we have blemished and scarred that body through social neglect and fear of being nonconformists.

There was a time when the church was very powerful. It was during that period when the early Christians rejoiced when they were deemed worthy to suffer for what they believed. In those days the church was not merely a thermometer that recorded the ideas and principles of popular opinion; it was a thermostat that transformed the mores of society. Wherever the early Christians entered a town the power structure got disturbed and immediately sought to convict them for being "disturbers of the peace" and "outside agitators." But they went on with the conviction that they were "a colony of heaven," and had to obey God rather than man. They were small in number but big in commitment. They were too God-intoxicated to be "astronomically intimidated." They brought an end to such ancient evils as infanticide and gladiatorial contest.

Things are different now. The contemporary church is often a weak, ineffectual voice with an uncertain sound. It is so often the arch-supporter of the status quo. Far from being disturbed by the presence of the church, the power structure of the average community is consoled by the church's silent and often vocal sanction of things as they are.

But the judgment of God is upon the church as never before. If the church of today does not recapture the sacrificial spirit of the early church, it will lose its authentic ring, forfeit the loyalty of millions, and be dismissed as an irrelevant social club with no meaning for the twentieth century. I am meeting young people every day whose disappointment with the church has risen to outright disgust.

Maybe again, I have been too optimistic. Is organized religion too inextricably bound to the status quo to save our nation and the world? Maybe I must turn my faith to the inner spiritual church, the church within the church, as the true *ecclesia* and the hope of the world. But again I am thankful to God that some noble souls from the ranks of organized religion have broken loose from the paralyzing chains of conformity and joined us as active partners in the struggle for freedom. They have left their secure congregations and walked the streets of Albany, Georgia, with us. They have gone through the highways of the South on tortuous rides for freedom. Yes, they have gone to jail with us. Some have been kicked out of their churches, and lost support of their bishops and fellow ministers. But they have gone with the faith that right defeated is stronger than evil triumphant. These men have been the leaven in the lump of the race. Their witness has been the spiritual salt that has preserved the true meaning of the gospel in these troubled times. They have carved a tunnel of hope through the dark mountain of disappointment.

I hope the church as a whole will meet the challenge of this decisive hour. But even if the church does not come to the aid of justice, I have no despair about the future. I have no fear about the outcome of our struggle in Birmingham, even if our motives are presently misunderstood. We will reach the goal of freedom in Birmingham and all over the nation, because the goal of America is freedom. Abused and scorned though we may be, our destiny is tied up with the destiny of America. Before the Pilgrims landed at Plymouth we were here. Before the pen of Jefferson etched across the pages of history the majestic words of the Declaration of Independence, we were here. For more than two centuries our foreparents labored in this country without wages; they made cotton king; and they built the homes of their masters in the midst of brutal injustice and shameful humiliation—and yet out of a bottomless vitality they continued to thrive and develop. If the inexpressive cruelties of slavery could not stop us, the opposition we now face will surely fail. We will win our freedom because the sacred heritage of our nation and the eternal will of God are embodied in our echoing demands.

I must close now. But before closing I am impelled to mention one other point in your statement that troubled me profoundly. You warmly commended the Birmingham police force for keeping "order" and "preventing violence." I don't believe you would have so warmly commended the police force if you had seen its angry violent dogs literally biting six unarmed, nonviolent Negroes. I don't believe you would so quickly commend the policemen if you would observe their ugly and inhuman treatment of Negroes here in the city jail; if you would watch them push and curse old Negro women and young Negro girls; if you would see them slap and kick old Negro men and young boys; if you will observe them, as they did on two occasions, refuse to give us food because we wanted to sing our grace together. I'm sorry that I can't join you in your praise for the police department.

It is true that they have been rather disciplined in their public handling of the demonstrators. In this sense they have been rather publicly "nonviolent." But for what purpose? To preserve the evil system of segregation. Over the last few years I have consistently preached that nonviolence demands that the means we use must be as pure as the ends we seek. So I have tried to make it clear that it is wrong to use immoral means to attain moral ends. But now I must affirm that it is just as wrong, or even more so, to use moral means to preserve immoral ends. Maybe Mr. Connor and his policemen have been rather publicly nonviolent, as Chief Pritchett was in Albany, Georgia, but they have used the moral means of nonviolence to maintain the immoral end of flagrant racial injustice. T. S. Eliot has said that there is no greater treason than to do the right deed for the wrong reason.

I wish you had commended the Negro sit-inners and demonstrators of Birmingham for their sublime courage, their willingness to suffer and their amazing discipline in the midst of the most inhuman provocation. One day the South will recognize its real heroes. They will be the James Merediths, courageously and with a majestic sense of purpose facing jeering and hostile mobs and the agonizing loneliness that characterizes the life of the pioneer. They will be old, oppressed, battered Negro women, symbolized in a seventy-two-year-old woman of Montgomery, Alabama, who rose up with a sense of dignity and with her people decided not to ride the segregated buses, and responded to one who inquired about her tiredness with ungrammatical profundity: "My feet is tired, but my soul is rested." They will be the young high school and college students, young ministers of the gospel and a host of their elders courageously and non-violently sitting-in at lunch counters and willingly going to jail for conscience's sake. One day the South will know that when these disinherited children of God sat down at lunch counters they were in reality standing up for the best in the American dream and the most sacred values in our Judeo-Christian heritage, and thusly, carrying our whole nation back to those great wells of democracy which were dug deep by the Founding Fathers in the formulation of the Constitution and the Declaration of Independence.

Never before have I written a letter this long (or should I say a book?). I'm afraid that it is much too long to take your precious time. I can assure you that it would have been much shorter if I had been writing from a comfortable desk, but what else is there to do when you are alone for days in the dull monotony of a narrow jail cell other than write long letters, think strange thoughts, and pray long prayers?

If I have said anything in this letter that is an overstatement of the truth and is indicative of an unreasonable impatience, I beg you to forgive me. If I have said anything in this letter that is an understatement of the truth and is indicative of my having a patience that makes me patient with anything less than brotherhood, I beg God to forgive me.

I hope this letter finds you strong in the faith. I also hope that circumstances will soon make it possible for me to meet each of you, not as an integrationist or a civil rights leader, but as a fellow clergyman and a Christian brother. Let us all hope that the dark clouds of racial prejudice will soon pass away and the deep fog of misunderstanding will be lifted from our fear-drenched communities and in some not too distant tomorrow the radiant stars of love and brotherhood will shine over our great nation with all of their scintillating beauty.

Yours for the cause of Peace and Brotherhood,
Martin Luther King, Jr.

FOR DISCUSSION AND WRITING

1. How does King justify nonviolent civil disobedience? Does he respond to his critics? What are alternative strategies to civil disobedience for people who have grievances? Which strategies do you think are most effective? Does your response depend on the situation? Explain. Find out which laws the civil disobedience violated.

2. King said, "We will have to repent in this generation not merely for the vitriolic words and actions of the bad people, but for the appalling silence of the good people." What does he mean by this statement about silence? What issues, from school policy to national policy to foreign policy, are good people silent about today?

3. Who is the audience King addresses in the letter? What are King's purposes in writing this letter? Has he succeeded? Use the letter to support your responses.

4. King thought that the moral climate in the United States was low when this letter was written in 1963. Do you think the moral climate in the United States today is higher or lower than when King wrote the letter? Discuss specific issues in explaining your views.

5. Do you see yourself as an "extremist for the cause of justice," as a moderate, or as removed from the cause of justice? Explain.

6. Create a time line of the main struggles of the civil rights movement. What were the aims and outcomes of these struggles?

I HAVE A DREAM
Martin Luther King, Jr.

In 1963 the struggle for civil rights was at its height. African-American young people who demonstrated for equality were battered by fire hoses and police dogs. Medgar Evers, a field secretary for the National Association for the Advancement of Colored People, was murdered on his front porch in Mississippi. Riots raged throughout the summer of 1963. That year was significant for Martin Luther King, Jr. and others fighting for civil rights because it was one hundred years after Abraham Lincoln's Emancipation Proclamation, and, as King said, "The Negro is still not free." These words are from King's most famous speech, "I Have a Dream," that he delivered before the Lincoln Memorial on August 28, 1963, to over 250,000 demonstrators of all ages and races. King was murdered in Memphis, Tennessee, in 1968, while helping to join the underprivileged of all races into a coalition against poverty.

I AM HAPPY TO JOIN WITH YOU TODAY in what will go down in history as the greatest demonstration for freedom in the history of our nation.

Fivescore years ago, a great American, in whose symbolic shadow we stand today, signed the Emancipation Proclamation. This momentous decree came as a great beacon light of hope to millions of Negro slaves who had been seared in the flames of withering injustice. It came as a joyous daybreak to end the long night of their captivity.

But one hundred years later, the Negro still is not free; one hundred years later, the life of the Negro is still sadly crippled by the manacles of segregation and the chains of discrimination; one hundred years later, the Negro lives on a lonely island of poverty in the midst of a vast ocean of material prosperity; one hundred years later, the Negro is still languished in the corners of American society and finds himself in exile in his own land.

So we've come here today to dramatize a shameful condition. In a sense we've come to our nation's capital to cash a check. When the architects of our republic wrote the magnificent words of the Constitution and the Declaration of Independence, they were signing a promissory note to which every American was to fall heir. This note was the promise that all men, yes, black men as well as white men, would be guaranteed the unalienable rights of life, liberty, and the pursuit of happiness.

It is obvious today that America has defaulted on this promissory note in so far as her citizens of color are concerned. Instead of honoring this sacred obligation, America has given the Negro people a bad check; a check which has come back marked "insufficient funds." We refuse to believe that there are insufficient funds in the great vaults of opportunity of this nation. And so we've come to cash this check, a check that will give us upon demand the riches of freedom and the security of justice.

We have also come to this hallowed spot to remind America of the fierce urgency of now. This is no time to engage in the luxury of cooling off or to take the tranquilizing drug of gradualism. Now is the time to make real the promises of democracy; now is the time to rise from the dark and desolate valley of segregation to the sunlit path of racial justice; now is the time to lift our nation from the quicksands of racial injustice to the solid rock of brotherhood; now is the time to make justice a reality for all God's children. It would be fatal for the nation to overlook the urgency of the moment. This sweltering summer of the Negro's legitimate discontent will not pass until there is an invigorating autumn of freedom and equality.

Nineteen sixty-three is not an end, but a beginning. And those who hope that the Negro needed to blow off steam and will now be content, will have a rude awakening if the nation returns to business as usual.

There will be neither rest nor tranquility in America until the Negro is granted his citizenship rights. The whirlwinds of revolt will continue to shake the foundations of our nation until the bright day of justice emerges.

But there is something that I must say to my people who stand on the warm threshold which leads into the palace of justice. In the process of gaining our rightful place we must not be guilty of wrongful deeds.

Let us not seek to satisfy our thirst for freedom by drinking from the cup of bitterness and hatred. We must forever conduct our struggle on the high plane of dignity and discipline. We must not allow our creative protest to degenerate into physical violence. Again and again we must rise to the majestic heights of meeting physical force with soul force.

The marvelous new militancy which has engulfed the Negro community must not lead us to a distrust of all white people, for many of our white brothers, as evidenced by their presence here today, have come to realize that their destiny is tied up with our destiny and they have come to realize that their freedom is inextricably bound to our freedom. This offense we share mounted to storm the battlements of injustice must be carried forth by a biracial army. We cannot walk alone.

Flip Schulke, Martin Luther King, Jr. with his son, *c. 1963*

And as we walk, we must make the pledge that we shall always march ahead. We cannot turn back. There are those who are asking the devotees of civil rights, "When will you be satisfied?" We can never be satisfied as long as the Negro is the victim of the unspeakable horrors of police brutality.

We can never be satisfied as long as our bodies, heavy with fatigue of travel, cannot gain lodging in the motels of the highways and the hotels of the cities. We cannot be satisfied as long as the Negro's basic mobility is from a smaller ghetto to a larger one.

We can never be satisfied as long as our children are stripped of their selfhood and robbed of their dignity by signs stating "for whites only." We cannot be satisfied as long as a Negro in Mississippi cannot vote and a Negro in New York believes he has nothing for which to vote. No, we are not satisfied, and we will not be satisfied until justice rolls down like waters and righteousness like a mighty stream.

I am not unmindful that some of you come here out of excessive trials and tribulation. Some of you have come fresh from narrow jail cells. Some of you have come from areas where your quest for freedom left you battered by the storms of persecution and staggered by the winds of police brutality. You have been the veterans of creative suffering. Continue to work with the faith that unearned suffering is redemptive.

Go back to Mississippi; go back to Alabama; go back to South Carolina; go back to Georgia; go back to Louisiana; go back to the slums and ghettos of the northern cities, knowing that somehow this situation can, and will be changed. Let us not wallow in the valley of despair.

So I say to you, my friends, that even though we must face the difficulties of today and tomorrow, I still have a dream. It is a dream deeply rooted in the American dream that one day this nation will rise up and live out the true meaning of its creed—we hold these truths to be self-evident, that all men are created equal.

I have a dream that one day on the red hills of Georgia, sons of former slaves and sons of former slave-owners will be able to sit down together at the table of brotherhood.

I have a dream that one day, even the state of Mississippi, a state sweltering with the heat of injustice, sweltering with the heat of oppression, will be transformed into an oasis of freedom and justice.

I have a dream my four little children will one day live in a nation where they will not be judged by the color of their skin but by the content of their character. I have a dream today!

I have a dream that one day, down in Alabama, with its vicious racists, with its governor having his lips dripping with the words of interposition and nullification, that one day, right there in Alabama, little black boys and black girls will be able to join hands with little white boys and white girls as sisters and brothers. I have a dream today!

I have a dream that one day every valley shall be exalted, every hill and mountain shall be made low, the rough places shall be made plain, and the crooked places shall be made straight and the glory of the Lord will be revealed and all flesh shall see it together.

This is our hope. This is the faith that I go back to the South with.

With this faith we will be able to hew out of the mountain of despair a stone of hope. With this faith we will be able to transform the jangling discords of our nation into a beautiful symphony of brotherhood.

With this faith we will be able to work together, to pray together, to struggle together, to go to jail together, to stand up for freedom together, knowing that we will be free one day. This will be the day when all of God's children will be able to sing with new meaning—"my country 'tis of thee; sweet land of liberty; of thee I sing; land where my fathers died, land of the pilgrim's pride; from every mountain side, let freedom ring"—and if America is to be a great nation, this must become true.

So let freedom ring from the prodigious hilltops of New Hampshire.

Let freedom ring from the mighty mountains of New York.

Let freedom ring from the heightening Alleghenies of Pennsylvania.

Let freedom ring from the snow-capped Rockies of Colorado.

Let freedom ring from the curvaceous slopes of California.

But not only that.

Let freedom ring from Stone Mountain of Georgia.

Let freedom ring from Lookout Mountain of Tennessee.

Let freedom ring from every hill and molehill of Mississippi, from every mountainside, let freedom ring.

And when we allow freedom to ring, when we let it ring from every village and hamlet, from every state and city, we will be able to speed up that day when all of God's children—black men and white men, Jews and Gentiles, Catholics and Protestants—will be able to join hands and to sing in the words of the old Negro spiritual, "Free at last, free at last; thank God Almighty, we are free at last."

FOR DISCUSSION AND WRITING

1. *Find instances in the speech in which King uses sentences and phrases from classic American speeches and songs.*

2. *In the speech King repeats phrases. Can you identify these phrases? What is the effect of these repetitions?*

3. *Who is the audience of the speech? What are the main purposes of his oration?*

4. *King says, "This is no time to engage in the luxury of cooling off or to take the tranquilizing drug of gradualism." What does he mean by "gradualism?" What might be examples of gradualism in public policy today. Do you agree or disagree with King on this point? Explain.*

5. *What is the relevance today of the words King wrote in 1963? Do they still articulate a dream? Are they outmoded? If so, what ideas take their place today? Explain.*

POEMS FROM *SONGS OF GOLD MOUNTAIN*

anonymous

Beginning in the 1840s, tens of thousands of Chinese people immigrated to the United States, where they found grueling work in the railroads, mines, in construction, and the fishing industry. In 1882, at the height of Chinese immigration, Congress passed the Chinese Exclusion Act which required that Chinese immigrants, hopeful for work, had to prove they were related by blood to a current United States citizen in order to immigrate to the United States. Thousands awaited interrogation, sometimes up to a year, in cramped wooden barracks at the Angel Island Immigration Station in San Francisco Bay. Many were deported to China. The following poems describe immigrants' first impressions of the United States, which they nicknamed Gold Mountain. The poems were originally included in an anthology published in 1911, and were recently translated into English.

I

AS SOON AS IT IS ANNOUNCED
    the ship has reached America:
I burst out cheering,
    I have found precious pearls.
How can I bear the detention upon arrival,
Doctors and immigration officials refusing
    to let me go?
All the abuse—
I can't describe it with a pen.
I'm held captive in a wooden barrack, like King Wen
    in Youli:[1]
No end to the misery and sadness in my heart.

---

1. King Wen (ca. 1200 B.C.), the first ruler of the Zhou dynasty, was detained in Youli for being an adversary of the ruling Shang.

Victor Fan, Chinese American History, *1988*

2
The moment I hear
  we've entered the port,
I am all ready:
  my belongings wrapped in a bundle.
Who would have expected joy to become sorrow:
Detained in a dark, crude, filthy room?
What can I do?
Cruel treatment, not one restful breath of air.
Scarcity of food, severe restrictions—all
  unbearable,
Here even a proud man bows his head low.

7
Detention is called "awaiting review."
No letter or message can get through to me.
My mind's bogged down with a hundred frustrations
  and anxieties,
My mouth balks at meager meals of rice gruel.
O, what can I do?
Just when can I go ashore?
Imprisoned in a coop, unable to breathe,
My countrymen are made into a herd of cattle!

8

America, I have come and landed,
And am stranded here, for more than a year.
Suffering thousands upon thousands of
      mistreatments.
Is it in retribution for a past life that I
      deserve such defilement?
It is outrageous—
Being humiliated repeatedly by them.
I pray my country will become strong and
      even the score
Send out troops, like Japan's war against
      Russia![2]

11

American laws, more ferocious than tigers:
Many are the people jailed inside wooden walls,
Detained, interrogated, tortured,
Like birds plunged into an open trap—
      What suffering!
To whom can I complain of the tragedy?
I shout to Heaven, but there is no way out!
Had I only known such difficulty in passing
      the Golden Gate . . .
Fed up with this treatment, I regret my journey here.

12

So, liberty is your national principle;
Why do you practice autocracy?
You don't uphold justice, you Americans,
You detain me in prison, guard me closely.
Your officials are wolves and tigers,
All ruthless, all wanting to bite me.
An innocent man implicated, such an injustice!
When can I get out of this prison and free
      my mind?

---

2. In the Russo-Japanese war of 1903, Japan defeated Russia in Manchuria, a region of
northeastern China, and emerged from this war as a world power.

19

Born into a rotten life,
Coming or going, all without leaving my mark.
Even after leaving the village for a foreign
      country,
Running about east and west, I've gained nothing.
Everything's turned upside down;
It's more disconcerting being away from home.
I have gone to the four corners of the world;
Alas, I am neither at ease while resting nor
      happy while moving.

20

Pitiful is the twenty-year sojourner,
Unable to make it home.
Having been everywhere—north, south, east,
      west—
Always obstacles along the way, pain knitting
      my brows.
Worried, in silence.
Ashamed, wishes unfulfilled.
A reflection on the mirror, a sudden fright:
      hair, half frost-white.
Frequent letters from home, all filled with much
      complaint.

23

I have walked to the very ends of the earth,
A dusty, windy journey.
I've toiled and I'm worn out, all for a miserable lot.
Nothing is ideal when I am down and out.
I think about it day and night—
Who can save a fish out of water?
From far away, I worry for my parents, my wife,
      my boy:
Do they still have enough firewood, rice, salt, and
      cooking oil?

24

Toiling in pain, east and west, all in vain;
Hurrying about, north and south, still more
      rushing.
What can a person do with a life full of mishap?
Searching, scheming, on all four sides, not
      one good lead in sight.
Eyes brimming with tears:
O, I just can't get rid of the misery.
My belly is full of frustration and grievance;
When life is at low ebb, I suffer dearly.

25

Drifting around, all over the place,
Seeking food everywhere, in all four directions.
Turning east, going west, always on an
      uncertain road;
Toiling, rushing about, much ado for nothing.
Fed by wind and frost,
I search for wealth, but all in vain.
If fate indeed has excluded me so, what more can
      I say?
After years of sojourn, I sigh in fear.

26

Look at that face in the mirror:
My appearance so completely changed.
Hair white as frost, long beard hanging;
Disheartening are the bald spots sparkling
      like stars.
Old age has arrived.
No longer is my face young and handsome.
Without my noticing, I am already over forty.
Shame is toiling in hardship, across the vast
      and distant oceans.

27

My ambition wouldn't allow me to stay cooped up
    in humility.
I took a raft and sailed the seas.
Rising early at dawn, with the stars above me,
    I traveled deep into the night, the moon my
    companion.
Who could have known it would be a journey full of
    rain and snow?
Winds pierced through my bones.
Hugging a blanket, my thighs trembling.
I wish to buy a fox-fur coat, but lack the money—
Right now I don't have the means even to fight
    the cold!

28

The Flowery Flag Nation is deep in frost and heavy
    with snow.
No one can withstand its winter without a fur
    coat.
Traveling is not at all like staying at home:
In thin clothing on wintry days, my shoulders and
    arms shrug and shiver in the cold.
Even if you are brave and strong,
The fierce wind will bend your back into a bow,
Prepare a cotton-padded gown and rush it to me!
Don't make this distant traveler wait anxiously
    for the journeying geese![3]

FOR DISCUSSION AND WRITING

1. What symbolic meanings did "Gold Mountain" have for Chinese immigrants?

2. Find out about the history of Chinese laborers who came to Gold Mountain. What were some of their main accomplishments in the United States?

3. What are the main emotions expressed in each poem?

---

3. Journeying geese—a metaphor for news messengers.

EACH YEAR GRAIN
Shawn Hsu Wong

This short story addresses the issues of Chinese laborers in the 1850s who dug gold mines and laid rail-road tracks in California. In a series of dream fragments, Shawn Hsu Wong describes how these Chinese immigrants were treated. Wong is a Chinese-American writer and professor of American Ethnic Studies. He believes that Asian-American authors should be more widely published, and to this end he has edited anthologies of Asian-American literature on his own and in collaboration with others.

*I*AM THE SON OF MY FATHER and I have a story to tell about my history and about a dream. I had the dream inside of a tree. I was child, walking through a forest of giant shade and I found a huge stump of a once giant redwood burned hollow so that you could step inside and look up and see the sky. I suddenly shouted into the charcoal darkness, into the soft charred soul of this tree. My shout was absorbed so quickly, I knew the tree was listening. And I spoke to the tree in my dream. The tree showed me its rings of growth and as I ran my fingers over each year grain, the tree showed me the year I was born and my history.

I asked the tree to show me the year I was born and the year of my father's birth and the tree said that it would not only show that year but would begin farther back in my history and show me my great-grandfather's country, the country that he came to, the land where he toiled day after day and the land where he was buried.

I came running down the grassy hills as fast as the wind moves down the waves of grass from shade to light. I came running down the long meadow of tumbling yellow greens racing wind across drifting grasses. I came running into a dream Appaloosa-like.

"Your great-grandfather's country was a rich land, the river's sand had gold dust in it. The water was fresh and clear, the sand sparkling beneath the surface of the water like the shiny skin of the trout that swam in the deep pools. This was California's gold country of the 1850's and your great-grandfather was there to reap the riches that California offered and to return home a rich man to live in comfort with his family."

I knew by the feeling of the land in my dream that great-grandfather did not live to return to China, nor to reap any riches. Instead he died here in northern California buried in the dark moist earth. And I heard my great-grandfather's voice in the wind speak, "Do not send my bones back to China. Bury me here beneath my tears."

The hawk glides in hot drafts of summer dust wind and drops the furry body of his meal into the brittle meadow grasses below and the body becomes the grass of next spring growing wet from light snow. And the land that makes each spring birth again is held moist in my hands. California north.

"Your great-grandfather was humiliated by the land and the people to which he gave his life. But unlike the other Chinese who died here and had their bones sent back to China, so that at least that much of them would return home away from the land that humiliated them and the life they loathed, your great-grandfather felt that since this land was important enough for him to give his life to, he should not leave and that his sons should follow him to this country, and his soul would protect them."

Woodsmoke drifts from Shasta, Trinity, Siskiyou, north to the wild Klamath River. Drift woodsmoke, bend and fall with the river near the people that live in your California heart! Klamath, Salmon, Eel, river running to a space where woodsmoke lives in the deep clover and moss on the breath of wind that passes down through the unmoving red-woods. California northcoast. Woodsmoke dissolves in a forest of mist from the sea cold, falling from jagged cliffs wearing by age. Points and coasts like Reyes, Bolinas, Monterey, take Sur Country energy into the black night ocean and repeat over and over the same silence.

I could see the gold country land in my dreams and I loved its sun, its wood, and the dark, loose and cool earth where my feet could dig in like roots. Then another vision came into my dream. It was not the same land. And the tree spoke to me, "One of the men you see working here was your great-grandfather building the railroad. It was the work that broke him and the work that he desperately held on to—to make a little place in this country. His brother was murdered."

My great-grandfather who drove rail spikes and laid track was speaking to me. "I left for San Francisco one month before my brother. In those days some ships were bringing us in illegally. They would drop a lifeboat outside the Golden Gate with the Chinese in it. Then the ship would steam in and at night the lifeboat would come in quietly and unload. If they were about to be caught, my people would be thrown overboard. But, you see, they couldn't swim because they were chained together. My brother died on that night and now his bones are chained to the bottom of the ocean. No burial ever. Now I am fighting to find a place in this country.

"We do not have our women here. My wife is coming to live here. We are staying. Nothing was sweet about those days I lived alone in the city, unless you can find sweetness in that kind of loneliness. I slept in the back of a kitchen by the grimy window where the light and noises of the wet city streets were ground in and out of me like the cold. The bed was so small I could hardly move away from my dreams. And when I awakened with the blue light of the moon shining in, there would be no dreams. That one moment when I wake, losing my dreams, my arms and heart imagining that she was near me moving closer and I float in her movements and light touch. But the blue light and the noise was always there and I would have nothing in my hands."

Great-grandfather's wife was a delicate, yet a strong and energetic lady. Insisting in her letters to Great-grandfather to let her come and join him. The loneliness was overpowering him, yet he resisted her pleas, telling her that life was too dangerous for a woman. "The people and the work move like hawks around me, I feel chained to the ground, unable even to cry for help. The sun blisters my skin, the winters leave me sick, the cold drains us. I look into the eyes of my friends and there is nothing, not even fear."

Upon receiving his letter, Great-grandmother told her friends that she was leaving to join her husband, saying that his fight to survive was too much for a single man to bear. And so she came and was happy and the hawks had retreated.

She lived in the city and gave birth to a son while Great-grandfather was still working in the Sierras building the railroad. He wrote to her, saying that the railroad would be finished in six months and he would return to the city and they would live together again as a family.

During the six months, the hawks came back into his vision. "The hawks had people faces laughing as they pulled me apart with their sharp talons, they had no voices just their mouths flapping open, a yellow hysteria of teeth." He knew that this was the beginning of sickness for his lover, he sensed her trouble and moments of pain, no word from her was necessary. "Your wounds are my wounds," he would say in the night, "the hawks that tear our flesh are disturbed by the perfect day, the pure sun that warms the wounds, I am singing and they cannot tear us apart."

She saw the sun as she woke that morning after waking all night long in moments of pain. The sun was so pure. She thought that this could not be the city, its stench, its noise replaced by this sweet air. She knew that this air, this breath, was her husband's voice. The ground was steaming dry, the humus became her soul, alive and vital with the moving and pushing of growth. She breathed deeply, the air was like sleep uninterrupted by pain, there was no more home to travel to, this moment was everything that loving could give and that was enough. She was complete and whole with that one breath, like the security of her childhood nights sleeping with mother, wrapping her arms around her, each giving the other the peace of touch, pure sun. There was a rush of every happiness in her life that she could feel and touch and as she let go, she thought of their son, and the joy of his birth jarred her and she tried desperately to reach out to wake, to hold on to that final fear, to grasp his childhood trust, but the smell of the humus, the moist decaying leaves struck by sunlight and steaming into her dreams was too much and she was moving too fast into sleep.

Great-grandfather had dreams, making vows to his son, seeing dark legends that moved on him like skeletons stomping down the metal spiral staircase of her grave. The hollow sounds of their white silk capes flapping in an updraft of hot dust.

"I shall take my son away from these hawks who cause me to mourn. I cannot cry. My tears leave scars on my face. There is no strength in pity. I will take my son away, move deeper into this country. I have heard stories about the South that there is no winter, only sun."

The images were strength for him. He had dreams of the South and they moved upon him like legends of faith. The hot dry dust and heat cleansing his skin, warming his back. The swamps were the visions of life's blood, there was something vital and deep red in the hiss of hot animal mouths and the humid steaming life that rose up to embrace him. There was a julep woman there for him, cool and she was the touch of green. She was silence, soft as meadow loam, sweet as a stream that he could lie in, letting her waters rush over his body, hearing the sound of leaves in the wind. The dream always ended with the scream of white fire. It was the magnolia. A huge magnolia tree afire, branches of flames moving around each white magnolia blossom. He saw them drop into the dust, a ball of white fire. The smell of the magnolia burning always woke him that smell lingering into morning like charred flesh, so cold.

Magnolia, magnolia your white blood
Is the fire of moons.
Your flower is winter to my flesh.

For Great-grandfather it was not enough anymore to say he was *Long-time Californ'*. He had lost faith in the land. He fell into deeper depressions, not from mourning his wife's death, but more from his loss of faith in the country. He had been defeated when he had vowed not to lose ground to the harsh land and cruel people. It was his son that finally carried him through, helped return the faith so that at least he would die at peace.

Slide, tumble down wide open tall grass hills, feel the warm sun on your face as you spin from earth to sky, fingers reaching into the moist earth and laugh uncontrolled or cry, it doesn't matter, just keep tumbling down that steep hill and finally when you roll slowly to a stop stained green stained brown and exhausted you will notice while catching your breath that you may have startled a blue heron which lifts its great wings up then down again rising from the meadow loam down the sun washed valley of tall trees. Watch until the low sun engulfs its silent flying guest. The moment is yours, take it with you into your own loneliness where sight becomes feeling. Instantaneously.

"The country that accepted your great-grandfather and his son now rejected them. The railroad was finished and the Chinese were chased out of the mines. They were allowed to live but not marry. The law was designed so that the Chinese would gradually die out, leaving no sons or daughters."

FOR DISCUSSION AND WRITING

1. What does the speaker learn about Chinese-American history from his dream? What do the history books at your school say about these issues?

2. Why do most Americans know so little about Chinese-American history? Are there ways to redress some of the wrongs that the author talks about? Explain.

3. Are there aspects of other cultures' histories that have been underemphasized in history textbooks? Why do you think this is so? Do you think it is important to know the history of other cultures?

THEY SAY THEM CHILD BRIDES DON'T LAST
Florence Reece interviewed by Kathy Kahn

Kathy Kahn conducted interviews of nineteen women from Appalachia and in 1972 compiled them into the book Hillbilly Women. *Some of these women were born and raised in the coal towns of Eastern Kentucky, Tennessee, and the Virginias. Others lived in the cotton mill towns and farming communities of Tennessee, North Carolina, and northern Georgia. The heritage of many people in this area is Scottish, Irish, and English. This heritage is reflected in the mountain music of the area which has its roots in the British Isles, and in turn is the main influence in modern country music. "They Say Them Child Brides Don't Last" is the story of Florence Reece, writer of the famous mineworker union song, "Which Side Are You On?"*

SAM WENT IN THE MINES WHEN HE WAS ELEVEN YEARS OLD. Sixty cents a day. And there wasn't no such thing as hours. He'd come out of there way in the dark of the night. And him just a little boy.

As soon as a boy'd get up to be ten or eleven years old, he'd have to go in the mines to help feed the others in his family. As soon as he got sixteen years old, he'd marry and it'd start revolving over.

I was fourteen when we got married and Sam was nineteen. Child bride. They say them child brides don't last, but they do. When the gun thugs was coming around we had eight children. We had ten altogether. And every one of them was born at home.

My father was killed in the coal mines. He was loading a ton and a half of coal for thirty cents, and pushing it. And that's what he got killed for, for nothing. That was Fork Ridge, Tennessee; they call it Mingo Holler now.

In the morning when they'd go to work before daylight, you could see the kerosene lamps they wore on their hats. It was just like fireflies all around the mountain. They'd go under that mountain every day, never knowing whether they'd come out alive. Most every day they'd bring out a dead man. Sometimes, two or three.

I never knew whether Sam would come out of the mines alive or not. I've seen him come home and his clothes would be froze into ice. He'd have to lay down in the water and dig the coal, and then carry a sack of coal home to keep us warm and to cook. But he had to go, had to go

Ben Shahn, Miners' Wives, *1948*

somewhere cause the children had to eat. Sam joined the union in nineteen and seventeen.

Well, it was in Harlan County, Kentucky, and they was on strike. John Henry Blair, see, he was the High Sheriff, and he'd hire these men to go and get the miners. He'd hire these men that was real tough, and they'd give them good automobiles to drive and good guns to carry and they'd give them whiskey to drink, to beat the miners down, keep them down so they couldn't went in the union. They called these men "deputy sheriffs" but they was gun thugs. That was the coal operators with John Henry Blair.

We was living in Molus in Harlan County, Kentucky, then. In 1930 the coal miners went out on strike against the coal operators. Well, Sam had a garage down below where we lived. The miners would come there and hang out and talk about how they wasn't going back to work. So some of the bosses and officials come and asked Sam if he'd go back to work and Sam said did that mean that they got the union contract. And they said no. So Sam said, well, he wouldn't go back to work. From that beginning they started on him.

First, they arrested him, they took him to jail, said he was selling whiskey, anything they could put on him. And he wasn't fooling with whiskey at all, no, not at all. That was in nineteen and thirty.

It seems like a bad dream when you think about it, that it happened to your own children. They didn't have no clothes, nor enough to eat, they was always sick and you could see they was hungry. We was all just starving, and so the miners would go out and kill cows or goats or just anything. They belonged to the coal companies, you know.

I've seen little children, their little legs would be so tiny and their stomachs would be so big from eating green apples, anything they could get. And I've seen grown men staggering they was so hungry. One of the company bosses said he hoped the children'd have to gnaw the bark off the trees.

In Molus they didn't have nothing to eat. The miners and their families was starving and a lot of people had that pellagra. One woman come to my house to get something to eat and she had that. All scaly all over, you know. Someone said, "Aren't you'll afraid you catch that from her?" I said, "No. She got that at the table cause she didn't have no food."

While we lived in Molus and Sam was away, he wasn't just hiding from the gun thugs. He was organizing with the union. One time he was gone a week and I didn't know where he was dead or alive. Well, one night he slipped in way long about one o'clock in the morning. We had a garden, it had corn and he slipped in through the back way, up through the corn. And I stayed up all that night watching for them to come after Sam.

The thugs made my mind up for me right off, which side I was on. They would come to our house in four and five carloads and they all had guns and belts around them filled with cartridges, and they had high powers. They'd come here looking for Sam cause he was organizing and on strike.

One night they killed eleven. That was "Evart's Fight." That was in May of 1931. It was at the Greenville crossing. A little boy heard the thugs a-talkin', saying they was going to meet the miners there at the railroad crossing and kill them. This little boy run and told his daddy and his daddy run and told the miners. The miners was there to meet the gun thugs and killed seven of them. Four miners got killed in the fight and the rest of them got sent to the penitentiary. One of them was a Negro man. But the thugs, they didn't get nothing.

Do you remember Harry Simms? He was from New York, he was a organizer. Sam was in the holler with Harry Simms, and Sam had just come out when the thugs backed Simms up on a flatcar and shot him. Well, the miners took him to Pineville after he was shot and he bled to death on the steps of the hospital. They wouldn't let him in cause he was a union man. They killed Harry Simms on Brush Creek. He was nineteen year old.

The gun thugs would take the union men out and kill them. The miners would go out in the woods and the cemeteries and hide. So then they had the state militia out after them. We'd find men's bones up there on Pine Mountain where they'd take them out and shoot them.

There was one man, a organizer, he come to our house. His back was beat to a bloody gore, he was beat all to pieces. He took off his shirt, went out back and laid in the sun for a long time. He stayed here all day. We pleaded with him not to go back. But he says, "Somebody's got to do it. I'm going back." When one gets killed, somebody's got to go back and take his place a-organizin'. And he went back and we never heard from him again.

One old man come to our house. Dan Brooks. They had a thousand or two thousand dollar on his head. I kept him in our house. He come in here from Pennsylvania to organize. He stayed two nights then left for a day. Then he came sneaking back to the house and that night he held a meeting on our porch. He told the miners, "Somebody's got to lose their lives in this, but won't it be better for them that's left?" And that's right. If we lose our lives a-doin' something like this, struggling, trying to get higher wages and better conditions for the workers, better homes, schools, hospitals, well then, if they kill us but yet if the people get those things, then it'd be better that we'd lose our lives for what'd help the workers.

Well, the thugs kept coming and coming. One day Sam went down to the garage and I saw them coming. I knowed from what had happened to other people that they was going to search the house.

Sam had a shotgun and he had a high power. Well, I was setting on the porch with my baby. They come on in and I got up and went in after them. My eleven-year-old daughter got that shotgun and that rifle and jumped out the window and ran, went up in the cornfields and hid.

We had shells hid inside the record player and I didn't want them to get them cause Sam would go hunting, you know. Well, one of them started to play the record player . . . it was one of them old ones you got to crank . . . he started a-crankin' it. I said, "You can't play that. It's broke." "Oh."

And he stopped cranking it. I knowed if they'd started a-playin' it they'd've killed every one of us cause there was shells in there.

They looked in the beds, under the beds, through the dirty clothes, through folded clean clothes. Said they was a-lookin' for guns and literature. I'd never studied papers, I'd never heared tell of the International Workers of the World till they come, I didn't know what it meant. So that worried me. I told them, I said, "I'm not used to such stuff as this. All I do is just stay at home and take care of my children and go to church." One of them said, "As long as these communists is in here, you'll have trouble." I didn't even know what a communist was, I never heared tell of a communist before. But every time a body starts to do one good thing, he's branded a communist.

So they kept harder and harder a-pushin' us. One day when Sam was gone, they come with high powers and a machine gun. They come down the back road they was a-guardin'. They was intending to get Sam. So I sent my son and my sister's son down the front road to Bell County to tell the miners not to come, the gun thugs was a-waitin' on them. The thugs didn't get nothing that time.

But then they was back again. Says, "Here we are back." I said. "There's nothing here but a bunch of hungry children." But they come in anyway. They hunted, they looked in suitcases, opened up the stove door, they raised up the mattresses. It was just like Hitler Germany.

Down at that little garage we had, there was a man that worked there, his name was Tuttle. The gun thugs thought he was so dumb he wouldn't listen at nothing, he was all dirty and greasy. Well, Tuttle heared something and come up and told me. Said, "They're going to get you or Harvey"—Harvey was my fourteen-year-old son—"and hold one of you till Sam comes." Well, I couldn't wait for nothing. Harvey was up at Wallens Creek tending to Sam's chickens and Tuttle went up there, told Harvey they was coming to get him. So Harvey come back down to the house. I told him, "Harvey, the thugs is going to get you or me and hold until your Daddy comes. Now," I says, "you go to Mrs. Brock's and tell her if she'll keep you all night till you can get out of here, I'll give her anything in my house, anything. And," I said, "tell her not to let them know you're there."

Well, he went. But he didn't stop at Mrs. Brock's at all. He went right on through the woods. The stooges was always a-watchin' the house and they saw him a-goin'. So Harvey walked eighteen miles through the woods, him fourteen year old. And they followed him along, these stooges did.

The next morning we was a-movin' out of our house, getting out fast. Tuttle was a-helpin' us and he was scared to death. So we come on down to Mrs. Brock's and we couldn't see Harvey nowhere. She said she hadn't seen him at all, he hadn't been there. We figured they got him between our place and Mrs. Brock's.

Well, we went down to Pineville. We called at the hospitals and the jails a-lookin' for Harvey. But we couldn't find him. So we went down to our friends, the Dilbecks. I said, "Has Harvey been here?" He says, "Yes, he come here last night and we put him in the bed. And," he said, "he'd got up and left it was peeping daylight." We went on then, with all our things, and made it to the Tennessee-Kentucky line. There, on the Tennessee side, a-settin' on the fence was Harvey a-waitin' on us.

I was thirty when I wrote "Which Side Are You On?" We couldn't get word out any way. So I just had to do something. It was the night Sam had sneaked in through the cornfields and I was up a-watchin' for the thugs to come after him. That's when I wrote the song. We didn't have any stationery cause we didn't get nothing, we was doing good to live. So I just took the calendar off the wall and wrote that song, "Which Side Are You On?":

WHICH SIDE ARE YOU ON?
By Florence Reece

Come all you poor workers,
Good news to you I'll tell,
How the good old union
Has come in here to dwell.

(Chorus:)
Which side are you on?
Which side are you on?

We're starting our good battle,
We know we're sure to win,
Because we've got the gun thugs
A-lookin' very thin.

(Chorus:)
Which side are you on?
Which side are you on?
If you go to Harlan County,
There is no neutral there,
You'll either be a union man
Or a thug for J. H. Blair.

(Chorus:)
Which side are you on?
Which side are you on?

They say they have to guard us
To educate their child,
Their children live in luxury,
Our children almost wild.

(Chorus:)
Which side are you on?
Which side are you on?

With pistols and with rifles
They take away our bread,
And if you miners hinted it
They'll sock you on the head.

(Chorus:)
Which side are you on?
Which side are you on?

Gentlemen, can you stand it?
Oh, tell me how you can?
Will you be a gun thug
Or will you be a man?

(Chorus:)
Which side are you on?
Which side are you on?

My daddy was a miner,
He's now in the air and sun[1]
He'll be with you fellow workers
Till every battle's won.

(Chorus:)
Which side are you on?
Which side are you on?

The music to the song is an old hymn. I can't remember what was that
hymn, but I've got to look in the songbooks and find out what that was a
tune to.

. . .

Now, I got a song, I like it, a lot of people like it:

We're tearing up an old recipe
Of poverty and war
We don't know why we're hungry
Nor what we're fighting for.

This old recipe is yellow with age
It's been used far too long
People are shuffling to and fro
They know there's something wrong.

If the sun would stand still
Till the people are fed, all wars cease to be
Houses, hospitals, schools, a-built . . .
We must have a new recipe.

Sam says it's better I don't have music with my songs cause then they
can understand every word you're saying. When you're past going out and
organizing, well, then maybe you can sing a song or write a song to help.

Sometimes I can cry, and sometimes I get hurt too bad, tears won't
come. I cry inside. It hurts worse. The ones that don't want the poor to
win, that wants to keep us down in slavery, they'll hire these gun thugs, like
they did over in Harlan County, to beat the workers down. And all in the

---

1. blacklisted and without a job.

world we people wanted was enough to feed and clothe and house our children. We didn't want what the coal operators had at all, just a decent living.

The workers offered all they had. They offered their hands, most of
them offered their prayers, they'd pray . . . well, they'd also drink moon-
shine. But they was good, them coal miners.

FOR DISCUSSION AND WRITING

1. What does Florence Reece mean when she says that child brides do last?

*2. Why were the coal company owners so set against unions that they used violent tactics to stop them?
Why did the miners and their families fight so hard for their rights even though the struggle was fraught
with so much danger?*

*3. Do you agree or disagree with these words of Florence Reece's song: "If you go to Harlan County,
there is no neutral there?" Do you think there were townspeople who said that the struggle was no business of theirs?*

TONY'S STORY
Leslie Marmon Silko

*Acclaimed writer and professor Leslie Marmon Silko grew up in Laguna Pueblo, New Mexico. She is of
Laguna Indian, Mexican, and European-American heritage, but she most identifies with her Laguna
background. Her writing demonstrates knowledge of and respect for Native-American languages and
traditions. In the space of a few pages, "Tony's Story" allows the reader to interpret a life-and-death situation from the viewpoint of Tony, a traditional Laguna Pueblo Indian. The glimpse into Tony's point
of view raises difficult questions about self-defense when confronted with hate and violence.*

ONE

IT HAPPENED ONE SUMMER when the sky was wide and hot and the summer rains did not come; the sheep were thin, and the tumbleweeds turned
brown and died. Leon came back from the army. I saw him standing by
the Ferris wheel across from the people who came to sell melons and chili
on San Lorenzo's Day. He yelled at me, "Hey Tony—over here!" I was

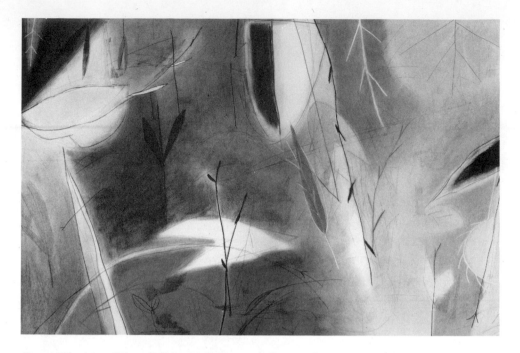

Emmi Whitehorse (Navajo), Rincon Marquez's Renewal, *1986*

embarrassed to hear him yell so loud, but then I saw the wine bottle with the brown-paper sack crushed around it.

"How's it going, buddy?"

He grabbed my hand and held it tight like a white man. He was smiling. "It's good to be home again. They asked me to dance tomorrow—it's only the Corn Dance, but I hope I haven't forgotten what to do."

"You'll remember—it will all come back to you when you hear the drum." I was happy, because I knew that Leon was once more a part of the pueblo. The sun was dusty and low in the west, and the procession passed by us, carrying San Lorenzo back to his niche in the church.

"Do you want to get something to eat?" I asked.

Leon laughed and patted the bottle. "No, you're the only one who needs to eat. Take this dollar—they're selling hamburgers over there." He pointed past the merry-go-round to a stand with cotton candy and a snow-cone machine.

It was then that I saw the cop pushing his way through the crowds of people gathered around the hamburger stand and bingo-game tent; he came steadily toward us. I remembered Leon's wine and looked to see if the cop was watching us; but he was wearing dark glasses and I couldn't see his eyes.

He never said anything before he hit Leon in the face with his fist. Leon collapsed into the dust, and the paper sack floated in the wine and pieces of glass. He didn't move and blood kept bubbling out of his mouth and nose. I could hear a siren. People crowded around Leon and kept pushing me away. The tribal policemen knelt over Leon, and one of them looked up at the state cop and asked what was going on. The big cop didn't answer. He was staring at the little patterns of blood in the dust near Leon's mouth. The dust soaked up the blood almost before it dripped to the ground—it had been a very dry summer. The cop didn't leave until they laid Leon in the back of the paddy wagon.

The moon was already high when we got to the hospital in Albuquerque. We waited a long time outside the emergency room with Leon propped between us. Siow and Gaisthea kept asking me, "What happened, what did Leon say to the cop?" and I told them how we were just standing there, ready to buy hamburgers—we'd never even seen him before. They put stitches around Leon's mouth and gave him a shot; he was lucky, they said—it could've been a broken jaw instead of broken teeth.

TWO

They dropped me off near my house. The moon had moved lower into the west and left the close rows of houses in long shadows. Stillness breathed around me, and I wanted to run from the feeling behind me in the dark; the stories about witches ran with me. That night I had a dream—the big cop was pointing a long bone at me—they always use human bones, and the whiteness flashed silver in the moonlight where he stood. He didn't have a human face—only little, round, white-rimmed eyes on a black ceremonial mask.

Leon was better in a few days. But he was bitter, and all he could talk about was the cop. "I'll kill the big bastard if he comes around here again," Leon kept saying.

With something like the cop it is better to forget, and I tried to make Leon understand. "It's over now. There's nothing you can do."

I wondered why men who came back from the army were troublemakers on the reservation. Leon even took it before the pueblo meeting. They discussed it, and the old men decided that Leon shouldn't have been drinking. The interpreter read a passage out of the revised pueblo law-and-order code about possessing intoxicants on the reservation, so we got up and left.

Then Leon asked me to go with him to Grants to buy a roll of barbed wire for his uncle. On the way we stopped at Cerritos for gas, and I went into the store for some pop. He was inside. I stopped in the doorway and turned around before he saw me, but if he really was what I feared, then he would not need to see me—he already knew we were there. Leon was waiting with the truck engine running almost like he knew what I would say.

"Let's go—the big cop's inside."

Leon gunned it and the pickup skidded back on the highway. He glanced back in the rear-view mirror. "I didn't see his car."

"Hidden," I said.

Leon shook his head. "He can't do it again. We are just as good as them."

The guys who came back always talked like that.

THREE

The sky was hot and empty. The half-grown tumbleweeds were dried-up flat and brown beside the highway, and across the valley heat shimmered above wilted fields of corn. Even the mountains high beyond the pale sandrock mesas were dusty blue. I was afraid to fall asleep so I kept my eyes on the blue mountains—not letting them close—soaking in the heat; and then I knew why the drought had come that summer.

Leon shook me. "He's behind us—the cop's following us!"

I looked back and saw the red light on top of the car whirling around, and I could make out the dark image of a man, but where the face should have been there were only the silvery lenses of the dark glasses he wore.

"Stop, Leon! He wants us to stop!"

Leon pulled over and stopped on the narrow gravel shoulder.

"What in the hell does he want?" Leon's hands were shaking.

Suddenly the cop was standing beside the truck, gesturing for Leon to roll down his window. He pushed his head inside, grinding the gum in his mouth; the smell of Doublemint was all around us.

"Get out. Both of you."

I stood beside Leon in the dry weeds and tall yellow grass that broke through the asphalt and rattled in the wind. The cop studied Leon's driver's license. I avoided his face—I knew that I couldn't look at his eyes, so I stared at his black half-Wellingtons, with the black uniform cuffs pulled over them; but my eyes kept moving, upward past the black gun belt. My legs were quivering, and I tried to keep my eyes away from his. But it was like the time when I was very little and my parents warned me not to look into the masked dancers' eyes because they would grab me, and my eyes would not stop.

"What's your name?" His voice was high-pitched and it distracted me from the meaning of the words.

I remember Leon said, "He doesn't understand English so good," and finally I said that I was Antonio Sousea, while my eyes strained to look beyond the silver frosted glasses that he wore; but only my distorted face and squinting eyes reflected back.

And then the cop stared at us for a while, silent; finally he laughed and chewed his gum some more slowly. "Where were you going?"

"To Grants." Leon spoke English very clearly. "Can we go now?"

Leon was twisting the key chain around his fingers, and I felt the sun everywhere. Heat swelled up from the asphalt and when cars went by, hot air and motor smell rushed past us.

"I don't like smart guys, Indian. It's because of you bastards that I'm here. They transferred me here because of Indians. They thought there wouldn't be as many for me here. But I find them." He spit his gum into the weeds near my foot and walked back to the patrol car. It kicked up gravel and dust when he left.

We got back in the pickup, and I could taste sweat in my mouth, so I told Leon that we might as well go home since he would be waiting for us up ahead.

"He can't do this," Leon said. "We've got a right to be on this highway."

I couldn't understand why Leon kept talking about "rights," because it wasn't "rights" that he was after, but Leon didn't seem to understand; he couldn't remember the stories that old Teofilo told.

I didn't feel safe until we turned off the highway and I could see the pueblo and my own house. It was noon, and everybody was eating—the village seemed empty—even the dogs had crawled away from the heat. The door was open, but there was only silence, and I was afraid that something had happened to all of them. Then as soon as I opened the screen door the little kids started crying for more Kool-Aid, and my mother said "no," and it was noisy again like always. Grandfather commented that it had been a fast trip to Grants, and I said "yeah" and didn't explain because it would've only worried them.

"Leon goes looking for trouble—I wish you wouldn't hang around with him." My father didn't like trouble. But I knew that the cop was something terrible, and even to speak about it risked bringing it close to all of us; so I didn't say anything.

That afternoon Leon spoke with the Governor, and he promised to send letters to the Bureau of Indian Affairs and to the State Police Chief. Leon seemed satisfied with that. I reached into my pocket for the arrowhead on the piece of string.

"What's that for?"

I held it out to him. "Here, wear it around your neck—like mine. See? Just in case," I said, "for protection."

"You don't believe in *that*, do you?" He pointed to a .30-30 leaning against the wall. "I'll take this with me whenever I'm in the pickup."

"But you can't be sure that it will kill one of them."

Leon looked at me and laughed. "What's the matter," he said, "have they brainwashed you into believing that a .30-30 won't kill a white man?" He handed back the arrowhead. "Here, you wear two of them."

FOUR

Leon's uncle asked me if I wanted to stay at the sheep camp for a while. The lambs were big, and there wouldn't be much for me to do, so I told him I would. We left early, while the sun was still low and red in the sky. The highway was empty, and I sat there beside Leon imagining what it was like before there were highways or even horses. Leon turned off the highway onto the sheep-camp road that climbs around the sandstone mesas until suddenly all the trees are piñons.

Leon glanced in the rear-view mirror. "He's following us!"

My body began to shake and I wasn't sure if I would be able to speak. "There's no place left to hide. It follows us everywhere."

Leon looked at me like he didn't understand what I'd said. Then I looked past Leon and saw that the patrol car had pulled up beside us; the piñon branches were whipping and scraping the side of the truck as it tried to force us off the road. Leon kept driving with the two right wheels in the rut—bumping and scraping the trees. Leon never looked over at it so he couldn't have known how the reflections kept moving across the mirror-lenses of the dark glasses. We were in the narrow canyon with pale sandstone close on either side—the canyon that ended with a spring where willows and grass and tiny blue flowers grow.

"We've got to kill it, Leon. We must burn the body to be sure."

Leon didn't seem to be listening. I kept wishing that old Teofilo could have been there to chant the proper words while we did it. Leon stopped the truck and got out—he still didn't understand what it was. I sat in the pickup with the .30-30 across my lap, and my hands were slippery.

The big cop was standing in front of the pickup, facing Leon. "You made your mistake, Indian. I'm going to beat the shit out of you." He raised the billy club slowly. "I like to beat Indians with this."

He moved toward Leon with the stick raised high, and it was like the long bone in my dream when he pointed it at me—a human bone painted brown to look like wood, to hide what it really was; they'll do that, you know—carve the bone into a spoon and use it around the house until the victim comes within range.

The shot sounded far away and I couldn't remember aiming. But he was motionless on the ground and the bone wand lay near his feet. The tumbleweeds and tall yellow grass were sprayed with glossy, bright blood. He was on his back, and the sand between his legs and along his left side was soaking up the dark, heavy blood—it had not rained for a long time, and even the tumbleweeds were dying.

"Tony! You killed him—you killed the cop!"

"Help me! We'll set the car on fire."

Leon acted strange, and he kept looking at me like he wanted to run. The head wobbled and swung back and forth, and the left hand and the legs left individual trails in the sand. The face was the same. The dark glasses hadn't fallen off and they blinded me with their hot-sun reflections until I pushed the body into the front seat.

The gas tank exploded and the flames spread along the underbelly of the car. The tires filled the wide sky with spirals of thick black smoke.

"My God, Tony. What's wrong with you? That's a state cop you killed." Leon was pale and shaking.

I wiped my hands on my Levis. "Don't worry, everything is O.K. now, Leon. It's killed. They sometimes take on strange forms."

The tumbleweeds around the car caught fire, and little heatwaves shimmered up toward the sky; in the west, rain clouds were gathering.

FOR DISCUSSION AND WRITING

1. Locate Laguna Pueblo Indian Reservation, Albuquerque, and Grants on a map of New Mexico.

2. Trace the change in Tony's attitude toward the cop from the beginning of the story to the end. How do you explain the change?

3. Do you think, as Tony's father suggests, that Leon "goes looking for trouble"?

4. What is your view of Tony's actions at the end of the story? How do you judge his character? Explain.

THIS IS THE LAND
Carlos Cortez

Carlos Cortez is a poet and poster designer of Mexican and German heritage who wrote this poem about the vast Great Plains of the United States. Cortez addresses a vast time period in this poem. He begins the story two thousand generations ago, when, as it is theorized, Asian tribes migrated across the Bering Strait and became the native peoples of the Western Hemisphere. With a few bold strokes, the author raises questions about the values of modern society and the ease with which people forget ancestral civilizations.

"This Is The Land" is written in two of the languages of the Western Hemisphere—English and Spanish. The poem also contains a number of Indian names. The variety of languages adds to the meaning of the poem. For instance, La Raza *expresses pride that is not part of the literal English translation, which is "Latin peoples of the Western Hemisphere."*

O N THE SUN-SWEPT *LLANOS* [1]
Where imperceptible chants of long-dead tribesmen
And imperceptible hoof beats of long-dead buffalo
Are lost on the ears of the speeding motorist
And the barreling semi driver,

The Sun beats down upon the parched grass
And naked rock-croppings
Of the horizon-less eternity of flatlands,

Flatlands of the Dakota, the Arapaho, the Kansa, the Kiowa [2]
And the escaped ante-bellum [3] fugitive slave
And the sod-busting homesteader
And the farmed-out Okies and Arkies
Y los braceros y los alambres y los mojados [4]

---

1. Plains. (Spanish)
2. The Dakota, the Arapaho, the Kansa, the Kiowa, tribes of the Great Plains.
3. Ante-bellum, before the Civil War.
4. Y los braceros y los alambres y los mojados, "and the farm-workers and the wire-cutters and the wetbacks." Braceros are legal immigrants from Mexico to the U.S.A. Alambres and mojados are derogatory terms for illegal border-crossers.

Where millenniums before *la Raza*
Rested on their long trek from the Bering Straits
To Anahuac, Tenochtitlan *y* Mayab[5]
Y dos mil generaciones después[6]
Are returning to their old tramping grounds,

Great endless sea of no water where a silent Jack Rabbit
Can be mistaken for a scrub tree
And where a scrub tree can be mistaken for a prairie dog
By the speeding motorist and barreling truck driver
Out in the distance-less infinity of unbroken sitting-duck sky
Where loneliness can be measured according to how much gas
Is left in the tank and how far it is to the next town

Where Goodyear four-plies rolling over asphalt and concrete
Tamp down the Western Earth that was once tamped down
By herds of buffalo stretching from horizon to horizon
Only to be slaughtered *en masse* by the invader
To starve the original plainsmen into submission
When gatling guns, rotgut whiskey, and typhoid-infected blankets
Were not doing the job fast enough.

And now the invader's grandsons press their speedometers
To get away from all this endlessness
And the Sun makes its exit from the western edge of the sky
When the land becomes an ocean of flame
Burning away into a flat mighty cinder
That emerges with an ashy pale glow
When the pallid flapjack tortilla moon
Comes out to pinch-hit for the Sun
And the flapjack tortilla moon is momentarily eclipsed

---

5. La Raza . . . Anajuac, Tenochtitlan y Mayab. La Raza refers to all Latin peoples of the New World, the first of whom were Asian tribes which migrated into the Western Hemisphere through Alaska. Tenochtitlan (now Mexico City) was the capital of the Aztec Empire in the valley of Anahuac. Mayab was a center of the Mayan culture south of the Aztecs in Mexico.
6. And two thousand generations after (Spanish).

And the flapjack tortilla moon is momentarily eclipsed
By an airliner with its human cargo
Of dozing night-light reading passengers
To whom the Great Plains is something vaguely remembered
From grammar school geography books
As they idly contemplate Disneyland and North Beach[7]

And somewhere
A coyote
Howls.

FOR DISCUSSION AND WRITING

1. Construct a time line of the major events Cortez refers to that took place on the Great Plains. Locate on a map the Bering Strait, the lands of the Okies and the Arkies, Tenochtitlan (now Mexico City), Disneyland, and North Beach.

2. Explain how the broad span of time Cortez covers in this poem affects how you think about the era in which you live.

3. Do you think the use of Spanish in this poem is effective? Explain.

---

7. Disneyland and North Beach, an amusement park near Los Angeles and a nightclub district of San Francisco.

P·E·R·S·O·N·A·L
I·D·E·N·T·I·T·Y

MY DUNGEON SHOOK: LETTER TO MY NEPHEW ON THE ONE HUNDREDTH ANNIVERSARY OF THE EMANCIPATION

James Baldwin

African-American author and humanitarian James Baldwin, who died in 1987, is one of the United States' most beloved and admired twentieth-century writers. Baldwin used the essay as an art form and garnered a reputation as one of the greatest American essayists. In most of his writing Baldwin probed the psychological dimensions of racism, both for the oppressed and the oppressor. He attempted to help destroy the myth of white superiority, arguing that this myth damages all Americans. Baldwin believed in the possibility of changing attitudes within the United States and imbued his writing with his urgency; he felt the United States must change fast or face great social upheaval.

"My Dungeon Shook" is a letter James Baldwin wrote to his fifteen-year-old nephew, James. As James grew into manhood, Baldwin urged him to look squarely at the world with his own eyes, not through the eyes of those who see him as inferior because he is black. Baldwin suggests to his nephew that he, along with other African Americans, has a destiny in healing the United States of the destructive effects of racism.

DEAR JAMES!

I have begun this letter five times and torn it up five times. I keep seeing your face, which is also the face of your father and my brother. Like him, you are tough, dark, vulnerable, moody—with a very definite tendency to sound truculent because you want no one to think you are soft. You may be like your grandfather in this, I don't know, but certainly both you and your father resemble him very much physically. Well, he is dead, he never saw you, and he had a terrible life; he was defeated long before he died because, at the bottom of his heart, he really believed what white people said about him. This is one of the reasons that he became so holy. I am sure that your father has told you something about all that. Neither you nor your father exhibit any tendency towards holiness: you really *are* of another era, part of what happened when the Negro left the land and came into what the late E. Franklin Frazier called "the cities of destruction." You can only be destroyed by believing that you really are what the white world calls a *nigger*. I tell you this because I love you, and please don't you ever forget it.

I have known both of you all your lives, have carried your Daddy in my arms and on my shoulders, kissed and spanked him and watched him learn to walk. I don't know if you've known anybody from that far back; if you've loved anybody that long, first as an infant, then as a child, then as a man, you gain a strange perspective on time and human pain and effort. Other people cannot see what I see whenever I look into your father's face, for behind your father's face as it is today are all those other faces which were his. Let him laugh and I see a cellar your father does not remember and a house he does not remember and I hear in his present laughter his laughter as a child. Let him curse and I remember him falling down the cellar steps, and howling, and I remember, with pain, his tears, which my hand or your grandmother's so easily wiped away. But no one's hand can wipe away those tears he sheds invisibly today, which one hears in his laughter and in his speech and in his songs. I know what the world has done to my brother and how narrowly he has survived it. And I know, which is much worse, and this is the crime of which I accuse my country and my countrymen, and for which neither I nor time nor history will ever forgive them, that they have destroyed and are destroying hundreds of thousands of lives and do not know it and do not want to know it. One can be, indeed one must strive to become, tough and philosophical concerning destruction and death, for this is what most of mankind has been best at since we have heard of man. (But remember: *most* of mankind is not *all* of mankind.) But it is not permissible that the authors of devastation should also be innocent. It is the innocence which constitutes the crime.

Now, my dear namesake, these innocent and well-meaning people, your countrymen, have caused you to be born under conditions not very far removed from those described for us by Charles Dickens in the London of more than a hundred years ago. (I hear the chorus of the innocents screaming, "No! This is not true! How *bitter* you are!"—but I am writing this letter to *you*, to try to tell you something about how to handle *them*, for most of them do not yet really know that you exist. I *know* the conditions under which you were born, for I was there. Your countrymen were *not* there, and haven't made it yet. Your grandmother was also there, and no one has ever accused her of being bitter. I suggest that the innocents check with her. She isn't hard to find. Your countrymen don't know that *she* exists, either, though she has been working for them all their lives.)

Well, you were born, here you came, something like fifteen years ago; and though your father and mother and grandmother, looking about the streets through which they were carrying you, staring at the walls into which they brought you, had every reason to be heavyhearted, yet they

Jacob Lawrence, Harriet Tubman series No. 9: Harriet Tubman dreamt of freedom ("Arise! Flee for your life!"), and in the visions of the night she saw the horsemen coming. Beckoning hands were ever motioning her to come, and she seemed to see a line dividing the land of slavery from the land of freedom. *1939–40*

were not. For here you were, Big James, named for me—you were a big baby, I was not—here you were: to be loved. To be loved, baby, hard, at once, and forever, to strengthen you against the loveless world. Remember that: I know how black it looks today, for you. It looked bad that day, too, yes, we were trembling. We have not stopped trembling yet, but if we had not loved each other none of us would have survived. And now you must survive because we love you, and for the sake of your children and your children's children.

This innocent country set you down in a ghetto in which, in fact, it intended that you should perish. Let me spell out precisely what I mean by that, for the heart of the matter is here, and the root of my dispute with my country. You were born where you were born and faced the future that you faced because you were black and *for no other reason.* The limits of your ambition were, thus, expected to be set forever. You were born into a society which spelled out with brutal clarity, and in as many ways as possible, that you were a worthless human being. You were not expected to aspire to excellence: you were expected to make peace with mediocrity. Wherever you have turned, James, in your short time on this earth, you have been told where you could go and what you could do (and *how* you could do it) and where you could live and whom you could marry. I know your countrymen do not agree with me about this, and I hear them saying, "You exaggerate." They do not know Harlem, and I do. So do you. Take no one's word for anything, including mine—but trust your experience. Know whence you came. If you know whence you came, there is really no limit to where you can go. The details and symbols of your life have been deliberately constructed to make you believe what white people say about you. Please try to remember that what they believe, as well as what they do and cause you to endure, does not testify to your inferiority but to their inhumanity and fear. Please try to be clear, dear James, through the storm which rages about your youthful head today, about the reality which lies behind the words *acceptance* and *integration*. There is no reason for you to try to become like white people and there is no basis whatever for their impertinent assumption that *they* must accept *you*. The really terrible thing, old buddy, is that *you* must accept *them*. And I mean that very seriously. You must accept them and accept them with love. For these innocent people have no other hope. They are, in effect, still trapped in a history which they do not understand; and until they understand it, they cannot be released from it. They have had to believe for many years, and for innumerable reasons, that black men are inferior to white men. Many of them, indeed, know better, but, as you will discover, people find it very difficult to act on what they know. To act is to be committed, and to be committed is to be in danger. In this case, the danger, in the minds of most white Americans, is the loss of their identity. Try to imagine how you would feel if you woke up one morning to find the sun shining and all the stars aflame. You would be frightened because it is out of the order of nature. Any upheaval in the universe is terrifying because it so profoundly attacks one's sense of one's own reality. Well, the black man has functioned in the white man's world as a fixed star, as an immovable pillar: and as he moves out of his place, heaven and earth are shaken to their foundations. You, don't be afraid I said that it was intended that you should perish in the ghetto, perish by never being allowed to go behind the white man's definitions, by never being allowed to spell your proper name. You have, and many of us have, defeated this intention; and, by a terrible law, a terrible paradox, those innocents who believed that your imprisonment made them safe are losing their grasp of reality. But these men are your brothers—your lost, younger brothers. And if the word *integration* means anything, this is what it means: that we, with love, shall force our brothers to see themselves as they are, to cease fleeing from reality and begin to change it. For this is your home, my friend, do not be driven from it; great men have done great things here, and will again, and we can make America what America must become. It will be hard, James, but you come from sturdy, peasant stock, men who picked cotton and dammed rivers and built railroads, and, in the teeth of the most terrifying odds, achieved an unassailable and monumental dignity. You come from a long line of great poets, some of the greatest poets since Homer. One of them said, *The very time I thought I was lost, My dungeon shook and my chains fell off.*

You know, and I know, that the country is celebrating one hundred years of freedom one hundred years too soon. We cannot be free until they are free. God bless you, James, and Godspeed.

Your uncle,

James

FOR DISCUSSION AND WRITING

1. What does Baldwin mean when he says that his country and his countrymen "have destroyed and are destroying hundreds of thousands of lives and do not know it and do not want to know it"?

2. According to Baldwin, how is his nephew as a young African-American male "supposed" to define or identify himself? What kind of aspirations, jobs, and self-image do his countrymen expect him to have? How is information about expected aspirations and roles communicated to people like Baldwin's nephew?

3. How does James Baldwin hope his fifteen-year-old nephew will view himself and his life? Which of Baldwin's comments do you think will most help his nephew form a positive identity?

4. What does Baldwin suggest about the life of young James's father?

5. In the beginning of The Fire Next Time, *which includes the letter to his nephew, James Baldwin writes: "God gave Noah the rainbow sign, No more water, the fire next time!" What do you think was Baldwin's purpose in including these words from a slave song?*

6. Do you ever feel that the expectations that people have of you are limiting? Explain.

ENDING POEM

Rosario Morales
Aurora Levins Morales

"Ending Poem" was written by and contains the voices of two poets—mother and daughter. Puerto Rican author Rosario Morales was raised in New York City and then returned to Puerto Rico to live with her Jewish-American husband. Their daughter Aurora Levins Morales was born and spent her early years in Puerto Rico on a coffee farm. Although the family eventually moved back to the mainland, readers can hear the islands in the Morales' poetry. In "Ending Poem," the poets celebrate the different cultures that have contributed to who they are today.

I AM WHAT I AM.
A child of the Americas.
A light-skinned mestiza of the Caribbean.
A child of many diaspora, born into this continent at a crossroads.
I am Puerto Rican. I am U.S. American.
I am New York Manhattan and the Bronx.
A mountain-born, country-bred, homegrown jíbara child,
up from the shtetl, a California Puerto Rican Jew
A product of the New York ghettos I have never known.
I am an immigrant
and the daughter and granddaughter of immigrants.
We didn't know our forbears' names with a certainty.
They aren't written anywhere.
First names only or mija, negra, ne, honey, sugar, dear

I come from the dirt where the cane was grown.
My people didn't go to dinner parties. They weren't invited.
I am caribeña, island grown.
Spanish is in my flesh, ripples from my tongue, lodges in my hips,
the language of garlic and mangoes.
Boricua. As Boricuas come from the isle of Manhattan.
I am of latinoamerica, rooted in the history of my continent.
I speak from that body. Just brown and pink and full of drums inside.

Sophie Rivera, Woman and Daughter in Subway, *1982*

I am not African.
Africa waters the roots of my tree, but I cannot return.

I am not Taína.
I am a late leaf of that ancient tree,
and my roots reach into the soil of two Americas.
Taíno is in me, but there is no way back.

I am not European, though I have dreamt of those cities.
Each plate is different.
wood, clay, papier mâché, metals basketry, a leaf, a coconut shell
Europe lives in me but I have no home there.

The table has a cloth woven by one, dyed by another,
embroidered by another still.
I am a child of many mothers.
They have kept it all going

All the civilizations erected on their backs.
All the dinner parties given with their labor.

We are new.
They gave us life, kept us going,
brought us to where we are.
Born at a crossroads.
Come, lay that dishcloth down. Eat, dear, eat.

History made us.
We will not eat ourselves up inside anymore.

And we are whole.

FOR DISCUSSION AND WRITING

1. In what sense does the poem show that the speakers are children "of many mothers"?

2. What does one of the speakers mean when she says at the end of the poem, "Come, lay that dishcloth down. Eat, dear, eat"?

3. What is the emotional tone of this poem? Give details from the poem to support your response.

◉ ◉

FREEWAY 280
Lorna Dee Cervantes

Lorna Dee Cervantes is a poet of Mexican descent. She is also the founder and senior editor of Mango Publications. *Born in San Francisco, Cervantes observed the ways freeways changed the local land-scape. In "Freeway 280," Cervantes intertwines her thoughts about nature and personal identity.*

LAS CASITAS[1] NEAR THE GRAY CANNERY,
nestled amid wild abrazos[2] of climbing roses
and man-high red geraniums
are gone now. The freeway conceals it
all beneath a raised scar.

But under the fake windsounds of the open lanes,
in the abandoned lots below, new grasses sprout,
wild mustard remembers, old gardens
come back stronger than they were,

---

1. Little houses.
2. Bear hugs.

trees have been left standing in their yards.
Albaricoqueros, cerezos, nogales . . .[3]

Viejitas[4] come here with paper bags to gather greens.
Espinaca, verdolagas, yerbabuena . . .[5]

I scramble over the wire fence
that would have kept me out.
Once, I wanted out, wanted the rigid lanes
to take me to a place without sun,
without the smell of tomatoes burning
on swing shift in the greasy summer air.

Maybe it's here
en los campos extraños de esta ciudad[6]
where I'll find it, that part of me
mown under
like a corpse
or a loose seed.

FOR DISCUSSION AND WRITING

1. What does the freeway symbolize to the speaker? Which objects and images in the poem does the author contrast with the freeway?

2. How does the speaker compare aspects of herself to aspects of nature?

3. How old do you estimate the speaker to be? Why do you think she may now be re-examining her identity? In what specific ways do you imagine that her life might change?

---

3. Apricot trees, cherry trees, walnut trees.
4. Old women.
5. Spinach, purslane, mint.
6. In the strange fields of this city.

FROM *I KNOW WHY THE CAGED BIRD SINGS*
Maya Angelou

Author and lecturer Maya Angelou is widely considered one of the great voices of contemporary litera-ture. She writes in her five-volume autobiography that she had been a Creole cook, a streetcar conductor, a cocktail waitress, a dancer, and an unwed mother by the time she was in her early twenties. She later became a successful singer, actress, playwright, lecturer, civil rights activist, and author. This selection from the first book of Angelou's autobiography reveals a great deal about the woman she would become. In this chapter, Angelou recollects what happened when her employer tried to force her to change her name. In addition to portraying the working conditions of a young southern girl from a poor black family in the early 1940s, Angelou highlights the importance names have in creating a person's identity.

RECENTLY A WHITE WOMAN FROM TEXAS, who would quickly describe herself as a liberal, asked me about my hometown. When I told her that in Stamps my grandmother had owned the only Negro general mer-chandise store since the turn of the century, she exclaimed, "Why, you were a debutante." Ridiculous and even ludicrous. But Negro girls in small Southern towns, whether poverty-stricken or just munching along on a few of life's necessities, were given as extensive and irrelevant prepa-rations for adulthood as rich white girls shown in magazines. Admittedly the training was not the same. While white girls learned to waltz and sit gracefully with a tea cup balanced on their knees, we were lagging behind, learning the mid-Victorian values with very little money to indulge them. (Come and see Edna Lomax spending the money she made picking cot-ton on five balls of ecru tatting thread. Her fingers are bound to snag the work and she'll have to repeat the stitches time and time again. But she knows that when she buys the thread.)

We were required to embroider and I had trunkfuls of colorful dish-towels, pillowcases, runners and handkerchiefs to my credit. I mastered the art of crocheting and tatting, and there was a lifetime's supply of dain-ty doilies that would never be used in sacheted dresser drawers. It went without saying that all girls could iron and wash but the finer touches around the home, like setting a table with real silver, baking roasts and cooking vegetables without meat, had to be learned elsewhere. Usually at the source of those habits. During my tenth year, a white woman's kitchen became my finishing school.

Mrs. Viola Cullinan was a plump woman who lived in a three-bedroom house somewhere behind the post office. She was singularly unattractive until she smiled, and then the lines around her eyes and mouth which made her look perpetually dirty disappeared, and her face looked like the mask of an impish elf. She usually rested her smile until late afternoon when her women friends dropped in and Miss Glory, the cook, served them cold drinks on the closed-in porch.

The exactness of her house was inhuman. This glass went here and only here. That cup had its place and it was an act of impudent rebellion to place it anywhere else. At twelve o'clock the table was set. At 12:15 Mrs. Cullinan sat down to dinner (whether her husband had arrived or not). At 12:16 Miss Glory brought out the food.

It took me a week to learn the difference between a salad plate, a bread plate and a dessert plate.

Mrs. Cullinan kept up the tradition of her wealthy parents. She was from Virginia. Miss Glory, who was a descendant of slaves that had worked for the Cullinans, told me her history. She had married beneath her (according to Miss Glory). Her husband's family hadn't had their money very long and what they had "didn't 'mount to much."

As ugly as she was, I thought privately, she was lucky to get a husband above or beneath her station. But Miss Glory wouldn't let me say a thing against her mistress. She was very patient with me, however, over the housework. She explained the dishware, silverware and servants' bells.

The large round bowl in which soup was served wasn't a soup bowl, it was a tureen. There were goblets, sherbet glasses, ice-cream glasses, wine glasses, green glass coffee cups with matching saucers, and water glasses. I had a glass to drink from, and it sat with Miss Glory's on a separate shelf from the others. Soup spoons, gravy boat, butter knives, salad forks and carving platter were additions to my vocabulary and in fact almost represented a new language. I was fascinated with the novelty, with the fluttering Mrs. Cullinan and her Alice-in-Wonderland house.

Her husband remains, in my memory, undefined. I lumped him with all the other white men that I had ever seen and tried not to see.

On our way home one evening, Miss Glory told me that Mrs. Cullinan couldn't have children. She said that she was too delicate-boned. It was hard to imagine bones at all under those layers of fat. Miss Glory went on to say that the doctor had taken out all her lady organs. I reasoned that a

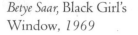

Betye Saar, Black Girl's Window, *1969*

pig's organs included the lungs, heart and liver, so if Mrs. Cullinan was walking around without those essentials, it explained why she drank alcohol out of unmarked bottles. She was keeping herself embalmed.

When I spoke to Bailey about it, he agreed that I was right, but he also informed me that Mr. Cullinan had two daughters by a colored lady and that I knew them very well. He added that the girls were the spitting image of their father. I was unable to remember what he looked like, although I had just left him a few hours before, but I thought of the Coleman girls. They were very light-skinned and certainly didn't look very much like their mother (no one ever mentioned Mr. Coleman).

My pity for Mrs. Cullinan preceded me the next morning like the Cheshire cat's smile. Those girls, who could have been her daughters, were beautiful. They didn't have to straighten their hair. Even when they were caught in the rain, their braids still hung down straight like tamed snakes. Their mouths were pouty little cupid's bows. Mrs. Cullinan didn't know what she missed. Or maybe she did. Poor Mrs. Cullinan.

For weeks after, I arrived early, left late and tried very hard to make up for her barrenness. If she had had her own children. she wouldn't have had to ask me to run a thousand errands from her back door to the back door of her friends. Poor old Mrs. Cullinan.

Then one evening Miss Glory told me to serve the ladies on the porch. After I set the tray down and turned toward the kitchen, one of the women asked, "What's your name, girl?" It was the speckled-faced one. Mrs. Cullinan said, "She doesn't talk much. Her name's Margaret."

"Is she dumb?"

"No. As I understand it, she can talk when she wants to but she's usually quiet as a little mouse. Aren't you, Margaret?"

I smiled at her. Poor thing. No organs and couldn't even pronounce my name correctly.

"She's a sweet little thing, though."

"Well, that may be, but the name's too long. I'd never bother myself. I'd call her Mary if I was you."

I fumed into the kitchen. That horrible woman would never have the chance to call me Mary because if I was starving I'd never work for her. I decided I wouldn't pee on her if her heart was on fire. Giggles drifted in off the porch and into Miss Glory's pots. I wondered what they could be laughing about.

Whitefolks were so strange. Could they be talking about me? Everybody knew that they stuck together better than the Negroes did. It was possible that Mrs. Cullinan had friends in St. Louis who heard about a girl from Stamps being in court and wrote to tell her. Maybe she knew about Mr. Freeman.

My lunch was in my mouth a second time and I went outside and relieved myself on the bed of four-o'clocks. Miss Glory thought I might be coming down with something and told me to go on home, that Momma would give me some herb tea, and she'd explain to her mistress.

I realized how foolish I was being before I reached the pond. Of course Mrs. Cullinan didn't know. Otherwise she wouldn't have given me the two nice dresses that Momma cut down, and she certainly wouldn't have called me a "sweet little thing." My stomach felt fine, and I didn't mention anything to Momma.

That evening I decided to write a poem on being white, fat, old and without children. It was going to be a tragic ballad. I would have to watch her carefully to capture the essence of her loneliness and pain.

The very next day, she called me by the wrong name. Miss Glory and I were washing up the lunch dishes when Mrs. Cullinan came to the doorway. "Mary? "

Miss Glory asked, "Who?"

Mrs. Cullinan, sagging a little, knew and I knew. "I want Mary to go down to Mrs. Randall's and take her some soup. She's not been feeling well for a few days."

Miss Glory's face was a wonder to see. "You mean Margaret, ma'am. Her name's Margaret."

"That's too long. She's Mary from now on. Heat that soup from last night and put it in the china tureen and, Mary, I want you to carry it carefully."

Every person I knew had a hellish horror of being "called out of his name." It was a dangerous practice to call a Negro anything that could be loosely construed as insulting because of the centuries of their having been called niggers, jigs, dinges, blackbirds, crows, boots and spooks.

Miss Glory had a fleeting second of feeling sorry for me. Then as she handed me the hot tureen she said, "Don't mind, don't pay that no mind. Sticks and stones may break your bones, but words . . . You know, I been working for her for twenty years."

She held the back door open for me. "Twenty years. I wasn't much older than you. My name used to be Hallelujah. That's what Ma named me, but my mistress give me 'Glory,' and it stuck. I likes it better too."

I was in the little path that ran behind the houses when Miss Glory shouted, "It's shorter too."

For a few seconds it was a tossup over whether I would laugh (imagine being named Hallelujah) or cry (imagine letting some white woman rename you for her convenience). My anger saved me from either outburst. I had to quit the job, but the problem was going to be how to do it. Momma wouldn't allow me to quit for just any reason.

"She's a peach. That woman is a real peach." Mrs. Randall's maid was talking as she took the soup from me, and I wondered what her name used to be and what she answered to now.

For a week I looked into Mrs. Cullinan's face as she called me Mary. She ignored my coming late and leaving early. Miss Glory was a little annoyed because I had begun to leave egg yolk on the dishes and wasn't putting much heart in polishing the silver. I hoped that she would complain to our boss, but she didn't.

Then Bailey solved my dilemma. He had me describe the contents of the cupboard and the particular plates she liked best. Her favorite piece was a casserole shaped like a fish and the green glass coffee cups. I kept his instructions in mind, so on the next day when Miss Glory was hanging out clothes and I had again been told to serve the old biddies on the porch, I dropped the empty serving tray. When I heard Mrs. Cullinan scream, "Mary!" I picked up the casserole and two of the green glass cups in readiness. As she rounded the kitchen door I let them fall on the tiled floor.

I could never absolutely describe to Bailey what happened next, because each time I got to the part where she fell on the floor and screwed up her ugly face to cry, we burst out laughing. She actually wobbled around on the floor and picked up shards of the cups and cried, "Oh, Momma. Oh, dear Gawd. It's Momma's china from Virginia. Oh, Momma, I sorry."

Miss Glory came running in from the yard and the women from the porch crowded around. Miss Glory was almost as broken up as her mistress. "You mean to say she broke our Virginia dishes? What we gone do?"

Mrs. Cullinan cried louder, "That clumsy nigger. Clumsy little black nigger."

Old speckled-face leaned down and asked, "Who did it, Viola? Was it Mary? Who did it?"

Everything was happening so fast I can't remember whether her action preceded her words, but I know that Mrs. Cullinan said, "Her name's Margaret, goddamn it, her name's Margaret! " And she threw a wedge of the broken plate at me. It could have been the hysteria which put her aim off, but the flying crockery caught Miss Glory right over her ear and she started screaming.

I left the front door wide open so all the neighbors could hear.

Mrs. Cullinan was right about one thing. My name wasn't Mary.

FOR DISCUSSION AND WRITING

1. How does Mrs. Cullinan treat the author? Use the story to support your response.

2. Why do Mrs. Cullinan and her friend want to rename Margaret? Do you think there are other reasons in addition to what is said in the story?

3. What is the difference between Margaret's and Miss Glory's attitude to Mrs. Cullinan and to life in general? Choose passages that most clearly reflect their differences.

4. Why is Margaret's name so important to her? Do you think Margaret reacts appropriately to the attempt to change her name, or do you believe she overreacts? Explain. How do you think you would react in her place?

5. Did you have any choice in choosing your name or nickname? Did you use your "veto" power on any name that someone gave you? Do you have a name in mind that you wish people would call you?

FROM *DONALD DUK*
Frank Chin

Frank Chin is an outspoken Chinese-American writer and editor who challenges Asian Americans to define their unique identities in a country that he believes classifies them as either foreign or "almost" white. One of Chin's major themes is the challenge to slash limiting stereotypes; he often communicates this serious message by using humor. The novel Donald Duk *is about twelve-year-old Donald Duk, a Chinese-American student who lives in San Francisco's Chinatown.*

WHO WOULD BELIEVE ANYONE NAMED DONALD DUK dances like Fred Astaire? Donald Duk does not like his name. Donald Duk never liked his name. He hates his name. He is not a duck. He is not a cartoon character. He does not go home to sleep in Disneyland every night. The kids that laugh at him are very smart. Everyone at his private school is smart. Donald Duk is smart. He is a gifted one, they say.

No one in school knows he takes tap dance lessons from a man who calls himself "The Chinese Fred Astaire." Mom talks Dad into paying for the lessons and tap shoes.

Fred Astaire. Everybody everywhere likes Fred Astaire in the old black-and-white movies. Late at night on TV, even Dad smiles when Fred Astaire dances. Mom hums along. Donald Duk wants to live the late night life in old black-and-white movies and talk with his feet like Fred Astaire, and smile Fred Astaire's sweet lemonade smile.

The music teacher and English teacher in school go dreamy eyed when they talk about seeing Fred Astaire and Ginger Rogers on the late-night

TV. "Remember when he danced with Barbara Stanwyck? What was the name of that movie . . . ?"

"Barbara Stanwyck?"

"Did you see the one where he dances with Rita Hayworth?"

"Oooh, Rita Hayworth!"

Donald Duk enjoys the books he reads in schools. The math is a curious game. He is not the only Chinese in the private school. But he is the only Donald Duk. He avoids the other Chinese here. And the Chinese seem to avoid him. This school is a place where the Chinese are comfortable hating Chinese. "Only the Chinese are stupid enough to give a kid a stupid name like Donald Duk," Donald Duk says to himself. "And if the Chinese were that smart, why didn't they invent tap dancing?"

Donald Duk's father's name is King. King Duk. Donald hates his father's name. He hates being introduced with his father. "This is King Duk, and his son Donald Duk." Mom's name is Daisy. "That's Daisy Duk, and her son Donald." Venus Duk and Penny Duk are Donald's sisters. The girls are twins and a couple of years older than Donald.

His own name is driving him crazy! Looking Chinese is driving him crazy! All his teachers are making a big deal about Chinese stuff in their classes because of Chinese New Year coming on soon. The teacher of California History is so happy to be reading about the Chinese. "The man I studied history under at Berkeley authored this book. He was a spellbinding lecturer," the teacher throbs. Then he reads, "The Chinese in America were made passive and nonassertive by centuries of Confucian thought and Zen mysticism. They were totally unprepared for the violently individualistic and democratic Americans. From their first step on American soil to the middle of the twentieth century, the timid, introverted Chinese have been helpless against the relentless victimization by aggressive, highly competitive Americans.

"One of the Confucian concepts that lends the Chinese vulnerable to the assertive ways of the West is 'the mandate of heaven.' As the European kings of old ruled by divine right, so the emperors of China ruled by the mandate of heaven." The teacher takes a breath and looks over his spellbound class. Donald wants to barf pink and green stuff all over the teacher's book.

"What's he saying?" Donald Duk's pal Arnold Azalea asks in a whisper.

"Same thing as everybody—Chinese are artsy, cutesy and chickendick." Donald whispers back.

Oh, no! Here comes Chinese New Year again! It is Donald Duk's worst time of year. Here come the stupid questions about the funny things Chinese believe in. The funny things Chinese do. The funny things Chinese eat. And, "Where can I buy some Chinese firecrackers?"

And in Chinatown it's *Goong hay fot choy* everywhere. And some gang kids do sell firecrackers. And some gang kids rob other kids looking for firecrackers. He doesn't like the gang kids. He doesn't like speaking their Chinese. He doesn't have to—this is America. He doesn't like China- town. But he lives here.

The gang kids know him. They call him by name. One day the Frog Twins wobble onto the scene with their load of full shopping bags. There is Donald Duk. And there are five gang boys and two girlfriends chewing gum, swearing and smirking. The gang kids wear black tanker jackets, white tee shirts and baggy black denim jeans. It is the alley in front of the Chinese Historical Society Museum. There are fish markets on each side of the Chinatown end of the alley. Lawrence Ferlinghetti's famous City Lights Bookstore is at the end that opens on Columbus Street. Suddenly there are the Frog Twins in their heavy black overcoats. They seem to be wearing all the clothes they own under their coats. Their coats bulge. Under their skirts they wear several pairs of trousers and slacks. They wear one knit cap over the other. They wear scarves tied over their heads and shawls over their shoulders.

That night, after he is asleep, Dad comes home from the restaurant and wakes him up. "You walk like a sad softie," Dad says. "You look like you want everyone to beat you up."

"I do not!" Donald Duk says.

"You look at yourself in the mirror," Dad says, and Donald Duk looks at himself in his full-length dressing mirror. "Look at those slouch- ing shoulders, that pouty face. Look at those hands holding onto each other. You look scared!" Dad's voice booms and Donald hears everyone's feet hit the floor. Mom and the twins are out in the hall looking into his open door.

"I am scared!" Donald Duk says.

"I don't care if you are scared," Dad says. His eyes sizzle into Donald Duk's frightened pie-eyed stare. "Be as scared as you want to be, but don't look scared. Especially when you walk through Chinatown."

"How do I look like I'm not scared if I am scared?" Donald Duk asks.

"You walk with your back straight. You keep your hands out of your pockets. Don't hunch your shoulders. Think of them as being down. Keep your head up. Look like you know where you're going. Walk like you know where you're going. And you say, 'Don't mess with me, horsepuckie!

Don't mess with me!' But you don't say it with your mouth. You say it with your eyes. You say it with your hands where everybody can see them. Anybody get two steps in front of you, you zap them with your eyes, and they had better nod at you or look away. When they nod, you nod. When you walk like nobody better mess with you, nobody will mess with you. When you walk around like you're walking now, all rolled up in a little ball and hiding out from everything, they'll get you for sure."

Donald does not like his dad waking him up like that and yelling at him. But what the old man says works. Outside among the cold San Francisco shadows and the early morning shoppers, Donald Duk hears his father's voice and straightens his back, takes his hands out of his pockets, says "Don't mess with me!" with his eyes and every move of his body. And, yes, he's talking with his body the way Fred Astaire talks, and shoots every gang kid who walks toward him in the eye with a look that says, "Don't mess with me." And no one messes with him. Dad never talks about it again.

Later, gang kids laugh at his name and try to pick fights with him during the afternoon rush hour, Dad's busy time in the kitchen. Donald is smarter than these lowbrow beady-eyed goons. He has to beat them without fighting them because he doesn't know how to fight. Donald Duk gets the twins to talk about it with Dad while they are all at the dining room table working on their model airplanes.

Dad laughs. "So he has a choice. He does not like people laughing at his name. He does not want the gangsters laughing at his name to beat him up. He mostly does not want to look like a sissy in front of them, so what can he do?"

"He can pay them to leave him alone," Venus says.

"He can not! That is so chicken it's disgusting!" Penelope says.

"So, our little brother is doomed."

"He can agree with them and laugh at his name," Dad says. "He can tell them lots of Donald Duk jokes. Maybe he can learn to talk that quack-quack Donald Duck talk."

"Whaaat?" the twins ask in one voice.

"If he keeps them laughing," Dad says, "even if he can just keep them listening, they are not beating him up, right? And they are not calling him a sissy. He does not want to fight? He does not have to fight. He has to use his smarts, okay? If he's smart enough, he makes up some Donald Duck jokes to surprise them and make them laugh. They laugh three times, he can walk away. Leave them there laughing, thinking Donald Duk is one terrific fella."

"So says King Duk," Venus Duk flips. The twins often talk as if everything they hear everybody say and see everybody do is dialog in a memoir they're writing or action in a play they're directing. This makes Mom feel like she's on stage and drives Donald Duk crazy.

"Is that Chinese psychology, dear?" Daisy Duk asks.

"Daisy Duk inquires," says Penelope Duk.

"And little Donnie Duk says, *Oh, Mom!* and sighs."

"I do not!" Donald Duk yelps at the twins.

"Well, then, say it," Penelope Duk says. "It's a good line. So *you* you, you know."

"Thank you," Venus says.

"Oh goshes, you all, your sympathy is so . . . so . . . so literary. So dramatic," Donald Duk says. "It is truly depressing."

"I thought it was narrative," Venus says.

"Listen up for some Chinese psychology, girls and boys," Daisy Duk says.

"No, that's not psychology, that's Bugs Bunny," Dad says.

"You don't mean, Bugs Bunny, dear. You always make that mistake."

"Br'er Rabbit!" Dad says.

"What does that mean?" Donald Duk asks the twins. They shrug their shoulders. Nobody knows what Br'er Rabbit has to do with Dad's way of avoiding a fight and not being a fool, but it works.

One bright and sunny afternoon, a gang boy stops Donald and talks to him in the quacking voice of Walt Disney's Donald Duck. The voice breaks Donald Duk's mind for a flash, and he is afraid to turn on his own Donald Duck voice. He tries telling a joke about Donald Duck not wearing trousers or shoes, when the gangster—in black jeans, black tee shirt, black jacket, black shades—says in a perfect Donald Duck voice, "Let's take the pants off Donald Duk!"

"Oh oh! I stepped in it now!" Donald Duk says in his Donald Duck voice and stuns the gangster and his two gangster friends and their three girlfriends. Everything is seen and understood very fast. Without missing a beat, his own perfect Donald Duck voice cries for help in perfect Cantonese *Gow meng ahhhh!* and they all laugh. Old women pulling little wire shopping carts full of fresh vegetables stop and stare at him. Passing children recognize the voice and say Donald Duck talks Chinese.

"Don't let these monsters take off my pants. I may be Donald Duk, but I am as human as you," he says in Chinese, in his Donald Duck voice, "I know how to use chopsticks. I use flush toilets. Why shouldn't I wear pants on Grant Street in Chinatown?" They all laugh more than three times. Their laughter roars three times on the corner of Grant and Jackson, and Donald Duk walks away, leaving them laughing, just the way Dad says he can. He feels great. Just great!

Donald Duk does not want to laugh about his name forever. There has to be an end to this. There is an end to all kidstuff for a kid. An end to diapers. An end to nursery rhymes and fairy tales. There has to be an end to laughing about his name to get out of a fight. Chinese New Year. Everyone will be laughing. He is twelve years old. Twelve years old is special to the Chinese. There are twelve years in the Asian lunar zodiac. For each year there is an animal. This year Donald will complete his first twelve-year cycle of his life. To celebrate, Donald Duk's father's old opera mentor, Uncle Donald Duk, is coming to San Francisco to perform a Cantonese opera. Donald Duk does not want Chinese New Year. He does not want his uncle Donald Duk to tell him again how Daddy was a terrible man to name his little boy Donald Duk, because all the *bok gwai*, the white monsters, will think he is named after that barebutt cartoon duck in the top half of a sailor suit and no shoes.

FOR DISCUSSION AND WRITING

1. Why does Donald Duk want to "barf" when the teacher lectures about the Chinese in the United States? Why does Donald hate Chinese New Year?

2. Do Donald and his father have a good relationship? Explain. How did Donald Duk get his name? Did his father do Donald a favor with this name?

3. Does Donald fit his teacher's image of the Chinese in the United States? Explain.

4. Do you have a relative, teacher, or friend who, like Donald's father, tries to guide you to become a certain kind of person? If so, do you appreciate this guidance? Explain.

FLYING HOME
Ralph Ellison

Many writers and critics consider Ralph Ellison one of the finest authors the United States has ever produced. At the Tuskegee Institute for African-American college students, Ellison developed a sensitivity to various kinds of literature and music. He read British, Russian, and American novels. He began to appreciate European classical music, and at the same time he loved African-American Blues. In New York City, Ellison deepened his roots in African-American literature when he met authors Richard Wright and Langston Hughes.

Ellison had a strong desire to join in his literature the forms and themes of various time periods or cultures. As Ellison said, "I was taken very early with a passion to link together all I loved within the Negro community and all those things I felt in the world which lay beyond." Just as Ellison felt free to create his own juxtaposition of forms in his writing, the main theme in his writing is the universal human struggle for freedom to define who one is.

The main character in "Flying Home" is an African-American pilot during World War II. At that time, African-American pilots were still denied the right by the United States Army to engage in combat. Ellison combines elements of folktales, realistic storytelling, and symbolism to create a story of a man who struggles to free himself of an identity others want him to take.

WHEN TODD CAME TO, HE SAW TWO FACES SUSPENDED ABOVE HIM in a sun so hot and blinding that he could not tell if they were black or white. He stirred, feeling a pain that burned as though his whole body had been laid open to the sun which glared into his eyes. For a moment an old fear of being touched by white hands seized him. Then the very sharpness of the pain began slowly to clear his head. Sounds came to him dimly. He done come to. Who are they? he thought. Naw he ain't, I coulda sworn he was white. Then he heard clearly:

"You hurt bad?"

Something within him uncoiled. It was a Negro sound.

"He's still out," he heard.

"Give 'im time. . . . Say, son, you hurt bad?"

Was he? There was that awful pain. He lay rigid, hearing their breathing and trying to weave a meaning between them and his being stretched painfully upon the ground. He watched them warily, his mind traveling back over a painful distance. Jagged scenes, swiftly unfolding as in a movie trailer, reeled through his mind, and he saw himself piloting a tail-spinning plane and landing and landing and falling from the cockpit and trying to stand. Then, as in a great silence, he remembered the sound of crunching bone, and now, looking up into the anxious faces of an old Negro man and a boy from where he lay in the same field, the memory sickened him and he wanted to remember no more.

"How you feel, son?"

Todd hesitated, as though to answer would be to admit an inacceptable weakness. Then, "It's my ankle," he said.

"Which one?"

"The left."

With a sense of remoteness he watched the old man bend and remove his boot, feeling the pressure ease.

"That any better?"

"A lot. Thank you."

He had the sensation of discussing someone else, that his concern was with some far more important thing, which for some reason escaped him.

"You done broke it bad," the old man said. "We have to get you to a doctor."

He felt that he had been thrown into a tailspin. He looked at his watch; how long had he been here? He knew there was but one important thing in the world, to get the plane back to the field before his officers were displeased.

"Help me up," he said. "Into the ship."

"But it's broke too bad. . . ."

"Give me your arm!"

"But, son . . ."

Clutching the old man's arm he pulled himself up, keeping his left leg clear, thinking, "I'd never make him understand," as the leather-smooth face came parallel with his own.

"Now, let's see."

He pushed the old man back, hearing a bird's insistent shrill. He swayed giddily. Blackness washed over him, like infinity.

"You best sit down."

"No, I'm OK."

"But, son. You jus' gonna make it worse. . . ."

It was a fact that everything in him cried out to deny, even against the flaming pain in his ankle. He would have to try again.

"You mess with that ankle they have to cut your foot off," he heard.

Holding his breath, he started up again. It pained so badly that he had to bite his lips to keep from crying out and he allowed them to help him down with a pang of despair.

"It's best you take it easy. We gon' git you a doctor."

Of all the luck, he thought. Of all the rotten luck, now I have done it. The fumes of high-octane gasoline clung in the heat, taunting him.

"We kin ride him into town on old Ned," the boy said.

Ned? He turned, seeing the boy point toward an ox team browsing where the buried blade of a plow marked the end of a furrow. Thoughts of himself riding an ox through the town, past streets full of white faces, down the concrete runways of the airfield made swift images of humiliation in his mind. With a pang he remembered his girl's last letter. "Todd," she had written, "I don't need the papers to tell me you had the intelligence to fly. And I have always known you to be as brave as anyone else. The papers annoy me. Don't you be contented to prove over and over again that you're brave or skillful just because you're black, Todd. I think they keep beating that dead horse because they don't want to say why you boys are not yet fighting. I'm really disappointed, Todd. Anyone with brains can learn to fly, but then what? What about using it, and who will you use it for? I wish, dear, you'd write about this. I sometimes think they're playing a trick on us. It's very humiliating. . . ." He wiped cold sweat from his face, thinking, What does she know of humiliation? She's never been down South. Now the humiliation would come. When you must have them judge you, knowing that they never accept your mistakes as your own, but hold it against your whole race—that was humiliation. Yes, and humiliation was when you could never be simply yourself, when you were always a part of this old black ignorant man. Sure, he's all right. Nice and kind and helpful. But he's not you. Well, there's one humiliation I can spare myself.

"No," he said, "I have orders not to leave the ship. . . ."

"Aw," the old man said. Then turning to the boy, "Teddy, then you better hustle down to Mister Graves and get him to come. . . ."

"No, wait!" he protested before he was fully aware. Graves might be white. "Just have him get word to the field, please. They'll take care of the rest."

He saw the boy leave, running.

"How far does he have to go?"

"Might' nigh a mile."

He rested back, looking at the dusty face of his watch. But now they know something has happened, he thought. In the ship there was a perfectly good radio, but it was useless. The old fellow would never operate it. That buzzard knocked me back a hundred years, he thought. Irony danced within him like the gnats circling the old man's head. With all I've learned I'm dependent upon this "peasant's" sense of time and space. His leg throbbed. In the plane, instead of time being measured by the rhythms of pain and a kid's legs, the instruments would have told him at a glance. Twisting upon his elbows he saw where dust had powdered the plane's fuselage, feeling the lump form in his throat that was always there when he thought of flight. It's crouched there, he thought, like the abandoned shell of a locust. I'm naked without it. Not a machine, a suit of clothes you wear. And with a sudden embarrassment and wonder he whispered, "It's the only dignity I have. . . ."

He saw the old man watching, his torn overalls clinging limply to him in the heat. He felt a sharp need to tell the old man what he felt. But that would be meaningless. If I tried to explain why I need to fly back, he'd think I was simply afraid of white officers. But it's more than fear . . . a sense of anguish clung to him like the veil of sweat that hugged his face. He watched the old man, hearing him humming snatches of a tune as he admired the plane. He felt a furtive sense of resentment. Such old men often came to the field to watch the pilots with childish eyes. At first it had made him proud; they had been a meaningful part of a new experience. But soon he realized they did not understand his accomplishments and they came to shame and embarrass him, like the distasteful praise of an idiot. A part of the meaning of flying had gone then, and he had not been able to regain it. If I were a prizefighter I would be more human, he thought. Not a monkey doing tricks, but a man. They were pleased simply that he was a Negro who could fly, and that was not enough. He felt cut off from them by age, by understanding, by sensibility, by technology and by his need to measure himself against the mirror of other men's appreciation. Somehow he felt betrayed, as he had when as a child he grew to discover that his father was dead. Now for him any real appreciation lay with his white officers; and with them he could never be sure. Between ignorant black men and condescending whites, his course of flight seemed mapped by the nature of things away from all needed and natural landmarks. Under some sealed orders, couched in ever more technical and mysterious terms, his path curved swiftly away from both the shame the old man symbolized and the cloudy terrain of white men's regard. Flying blind, he knew but one point of landing and there he would receive his wings. After that the enemy would appreciate his skill and he would assume his deepest meaning, he thought sadly, neither from those who condescended nor from those who praised without understanding, but from the enemy who would recognize his manhood and skill in terms of hate. . . .

He sighed, seeing the oxen making queer, prehistoric shadows against the dry brown earth.

"You just take it easy, son," the old man soothed. "That boy won't take long. Crazy as he is about airplanes."

"I can wait," he said.

"What kinda airplane you call this here'n?"

"An Advanced Trainer," he said, seeing the old man smile. His fingers were like gnarled dark wood against the metal as he touched the low-slung wing.

"'Bout how fast can she fly?"

"Over two hundred an hour."

"Lawd! That's so fast I bet it don't seem like you moving!"

Holding himself rigid, Todd opened his flying suit. The shade had gone and he lay in a ball of fire.

"You mind if I take a look inside? I was always curious to see. . . ."

"Help yourself. Just don't touch anything."

He heard him climb upon the metal wing, grunting. Now the questions would start. Well, so you don't have to think to answer. . . .

He saw the old man looking over into the cockpit, his eyes bright as a child's.

"You must have to know a lot to work all these here things."

He was silent, seeing him step down and kneel beside him.

"Son, how come you want to fly way up there in the air?"

Because it's the most meaningful act in the world . . . because it makes me less like you, he thought.

But he said: "Because I like it, I guess. It's as good a way to fight and die as I know."

"Yeah? I guess you right," the old man said. "But how long you think before they gonna let you all fight?"

He tensed. This was the question all Negroes asked, put with the same timid hopefulness and longing that always opened a greater void within him than that he had felt beneath the plane the first time he had flown. He felt light-headed. It came to him suddenly that there was something sinister about the conversation, that he was flying unwillingly into unsafe and uncharted regions. If he could only be insulting and tell this old man who was trying to help him to shut up!

"I bet you one thing . . ."

African-American Pilots in Italy during World War II

"Yes ?"

"That you was plenty scared coming down."

He did not answer. Like a dog on a trail the old man seemed to smell out his fears and he felt anger bubble within him.

"You sho' scared me. When I seen you coming down in that thing with it a-rollin' and a-jumpin' like a pitchin' hoss, I thought sho' you was a goner. I almost had me a stroke!"

He saw the old man grinning, "Ever'thin's been happening round here this morning, come to think of it."

"Like what?" he asked.

"Well, first thing I know, here come two white fellers looking for Mister Rudolph, that's Mister Graves's cousin. That got me worked up right away...."

"Why ?"

"Why? 'Cause he done broke outta the crazy house, that's why. He liable to kill somebody," he said. "They oughta have him by now though. Then here you come. First I think it's one of them white boys. Then doggone if you don't fall outta there. Lawd, I'd done heard about you boys but I haven't never seen one o' you-all. Cain't tell you how it felt to see somebody what look like me in a airplane!"

The old man talked on, the sound streaming around Todd's thoughts like air flowing over the fuselage of a flying plane. You were a fool, he thought, remembering how before the spin the sun had blazed bright against the billboard signs beyond the town, and how a boy's blue kite had bloomed beneath him, tugging gently in the wind like a strange, odd-shaped flower. He had once flown such kites himself and tried to find the boy at the end of the invisible cord. But he had been flying too high and too fast. He had climbed steeply away in exultation. Too steeply, he thought. And one of the first rules you learn is that if the angle of thrust is too steep the plane goes into a spin. And then, instead of pulling out of it and going into a dive you let a buzzard panic you. A lousy buzzard !

"Son, what made all that blood on the glass?"

"A buzzard," he said, remembering how the blood and feathers had sprayed back against the hatch. It had been as though he had flown into a storm of blood and blackness.

"Well, I declare! They's lots of 'em around here. They after dead things. Don't eat nothing what's alive."

"A little bit more and he would have made a meal out of me," Todd said grimly.

"They bad luck all right. Teddy's got a name for 'em, calls 'em jimcrows," the old man laughed.

"It's a damned good name."

"They the damnedest birds. Once I seen a hoss all stretched out like he was sick, you know. So I hollers, 'Gid up from there, suh!' Just to make sho! An' doggone, son, if I don't see two ole jimcrows come flying right up outa that hoss's insides! Yessuh! The sun was shinin' on 'em and they couldn't a been no greasier if they'd been eating barbecue."

Todd thought he would vomit, his stomach quivered.

"You made that up," he said.

"Nawsuh! Saw him just like I see you."

"Well, I'm glad it was you."

"You see lots a funny things down here, son."

"No, I'll let you see them," he said.

"By the way, the white folks round here don't like to see you boys up there in the sky. They ever bother you?"

"No."

"Well, they'd like to."

"Someone always wants to bother someone else," Todd said. "How do you know?"

"I just know."

"Well," he said defensively, "no one has bothered us."

Blood pounded in his ears as he looked away into space. He tensed, seeing a black spot in the sky, and strained to confirm what he could not clearly see.

"What does that look like to you?" he asked excitedly.

"Just another bad luck, son."

Then he saw the movement of wings with disappointment. It was gliding smoothly down, wings outspread, tail feathers gripping the air, down swiftly—gone behind the green screen of trees. It was like a bird he had imagined there, only the sloping branches of the pines remained, sharp against the pale stretch of sky. He lay barely breathing and stared at the point where it had disappeared, caught in a spell of loathing and admiration. Why did they make them so disgusting and yet teach them to fly so well? It's like when I was up in heaven, he heard, starting.

The old man was chuckling, rubbing his stubbled chin.

"What did you say?"

"Sho', I died and went to heaven . . . maybe by time I tell you about it they be done come after you."

"I hope so," he said wearily.

"You boys ever sit around and swap lies?"

"Not often. Is this going to be one?"

"Well, I ain't so sho', on account of it took place when I was dead."

The old man paused, "That wasn't no lie 'bout the buzzards, though."

"All right," he said.

"Sho' you want to hear 'bout heaven?"

"Please," he answered, resting his head upon his arm.

"Well, I went to heaven and right away started to sproutin' me some wings. Six good ones, they was. Just like them the white angels had. I couldn't hardly believe it. I was so glad that I went off on some clouds by myself and tried 'em out. You know, 'cause I didn't want to make a fool outta myself the first thing. . . ."

It's an old tale, Todd thought. Told me years ago. Had forgotten. But at least it will keep him from talking about buzzards.

He closed his eyes, listening.

". . . First thing I done was to git up on a low cloud and jump off. And doggone, boy, if them wings didn't work! First I tried the right; then I tried the left; then I tried 'em both together. Then Lawd, I started to move on out among the folks. I let 'em see me. . . ."

He saw the old man gesturing flight with his arms, his face full of mock pride as he indicated an imaginary crowd, thinking, It'll be in the newspapers, as he heard, ". . . so I went and found me some colored angels—somehow I didn't believe I was an angel till I seen a real black one, ha, yes! Then I was sho'—but they tole me I better come down 'cause us colored folks had to wear a special kin' a harness when we flew. That was how come they wasn't flyin'. Oh yes, an' you had to be extra strong for a black man even, to fly with one of them harnesses. . . ."

This is a new turn, Todd thought, what's he driving at?

"So I said to myself, I ain't gonna be bothered with no harness! Oh naw! 'Cause if God let you sprout wings you oughta have sense enough not to let nobody make you wear something what gits in the way of flyin'. So I starts to flyin'. Heck, son," he chuckled, his eyes twinkling, "you know I had to let eve'ybody know that old Jefferson could fly good as anybody else. And I could too, fly smooth as a bird! I could even loop-the-loop—only I had to make sho' to keep my long white robe down roun' my ankles. . . ."

Todd felt uneasy. He wanted to laugh at the joke, but his body refused, as of an independent will. He felt as he had as a child when after he had chewed a sugar-coated pill which his mother had given him, she had laughed at his efforts to remove the terrible taste.

". . . Well," he heard, "I was doing all right 'til I got to speeding. Found out I could fan up a right strong breeze, I could fly so fast. I could do all kin'sa stunts too. I started flying up to the stars and divin' down and zooming roun' the moon. Man, I like to scare the devil outa some ole white angels. I was raisin' hell. Not that I meant any harm, son. But I was just feeling good. It was so good to know I was free at last. I accidentally knocked the tips offa some stars and they tell me I caused a storm and a coupla lynchings down here in Macon County—though I swear I believe them boys what said that was making up lies on me. . . ."

He's mocking me, Todd thought angrily. He thinks it's a joke. Grinning down at me . . . His throat was dry. He looked at his watch; why the hell didn't they come? Since they had to, why? One day I was flying down one of them heavenly streets. You got yourself into it, Todd thought. Like Jonah in the whale.

"Justa throwin' feathers in everybody's face. An' ole Saint Peter called me in. Said, 'Jefferson, tell me two things, what you doin' flyin' without a harness; an' how come you flyin' so fast?' So I tole him I was flyin' without a harness 'cause it got in my way, but I couldn'ta been flyin' so fast, 'cause I wasn't usin' but one wing. Saint Peter said, 'You wasn't flyin' with but one wing?' 'Yessuh,' I says, scared-like. So he says, 'Well, since you got sucha extra fine pair of wings you can leave off yo' harness awhile. But from now on none of that there one-wing flyin', 'cause you gittin' up too damn much speed!'"

And with one mouth full of bad teeth you're making too damned much talk, thought Todd. Why don't I send him after the boy? His body ached from the hard ground and seeking to shift his position he twisted his ankle and hated himself for crying out.

"It gittin' worse?"

"I . . . I twisted it," he groaned.

"Try not to think about it, son. That's what I do."

He bit his lip, fighting pain with counter-pain as the voice resumed its rhythmical droning. Jefferson seemed caught in his own creation.

". . . After all that trouble I just floated roun' heaven in slow motion. But I forgot, like colored folks will do, and got to flyin' with one wing again. This time I was restin' my old broken arm and got to flyin' fast enough to shame the devil. I was comin' so fast, Lawd, I got myself called befo' ole Saint Peter again. He said, 'Jeff, didn't I warn you 'bout that speedin'?' 'Yessuh,' I says, 'but it was an accident.' He looked at me sad-like and shook his head and I knowed I was gone. He said, 'Jeff, you and that speedin' is a danger to the heavenly community. If I was to let you keep on flyin', heaven wouldn't be nothin' but uproar. Jeff, you got to go!' Son, I argued and pleaded with that old white man, but it didn't do a bit of good. They rushed me straight to them pearly gates and gimme a parachute and a map of the state of Alabama . . ."

Todd heard him laughing so that he could hardly speak, making a screen between them upon which his humiliation glowed like fire.

"Maybe you'd better stop awhile," he said, his voice unreal.

"Ain't much more," Jefferson laughed. "When they gimme the parachute ole Saint Peter ask me if I wanted to say a few words before I went. I felt so bad I couldn't hardly look at him, specially with all them white angels standin' around. Then somebody laughed and made me mad. So I tole him, 'Well, you done took my wings. And you puttin' me out. You got charge of things so's I can't do nothin' about it. But you got to admit just this: While I was up here I was the flyinest sonofabitch what ever hit heaven!'"

At the burst of laughter Todd felt such an intense humiliation that only great violence would wash it away. The laughter which shook the old man like a boiling purge set up vibrations of guilt within him which not even the intricate machinery of the plane would have been adequate to transform and he heard himself screaming, "Why do you laugh at me this way?"

He hated himself at that moment, but he had lost control. He saw Jefferson's mouth fall open, "What—?"

"Answer me!"

His blood pounded as though it would surely burst his temples and he tried to reach the old man and fell, screaming, "Can I help it because they won't let us actually fly? Maybe we are a bunch of buzzards feeding on a dead horse, but we can hope to be eagles, can't we? Can't we?"

He fell back, exhausted, his ankle pounding. The saliva was like straw in his mouth. If he had the strength he would strangle this old man. This grinning, gray-headed clown who made him feel as he felt when watched by the white officers at the field. And yet this old man had neither power, prestige, rank nor technique. Nothing that could rid him of this terrible feeling. He watched him, seeing his face struggle to express a turmoil of feeling.

"What you mean, son? What you talking 'bout . . . ?"

"Go away. Go tell your tales to the white folks."

"But I didn't mean nothing like that. . . . I . . . I wasn't tryin' to hurt your feelings. . . ."

"Please. Get the hell away from me!"

"But I didn't, son. I didn't mean all them things a-tall."

Todd shook as with a chill, searching Jefferson's face for a trace of the mockery he had seen there. But now the face was somber and tired and old. He was confused. He could not be sure that there had ever been laughter there, that Jefferson had ever really laughed in his whole life. He saw Jefferson reach out to touch him and shrank away, wondering if anything except the pain, now causing his vision to waver, was real. Perhaps he had imagined it all.

"Don't let it get you down, son," the voice said pensively.

He heard Jefferson sigh wearily, as though he felt more than he could say. His anger ebbed, leaving only the pain.

"I'm sorry," he mumbled.

"You just wore out with pain, was all. . . ."

He saw him through a blur, smiling. And for a second he felt the embarrassed silence of understanding flutter between them.

"What you was doin' flyin' over this section, son? Wasn't you scared they might shoot you for a cow?"

Todd tensed. Was he being laughed at again? But before he could decide, the pain shook him and a part of him was lying calmly behind the screen of pain that had fallen between them, recalling the first time he had ever seen a plane. It was as though an endless series of hangars had been shaken ajar in the air base of his memory and from each, like a young wasp emerging from its cell, arose the memory of a plane.

The first time I ever saw a plane I was very small and planes were new in the world. I was four-and-a-half and the only plane that I had ever seen was a model suspended from the ceiling of the automobile exhibit at the State Fair. But I did not know that it was only a model. I did not know how large a real plane was, nor how expensive. To me it was a fascinating toy, complete in itself, which my mother said could only be owned by rich little white boys. I stood rigid with admiration, my head straining backwards as I watched the gray little plane describing arcs above the gleaming tops of the automobiles. And I vowed that, rich or poor, someday I would own such a toy. My mother had to drag me out of the exhibit and not even the merry-go-round, the Ferris wheel, or the racing horses could hold my attention for the rest of the Fair. I was too busy imitating the tiny drone of the plane with my lips, and imitating with my hands the motion, swift and circling, that it made in flight.

After that I no longer used the pieces of lumber that lay about our back yard to construct wagons and autos . . . now it was used for airplanes. I built biplanes, using pieces of board for wings, a small box for the fuselage, another piece of wood for the rudder. The trip to the Fair had brought something new into my small world. I asked my mother repeatedly when the Fair would come back again. I'd lie in the grass and watch the sky, and each fighting bird became a soaring plane. I would have been good a year just to have seen a plane again. I became a nuisance to everyone with my questions about airplanes. But planes were new to the old folks, too, and there was little that they could tell me. Only my uncle knew some of the answers. And better still, he could carve propellers from pieces of wood that would whirl rapidly in the wind, wobbling noisily upon oiled nails.

I wanted a plane more than I'd wanted anything; more than I wanted the red wagon with rubber tires, more than the train that ran on a track with its train of cars. I asked my mother over and over again:

"Mamma?"

"What do you want, boy?" she'd say.

"Mamma, will you get mad if I ask you?" I'd say.

"What do you want now? I ain't got time to be answering a lot of fool questions. What you want?"

"Mamma, when you gonna get me one . . . ?" I'd ask.

"Get you one what?" she'd say.

"You know, Mamma; what I been asking you. . . ."

"Boy," she'd say, "if you don't want a spanking you better come an' tell me what you talking about so I can get on with my work."

"Aw, Mamma, you know. . . ."

"What I just tell you?" she'd say.

"I mean when you gonna buy me a airplane."

"Airplane! Boy, is you crazy? How many times I have to tell you to stop that foolishness. I done told you them things cost too much. I bet I'm gon' wham the living daylight out of you if you don't quit worrying me 'bout them things!"

But this did not stop me, and a few days later I'd try all over again.

Then one day a strange thing happened. It was spring and for some reason I had been hot and irritable all morning. It was a beautiful spring. I could feel it as I played barefoot in the backyard. Blossoms hung from the thorny black locust trees like clusters of fragrant white grapes. Butterflies flickered in the sunlight above the short new dew-wet grass. I had gone in the house for bread and butter and coming out I heard a steady unfamiliar drone. It was unlike anything I had ever heard before. I tried to place the sound. It was no use. It was a sensation like that I had when searching for my father's watch, heard ticking unseen in a room. It made me feel as though I had forgotten to perform some task that my mother had ordered . . . then I located it, overhead. In the sky, flying quite low and about a hundred yards off was a plane! It came so slowly that it seemed barely to move. My mouth hung wide; my bread and butter fell into the dirt. I wanted to jump up and down and cheer. And when the idea struck I trembled with excitement: "Some little white boy's plane's done flew away and all I got to do is stretch out my hands and it'll be mine!" It was a little plane like that at the Fair, flying no higher than the eaves of our roof. Seeing it come steadily forward I felt the world grow warm with promise. I opened the screen and climbed over it and clung there, waiting. I would catch the plane as it came over and swing down fast and run into the house before anyone could see me. Then no one could come to claim the plane. It droned nearer. Then when it hung like a silver cross in the blue directly above me I stretched out my hand and grabbed. It was like sticking my finger through a soap bubble. The plane flew on, as though I had simply blown my breath after it. I grabbed again, frantically, trying to catch the tail. My fingers clutched the air and disappointment surged tight and hard in my throat. Giving one last desperate grasp, I strained forward. My fingers ripped against the screen. I was falling. The ground burst hard against me. I drummed the earth with my heels and when my breath returned, I lay there bawling.

My mother rushed through the door.

"What's the matter, chile! What on earth is wrong with you?"

"It's gone! It's gone!"

"What gone?"

"The airplane . . ."

"Airplane?"

"Yessum, jus' like the one at the Fair. . . . I . . . I tried to stop it an' it kep' right on going. . . ."

"When, boy?"

"Just now," I cried, through my tears.

"Where it go, boy, what way?"

"Yonder, there . . ."

She scanned the sky, her arms akimbo and her checkered apron flapping in the wind as I pointed to the fading plane. Finally she looked down at me, slowly shaking her head.

"It's gone! It's gone!" I cried.

"Boy, is you a fool?" she said. "Don't you see that there's a real airplane 'stead of one of them toy ones?"

"Real . . . ?" I forgot to cry. "Real?"

"Yass, real. Don't you know that thing you reaching for is bigger'n a auto? You here trying to reach for it and I bet it's flying 'bout two hundred miles higher'n this roof." She was disgusted with me. "You come on in this house before somebody else sees what a fool you done turned out to be. You must think these here lil ole arms of you'n is mighty long. . . ."

I was carried into the house and undressed for bed and the doctor was called. I cried bitterly, as much from the disappointment of finding the plane so far beyond my reach as from the pain.

When the doctor came I heard my mother telling him about the plane and asking if anything was wrong with my mind. He explained that I had had a fever for several hours. But I was kept in bed for a week and I constantly saw the plane in my sleep, flying just beyond my fingertips, sailing so slowly that it seemed barely to move. And each time I'd reach out to grab it I'd miss and through each dream I'd hear my grandma warning:

> Young man, young man,
> Yo' arms too short
> To box with God. . . .

"Hey, son!"

At first he did not know where he was and looked at the old man pointing, with blurred eyes.

"Ain't that one of you-all's airplanes coming after you?"

As his vision cleared he saw a small black shape above a distant field, soaring through waves of heat. But he could not be sure and with the pain he feared that somehow a horrible recurring fantasy of being split in twain by the whirling blades of a propeller had come true.

"You think he sees us?" he heard.

"See? I hope so."

"He's coming like a bat outa hell!"

Straining, he heard the faint sound of a motor and hoped it would soon be over.

"How you feeling?"

"Like a nightmare," he said.

"Hey, he's done curved back the other way!"

"Maybe he saw us," he said. "Maybe he's gone to send out the ambulance and ground crew." And, he thought with despair, maybe he didn't even see us.

"Where did you send the boy?"

"Down to Mister Graves," Jefferson said. "Man what owns this land."

"Do you think he phoned?"

Jefferson looked at him quickly.

"Aw sho'. Dabney Graves is got a bad name on accounta them killings but he'll call though. . . ."

"What killings?"

"Them five fellers . . . ain't you heard?" he asked with surprise.

"No."

"Everybody knows 'bout Dabney Graves, especially the colored. He done killed enough of us."

Todd had the sensation of being caught in a white neighborhood after dark.

"What did they do?" he asked.

"Thought they was men," Jefferson said. "An' some he owed money, like he do me. . . ."

"But why do you stay here?"

"You black, son."

"I know, but . . ."

"You have to come by the white folks, too."

He turned away from Jefferson's eyes, at once consoled and accused.

And I'll have to come by them soon, he thought with despair. Closing his eyes, he heard Jefferson's voice as the sun burned blood-red upon his lips.

"I got nowhere to go," Jefferson said, "an' they'd come after me if I did. But Dabney Graves is a funny fellow. He's all the time making jokes. He can be mean as hell, then he's liable to turn right around and back the colored against the white folks. I seen him do it. But me, I hates him for that more'n anything else. 'Cause just as soon as he gits tired helping a man he don't care what happens to him. He just leaves him stone cold. And then the other white folks is double hard on anybody he done helped. For him it's just a joke. He don't give a hilla beans for nobody—but hisself. . . ."

Todd listened to the thread of detachment in the old man's voice. It was as though he held his words arm's length before him to avoid their destructive meaning.

"He'd just as soon do you a favor and then turn right around and have you strung up. Me, I stays outa his way 'cause down here that's what you gotta do."

If my ankle would only ease for a while, he thought. The closer I spin toward the earth the blacker I become, flashed through his mind. Sweat ran into his eyes and he was sure that he would never see the plane if his head continued whirling. He tried to see Jefferson, what it was that Jefferson held in his hand? It was a little black man, another Jefferson! A little black Jefferson that shook with fits of belly-laughter while the other Jefferson looked on with detachment. Then Jefferson looked up from the thing in his hand and turned to speak, but Todd was far away searching the sky for a plane in a hot dry land on a day and age he had long forgotten. He was going mysteriously with his mother through empty streets where black faces peered from behind drawn shades and someone was rapping at a window and he was looking back to see a hand and a frightened face frantically beckoning from a cracked door and his mother was looking down the empty perspective of the street and shaking her head and hurrying him along and at first it was only a flash he saw and a motor was droning as through the sun-glare he saw it gleaming silver as it circled and he was seeing a burst like a puff of white smoke and hearing his mother yell, Come along, boy, I got no time for them fool airplanes, I got no time, and he saw it a second time, the plane flying high, and the burst appeared suddenly and fell slowly, billowing out and sparkling like fireworks and he was watching and being hurried along as the air filled with a flurry of white pinwheeling cards that caught in the wind and scattered over the rooftops and into the gutters and a woman was running and snatching a card and reading it and screaming and he darted into the shower, grabbing as in winter he grabbed for snowflakes and bounding away at his mother's, Come on here, boy! Come on, I say! and he was watching as she took the card away, seeing her face grow puzzled and turning taut as her voice quavered, "Niggers Stay From the Polls," and died to a moan of terror as he saw the eyeless sockets of a white hood staring at him from the card and above he saw the plane spiraling gracefully, agleam in the sun like a fiery sword. And seeing it soar he was caught, transfixed between a terrible horror and a horrible fascination.

The sun was not so high now, and Jefferson was calling and gradually he saw three figures moving across the curving roll of the field.

"Look like some doctors, all dressed in white," said Jefferson.

They're coming at last, Todd thought. And he felt such a release of tension within him that he thought he would faint. But no sooner did he close his eyes than he was seized and he was struggling with three white men who were forcing his arms into some kind of coat. It was too much for him, his arms were pinned to his sides and as the pain blazed in his eyes, he realized that it was a straitjacket. What filthy joke was this?

"That oughta hold him, Mister Graves," he heard.

His total energies seemed focused in his eyes as he searched their faces. That was Graves; the other two wore hospital uniforms. He was poised between two poles of fear and hate as he heard the one called Graves saying, "He looks kinda purty in that there suit, boys. I'm glad you dropped by."

"This boy ain't crazy, Mister Graves," one of the others said. "He needs a doctor, not us. Don't see how you led us way out here anyway. It might be a joke to you, but your cousin Rudolph liable to kill somebody. White folks or niggers, don't make no difference. . . ."

Todd saw the man turn red with anger. Graves looked down upon him, chuckling.

"This nigguh belongs in a straitjacket, too, boys. I knowed that the minit Jeff's kid said something 'bout a nigguh flyer. You all know you cain't let the nigguh git up that high without his going crazy. The nigguh brain ain't built right for high altitudes. . . ."

Todd watched the drawling red face, feeling that all the unnamed horror and obscenities that he had ever imagined stood materialized before him.

"Let's git outta here," one of the attendants said.

Todd saw the other reach toward him, realizing for the first time that he lay upon a stretcher as he yelled.

"Don't put your hands on me!"

They drew back, surprised.

"What's that you say, nigguh?" asked Graves.

He did not answer and thought that Graves's foot was aimed at his head. It landed on his chest and he could hardly breathe. He coughed helplessly, seeing Graves's lips stretch taut over his yellow teeth, and tried to shift his head. It was as though a half-dead fly was dragging slowly across his face and a bomb seemed to burst within him. Blasts of hot, hysterical laughter tore from his chest, causing his eyes to pop and he felt that the veins in his neck would surely burst. And then a part of him stood behind it all, watching the surprise in Graves's red face and his own hysteria. He thought he would never stop, he would laugh himself to death. It rang in his ears like Jefferson's laughter and he looked for him, centering his eyes desperately upon his face, as though somehow he had become his sole salvation in an insane world of outrage and humiliation. It brought a certain relief. He was suddenly aware that although his body was still contorted it was an echo that no longer rang in his ears. He heard Jefferson's voice with gratitude.

"Mister Graves, the Army done tole him not to leave his airplane."

"Nigguh, Army or no, you gittin' off my land! That airplane can stay 'cause it was paid for by taxpayers' money. But you gittin' off. An' dead or alive, it don't make no difference to me."

Todd was beyond it now, lost in a world of anguish.

"Jeff," Graves said, "you and Teddy come and grab holt. I want you to take this here black eagle over to that nigguh airfield and leave him."

Jefferson and the boy approached him silently. He looked away, realizing and doubting at once that only they could release him from his overpowering sense of isolation.

They bent for the stretcher. One of the attendants moved toward Teddy.

"Think you can manage it, boy?"

"I think I can, suh," Teddy said.

"Well, you better go behind then, and let yo' pa go ahead so's to keep that leg elevated."

He saw the white men walking ahead of Jefferson and the boy carried him along in silence. Then they were pausing and he felt a hand wiping his face; then he was moving again. And it was as though he had been lifted out of his isolation, back into the world of men. A new current of communication flowed between the man and boy and himself. They moved him gently. Far away he heard a mockingbird liquidly calling. He raised his eyes, seeing a buzzard poised unmoving in space. For a moment the whole afternoon seemed suspended and he waited for the horror to seize him again. Then like a song within his head he heard the boy's soft humming and saw the dark bird glide into the sun and glow like a bird of flaming gold.

FOR DISCUSSION AND WRITING

1. How at ease is Todd with himself in the early part of the story? Do you think he has high self-esteem? Use the story to support your response.

2. What does Todd think of the old man (Jefferson) when the story begins? How does Todd feel about his white officers? Use passages from the story to support your response.

3. When in the story do you feel Todd's attitude toward Jefferson begins to change? Why does Todd's attitude change? How would you characterize Jefferson?

4. What discoveries does Todd make about his own past? In the last paragraph of the story, Ellison says of Todd, "And it was as though he had been lifted out of his isolation, back into the world of men." What does this mean? Why does Todd feel this way?

5. Ellison uses symbols and stark images in "Flying Home." Which ones help you understand the main issues in the story?

6. Compare how Todd sees himself at the beginning of the story to how he sees himself at the end of the story.

AUTUMN GARDENING
Siu Wai Anderson

Siu Wai Anderson was born in Hong Kong, China, and was adopted and raised by a European-American family in the United States. Besides working for a major publishing company, she is a book reviewer for an Asian-American newsletter. The principal character of "Autumn Gardening" is Mariko, a hibakusha, *a survivor of the atomic bomb, who shows how even older people can choose new paths in life.*

*I*T WAS A MILD MORNING FOR EARLY NOVEMBER, sunny and cool with only a hint of frost. The heavy rains that had flooded the gutters for the past week were gone now. Patches of mud amid sparse wet spikes of grass made the yard treacherous. Along the cyclone fence clusters of sun-dappled brown and yellow leaves rustled in the light breeze. They drifted to the ground and skittered across the small yard, coming to rest against the splintered white wall of the dilapidated garage. The breeze became a steady wind.

Mariko Abe opened the screen door and shuffled onto her back porch, blinking in the bright sunlight. She moved over to a rusty lawn chair and sat down heavily, gasping from the effort. When she had caught her breath she sniffed the air, enjoying the tangy scent that made her think of dry crackling leaves and wood-burning stoves—the heady smell of autumn in New England.

As she exhaled with a long sigh, a sharper, more pungent smell intruded on her senses. It seemed to come from the laundry snapping on the line strung across her next-door-neighbor's porch. Mariko wrinkled her nose. Whatever kind of detergent that was, it reminded her of the starched uniforms of American soldiers.

As she settled herself in the chair and drew her sweater closer about her shoulders, she glanced at the porch railing and noticed that the paint was peeling badly. Better tell Paul to buy some sandpaper so he could scrape off the old paint before putting on a fresh coat. If he let it go until spring, it would probably never get done.

There never seemed to be enough time to do all the tedious little
upkeep tasks that an old house required. Now that her asthma was worse,
she found it even harder to manage. Paul was a big help, but he had his
own family to mind on the weekends. Sometimes when he did odd jobs
for Mariko he brought the children along, but not often. They were too
wild for her, these *Sansei*. She and Paul had been raised with old-fashioned
Japanese manners, but he seemed to have forgotten his when it came time
to raising his own kids.

These days it was a rare luxury to just sit and think as she was doing
now. Usually she preferred it that way. If she kept busy during the daytime hours she was more likely to sleep soundly at night, instead of tossing and turning with nervous thoughts or waking up screaming from a
nightmare.

The sharp edges of folded paper in her pocket reminded Mariko of the
letter. Slowly she withdrew it and smoothed it out on her lap, staring at
the flowing handwriting until the words blurred and ran together. A sudden gust of wind threatened to pull the letter from her grasp. Her fingers
tightened automatically and she rubbed her thumb across the slightly
rough surface of the paper as she re-read the first page.

Dear Mariko:

*How have you been this fall? I hope you've managed to stay well. I'm doing much bet-
ter since my leukemia went into remission. Here's hoping it stays that way.*

Recently I joined a group of hibakusha *who meet once a month to talk about our problems. It's not as terrible as it sounds! Sometimes we talk about the Bomb, but mostly we think about ways to make people aware of us.*

They want me to speak at the next Hiroshima anniversary event and tell about my life. It's going to be on television. Imagine that!

Mariko smiled and shook her head. Her friend Mitsuye was never one to turn down a chance to be in the spotlight. Mariko had told her many times that she should have been an actress. Mitsuye brought a dramatic flair to everything she did. And her scars were hardly noticeable.

The sound of a distant plane caused Mariko to raise her head and peer nervously at the sky. Scanning the milky blue expanse, she instinctively shielded her eyes from the sun's glare. A black dot appeared in the east. She followed the jet's white trail as it passed overhead, probably heading for the Air Force base twenty miles out of town. Only when the faint whine had completely faded did she sit down again and rub her eyes wearily.

"Stop this nonsense," she scolded herself. "You've been in America for nearly forty years. The war is over. Are you going to jump like a rabbit every time an airplane passes overhead?" For several minutes a painful tightness gripped her chest, then gradually subsided. Slowly her breathing returned to normal and she resumed reading the letter.

The group asked me if I knew of any other hibakusha *who would talk. I thought of you right away. You and I have never talked about what happened to us but I have never forgotten and I know you haven't either. Marichan, will you join me?*

A chill passed through Mariko; she shut her eyes and shivered. The wind had grown stronger, picking up the leaves by the fence and relentlessly spinning them through the air. Fast-moving clouds obscured the sun and cast shadows across the yard. The mild sunny morning was rapidly turning into a gloomy afternoon, but Mariko hardly noticed the sudden change in weather conditions. Her discomfort came from within.

Mitsuye knew her too well. The two women had been friends since childhood. Both had lived on farms in California's San Joaquin Valley back in the thirties. Until they turned thirteen, the two girls were almost inseparable. Then their *Issei* parents had sent the girls back to Hiroshima to get a "good" Japanese education.

The girls ended up in different schools and seldom saw one another. After graduating from high school, Mariko had gone to Tokyo to receive training as a nurse. She moved back to Hiroshima in 1940 when a position opened at Taruya Surgical Clinic. Meanwhile, Mitsuye had married a restaurant owner and settled in the nearby town of Fukuyama. Mariko managed to visit her friend on occasion.

Mariko and Mitsuye were on opposite sides of Hiroshima the day the

Bomb was dropped. Mitsuye had come to do some shopping at Fukuya's less than a mile from the explosion. Miraculously she managed to escape with only a few small burns. Aside from a persistent feeling of tiredness, she seemed to have no obvious problems. It wasn't until thirty years later, after her husband had died of radiation sickness, that she began to suffer symptoms of leukemia.

Mariko had just begun her day at the clinic on the outskirts when the *pika* flashed over downtown, two miles away. Falling debris knocked her to the ground and flying shards of glass left her with several cuts on her face. There was no time to wonder what had happened. She and the few surviving doctors and nurses were soon caught up with taking care of others who had been more badly injured.

Like Mitsuye, she seemed to have survived the Bomb with no serious effects. Then when she was forty-two she began to experience sharp pains in her face. Tiny pieces of glass had worked their way through her skin and had to be picked out. Several facial nerves were damaged by the emerging glass. When they healed, her mouth was stretched to one side, giving it a permanent cynical twist.

Lately her health had taken a turn for the worse. The asthma she'd had since childhood was becoming more severe. She often woke up in the morning gasping for breath. Whether it was in any way related to the Bomb, she could only speculate. Her trips to the doctor were much more frequent these days, and she dared not tell him the full truth. She knew she would lose her medical benefits if it were known she was an A-bomb survivor.

After the war Mariko had returned to the United States. She was unprepared for the all-pervasive hatred of the Japanese in California. Her family had been interned in one of the so-called relocation camps ordered by President Roosevelt to contain all the "traitorous" Japanese American citizens. Her parents and brothers were released in 1944 and sent east to Boston and New York. Mariko joined them shortly after her return from Japan. After her parents died she settled in Boston near her brother Paul and his family.

Mariko never married. She was always aware of the scars on her face and blamed them for making her unattractive. They were also a constant reminder of what she'd been through. Over the years the memories had never faded. When an occasional man did show interest in her, she quickly backed off from getting involved. She was afraid to get too close to anyone, not wishing to burden anyone with her memories and her nightmares. Her only real friend was Mitsuye, whose silent understanding helped Mariko feel she was not totally alone.

Through some cousins in New York Mariko had learned that Mitsuye had also returned from Hiroshima and was living in Queens. They quickly renewed their old friendship, although they seldom talked about their years in Hiroshima. Every two or three months Mariko would visit Mitsuye in New York, or Mitsuye would come up to Boston.

And now Mitsuye was asking her to get up in front of a TV camera and relive the awful events she had spent years trying to forget. She would also risk losing her insurance. Brave, foolish Mitsuye . . . how could she even think of doing such a thing since her bout with leukemia? What purpose would it serve?

With difficulty Mariko got to her feet and put the letter back in her pocket. She pursed her lips as she made her way down the porch steps and towards the garage. Mitsuye was a dear friend but there were limits to what one could do, even for a friend. Tomorrow she would write back and say no.

Today was for chores, raking the leaves and perhaps some weeding. She didn't want to think anymore. As she tugged open the creaking garage door just wide enough to squeeze through, she felt a growing irritation. How could Mitsuye consider speaking about such private things? The guilt for still being alive when so many had died. The horror of crawling half-naked and bloody through rubble that only moments before had been a gleaming modern clinic, the pride and joy of its staff. And all the years since then. She often felt as if she were neither dead nor alive, only an organism living out her allotted timespan because fate had chosen not to take her life that day.

Mariko groped about the dim interior of the garage and put on an old jacket and a pair of gardening gloves. Now where had Paul left the rake last Saturday? She found she was trembling and suddenly anxious to get out of the small dark room. In her haste, she tripped over something and nearly fell. It was the long handle of the rake. Paul must have carelessly tossed it there. Suddenly she was unreasonably angry with him. Didn't he care whether his sister got hurt?

The sudden upwelling of emotion caused Mariko to gasp for breath. She forced herself to calm down and breathe more slowly. It would do no good to have an asthma attack in this miserable shed where no one could hear her or come to her aid. A survivor of something as catastrophic as the atom bomb deserved a more dignified end. She shook free of her self-pity long enough to smile at her own joke. Then she picked up the rake and went outside.

The cool fresh air cleared her head. The wind had died down and scattered its hapless burden of leaves across the wet grass. Mariko began to rake them into a neat pile. The slow mechanical action of swinging the rake helped further to calm her down. For a while, her mind was at ease.

Calmly, she began to reminisce about her years as a nursing student at Tokyo's General Hospital. How she had enjoyed the lively debates she had engaged in with her girlfriends! They cheerfully argued medical ethics in what little spare time they could find between nursing rounds and academic studies. Their favorite topic was what one would call "lifeboat ethics"—making choices in dire circumstances. Playing God— or Buddha, as it were—with their patients' lives.

If you were trapped in a bomb shelter with a very sick child and a feeble old man and you only had enough food and medicine for one of them, whom should you try to save? Was it more important to honor one's elders and preserve a life that was a dying ember, or should one invest in the future and fight to keep alive the newer spark? Whose life was more valuable? Did mere human beings have the right to decide such a thing?

Mariko shook her head ruefully as she recalled the ease with which she and her friends had argued the question, arrogantly confident that they would be able to make such a decision if forced to. None of them ever expected to encounter such a situation in real life. Yet she had, during the nightmarish aftermath of the Bomb. She was haunted by the faces of those she had passed by because their wounds looked far too difficult to deal with.

Mariko stopped raking. She leaned on the handle and bowed her head. Oh, Mitsuye, you are asking too much of me. How could I tell strangers what I did—leaving people to die because I couldn't deal with their awful injuries? She wasn't sure if there were words to describe the stunned lips locked against pain, others contorted in anguish. She had felt overwhelmed and frustrated as a lone nurse working with meager supplies salvaged from the ruins of the hospital. She did what she could to stem a never-ending tide of burns and wounds and dysentery.

The bandages and ointments were depleted within an hour after the Bomb was dropped and still the people came, clutching their torn bleeding faces and carrying dying family members, friends or co-workers on their backs. She had to resort to treating burns with cooking oil, animal fat, and even sliced cucumbers. All through that first night and for the next two days, she and the few surviving nurses and doctors had struggled to ease the pain of those who came begging for help. It was a losing battle.

Paradoxically, some of the victims with the worst injuries eventually recovered, while others who appeared unscathed suddenly died. Making decisions based on conventional medical knowledge became impossible in the face of this strange radiation sickness. Mariko knew she had done her best in the horrifying circumstances, but her feelings of guilt lingered nonetheless.

It had been almost a relief when the last of her improvised bandages and salves had run out and she could no longer even attempt to treat the many victims that still came seeking help. Though it was agonizing to have to abandon people in pain, the burden of choosing who would live and who would die had been lifted from her shoulders.

Exhausted by her round-the-clock nursing and in pain from the cuts on her face, Mariko had finally left the clinic and caught a ride on an army truck to her uncle's house in Tomo Village several miles away. Her cuts became infected and refused to heal for months. She was ashamed to show herself in public. The villagers thought she brought bad luck with her, and avoided her whenever she went out. At last her skin healed enough for her to return to work. As soon as she had saved the money to return to America she left Japan with a sigh of relief.

Mariko was brought back to the present by the loud barking of her neighbor's German Shepherd on the other side of the wire fence. She glanced at her watch—it was nearly two. The dog always barked at the jabbering groups of schoolchildren streaming past on their way home from the bus stop. You could set your clock by that foolish dog's daily howling and pawing at the fence.

She was surprised to see that she had been outside since eleven-thirty. Her bones were beginning to feel the autumn dampness. Winter would be coming soon, but the flowerbeds could use some weeding. She looked forward to spring when she would plant chrysanthemums along the side of the house. They reminded her of her father's garden.

As she put the wire rake in a corner of the garage, making sure that no one would trip over it, she paused to deliberate. Should she start working in the flowerbeds today? The rest of the afternoon stretched before her and she felt a need to fill it with activity. Her friend's letter had unsettled her. She needed time to push aside the ghosts of the past. Something fell from her pocket and fluttered to the floor. Huffing with the effort, Mariko stooped to pick it up. Her hand trembled. Somehow the folded letter had opened up as it fell to the ground. The words "speak for the dead" caught her eye, and she shivered as she straightened up. She read the rest of the letter.

. . . I know I'm asking a lot of you. These things are painful to remember. But we hibakusha *are the only ones who've seen firsthand what the* gembaku *can do to human beings. The world needs to hear from us, but we're getting old. Pretty soon there won't be anyone left who was actually there.*

You and I owe it to all those people who lost their lives. They can't speak for themselves.

I firmly believe that that is why some of us have survived. If we don't speak for the dead, none of it will mean anything to anyone anymore. Does that make sense?

"We can speak for the dead . . ." Mariko had never thought of it in that light before. Was that why her life had been spared? Could she find a purpose to her seemingly empty existence? The letter blurred before her eyes.

I guess you could call this "bearing witness," as the Jewish people did to get through the concentration camps. Oh Mari, I can't tell you how much better I feel to be doing something like this. After all those years of wishing I'd never survived, now I feel I'm doing something worthwhile.

Well, please think about it. Call me when you can, or I'll call you. I miss you. My love to Paul.

Sayonara,

Mitsuye

Mariko slowly squatted in front of her empty flowerbeds and began pulling weeds, her mind turning over her friend's words. She said aloud, "*Kuri kaesa-nai* . . . it should never be repeated." She saw once again the child who had died in her arms, his bewildered eyes asking her how it had come to pass that one minute he was playing in the street, the next he lay dying. The young mother who tried in vain to keep her baby alive by nursing it even as she herself was bleeding to death. And the man whose entire body was one raw burn. There were more faces than she could count. Perhaps with Mitsuye's help, Mariko could pass on their memories.

She folded the letter and put it carefully back into the pocket of her work pants. Her hands in their thick cotton gloves cleared away the weeds with smooth, strong motions, deftly untangling them and tossing them aside. The mid-afternoon sun reappeared and warmed her back as she patted the rich moist soil and prepared it for the flowers that she would plant there next spring.

FOR DISCUSSION AND WRITING

1. How does Mariko's conception of who she is change during the course of the story?

2. What is the meaning of the title?

SOUTH BROOKLYN, 1947
Fran Claro

Fran Claro is a writer and an editor of a teen magazine. In "South Brooklyn, 1947," Claro writes about how her mother disliked her own Italian heritage. This essay explores the paradox many Americans face: the desire to be a certain kind of person may conflict with the desire to maintain one's ethnic identity.

M Y MOTHER'S NAME WAS MARY. Maria Luisa was her given name. It was a beautiful name—it could have been contracted to Marisa—a very fashionable name for girls today.

Instead she chose to call herself *Mary*—good old American *Mary*. I remember my father singing to her:

Mary . . . Mary . . . plain as any name could be . . .

My mother delighted in the song until she heard the lines:

But with pro-pri-e-ty
So-ci-e-ty
Will say Mar-ie.

Then she'd say, "Oh, I hate that 'Marie.' My name is *Mary.*"

When we went to the stores, she'd meet her old classmates. "Hello, Marie," they would say, because this is what the nuns in school used to call her.

When she started elementary school, she spoke only Italian. She was the oldest child in the family, and she would eventually be responsible for overseeing the education—and the Americanization—of five younger brothers and sisters.

Her introduction to formal adult English started when she was about 11. Those were the depression years, and she would translate into Italian for my grandparents all the letters they received from the bank.

Years later, she remembered reading them the letter which told them that their mortgage had been foreclosed.

She escaped from her Italian world by reading. *Rebecca of Sunnybrook Farm* became her favorite book. For long hours—after she finished helping my grandmother with the younger children and the sewing homework— she would sit and read. Her heroines were fair-skinned, blond-haired, blue-eyed. She could not identify with them, but their world intrigued her. She wanted to absorb the culture of these American heroines. Because her parents were not educated, she grew up listening to Italian soap operas and being entertained at street festivals. She rebelled against this gaudy, flashy brand of entertainment. As she grew into adulthood, her childhood dreams of American respectability grew into a determination to separate her children from a culture she had learned to despise.

She would never allow her children to get involved in any of the activities which were dear to her parents' hearts. Their culture, she believed, was not one to pass to a new generation.

I remember the Saints' days, especially the parades and the feasts. Early on a Saturday morning, the band would line up outside the church, and the marchers would assemble.

"Open the window!" I would call to my brother. "Quick, I hear the parade coming!"

My mother would say, "Run, get a pillow for my elbows."

We were safely aloof in our second-floor apartment. So my mother could join us in watching the parade, without feeling that she was taking part in it.

As the band passed, my brother would sing along:

Oh, the monkeys have no tail in Zambawanga,

In Zambawanga . . .

"Ma, look! The girls with the collection trays!"

"Hurry," she'd tell my brother, "get some change. No, not a quarter, a dime."

She'd thrust the money into my hand. "Here. Throw it out the window." I'd toss the coin and yell, "Look, Ma, she got it!"

The girl would look up and smile. She was always a little too fat for the blue rayon dress she wore.

We never watched the parade from the curb. If you were there, you were expected to give a dollar. The maids on the Saint's float would pin the bills to the sash on the statue and give you a holy picture.

My brother and I concentrated on the parade. My mother watched, keeping her distance. She was safe in our little apartment.

The committee came first. These were the men who collected money all year to pay for the affair in honor of St. Lucy—St. Michael—St. Ann—it depended on the province they came from.

They wore red, white, and green sashes and a lapel pin printed with the word COMMITTEE. The median age of the committee members was 65. The parish's Italian-speaking priest walked with them.

The band played. (There were many tubas.) After the band came the float, pulled by the strongest—and, often, the most simple-minded—young men in the neighborhood.

Of course, it wasn't called a float. It was The Saint. Ripe young virgins in cheap party dresses pinned the money on the overpainted statue amid a setting of fake grass and fake flowers. It was a living Woolworth's window, decked out for Mother's Day.

The widows followed The Saint. They were dressed in black, with black rosaries wrapped around their hands. When they caught your eye, they would perform an elaborate sign of the cross, kiss their fingers, raise their eyes, and point the kiss in the direction of The Saint.

In the row of committeemen, I would see my grandfather, his face flushed, sweating, and proud. This was *his* parade. His good grey suit—with the COMMITTEE pin prominently displayed—was used for this one time every year.

Oh, how I wanted to be part of that parade. I wanted to be on that float. I dreamed about pinning bills on The Saint. But my mother was becoming an American.

"That's not for you," she would say. "Even when you're old enough, we're not gonna let you do that."

My father did not interfere. He deferred to her in all decisions about raising us.

My father was the local high school graduate, and he took some pride in being a man of letters. He could be counted on to fill out alien registration forms and to address the tags for the packages everyone sent overseas.

"Mike, you got any boxes?" my mother would ask the grocer. "I'm making a package for Italy. I need a box."

These packages were not "for the relatives," or "for home." They were *for Italy.*

I used to think that a man stood on the dock in Naples and gave all my old clothes to everyone in Italy.

My father worked very hard, but I was never impressed with his civil service job, or even with the time he spent in Korea during World War II. All of it never impressed me the way my grandfather's work did.

My grandfather—and almost all his friends—*dug*. I was never really sure just what they dug, although I knew it had something to do with buildings.

At five o'clock, my brother and I would walk the six blocks to meet him at the subway. His heavy shoes would be caked with mud and plaster. His hands were hard and brittle, like plastic. His complexion was almost Indian red. On the way home from the subway, he would joke with us, half in English, half in Italian.

As soon as we got to his house, we would bring him hot coffee with milk and sugar. We would sit on the window sill in his kitchen, lean out on the fire escape, and see the back of our own apartment.

My grandfather smiled most of the time. He liked to play with us, and he felt proud when we walked with him. We loved being with him.

But what I found charming about him, his daughter—my mother—found embarrassing. It was to please him that she had to attend the feast that followed the parade.

Oh, the feast.

The street from avenue to avenue festooned with curlicues of colored lights and Italian flags. In the middle of the block, a bandstand erected on a level with a second-story window.

The smell of the grease, fried, refried, and refried.

The Saint's dais—a storefront where the statue stood, guarded by members of The Committee.

"Zeppole, calzone, salsiccia forte!" shouted the vendors.

My mother, in her patented stage whisper: "Don't eat from those stands! Look, they're filthy! He just blew his nose! Oh, it's disgusting!"

This was her litany, as she unwillingly soiled herself by dragging us through the crowd on a Saturday night.

"Please, Ma, let us stay a little while," my brother would beg.

"Only until we see your grandfather. So he knows we came."

"Here's a dime," my father would say to my brother. "Go try that game."

"No, you do it, Dad." My brother stepped aside so my father could wind up with the small, soft ball.

My father, the almost ball-player, winding up. For a minute, he forgot he was 27 and the father of two. He was 16, and trying out for the high school team. He made the team, but he never played a game. He had to work after school.

"C'mon, Dad!" my brother cheered.

The man with the greasy black change apron: "Here, Mister. Pick your prize."

"Take the snake on the stick!" my brother said.

The snake was black and silver and white crinkled paper with one rhinestone eye. It twirled around a skinny dowel. We waved it at each other.

"Ma," I said, "I'm hungry."

She hesitated. Then, "All right. When we walk up the street, we'll get a lemon ice. At least it's clean in the pasticceria."

"*Canta, canta Napoli,*" beseeched the voices of the widows, who brought folding chairs to set up under the bandstand. The music followed us up the street.

If we slowed down, my mother tugged at us.

"Don't dirty your dress. Watch out for that hot grease."

"Look," my father said to us, "there's your grandfather."

"Grandpa, Grandpa, look what we won!"

"*E bello,*" he beamed at us. He turned to his friend. "*Luigi, questo mio nepoti.*"

"*Una bella ragazza,*" Luigi said.

"*Maria,*" my grandfather said, "wait. *Zia* Caterina is coming."

"No, Pa. The kids want a lemon ice. Tell her I'll see her next week. Good night, *Cumpari.* Good night, Pa."

On the way up the street, we met the priest. My mother looked as if she might die. She felt naked. She had come to the feast to please her father. Now she had to face the Irish priest.

"Hello, Mary," he smiled.

"Hello, Father. The kids wanted to walk down and see what was going on," she said, blushing. Under the lights, I could see a tear in her eye.

I felt her stiffen and grab my hand. To herself, she was saying:

Good Irish father, forgive me, but my children don't know what they're doing. You can be here because you're not one of us. You can be here because *Cumpari* Sal will put a table and chair from his bar at the curb for you and bring you a free cold beer. You can be an observer. But my kids, they want to listen to the music and eat the food and play the games. And my father, he's proud. He thinks this stinking, filthy display will do honor to a saint.

She continued to blush and smile at the priest.

"Well," he said, moving on to greet others, "I'll see you all at the nine tomorrow."

"Good night, Father," we all said.

The walk up the street to the pasticceria was my mother's Gethsemane.

My father met an old bachelor friend. "Hey, Frankie," my father called, "is Sonny here with you?"

"Yeah. He's over there with *Cump' Angelo.* You and Mary leaving already?"

'Yeah, well, you know—the kids. Tomorrow's church and all." My father was embarrassed.

Cumari Amelia, Frankie's mother, approached my mother. "Maria, you see *Cumpa* Giuan? He's with your father, no?"

Just being talked to here was humiliating for my mother. "They're over there, *Cumari,* by The Saint."

Didn't these people realize that she had to get off this street? She didn't belong here. Her children must not enjoy this!

"Listen," Frankie said, "don't forget stickball tomorrow at 11 on 18th Street. "

"Yeah," my father answered. "I'll be there after we stop up and see Nana. "

"G'night, Mary," Frankie said. "G'night kids."

My mother said, "Good night, *Cumari.*"

'Sta bene, Maria."

Finally, we arrived at the pasticceria. My father bought nickel cups of lemon ice, just for the kids. He and my mother would take only a taste.

The mixture inside the pleated, slightly waxed cup had a snowy-granular-sour-sweet taste. As the ice softened, you squeezed the cup, and the delicious lemony flavor came into the corners of your mouth. It made you lick the corners of your lips.

"Should we stop at your mother's on the way home?" my father asked.

"No, my brother's bringing his girl over tonight. We'll just go home." She sounded very tired.

The lemon ice got softer. If you folded the cup vertically in two and bit down on the waxy cup, the syrup dribbled down your throat.

My brother tried to grab the snake from me.

"C'mon, let me hold it for a while."

"Hey, stop fighting with your sister." My father rolled the snake around the stick and tucked it under his arm.

"Next year," my mother said, "we're not going anywhere near that feast."

The music became vague and distant as we neared home. But I could still hear the voice singing:

Mama . . . Mama . . . solo per te la mia canzone vola . . .

The next morning, my father—the usher—led us to our pew at the nine o'clock Mass. It was a front row seat. My mother sent us to Catholic school so we would be allowed to sit in the front of the church on Sunday. Years earlier, she had been forced to sit in the back, because she went to public school.

She was going to Americanize her children primarily through the church. She wanted her children to become Rosarians, to join the Holy Name Society and the Sodalities.

Her children would never walk the streets soliciting contributions for a saint's feast day. But every Tuesday, they might "help the pastor out with Bingo."

The "fine ladies" of the Rosary Society impressed my mother as being modern, secure, and attractive. She thought the way they let their ice cream melt in their coffee was very stylish. She admired their appearance, so different from her very dark and very Italian beauty.

She admired them without stopping to realize that she was in awe, not of Ladies of the Manor, but of Brooklyn Irish Catholics.

The church did its Americanizing well. By the time I was ready for high school—having lived through the Irish nuns under the direction of an Italian pastor—I had no real identity. I acted like all my Irish classmates, dressed like them, and excelled over most of them in grades.

But no matter what I did, I just didn't *look* like them. All the Peter Pan collars and washing granules in the world could not erase my Italianness.

In college, I started thinking about why my Italianness bothered me. Gradually, I came to realize that it bothered my mother, and not me.

I became interested in the language and the music. I learned a lot that I should have learned years earlier, and I talked to my mother about what I was learning.

My mother—because she revered education—began to listen seriously to what I was talking about. She came to realize that there could be beauty in Italian music and elegance in Italian food.

She learned that there was charm and joy and zest in the enthusiasm my grandfather shared with his friends in planning a feast.

After my brother and I became the adults she wanted us to be, she stepped back and took a long look at us. She realized that without the feasts and the church and the dozens of relatives, we would not have been the same people. After all those years, she was ready to learn about and enjoy her own culture.

She had decided to become an Italian.

1. What does "Americanization" mean to Maria Louisa, the speaker's mother?

To get the other children in her family to be m Americ [handwritten]

2. Why does the author's mother try to be unlike the Italians of the street festivals and even her own father? What does she find attractive about the style of the "fine ladies" of the Rosary Society?

because she wants her children to be Americanized. Ice cream coffee Appearanc [handwritten]

3. Why do you think the speaker had good associations with being Italian?

Because she was Italian. And this was abou what had happened to [handwritten]

4. Have you or any one you know felt like Maria Louisa did about her background? Explain.

No [handwritten]

ELLIS ISLAND
Joseph Bruchac

In "Ellis Island," well-known poet, teacher, and publisher Joseph Bruchac explains how he descended from grandparents of Slovak and Abnaki Indian nationalities. The poem shows how Bruchac's dual heritage encouraged him to see from both perspectives. While in college, Bruchac was active in the civil rights and antiwar movements. He later taught high school in Ghana, West Africa. He says the most important fact he learned is "how human people are everywhere—which may be the one grace that can save us all."

BEYOND THE RED BRICK OF ELLIS ISLAND
where the two Slovak children
who became my grandparents
waited the long days of quarantine,
after leaving the sickness,
the old Empires of Europe,
a Circle Line ship slips easily
on its way to the island
of the tall woman, green
as dreams of forests and meadows
waiting for those who'd worked
a thousand years
yet never owned their own.

Like millions of others,
I too come to this island,
nine decades the answerer
of dreams.

Yet only one part of my blood loves that memory.
Another voice speaks
of native lands
within this nation.
Lands invaded
when the earth became owned.
Lands of those who followed
the changing Moon,
knowledge of the seasons
in their veins.

FOR DISCUSSION AND WRITING

1. *What shows that Bruchac can see from the perspectives of both sets of grandparents?*

2. *How could the author reconcile the two different dreams in his own lifestyle?*

GOING HOME
Maurice Kenny

In this autobiographical poem, Maurice Kenny, a prominent and prolific poet of Mohawk descent, writes about returning to his childhood home. Kenny was born and raised in upper New York State, near the St. Lawrence River, and lived for a time in Brooklyn, New York.

THE BOOK LAY UNREAD IN MY LAP
snow gathered at the window
from Brooklyn it was a long ride
the Greyhound followed the plow
from Syracuse to Watertown

to country cheese and maples
tired rivers and closed paper mills
home to gossipy aunts . . .
their dandelions and pregnant cats . . .
home to cedars and fields of boulders
cold graves under willow and pine
home from Brooklyn to the reservation
that was not home
to songs I could not sing
to dances I could not dance
from Brooklyn bars and ghetto rats
to steaming horses stomping frozen earth
barns and privies lost in blizzards
home to a Nation, Mohawk
to faces, I did not know
and hands which did not recognize me
to names and doors
my father shut

1. Which of Kenny's images are most striking?

2. What might have led to the speaker's choice to return home? In turn, might this choice have affected the speaker's subsequent life?

3. Research the history of the Mohawk Indians. Find out about interactions between Mohawks and European Americans. What are some current issues facing Mohawks?

4. Do you feel that your area of the United States or your city or town suits your personality? If not, where would you want to live? Explain.

*Jeffrey M. Thomas
(Onondaga/Cayuga),
4 Dancers, Niagara Falls,
New York, 1985*

CHOICES
Jimmy Santiago Baca

Jimmy Santiago Baca is an acclaimed poet of Chicano and Apache descent. In the poem "Choices," the speaker's friend decides to leave farming and to take an engineering job at Los Alamos Laboratories in Los Alamos, New Mexico. What makes this decision more important than an ordinary career choice is the fact that the laboratories are involved in atomic weapons testing and production. Nuclear weapons production came to Los Alamos, New Mexico in 1942. The United States government began atomic research at Los Alamos, and the first atomic bombs, including those dropped on Hiroshima and Nagasaki, were produced there. Baca uses images of his beloved New Mexico to express feelings about the choice to be part of the Los Alamos laboratories.

AN ACQUAINTANCE AT LOS ALAMOS LABS
who engineers weapons
black x'd a mark where I live
on his office map.
Star-wars humor. . . .
He exchanged muddy boots
and patched jeans
for a white intern's coat
and black polished shoes.
A month ago, after butchering a gouged bull,
we stood on a pasture hill,
and he wondered with pained features
where money would come from
to finish his shed, plant alfalfa,
and fix his tractor.
Now his fingers
yank horsetail grass,
he crimps herringbone tail-seed
between teeth, and grits out words,
"Om gonna buy another tractor
next week. More land too."

Silence between us is gray water
let down in a tin pail
in a deep, deep well,
a silence
milled in continental grindings
millions of years ago.
I throw my heart
into the well, and it falls
a shimmering pebble to the bottom.
Words are hard
to come by. "Would have lost everything
I've worked for, not takin' the job."

His words try to
retrieve
my heart
from the deep well.
We walk on in silence,
our friendship
rippling away.

FOR DISCUSSION AND WRITING

1. Why does the speaker feel that friendship is "rippling away?"

2. What choices do both people make in the poem?

3. What images does the speaker use to convey the magnitude of the difference between him and his old friend?

4. How would you feel if your friend took an engineering job at Los Alamos? What paths in life could a close friend choose that might jeopardize your friendship? Explain.

5. Are there jobs that you would not take even if your choice resulted in a substantial cut in your standard of living? Explain.

C·E·L·E·B·R·A·T·I·O·N·S

✳ ✳ ✳ ✳ ✳ ✳ ✳ ✳ ✳ ✳ ✳ ✳ ✳ ✳ ✳ ✳

CHUMASH MAN
Georgiana Voloyce Sanchez

Georgiana Valoyce Sanchez is of O'odham and Chumash descent and is a poet and teacher of American Indian literature. She lives in coastal southern California, home of the Chumash Indians, where she was inspired to write this tribute to her heritage.

"SHOO-MASH," he says
and when he says it
I think of ancient sea lion hunts
and salt spray windswept
across my face

They tell him
his people are dead
"Terminated"
　　It's official
　　U.S. rubber-stamped official
　　CHUMASH: Terminated
　　a People who died
　　they say
　　a case for anthropologists

Ah, but this old one
this old one whose face is
ancient prayers come to rest
this old one knows
who he is

"Shoo-mash," he says
and somewhere sea lions still gather
along the California coast

and salt spray
rises
rainbow mist
above the constant breaking
of the waves

FOR DISCUSSION AND WRITING

1. What emotions does this poem evoke in you?

2. Read the poem aloud. Does the sound of the language vary from stanza to stanza? How do the varying rhythms and sounds affect the tone?

* * * * * * * * * * * * * * *

AIN'T THAT BAD? *and*
CALL LETTERS: MRS. V. B.
Maya Angelou

Maya Angelou, one of the United States' most loved and prominent authors, expresses through her writing the art, poetry, and vitality found in many African-American communities across the country. Readers of all cultures may find the positive attitudes expressed in these poems applicable to their own lives.

AIN'T THAT BAD?

DANCIN' THE FUNKY CHICKEN
Eatin' ribs and tips
Diggin' all the latest sounds
And drinkin' gin in sips.

Puttin' down that do-rag
Tightenin' up my 'fro
Wrappin' up in Blackness
Don't I shine and glow?

Hearin' Stevie Wonder
Cookin' beans and rice
Goin' to the opera
Checkin' out Leontyne Price.
Get down, Jesse Jackson
Dance on, Alvin Ailey
Talk, Miss Barbara Jordan
Groove, Miss Pearlie Bailey.

Now ain't they bad?
An' ain't they Black?
An' ain't they Black?
An' ain't they Bad?
An' ain't they bad?
An' ain't they Black?
An' ain't they fine?

Black like the hour of the night
When your love turns and wriggles close to your side
Black as the earth which has given birth
To nations, and when all else is gone will abide.

Bad as the storm that leaps raging from the heavens
Bringing the welcome rain
Bad as the sun burning orange hot at midday
Lifting the waters again.

Arthur Ashe on the tennis court
Muhammad Ali in the ring
André Watts and Andrew Young
Black men doing their thing.

Dressing in purples and pinks and greens
Exotic as rum and Cokes
Living our lives with flash and style
Ain't we colorful folks?

Now ain't we bad?
An' ain't we Black?
An' ain't we Black?

Amos Ferguson, Beeded Hair, *1984*

An' ain't we bad?
An' ain't we bad?
An' ain't we Black?
An' ain't we fine?

CALL LETTERS: MRS. V. B.

SHIPS?
Sure I'll sail them.
Show me the boat,
If it'll float,
I'll sail it.

Men?
Yes I'll love them.
If they've got the style,
To make me smile,
I'll love them.

Life?
'Course I'll live it.
Let me have breath,
Just to my death,
And I'll live it.

Failure?
I'm not ashamed to tell it,
I never learned to spell it.
Not Failure.

FOR DISCUSSION AND WRITING

1. Do you know people like the speaker in the poem? Would you like to know the speaker of the poem? Explain.

2. How would you describe the tone of the poem? What devices does Angelou use to create the tone?

THERESA'S FRIENDS
Robert Creeley

Robert Creeley is an award-winning and influential Irish-American poet. Many of his poems are like mental movies that record a person's thought process. "Theresa's Friends" describes how the author learned that he was Irish. Creeley considers the spoken word an important part of his heritage and often reads his poems aloud to audiences.

FROM THE OUTSET CHARMED
by the soft, quick speech
of those men and women,
Theresa's friends—and the church

she went to, the "other,"
not the white plain Baptist
I tried to learn God in.
Or, later, in Boston the legend

of "being Irish," the lore, the magic,
the violence, the comfortable
or uncomfortable drunkenness.
But most, that endlessly present talking,

as Mr. Connealy's, the ironmonger,
sat so patient in Cronin's Bar,
and told me sad, emotional stories
with the quiet air of an elder

does talk to a younger man.
Then, when at last I was twenty-one,
my mother finally told me
indeed the name *Creeley* was Irish—

and the heavens opened, birds sang,
and the trees and the ladies spoke
with wondrous voices. The power of the glory
of poetry—was at last mine.

FOR DISCUSSION AND WRITING

1. Why was the author so happy when his mother said that he was of Irish heritage? What does being Irish mean to him?

2. Why do you think the poet's mother waited until he was twenty-one to tell him about his heritage? Do you think the author suspected that he was Irish all along? Use the poem to support your response.

3. Research the history of the Irish in the United States. When did Irish immigrants begin to arrive in the United States? Why did they immigrate? What kinds of jobs did they have in the United States?

✳ ✳ ✳ ✳ ✳ ✳ ✳ ✳ ✳ ✳ ✳ ✳ ✳ ✳ ✳ ✳ ✳

FLIPOCHINOS
Cyn. Zarco

Cyn. Zarco was born in Manila in the Philippines and now lives in California. She won the American Book Award in 1986 for her book Cir'cum-nav'i-ga'tion. *Although brief, "Flipochinos" provides a glimpse of the diversity of the Philippine population as well as Zarco's attitude toward her heritage.*

W HEN A BROWN PERSON
  gets together
  with a yellow person
  it is something like
  the mating of a chico[1] and a banana

  the brown meat of the chico
  plus the yellow skin of the banana
  take the seed of the chico for eyes
  peel the banana for sex appeal
  lick the juice from your fingers
  and watch your step

FOR DISCUSSION AND WRITING

1. What qualities of Filipinos does the author suggest in the poem? What is the tone of the poem? What do you think the author means by the last line?

2. Research the history of Filipinos. What is meant by the reference in the poem to the brown and yellow heritage of Filipinos? What languages are spoken in the Philippines?

---

1. Greasewood; a thorny plant with fleshy leaves and dry papery fruit found in the deserts of the American West.

✳ ✳ ✳ ✳ ✳ ✳ ✳ ✳ ✳ ✳ ✳ ✳ ✳ ✳ ✳ ✳

POWWOW 79, DURANGO
Paula Gunn Allen

Paula Gunn Allen is an author and professor of Sioux-Laguna and Lebanese-Jewish heritage who was exposed to five languages in her home as a child. In 1990 Allen was awarded both the Native American Prize for literature and the American Book Award for Spider Woman's Granddaughters: Traditional Tales and Contemporary Writing by Native American Women. *Much of Allen's writing, like "Powwow 79, Durango," acknowledges the value of traditions and encourages readers to examine their own traditions.*

*h*AVEN'T BEEN TO ONE IN ALMOST THREE YEARS
there's six drums and 200 dancers a few
booths piled with jewelry and powwow stuff
some pottery and oven bread
everyone gathers
stands for the grand entry
two flag songs
and the opening prayer by some guy
works for the BIA[1]
who asks our father
to bless our cars
to heal our hearts
to let the music here tonight
make us better, cool
hurts and unease
in his son's name, amen.
my daughter arrives, stoned,

brown face ashy from the weed,
there's no toilet paper
in the ladies room she accuses me
there's never any toilet paper

---

1. Bureau of Indian Affairs, an office of the Federal Government.

in the *ladies* room at a powwow she glares
changes
calms
it's like being home after a long time
are you gonna dance I ask
here's my shawl
not dressed right she says
the new beaded ties I bought her swing
from her long dark braids
why not you have dark blue on I say
look.
we step inside the gym
eyes sweep the rubber floor
jackets, jeans, down-filled vests,
sweatshirts all dark blue.
have to look close to pick out
occasional brown or red on older folks
the dark brown faces rising on the bleachers
the dark hair on almost every head
ever see so many Indians
you're dressed right
we look at the bleachers
quiet like shadows
the people sit watching the floor below
where dancers circle the beating drums
exploding color in the light.

FOR DISCUSSION AND WRITING

1. What are the speaker's feelings about the powwow?

2. What do you think are the daughter's feelings about the powwow? Do they change? Explain.

3. Have you ever been to a powwow? If so, does this poem fit with your impressions of powwows? If not, does this poem change the way you think about powwows? Why or why not?

John Running, Little Shell Pow Wow

* * * * * * * * * * * * * * * * *

DEER WOMAN
Paula Gunn Allen

In the short story "Deer Woman," Paula Gunn Allen uses elements of myth and down-to-earth humor to pay tribute to traditional ways. In addition, the story raises questions about what is real: Are there aspects of reality that are not visible to the modern eye?

TWO YOUNG MEN WERE OUT SNAGGING ONE AFTERNOON. They rode around in their pickup, their Ind'in Cadillac, cruising up this road and down that one through steamy green countryside, stopping by friends' places here and there to lift a few beers. The day was sultry and searing as summer days in Oklahoma get, hot as a sweat lodge.

Long after dark they stopped at a tavern twenty or thirty miles outside of Anadarko, and joined some skins gathered around several tables. After the muggy heat outside, the slowly turning fan inside felt cool. When they'd been there awhile, one of the men at their table asked them if they were headed to the stomp dance. "Sure," they said, though truth to tell, they hadn't known there was a stomp dance that night in the area. The three headed out to the pickup.

They drove for some distance along narrow country roads, turning occasionally at unmarked crossings, bumping across cattle guards, until at length they saw the light of the bonfire, several unshaded lights hanging from small huts that ringed the danceground, and headlights from a couple of parking cars.

They pulled into a spot in the midst of a new Winnebago, a Dodge van, two Toyotas, and a small herd of more battered models, and made their way to the danceground. The dance was going strong, and the sound of turtle shell and aluminum can rattles and singing, mixed with occasional laughter and bits of talk, reached their ears. "All right!" Ray, the taller and heavier of the two exclaimed, slapping his buddy's raised hand in glee. "Gnarly!" his pal Jackie responded, and they grinned at each other in the unsteady light. Slapping the man who'd ridden along with them on the back, the taller one said, "Man, let's go find us some snags!"

They hung out all night, occasionally starting a conversation with one good-looking woman or another, but though the new brother who had accompanied them soon disappeared with a long-legged beauty named Lurine, the two anxious friends didn't score. They were not the sort to feel disheartened, though. They kept up their spirits, dancing well and singing even better. They didn't really care so much about snagging as it gave them something to focus on while they filled the day and night with interesting activity. They were among their own, and they were satisfied with their lives and themselves.

Toward morning, though, Ray spotted two strikingly beautiful young women stepping onto the danceground. Their long hair flowed like black rivers down their backs. They were dressed out in traditional clothes, and something about them—something elusive—made Ray shiver with a feeling almost like recognition, and at the same time, like dread. "Who are they?" he asked his friend, but Jackie shrugged silently. Ray could see his eyes shining for a moment as the fire near them flared suddenly.

At the same moment, they both saw the young women looking at them out of the corners of their eyes as they danced modestly and almost gravely past. Jackie nudged Ray and let out a long, slow sigh. "All right," he said in a low, almost reverent voice. "All right!"

When the dance was ended, the young women made their way to where the two youths were standing, "Hey, dude," one of them said. "My friend and I need a ride to Anadarko, and they told us you were coming from there." As she said that she gestured with her chin over her left shoulder toward a vaguely visible group standing across the danceground.

"What's your friend's name?" Ray countered.

"Linda," the other woman said. "Hers is Junella."

"My friend's name's Jackie," Ray said, grinning, "When do you want to take off?"

"Whenever," Junella answered. She held his eyes with hers. "Where are you parked?"

They made their way to the pickup and got in. It was a tight fit, but nobody seemed to mind. Ray drove, backing the pickup carefully to thread among the haphazardly parked vehicles that had surrounded theirs while they were at the dance. As he did, he glanced down for a second, and thought he saw the feet of both women as deer hooves. Man, he thought. I gotta lay off the weed. He didn't remember he'd quit smoking it months before, and hadn't had a beer since they'd left the tavern hours before. The women tucked their feet under their bags, and in the darkness he didn't see them anymore. Besides, he had more soothing things on his mind.

They drove companionably for some time, joking around telling a bit about themselves, their tastes in music, where they'd gone to school, when they'd graduated. Linda kept fiddling with the dial, reaching across Junella to get to the knob. Her taste seemed to run to hard-core country and western or what Ray privately thought of as "space" music.

She and Linda occasionally lapsed into what seemed like a private conversation, or joke; Ray couldn't be sure which. Then as though remembering themselves, they'd laugh and engage the men in conversation again.

After they'd traveled for an hour or so, Linda suddenly pointed to a road that intersected the one they were on. "Take a left," she said, and Ray complied. He didn't even think about it, or protest that they were on the road to Anadarko already. A few hundred yards further, she said "Take a right." Again he complied, putting the brake on suddenly as he went into the turn, spilling Junella hard against him. He finished shifting quickly and put his arm around her. She leaned into him, saying nothing, and put her hand on his thigh.

The road they had turned onto soon became gravel, and by the time they'd gone less than a quarter of a mile, turned into hard-packed dirt. Ray could smell water, nearby. He saw some trees standing low on the horizon and realized it was coming light.

"Let's go to the water," Linda said. "Junella and I are kind of traditional, and we try to wash in fresh running water every morning."

"Yeah," Junella murmured. "We were raised by our mother's grandmother, and the old lady was real strict about some things. She always made sure we prayed to Long Man every day. Hope it's okay."

Jackie and Ray climbed out of the truck, the women following. They made their way through the thickest of scrub oak and bushes and clambered down the short bank to the stream, the men leading the way. They stopped at the edge of the water, but the young women stepped right in, though still dressed in their dance clothes. They bent and splashed water on their faces, speaking the old tongue softly as they did so. The men removed their tennis shoes and followed suit, removing their caps and tucking them in the hip pockets of their jeans.

After a suitable silence, Junella pointed to the opposite bank with her uplifted chin. "See that path," she asked the men. "I think it goes to our old house. Let's go up there and see."

"Yes," Linda said, "I thought it felt familiar around here. I bet it is our old place." When the women didn't move to cross the shallow river and go up the path, the men took the lead again. Ray briefly wondered at his untypical pliability, but banished the thought almost as it arose. He raised his head just as he reached the far bank and saw that the small trees and brush were backed by a stone bluff that rose steeply above them. As he tilted his head back to spot the top of the bluff, he had a flashing picture of the small round feet he'd thought he'd seen set against the floorboard of the truck. But as the image came into his mind, the sun rose brilliantly just over the bluff, and the thought faded as quickly as it had come, leaving him with a slightly dazed feeling and a tingling that climbed rapidly up his spine. He put on his cap.

Jackie led the way through the thicket, walking as rapidly as the low branches would allow, bending almost double in places. Ray followed him, and the women came after. Shortly, they emerged from the trees onto a rocky area that ran along the foot of the bluff like a narrow path. When he reached it, Jackie stopped and waited while the others caught up. "Do you still think this is the old homestead?" he quipped. The women laughed sharply, then fell into animated conversation in the old language. Neither Ray nor Jackie could talk it, so they stood waiting, admiring the beauty of the morning, feeling the cool dawn air on their cheeks and the water still making their jeans cling to their ankles. At least their feet were dry, and so were the tennies they'd replaced after leaving the river.

After a few animated exchanges, the women started up the path, the men following. "She says it's this way," Linda said over her shoulder. "It can't be far." They trudged along for what seemed a long time, following the line of the bluff that seemed to grow even higher. After a time Junella turned into a narrow break in the rock and began to trudge up its gradual slope, which soon became a steep rise.

"I bet we're not going to Grandma's house," Jackie said in quiet tones to his friend.

"I didn't know this bluff was even here," Ray replied.

"It's not much farther," Junella said cheerfully. "What's the matter? You dudes out of shape or something?"

"Well, I used to say I'd walk a mile for a camel," Jackie said wryly, "but I didn't say anything about snags!" He and Ray laughed, perhaps more heartily than the joke warranted.

"This is the only time I've heard of Little Red Riding Hood leading the wolves to Grandma's," Ray muttered.

"Yah," Linda responded brightly. "And wait'll you see what I'm carrying in my basket of goodies." Both women laughed, the men abashedly joining in.

"Here's the little creek I was looking for," Junella said suddenly. "Let's walk in it for a while." Ray looked at Jackie quizzically.

"I don't want to walk in that," Jackie said quickly. "I just got dry from the last dip." The women were already in the water walking upstream.

"Not to worry," Junella said. "It's not wet; it's the path to the old house."

"Yeah, right," Ray mumbled, stepping into the water with a sigh. Jackie followed him, falling silent. But as they stepped into what they thought was a fast-running stream of water their feet touched down on soft grass. "Hey!" Ray exclaimed. "What's happening?" He stopped abruptly and Jackie plowed into him.

"Watch it, man," the smaller man said. He brushed past Ray and made after the women who were disappearing around a sharp turn.

Ray stood rooted a moment, then hurried after him. "Wait up," he called. His voice echoed loudly against the cliff.

As Ray turned the corner he saw Linda reaching upward along the cliff where a tall rock slab leaned against it. She grasped the edge of the slab and pulled. To the men's astonishment it swung open, for all the world like an ordinary door. The women stepped through.

Ray and Jackie regarded each other for long moments. Finally, Ray shrugged and Jackie gestured with his outspread arm at the opening in the cliff. They followed the women inside.

Within, they were greeted with an astonishing scene. Scores of people, perhaps upward of two hundred, stood or walked about a green land.

Frank LaPena (Wintu, Sacramento), Big Head Spirit, *1987*

Houses stood scattered in the near distance, and smoke arose from a few chimneys. There were tables spread under some large trees, sycamore or elm, Ray thought, and upon them, food in large quantities and tantalizing variety beckoned to the men. Suddenly aware they hadn't eaten since early the day before, they started forward. But before they'd taken more than a few steps Linda and Junella took their arms and led them away from the feast toward the doorway of one of the houses. There sat a man who seemed ancient to the young men. His age wasn't so much in his hair, though it hung in waist-long white strands.

It wasn't even so much in his skin, wrinkled and weathered though it was beneath the tall crowned hat he wore. It was just that he seemed to be age personified. He seemed to be older than the bluff, than the river, than even the sky.

Next to him lay two large mastiffs, their long, lean bodies relaxed, their heads raised, their eyes alert and full of intelligence. "So," the old one said to the women, "I see you've snagged two strong young men." He shot a half-amused glance at the young men's direction. "Go, get ready," he directed the women, and at his words they slipped into the house, closing the door softly behind themselves.

The young men stood uneasily beside the old man who, disregarding them completely, seemed lost in his own thoughts as he gazed steadily at some point directly before him.

After maybe half an hour had passed, the old man addressed the young men again. "It's a good thing you did," he mused "following my nieces here. I wonder that you didn't give up or get lost along the way." He chuckled quietly as at a private joke. "Maybe you two are intelligent men." He turned his head suddenly and gave them an appraising look. Each of the young men shifted under that knowing gaze uncomfortably. From somewhere, the ground, the sky, they didn't feel sure, they heard thunder rumbling. "I have told everybody that they did well for themselves by bringing you here."

Seeing the surprised look on their faces, he smiled. "Yes, you didn't hear me, I know. I guess we talk different here than you're used to where you come from. Maybe you'll be here long enough to get used to it," he added. "That is, if you like my nieces well enough. We'll feed you soon," he said. "But first there are some games I want you to join in." He pointed with pursed lips in the direction of a low hill that rose just beyond the farthest dwelling. Again the thunder rumbled, louder than before.

A moment later the women appeared. Their long, flowing hair was gone, and their heads shone in the soft light that filled the area, allowing distant features to recede into its haze. The women wore soft clothing that completely covered their bodies, even their hands and feet. It seemed to be of a bright, gleaming cloth that reflected the light at the same intensity as their bald heads. Their dark eyes seemed huge and luminous against skin that somehow gave off a soft radiance. Seeing them, both men were nearly overcome with fear. They have no hair at all, Ray thought. Where is this place? He glanced over at Jackie, whose face mirrored his own unease. Jackie shook his head almost imperceptibly, slowly moving it from side to side in a gesture that seemed mournful, and at the same time, oddly resigned.

Linda and Junella moved to the young men, each taking the hand of one and drawing him toward the central area nearby. In a daze Ray and Jackie allowed themselves to be led into the center of the area ringed by heavily laden tables, barely aware that the old man had risen from his place and with his dogs was following behind them. They were joined by a number of other young men, all wearing caps like the ones Ray and Jackie wore. Two of the men carried bats, several wore gloves, and one was tossing a baseball in the air as he walked. Slowly the throng made their way past the tables and came to an open area where Jackie and Ray saw familiar shapes. They were bases, and the field that the soft light revealed to them was a baseball diamond.

The old man took his place behind first base, and one of the young men crouched before him as a loud peal of thunder crashed around them. "Play ball!" the old man shouted, and the men took up their places as the women retired to some benches at the edge of the field behind home plate where they sat.

The bewildered young men found their positions and the game was on. It was a hard-played game, lasting some time. At length, it reached a rowdy end, the team Jackie and Ray were on barely edging out the opposition in spite of a couple of questionable calls the old man made against them. Their victory was due in no small measure to a wiry young man's superb pitching. He'd pitched two no-hit innings and that had won them the game.

As they walked with the other players back toward the houses the old man came up to them. Slapping each on the back a couple of times, he told them he thought they were good players. "Maybe that means you'll be ready for tomorrow's games," he said, watching Jackie sharply. "They're not what you're used to, I imagine, but you'll do all right."

They reached the tables and were helped to several large portions of food by people whose faces never seemed to come quite into focus but whose goodwill seemed unquestionable. They ate amid much laughter and good-natured joshing, only belatedly realizing that neither Linda nor Junella was among the revelers. Ray made his way to Jackie, and asked him if he'd seen either woman. Replying in the negative, Jackie offered to go look around for them.

They agreed to make a quick search and rendezvous at the large tree near the old man's house. But after a fruitless hour or so Ray went to the front of the house and waited for his friend, who didn't come. At last, growing bored, he made his way back to the tables where a group had set up a drum and were singing lustily. A few of the younger people had formed a tight circle around the drummers and were slowly stepping around in it, their arms about each others' waists and shoulders. All right! Ray thought, cheered. "49's." He joined the circle between two women he hadn't seen before, who easily made way for him, and smoothly closed the circle about him again as each wrapped an arm around his waist. He forgot all about his friend.

.   .   .

When Ray awoke the sun was beating down on his head. He sat up, and realized he was lying near the river's edge, his legs in the thicket, his head and half-turned face unshielded from the sun. It was about a third of the way up in a clear sky. As he looked groggily around, he discovered Junella sitting quietly a few yards away on a large stone. "Hey," she said, smiling.

"How'd I get here?" Ray asked. He stood and stretched, surreptitiously feeling to see if everything worked. His memory seemed hesitant to return clearly, but he had half-formed impressions of a baseball game and eating and then the 49. He looked around. "Where's Jackie and, uh—"

"Linda?" Junella supplied as he paused.

"Yeah, Linda," he finished.

"Jackie is staying there," she told him calmly. She reached into her bag and brought out a man's wristwatch. "He said to give you this," she said, holding it out to him.

Ray felt suddenly dizzy. He swayed for a moment while strange images swept through him. Junella with no hair and that eerie light; the one that was some pale tan but had spots or a pattern of soft gray dots that sort of fuzzed out at the edges to blend into the tan. The old man.

He took a step in her direction. "Hey," he began "What the hell's—" but broke off. The rock where she sat was empty. On the ground next to it lay Jackie's watch.

.   .   .

When Ray told me the story, about fifteen months afterward, he had heard that Jackie had showed up at his folks' place. They lived out in the country, a mile or so beyond one of the numerous small towns that dot the Oklahoma landscape. The woman who told him about Jackie's return, Jackie's cousin Ruth Ann, said he had come home with a strange woman who was a real fox. At thirteen, Ruth Ann had developed an eye for good looks and thought herself quite a judge of women's appearance. They hadn't stayed long, he'd heard. Mainly they packed up some of Jackie's things and visited with his family. Ray had been in Tulsa and hadn't heard Jackie was back until later. None of their friends had seen him either. There had been a child with them, he said, maybe two years old, Ruth Ann had thought, because she could walk by herself.

"You know," Ray had said thoughtfully, turning a Calistoga slowly between his big hands, a gesture that made him seem very young and somehow vulnerable, "one of my grandma's brothers, old Jess, used to talk about the little people a lot. He used to tell stories about strange things happening around the countryside here. I never paid much attention. You know how it is. I just thought he was putting me on, or maybe he was pining away for the old days. He said that Deer Woman would come to dances sometimes, and if you weren't careful she'd put her spell on you and take you inside the mountain to meet her uncle. He said her uncle was really Thunder, one of the old gods or supernaturals whatever the traditionals call them."

He finished his drink in a couple of swallows and pushed away from the table we were sitting at. "I dunno," he said, and gave me a look that I still haven't forgotten, a look that was somehow wounded and yet with a kind of wild hope mixed in. "Maybe those old guys know something, eh?"

It was a few years before I saw him again. Then I ran into him unexpectedly in San Francisco a couple of years ago. We talked for a while, standing on the street near the Mission BART station. He started to leave when my curiosity got the better of my manners. I asked if he'd ever found out what happened to Jackie.

Well, he said that he'd heard that Jackie came home off and on, but the woman—probably Linda, though he wasn't sure— was never with him. Then he'd heard that someone had run into Jackie, or a guy they thought was him, up in Seattle. He'd gone alcoholic. Later, they'd heard he'd died. "But you know," Ray said, "the weird thing is that he'd evidently been telling someone all about that time inside the mountain, and that he'd married her, and about some other stuff, stuff I guess he wasn't supposed to tell." Another guy down on his luck, he guessed. "Remember how I was telling you about my crazy uncle, the one who used to tell about Deer Woman? Until I heard about Jackie, I'd forgotten that the old man used to say that the ones who stayed there were never supposed to talk about it. If they did, they died in short order."

After that, there didn't seem to be much more to say. Last time I saw Ray, he was heading down the steps to catch BART. He was on his way to a meeting and he was running late.

FOR DISCUSSION AND WRITING

1. Which details in the story foreshadow the turn of events that go beyond everyday reality? What was your earliest indication of something out of the ordinary?

2. How objective an observer is Ray? Does he exaggerate evidence of the supernatural? Use the story to support your response.

3. What attitude does Ray express about his experiences and the stories of the "traditionals" when he recounts them to the narrator? Explain with evidence from the story.

4. What do you imagine Ray's life to be like at the end of the story? Why?

5. In addition to entertaining readers, what might have been the author's purpose in writing this story?

✳ ✳ ✳ ✳ ✳ ✳ ✳ ✳ ✳ ✳ ✳ ✳ ✳ ✳ ✳ ✳

IN THE BEGINNING
Sandra Maria Esteves

Sandra Maria Esteves was born and raised in New York's South Bronx, where she still lives. She plays an important role in bringing Puerto Rican literature and arts to the public. She is a poet, essayist, graphic artist, performer, and director/producer. Whether her writing expresses anger at the cruelty of a negligent landlord or celebrates music, as does "In The Beginning," a sense of the Puerto Rican community informs her voice.

I N THE BEGINNING WAS THE SOUND
Like the universe exploding
It came, took form, gave life
And was called Conga

And Conga said:
Let there be night and day
And was born el Quinto y el Bajo

And Quinto said: Give me female
There came Campana
And Bajo said: Give me son
There came Bongoses

They merged produced force
Maracas y Claves
Chequere y Timbales

Que viva la musica!
So it was written
On the skin of the drum

Que viva la gente!
So it was written
In the hearts of the people

Que viva Raza!

So it was written.

FOR DISCUSSION AND WRITING

1. Look up the following Spanish words in a dictionary: Conga, Quinto, Bajo, Campana, Bongo, Maracas, Claves, Chequere, *and* Timbales. *Do the words mean what you thought they did? You may need to use both English and Spanish dictionaries.*

2. Why do you think the author chose biblical language to express her thoughts? Do you share her feelings about music? Explain.

✳ ✳ ✳ ✳ ✳ ✳ ✳ ✳ ✳ ✳ ✳ ✳ ✳ ✳ ✳ ✳

THE LATEST LATIN DANCE CRAZE
Victor Hernández Cruz

Victor Hernández Cruz is one of the most widely read of New York's Puerto Rican poets, perhaps because he tries to bridge the Puerto Rican community and the rest of the population. He delights in the fact that Puerto Ricans and other people from the Caribbean have tropicalized New York City and other cities.

FIRST
You throw your head back twice
Jump out onto the floor like a
Kangaroo
Circle the floor once
Doing fast scissor work with your
Legs
Next
Dash towards the door
Walking in a double cha cha cha
Open the door and glide down
The stairs like a swan
Hit the street
Run at least ten blocks
Come back in through the same
Door
Doing a mambo-minuet
Being careful that you don't fall
And break your head on that one
You have just completed your first
Step.

FOR DISCUSSION AND WRITING

1. Can you follow the sequence of Cruz's steps? Do you think he really describes a dance? Explain.

2. What kinds of dancing styles do you like?

CARLOS DE OXNARD
Javier Barrales Pacheco

Javier Barrales Pacheco is a doctoral student in Latino music history and a performance artist. He recites poems accompanied by mixed media including piano, vocals, and cassette tapes. One can imagine him performing "Carlos De Oxnard," a mock movie advertisement, as if he were an announcer on a Mexican-American radio station. His tone would promise one incredible movie! Carlos, the modern day Chicano hero, effortlessly blends Mexican traditions and Southern California collegiate styles. Oxnard, a town near Los Angeles with a non-Mexican-sounding name, is home to many Mexican-American farmworkers and their families.

AND NOW,
three years in the making!
The story they said could not be told!!

Beyond the wall of light,
no beginning
no end
continual process—flow—
beyond space/time/infinity/change
(as some once knew it)
the unexplainable takes form
harbinger of quantum foam
carrier of consciousness
molded into human seed
manifesting itself;
light,
potential,
change through each stage
to perfection . . .
completion.

In the time of the Olmecs,
he was known as TSÚ MECHA
During the Toltec era
he was CAHUITZTLI OXÁN

During the Aztec reign
he was CALOXNATL

During the Spanish Inquisition
he was CARLOS LUCERO.

Having mastered many karmic lessons on the human plane
he would return one day again,
reincarnate
into
the twentieth century!
One last time as a human bean,
to complete his journey
among la graza and megalomania
with a new identity, papers, face,
to assume his position, his destiny
as a modern-day saint
in the land of chicaspatas
northern Aztlán,
California (looking forward)
as a liberator of Mexican/hyphen/Americans:

The prophet of el Barrio is born!

Christened: CARLOS DE OXNARD!!

Chicano, liberated pocho,
born and raised on carnitas and cilantro
pendletons and khakis.
Son of Fidencio and Chamula,
also
de Oxnard.

Familia humilde, farm workers, laborers;
people who put in more than an honest day's work
for their few possessions, tacones y chaquetas.

In his formative years,
the boy would find out about Bakke
and red lining
amidst the squalor and salty-earth decor,
about the "land of opportunity" that exists on television.

But he was of a higher calling—the cosmic Chicano!
Personification of consciousness;
able to leap tall fences in a single bound,
leader who does not lead
prophet without a prophecy
the unmessianic messiah!!
Visionary a la 20/20,
breaking the chain of the struggle
between the individual and society
work and the fiesta
action in unity!

And who
in his growing years
developed a body of pragmatic knowledge and natural curing,
gave the word "commitment" a new meaning!

CARLOS DE OXNARD!

Watch the child unfold,
grow with him,
experience the trials and tribulations
and become the one, transformed,
fully grown adult rebel!

CARLOS DE OXNARD!

El carnal incarnate!

(Coming soon to a teatro near you!)

1. What is the significance of describing Carlos as being raised on carnitas and cilantro, pendletons and khakis?

2. What is the author's attitude toward Carlos? Do you think the author knows anyone like Carlos? Would he be friendly with him if he knew him? Explain.

3. What is Carlos's attitude toward life and himself? Use the poem to support your response.

---

* * * * * * * * * * * * * * * *

THE WOMAN WHO MAKES SWELL DOUGHNUTS
Toshio Mori

"The Woman Who Makes Swell Doughnuts" is one of the stories in the collection Yokohama, California. *These stories are about Japanese-American life during the twenties and thirties in a fictional town somewhere in the East Bay area of San Francisco. The book was to be published in 1941, but World War II and Japanese-American internment camps intervened. When* Yokohama, California *was published in 1949, the book received very little of the recognition it deserved. In 1974 this classic could only be found in used bookstores for twenty-five cents. Due to the efforts of contemporary Asian-American scholars and authors, Toshio Mori's work has been republished in other anthologies.*

T HERE IS NOTHING I LIKE TO DO BETTER than to go to her house and knock on the door and when she opens the door, to go in. It is one of the experiences I will long remember—perhaps the only immortality that I will ever be lucky to meet in my short life—and when I say experienced I do not mean the actual movement, the motor of our lives. I mean by experience the dancing of emotions before our eyes and inside of us, the dance that is still but is the roar and the force capable of stirring the earth and the people.

Of course, she, the woman I visit, is old and of her youthful beauty there is little left. Her face of today is coarse with hard water and there is no question that she has lived her life: given birth to six children, worked side by side with her man for forty years, working in the fields, working in the house, caring for the grandchildren, facing the summers and winters and also the springs and autumns, running the household that is completely her little world. And when I came on the scene, when I discovered her in her little house on Seventh Street, all of her life was behind, all of her task in this world was tabbed, looked into, thoroughly attended, and all that is before her in life and the world, all that could be before her now was to sit and be served; duty done, work done, time clock punched; old-age pension and old-age security; easy chair; soft serene hours till death take her. But this was not of her, not the least bit of her.

When I visit her she takes me to the coziest chair in the living room, where are her magazines and books in Japanese and English. "Sit down," she says. "Make yourself comfortable. I will come back with some hot doughnuts just out of oil."

And before I can turn a page of a magazine she is back with a plateful of hot doughnuts. There is nothing I can do to describe her doughnut; it is in a class by itself, without words, without demonstration. It is a doughnut, just a plain doughnut just out of oil but it is different, unique. Perhaps when I am eating her doughnuts I am really eating her; I have this foolish notion in my head many times and whenever I catch myself doing so I say, that is not so, that is not true. Her doughnuts really taste swell, she is the best cook I have ever known, oriental dishes or American dishes.

I bow humbly that such a room, such a house exists in my neighborhood so I may dash in and out when my spirit wanes, when hell is loose. I sing gratefully that such a simple and common experience becomes an event, an event of necessity and growth. It is an event that is a part of me, an addition to the elements of the earth, water, fire, and air, and I seek the day when it will become a part of everyone.

All her friends, old and young, call her Mama. Everybody calls her Mama. That is not new, it is logical. I suppose there is in every block of every city in America a woman who can be called Mama by her friends and the strangers meeting her. This is commonplace, it is not new and the old sentimentality may be the undoing of the moniker. But what of a woman who isn't a mama but is, and instead of priding in the expansion of her little world, takes her little circle, living out her days in the little circle, perhaps never to be exploited in a biography or on everybody's tongue, but enclosed, shut, excluded from world news and newsreels; just sitting, just moving, just alive, planting the plants in the fields, caring for the children and the grandchildren and baking the tastiest doughnuts this side of the next world.

When I sit with her I do not need to ask deep questions, I do not need to know Plato or The Sacred Books of the East or dancing. I do not need to be on guard. But I am on guard and foot-loose because the room is alive.

"Where are the grandchildren?" I say. "Where are Mickey, Tadao, and Yaeko?"

"They are out in the yard," she says. "I say to them, play, play hard, go out there and play hard. You will be glad later for everything you have done with all your might."

Sometimes we sit many minutes in silence. Silence does not bother her. She says silence is the most beautiful symphony, she says the air breathed in silence is sweeter and sadder. That is about all we talk of. Sometimes I sit and gaze out the window and watch the Southern Pacific trains rumble by and the vehicles whizz with speed. And sometimes she catches me doing this and she nods her head and I know she understands that I think the silence in the room is great, and also the roar and the dust of the outside is great, and when she is nodding I understand that she is saying that this, her little room, her little circle, is a depot, a pause, for the weary traveler, but outside, outside of her little world there is dissonance, hugeness of another kind, and the travel to do. So she has her little house, she bakes the grandest doughnuts, and inside of her she houses a little depot.

Most stories would end with her death, would wait till she is peacefully dead and peacefully at rest but I cannot wait that long. I think she will grow, and her hot doughnuts just out of the oil will grow with softness and touch. And I think it would be a shame to talk of her doughnuts after she is dead, after she is formless.

Instead I take today to talk to her and her wonderful doughnuts when the earth is something to her, when the people from all the parts of the earth may drop in and taste the flavor, her flavor, which is everyone's and all flavor; talk to her, sit with her, and also taste the silence of her room and the silence that is herself; and finally go away to hope and keep alive what is alive in her, on earth and in men, expressly myself.

FOR DISCUSSION AND WRITING

1. How important are the doughnuts in making the woman's house a special place? Explain.

2. Have you ever experienced a place that is a "depot," a safe place out of the "roar and dust" of the fast lane? Is there a relative, teacher, or friend who plays the role for you of the woman in the story? Do you wish you had such a place?

✳ ✳ ✳ ✳ ✳ ✳ ✳ ✳ ✳ ✳ ✳ ✳ ✳ ✳ ✳ ✳

RAVIOLI
Anna Bart

Anna Bart, Italian-American poet and textile designer, was born in Buffalo, New York. Her poem "Ravioli" highlights the rituals of preparing a favorite Italian dish.

GRANDMA'S LONG BLACK DRESS   BLACK IRON STOVE
narrow windows on a narrow alley
the Roma Street kitchen a shadowy cave
but the back door opens to a sunny yard

She breaks eggs into a flour volcano-crater
mixing, kneading, rolling it smooth on the dough board
cutting circles with a coffee can lid
spooning ricotta in each circle
folding them into half-moon pillows

At five I can press the fork tines round the edge
crisp bird tracks in the dough
press my thumb to make a dimple
in the powdered skin

　　　Cover them with a towel
　　　they need to rest awhile
　　　Let's go and feed
　　　the Pee-Pees

Buoyant air bright with sunny ferment
jostling each other hungry chicks
lift red wire legs beaks stretched
in frantic Pee-ee-eep!
Pee-ee-eep! Pee-eeeep!

1. In whose voice is this poem written? What is the mood of this recollection? Use the poem to support your response.

2. Do you remember experiences in which you have cooked meals or baked delicious desserts with relatives? Describe these experiences.

3. How important do you think it is to have relationships such as the one described in "Ravioli"? Explain.

✳ ✳ ✳ ✳ ✳ ✳ ✳ ✳ ✳ ✳ ✳ ✳ ✳ ✳ ✳ ✳

RICE PLANTING
Amy Uyematsu

Amy Uyematsu is a Sansei (third-generation Japanese-American) poet from San Francisco. "Rice Planting" describes an impressive number of culinary and other uses of rice.

> *In the sky at night*
> *stars known as the "rice basket"*
> *blossom like flowers.*
> *All day I make rice baskets;*
> *at night I view these flowers.*
> *— 16th c. Japanese tanka*

*E*VEN MY MOTHER HAS TAUGHT HERSELF
to acquire the taste of butter & bread,
but I refuse. Every night I must make
two cups of rice—
after washing the grains,
the level of water measured exactly,
only as high as the first groove
on my third finger.
This is essential,
for Japanese rice is wetter than others.
We say Chinese rice falls apart

too easily (they say ours is too sticky).
A newlywed bride has ruined many meals
by a rice too dry or too moist.

I plan every dinner around rice.
I know it's a starch like potatoes or noodles,
but I'm sure rice has so many more uses.
I can cook it with any meat,
fish, or casserole. I even serve rice with spaghetti.
And leftover rice is just as good—
fried with last night's scraps
or the cold rice I reheat with tea
then sprinkle with bonito shavings
to become a hot soup
to be slurped the next day.

Of course there's the vinegared rice
that's the basis for sushi,
then on special occasions
a wine-colored rice
flavored with dark red azuki beans.
Rice goes in our Thanksgiving stuffing,
it's a cracker for munching with beer,
and pounded, rice can be molded
into New Year's mochi cakes
or sweetened for manju
in pink-and-white stripes.

When we go to the mountains or beach,
the best part of the trip is our picnic lunch—
triangles and spool shapes of rice,
covered with roasted sesame seeds
or green and black wrappers of dried seaweed.
These onigiro always go well with fried
chicken or slices of ham.

If I'm sick mother boils
a heavy rice gruel which will
settle my stomach.
And when we don't feel like cooking,

there's that breakfast rice
which can only be ordered in Buddhahead
towns like Honolulu or Gardena—
rice heaped on a platter,
two eggs over easy,
your choice of Portuguese sausage,
bacon, or Chinese roast pork—
a typical Japanese American meal.

I can remember when I couldn't boast
like this about rice. My father told us
the upper classes never
ate rice with their main course
like we did. Now I can even put rice
in my son's sack lunches—
when I ask him again if friends joke or stare,
I am back in the sixth grade
at my all-white school
in a less sophisticated time before sushi
became just another California fastfood.

There is also the rice not eaten.
Moistened and mashed it's reliable glue.
Uncooked it's a good luck sign
to be thrown at weddings.
When rice is fermented as sake,
it's served chilled in wood boxes
with lemon and ice,
or so hot it melts the body
and is likely to make me dance and sing.
In craftsmen's hands it's passed on
as a fine rice paper,
barely transparent and suited for lanterns
or poems brushed in ink.

But above all rice is a plain people's food.
Before temples and imperial palaces,
my peasant ancestors planted
until the land and grain were the harvest,
the rhythm we lived by.

Rice is the staple of farmers and monks—
nothing is wasted.
It has fed me on many long journeys—
and though my family no longer grows rice
and our women no longer bend
to a rice planting song,
I am thankful when my own son
from the fourth generation
tells me he's hungry and smiles
when I hand him a riceball
the size of my fist.

FOR DISCUSSION AND WRITING

1. What does the author mean when she says that we live in a more "sophisticated" time than when she was in sixth grade?

2. Why is the poem titled "Rice Planting"?

3. Are there certain foods that are particularly important to people of your family or heritage? What foods of different cultural groups (including your own) do you enjoy?

✳ ✳ ✳ ✳ ✳ ✳ ✳ ✳ ✳ ✳ ✳ ✳ ✳ ✳ ✳ ✳

TO SATCH: AMERICAN GOTHIC
Samuel Allen (Paul Vesey)

African-American author Paul Vesey was born in 1917 and has worked in both the United States and Europe. When he was a lawyer with the Armed Forces in France after World War II, he became involved with African and Caribbean writers who were living in Paris. These black writers inspired Vesey to write poetry that reflected the rich heritage of African and African-American communities. In the poem "American Gothic," Vesey wrote about Satchel Paige, the brilliant African-American baseball pitcher who was barred from the major leagues until 1948, when he was nearly fifty years old.

SOMETIMES I FEEL LIKE I WILL *NEVER* STOP
Just go on forever
'Til one fine mornin'
I'm gonna reach up and grab me a handfulla stars
Swing out my long lean leg
And whip three hot strikes burnin' down the heavens
And look over at God and say
How about that!

FOR DISCUSSION AND WRITING

1. Research the life of Satchel Paige. What caliber pitcher was he? How did he finally enter the major leagues?

2. In whose voice is this poem written? Considering Paige's history, do you feel that this poem is an appropriate tribute to the ballplayer?

Linda Lomahaftewa (Hopi/Choctaw), Star Gatherers, *1990*

THE ENGLISH LESSON
Nicholasa Mohr

Nicholasa Mohr writes and illustrates prizewinning books about New York's Puerto Rican community. "The English Lesson" is a story about immigrants from many different countries who meet in an English-as-a-Second-Language class. Although the story does not portray an unrealistically glowing picture of the United States, "The English Lesson" suggests that there are important freedoms and opportunities in the United States that can expand the horizons for many new immigrants.

REMEMBER OUR ASSIGNMENT FOR TODAY EVERYBODY! I'm so confident that you will all do exceptionally well!" Mrs. Susan Hamma smiled enthusiastically at her students. "Everyone is to get up and make a brief statement as to why he or she is taking this course in Basic English. You must state your name, where you originally came from, how long you have been here, and . . . uh . . . a little something about yourself, if you wish. Keep it brief, not too long; remember, there are twenty-eight of us. We have a full class, and everyone must have a chance." Mrs. Hamma waved a forefinger at her students. "This is, after all, a democracy, and we have a democratic class: fairness for all!"

Lali grinned and looked at William, who sat directly next to her. He winked and rolled his eyes toward Mrs. Hamma. This was the third class they had attended together. It had not been easy to persuade Rudi that Lali should learn better English.

"Why is it necessary, eh?" Rudi had protested. "She works here in the store with me. She don't have to talk to nobody. Besides, everybody that comes in speaks Spanish—practically everybody, anyway."

But once William had put the idea to Lali and explained how much easier things would be for her, she kept insisting until Rudi finally agreed. "Go on, you're both driving me nuts. But it can't interfere with business or work—I'm warning you!"

Adult Education offered Basic English, Tuesday evenings from 6:30 to 8:00, at a local public school. Night customers did not usually come into Rudi's Luncheonette until after eight. William and Lali promised that they would leave everything prepared and make up for any inconvenience by working harder and longer than usual, if necessary.

The class admitted twenty-eight students, and because there were only twenty-seven registered, Lali was allowed to take the course even after missing the first two classes. William had assured Mrs. Hamma that he would help Lali catch up; she was glad to have another student to make up the full registration.

Most of the students were Spanish-speaking. The majority were American citizens—Puerto Ricans who had migrated to New York and spoke very little English. The rest were immigrants admitted to the United States as legal aliens. There were several Chinese, two Dominicans, one Sicilian, and one Pole.

Every Tuesday Mrs. Hamma traveled to the Lower East Side from Bayside, Queens, where she lived and was employed as a history teacher in the local junior high school. She was convinced that this small group of people desperately needed her services. Mrs. Hamma reiterated her feelings frequently to just about anyone who would listen. "Why, if these people can make it to class after working all day at those miserable, dreary, uninteresting, and often revolting jobs, well, the least I can do is be there to serve them, making every lesson count toward improving their conditions! My grandparents came here from Germany as poor immigrants, working their way up. I'm not one to forget a thing like that!"

By the time class started most of the students were quite tired. And after the lesson was over, many had to go on to part-time jobs, some even without time for supper. As a result there was always sluggishness and yawning among the students. This never discouraged Mrs. Hamma, whose drive and enthusiasm not only amused the class but often kept everyone awake.

"Now this is the moment we have all been preparing for." Mrs. Hamma stood up, nodded, and blinked knowingly at her students. "Five lessons, I think, are enough to prepare us for our oral statements. You may read from prepared notes, as I said before, but please try not to read every word. We want to hear you speak; conversation is what we're after. When someone asks you about yourself, you cannot take a piece of paper and start reading the answers, now can you? That would be foolish. So . . ."

Standing in front of her desk, she put her hands on her hips and spread her feet, giving the impression that she was going to demonstrate calisthenics.

"Shall we begin?"

Mrs. Hamma was a very tall, angular woman with large extremities. She was the tallest person in the room. Her eyes roamed from student to student until they met William's.

"Mr. Colón, will you please begin?"

Nervously William looked around him, hesitating.

"Come on now, we must get the ball rolling. All right now . . . did you hear what I said? Listen, 'getting the ball rolling' means getting started. Getting things going, such as—" Mrs. Hamma swiftly lifted her right hand over her head, making a fist, then swung her arm around like a pitcher and, with an underhand curve, forcefully threw an imaginary ball out at her students. Trying to maintain her balance, Mrs. Hamma hopped from one leg to the other. Startled, the students looked at one another. In spite of their efforts to restrain themselves, several people in back began to giggle. Lali and William looked away, avoiding each other's eyes and trying not to laugh out loud. With assured countenance, Mrs. Hamma continued.

"An idiom!" she exclaimed, pleased. "You have just seen me demonstrate the meaning of an idiom. Now I want everyone to jot down this information in his notebook." Going to the blackboard, Mrs. Hamma explained, "It's something which literally says one thing, but actually means another. Idiom . . . idiomatic." Quickly and obediently, everyone began to copy what she wrote. "Has everyone got it? OK, let's GET THE BALL ROLLING, Mr. Colón!

Uneasily William stood up; he was almost the same height standing as sitting. When speaking to others, especially in a new situation, he always preferred to sit alongside those listening; it gave him a sense of equality with other people. He looked around and cleared his throat; at least everyone else was sitting. Taking a deep breath, William felt better.

"My name is William Horacio Colón," he read from a prepared statement. "I have been here in New York City for five months. I coming from Puerto Rico. My town is located in the mountains in the central part of the island. The name of my town is Aibonito, which means in Spanish 'oh how pretty.' It is name like this because when the Spaniards first seen that place they was very impressed with the beauty of the section and—"

"Make it brief, Mr. Colón," Mrs. Hamma interrupted, "there are others, you know."

William looked at her, unable to continue.

"Go on, go on, Mr. Colón, please!"

"I am working here now, living with my mother and family in Lower East Side of New York City," William spoke rapidly. "I study Basic English por que . . . because my ambition is to learn to speak and read English very good. To get a better job. Y—y también, to help my mother y familia." He shrugged. "Y do better, that's all."

"That's all? Why, that's wonderful! Wonderful! Didn't he do well, class?" Mrs. Hamma bowed slightly toward William and applauded him. The students watched her and slowly each one began to imitate her. Pleased, Mrs. Hamma looked around her; all together they gave William a healthy round of applause.

Next, Mrs. Hamma turned to a Chinese man seated at the other side of the room.

"Mr. Fong, you may go next."

Mr. Fong stood up; he was a man in his late thirties, of medium height and slight build. Cautiously he looked at Mrs. Hamma, and waited.

"Go on, Mr. Fong. Get the ball rolling, remember?"

"All right. Get a ball rolling . . . is idiot!" Mr. Fong smiled.

"No, Mr. Fong, idiommmmmm!" Mrs. Hamma hummed her m's, shaking her head. "Not an—It's idiomatic!"

"What I said!" Mr. Fong responded with self-assurance, looking directly at Mrs. Hamma. "Get a ball rolling, idiomit."

"Never mind." She cleared her throat. "Just go on."

"I said OK?" Mr. Fong waited for an answer.

"Go on, please."

Mr. Fong sighed, "My name is Joseph Fong. I been here in this country United States New York City for most one year." He too read from a prepared statement. "I come from Hong Kong but original born in city of Canton, China. I working delivery food business and live with my brother and his family in Chinatown. I taking the course in Basic English to speak good and improve my position better in this country. Also to be eligible to become American citizen."

Mrs. Hamma selected each student who was to speak from a different part of the room, rather than in the more conventional orderly fashion of row by row, or front to back, or even alphabetical order. This way, she reasoned, no one will know who's next; it will be more spontaneous. Mrs. Hamma enjoyed catching the uncertain looks on the faces of her students. A feeling of control over the situation gave her a pleasing thrill, and she made the most of these moments by looking at several people more than once before making her final choice.

There were more men than women, and Mrs. Hamma called two or three men for each woman. It was her way of maintaining a balance. To her distress, most read from prepared notes, despite her efforts to discourage this. She would interrupt them when she felt they went on too long, then praise them when they finished. Each statement was followed by applause from everyone.

All had similar statements. They had migrated here in search of a better future, were living with relatives, and worked as unskilled laborers. With the exception of Lali, who was childless, every woman gave the ages and sex of her children; most men referred only to their "family." And, among the legal aliens, there was only one who did not want to become an American citizen, Diego Torres, a young man from the Dominican Republic, and he gave his reasons.

". . . and to improve my economic situation." Diego Torres hesitated, looking around the room. "But is one thing I no want, and is to become American citizen"—he pointed to an older man with a dark complexion, seated a few seats away—"like my fellow countryman over there!" The man shook his head disapprovingly at Diego Torres, trying to hide his annoyance. "I no give up my country, Santo Domingo, for nothing," he went on, "nothing in the whole world. OK, man? I come here, pero I cannot help. I got no work at home. There, is political. The United States control most the industry which is sugar and tourismo. Y—you have to know somebody. I tell you, is political to get a job, man! You don't know nobody and you no work, eh? So I come here from necessity, pero this no my country—"

"Mr. Torres," Mrs. Hamma interrupted, "we must be brief, please, there are—"

"I no finish lady!" he snapped. "You wait a minute when I finish!"

There was complete silence as Diego Torres glared at Susan Hamma. No one had ever spoken to her like that, and her confusion was greater than her embarrassment. Without speaking, she lowered her eyes and nodded.

"OK, I prefer live feeling happy in my country, man. Even I don't got too much. I live simple but in my own country I be contento. Pero this is no possible in the situation of Santo Domingo now. Someday we gonna run our own country and be jobs for everybody. My reasons to be here is to make money, man, and go back home buy my house and property. I no be American citizen, no way. I'm Dominican and proud! That's it. That's all I got to say." Abruptly, Diego Torres sat down.

"All right." Mrs. Hamma had composed herself. "Very good; you can come here and state your views. That is what America is all about! We may not agree with you, but we defend your right to an opinion. And as long as you are in this classroom, Mr. Torres, you are in America. Now, everyone, let us give Mr. Torres the same courtesy as everyone else in this class." Mrs. Hamma applauded with a polite light clap, then turned to find the next speaker.

"Bullshit," whispered Diego Torres.

Practically everyone had spoken. Lali and the two European immigrants were the only ones left. Mrs. Hamma called upon Lali.

"My name is Rogelia Dolores Padillo. I come from Canovanas in Puerto Rico. Is a small village in the mountains near El Yunque Rain Forest. My family is still living there. I marry and live here with my husband working in his business of restaurant. Call Rudi's Luncheonette. I been here New York City Lower East Side since I marry, which is now about one year. I study Basic English to improve my vocabulario and learn more about here. This way I help my husband in his business and I do more also for myself, including to be able to read better in English. Thank you."

Aldo Fabrizi, the Sicilian, spoke next. He was a very short man, barely five feet tall. Usually he was self-conscious about his height, but William's presence relieved him of these feelings. Looking at William, he thought being short was no big thing; he was, after all, normal. He told the class that he was originally from Palermo, the capital of Sicily, and had gone to Milano, in the north of Italy, looking for work. After three years in Milano, he immigrated here six months ago and now lived with his sister. He had a good steady job, he said, working in a copper wire factory with his brother-in-law in Brooklyn. Aldo Fabrizi wanted to become an American citizen and spoke passionately about it, without reading from his notes.

"I be proud to be American citizen. I no come here find work live good and no have responsibility or no be grateful." He turned and looked threateningly at Diego Torres. "Hey? I tell you all one thing, I got my nephew right now fighting in Vietnam for this country!" Diego Torres stretched his hands over his head, yawning, folded his hands, and lowered his eyelids. "I wish I could be citizen to fight for this country. My whole family is citizens—we all Americans and we love America!" His voice was quite loud. "That's how I feel."

"Very good," Mrs. Hamma called, distracting Aldo Fabrizi. "That was well stated. I'm sure you will not only become a citizen, but you will also be a credit to this country."

The last person to be called on was the Pole. He was always neatly dressed in a business suit, with a shirt and tie, and carried a briefcase. His manner was reserved but friendly.

"Good evening fellow students and Madame Teacher." He nodded politely to Mrs. Hamma. "My name is Stephan Paczkowski. I am originally from Poland about four months ago. My background is I was born in capital city of Poland, Warsaw. Being educated in capital and also graduating from the University with degree of professor of music with specialty in the history of music."

Stephan Paczkowski read from his notes carefully, articulating every word. "I was given appointment of professor of history of music at University of Krakow. I work there for ten years until about year and half ago. At this time the political situation in Poland was so that all Jewish people were requested by the government to leave Poland. My wife who also is being a professor of economics at University of Krakow is of Jewish parents. My wife was told she could not remain in position at University or remain over there. We made arrangements for my wife and daughter who is seven years of age and myself to come here with my wife's cousin who is to be helping us.

"Since four months I am working in large hospital as position of porter in maintenance department. The thing of it is, I wish to take Basic English to improve my knowledge of English language, and be able to return to my position of professor of history of music. Finally, I wish to become a citizen of United States. That is my reasons. I thank you all."

After Stephan Paczkowski sat down, there was a long awkward silence and everyone turned to look at Mrs. Hamma. Even after the confrontation with Diego Torres, she had applauded without hesitation. Now she seemed unable to move.

"Well," she said, almost breathless, "that's admirable! I'm sure, sir, that you will do very well . . . a person of your . . . like yourself, I mean . . . a professor, after all, it's really just admirable." Everyone was listening intently to what she said. "That was well done, class. Now, we have to get to next week's assignment." Mrs. Hamma realized that no one had applauded Stephan Paczkowski. With a slightly pained expression, she began to applaud. "Mustn't forget Mr. Paczkowski; everybody here must be treated equally. This is America!" The class joined her in a round of applause.

As Mrs. Hamma began to write the next week's assignment on the board, some students looked anxiously at their watches and others asked about the time. Then they all quickly copied the information into their notebooks. It was almost eight o'clock. Those who had to get to second jobs did not want to be late; some even hoped to have time for a bite to eat first. Others were just tired and wanted to get home.

Lali looked at William, sighing impatiently. They both hoped Mrs. Hamma would finish quickly. There would be hell to pay with Rudi if the night customers were already at the luncheonette.

"There, that's next week's work, which is very important, by the way. We will be looking at the history of New York City and the different ethnic groups that lived here as far back as the Dutch. I can't tell you how proud I am of the way you all spoke. All of you—I have no favorites, you know."

Mrs. Hamma was interrupted by the long, loud buzzing sound, bringing the lesson to an end. Quickly everyone began to exit.

"Good night, see you all next Tuesday!" Mrs. Hamma called out. "By the way, if any of you here wants extra help, I have a few minutes this evening." Several people bolted past her, excusing themselves. In less than thirty seconds, Mrs. Hamma was standing in an empty classroom.

.   .   .

William and Lali hurried along, struggling against the cold, sharp March wind that whipped across Houston Street, stinging their faces and making their eyes tear.

In a few minutes they would be at Rudi's. So far, they had not been late once.

"You read very well—better than anybody in class. I told you there was nothing to worry about. You caught up in no time."

"Go on. I was so nervous, honestly! But, I'm glad she left me for one of the last. If I had to go first, like you, I don't think I could open my mouth. You were so calm. You started the thing off very well."

"You go on now, I was nervous myself!" He laughed, pleased.

"Mira, Chiquitín," Lali giggled, "I didn't know your name was Horacio. William Horacio. Ave Maria, so imposing!"

"That's right, because you see, my mother was expecting a valiant warrior! Instead, well"—he threw up his hands—"no one warned me either. And what a name for a Chiquitín like me."

Lali smiled, saying nothing. At first she had been very aware of William's dwarfishness. Now it no longer mattered. It was only when she saw others reacting to him for the first time that she was once more momentarily struck with William's physical difference.

"We should really try to speak in English, Lali. It would be good practice for us."

"Dios mío . . . I feel so foolish, and my accent is terrible!"

"But look, we all have to start some place. Besides, what about the

Americanos? When they speak Spanish, they sound pretty awful, but we accept it. You know I'm right. And that's how people get ahead, by not being afraid to try."

They walked in silence for a few moments. Since William had begun to work at Rudi's, Lali's life had become less lonely. Lali was shy by nature; making friends was difficult for her. She had grown up in the sheltered environment of a large family living in a tiny mountain village. She was considered quite plain. Until Rudi had asked her parents for permission to court her, she had only gone out with two local boys. She had accepted his marriage proposal expecting great changes in her life. But the age difference between her and Rudi, being in a strange country without friends or relatives, and the long hours of work at the luncheonette confined Lali to a way of life she could not have imagined. Every evening she found herself waiting for William to come in to work, looking forward to his presence.

Lali glanced over at him as they started across the wide busy street. His grip on her elbow was firm but gentle as he led her to the sidewalk.

"There you are, Miss Lali, please to watch your step!" he spoke in English.

His thick golden-blond hair was slightly mussed and fell softly, partially covering his forehead. His wide smile, white teeth, and large shoulders made him appear quite handsome. Lali found herself staring at William. At that moment she wished he could be just like everybody else.

"Lali?" William asked, confused by her silent stare. "Is something wrong?"

"No." Quickly Lali turned her face. She felt herself blushing. "I . . . I was just thinking how to answer in English, that's all."

"But that's it . . . don't think! What I mean is, don't go worrying about what to say. Just talk natural. Get used to simple phrases and the rest will come, you'll see."

"All right," Lali said, glad the strange feeling of involvement had passed, and William had taken no notice of it. "It's an interesting class, don't you think so? I mean—like that man, the professor. Bendito! Imagine, they had to leave because they were Jewish. What a terrible thing!"

"I don't believe he's Jewish; it's his wife who is Jewish. She was a professor too. But I guess they don't wanna be separated . . . and they have a child."

"Tsk, tsk, los pobres! But, can you imagine, then? A professor from a university doing the job of a porter? My goodness!" Lali sighed. "I never heard of such a thing!"

"But you gotta remember, it's like Mrs. Hamma said, this is America, right? So . . . everybody got a chance to clean toilets! Equality, didn't she say that?"

They both laughed loudly, stepping up their pace until they reached Rudi's Luncheonette.

The small luncheonette was almost empty. One customer sat at the counter.

"Just in time," Rudi called out. "Let's get going. People gonna be coming in hungry any minute. I was beginning to worry about you two!"

William ran in the back to change into his workshirt.

Lali slipped into her uniform and soon was busy at the grill.

"Well, did you learn anything tonight?" Rudi asked her.

"Yes."

"What?"

"I don't know," she answered, without interrupting her work. "We just talked a little bit in English."

"A little bit in English—about what?"

Lali busied herself, ignoring him. Rudi waited, then tried once more.

"You remember what you talked about?" He watched her as she moved, working quickly, not looking in his direction.

"No." Her response was barely audible.

Lately Rudi had begun to reflect on his decision to marry such a young woman. Especially a country girl like Lali, who was shy and timid. He had never had children with his first wife and wondered if he lacked the patience needed for the young. They had little in common and certainly seldom spoke about anything but the business. Certainly he could not fault her for being lazy; she was always working without being asked. People would accuse him in jest of overworking his young wife. He assured them there was no need, because she had the endurance of a country mule. After almost one year of marriage, he felt he hardly knew Lali or what he might do to please her.

William began to stack clean glasses behind the counter.

"Chiquitín! How about you and Lali having something to eat? We gotta few minutes yet. There's some fresh rice pudding."

"Later . . . I'll have mine a little later, thanks."

"Ask her if she wants some," Rudi whispered, gesturing toward Lali.

William moved close to Lali and spoke softly to her.

"She said no." William continued his work.

"Listen, Chiquitín, I already spoke to Raquel Martinez who lives next door. You know, she's got all them kids? In case you people are late, she can cover for you and Lali. She said it was OK."

"Thanks, Rudi, I appreciate it. But we'll get back on time."

"She's good, you know. She helps me out during the day whenever I need extra help. Off the books, I give her a few bucks. But, mira, I cannot pay you and Raquel both. So if she comes in, you don't get paid. You know that then, OK?"

"Of course. Thanks, Rudi."

"Sure, well, it's a good thing after all. You and Lali improving yourselves. Not that she really needs it, you know. I provide for her. As I said, she's my wife, so she don't gotta worry. If she wants something, I'll buy it for her. I made it clear she didn't have to bother with none of that, but"— Rudi shrugged—"if that's what she wants, I'm not one to interfere."

The door opened. Several men walked in.

"Here they come, kids!"

Orders were taken and quickly filled. Customers came and went steadily until about eleven o'clock, when Rudi announced that it was closing time.

.   .   .

The weeks passed, then the months, and this evening, William and Lali sat with the other students listening to Mrs. Hamma as she taught the last lesson of the Basic English course.

"It's been fifteen long hard weeks for all of you. And I want you to know how proud I am of each and every one here."

William glanced at Lali; he knew she was upset. He felt it too, wishing that this was not the end of the course. It was the only time he and Lali had free to themselves together. Tuesday had become their evening.

Lali had been especially irritable that week, dreading this last session. For her, Tuesday meant leaving the world of Rudi, the luncheonette, that street, everything that she felt imprisoned her. She was accomplishing something all by herself, and without the help of the man she was dependent upon.

Mrs. Hamma finally felt that she had spent enough time assuring her students of her sincere appreciation.

"I hope some of you will stay and have a cup of coffee or tea, and cookies. There's plenty over there." She pointed to a side table where a large electric coffeepot filled with hot water was steaming. The table was set for instant coffee and tea, complete with several boxes of assorted cookies. "I do this every semester for my classes. I think it's nice to have a little informal chat with one another; perhaps discuss our plans for the future and so on. But it must be in English! Especially those of you who are Spanish-speaking. Just because you outnumber the rest of us, don't you think you can get away with it!" Mrs. Hamma lifted her forefinger threateningly but smiled. "Now, it's still early, so there's plenty of time left. Please turn in your books."

Some of the people said good-bye quickly and left, but the majority waited, helping themselves to coffee or tea and cookies. Small clusters formed as people began to chat with one another.

Diego Torres and Aldo Fabrizi were engaged in a friendly but heated debate on the merits of citizenship.

"Hey, you come here a minute, please," Aldo Fabrizi called out to William, who was standing with a few people by the table, helping himself to coffee. William walked over to the two men.

"What's the matter?"

"What do you think of your paisano. He don't wanna be citizen. I say—my opinion—he don't appreciate what he got in this country. This a great country! You the same like him, what do you think?"

"Mira, please tell him we no the same," Diego Torres said with exasperation. "You a citizen, pero not me. Este tipo no comprende, man!"

"Listen, you comprendo . . . yo capito! I know what you say. He be born in Puerto Rico. But you see, we got the same thing. I be born in Sicily— that is another part of the country, separate. But I still Italiano, capito?"

"Dios mio!" Diego Torres smacked his forehead with an open palm. "Mira"—he turned to William—"explain to him, por favor."

William swallowed a mouthful of cookies. "He's right. Puerto Rico is part of the United States. And Sicily is part of Italy. But not the Dominican Republic where he been born. There it is not the United States. I was born a citizen, do you see?"

"Sure!" Aldo Fabrizi nodded. "Capito. Hey, but you still no can vote, right?"

"Sure I can vote; I got all the rights. I am a citizen, just like anybody else," William assured him.

"You some lucky guy then. You got it made! You don't gotta worry like the rest of—"

"Bullshit," Diego Torres interrupted. "Why he got it made, man? He force to leave his country. Pendejo, you no capito nothing, man . . ."

As the two men continued to argue, William waited for the right moment to slip away and join Lali.

She was with some of the women, who were discussing how sincere and devoted Mrs. Hamma was.

"She's hardworking . . ."

"And she's good people . . ." an older woman agreed.

Mr. Fong joined them, and they spoke about the weather and how nice and warm the days were.

Slowly people began to leave, shaking hands with their fellow students and Mrs. Hamma, wishing each other luck.

Mrs. Hamma had been hoping to speak to Stephan Paczkowski privately this evening, but he was always with a group. Now he offered his hand.

"I thank you very much for your good teaching. It was a fine semester."

"Oh, do you think so? Oh, I'm so glad to hear you say that. You don't know how much it means. Especially coming from a person of your caliber. I am confident, yes, indeed, that you will soon be back to your profession, which, after all, is your true calling. If there is anything I can do, please . . ."

"Thank you, miss. This time I am registering in Hunter College, which is in Manhattan on Sixty-eighth Street in Lexington Avenue, with a course of English Literature for beginners." After a slight bow, he left.

"Good-bye." Mrs. Hamma sighed after him.

Lali, William, and several of the women picked up the paper cups and napkins and tossed them into the trash basket.

"Thank you so much, that's just fine. Luis the porter will do the rest. He takes care of these things. He's a lovely person and very helpful. Thank you."

William shook hands with Mrs. Hamma, then waited for Lali to say good-bye. They were the last ones to leave.

"Both of you have been such good students. What are your plans? I hope you will continue with your English."

"Next term we're taking another course," Lali said, looking at William.

"Yes," William responded, "it's more advance. Over at the Washington Irving High School around Fourteenth Street."

"Wonderful." Mrs. Hamma hesitated. "May I ask you a question before you leave? It's only that I'm a little curious about something."

"Sure, of course." They both nodded.

"Are you two related? I mean, you are always together and yet have different last names, so I was just . . . wondering."

"Oh, we are just friends," Lali answered, blushing.

"I work over in the luncheonette at night, part-time."

"Of course." Mrs. Hamma looked at Lali. "Mrs. Padillo, your husband's place of business. My, that's wonderful, just wonderful! You are all just so ambitious. Very good . . ."

They exchanged farewells.

Outside, the warm June night was sprinkled with the sweetness of the new buds sprouting on the scrawny trees and hedges planted along the sidewalks and in the housing project grounds. A brisk breeze swept over the East River on to Houston Street, providing a freshness in the air.

This time they were early, and Lali and William strolled at a relaxed pace.

"Well," Lali shrugged, "that's that. It's over!"

"Only for a couple of months. In September we'll be taking a more advanced course at the high school."

"I'll probably forget everything I learned by then."

"Come on, Lali, the summer will be over before you know it. Just you wait and see. Besides, we can practice so we don't forget what Mrs. Hamma taught us."

"Sure, what do you like to speak about?" Lali said in English.

William smiled, and clasping his hands, said, "I would like to say to you how wonderful you are, and how you gonna have the most fabulous future . . . after all, you so ambitious!"

When she realized he sounded just like Mrs. Hamma, Lali began to laugh.

"Are you"—Lali tried to keep from giggling, tried to pretend to speak in earnest—"sure there is some hope for me?"

"Oh, heavens, yes! You have shown such ability this"—William was beginning to lose control, laughing loudly—"semester!"

"But I want"—Lali was holding her sides with laughter—"some guarantee of this. I got to know."

"Please, Miss Lali." William was laughing so hard tears were coming to his eyes. "After . . . after all, you now a member in good standing . . . of the promised future!"

William and Lali broke into uncontrollable laughter, swaying and limping, oblivious to the scene they created for the people who stared and pointed at them as they continued on their way to Rudi's.

1. Do you think Mrs. Hamma handles Diego Torres's oral statement well? If you think she did not handle the situation well, describe what else she could have said or done.

2. What does Mrs. Hamma believe about opportunities in the United States? Do you think her views are accurate? Do the students in the class believe her views are accurate? Does her practice fit her beliefs? Explain.

3. Do you think Mrs. Hamma's class creates opportunities for Lali and Rudi?

4. Imagine that you are a student in Mrs. Hamma's class. What would you find attractive about life in the United States?

Cyn. Zarco, "Flipochinos," from *Cir'cum-nav-i-gation*, Tooth of Time Books.

Paula Gunn Allen, "Powwow Durango," from *Shadow Country*, copyright © 1982 by The Regents of the University of California. Published by The American Indian Studies Center, University of California, Los Angeles.

Paula Gunn Allen, "Deer Woman," from *Grandmothers of the Light*, copyright © 1991 by Paula Gunn Allen. Reprinted by permission of Beacon Press.

Sandra Maria Esteves, "In the Beginning," from *Puerto Rican Writers at Home in the USA*, by Open Hand Publishing, Inc., 1991. Originally published in *Tropical Rains*, African Caribbean Theatre. Copyright © 1984 by Sandra Maria Esteves.

Victor Hernández Cruz, "Latest Latin Dance Craze," copyright © 1976 by Victor Hernández Cruz, first published in *Tropicalization* (Reed, Cannon & Johnson, 1976).

Javier Pachecho, "Carlos De Oxnard," *Invocation L.A.: Urban Multicultural Poetry*, copyright © 1989, by West End Press, Michelle T. Clinton et al., eds. West End Press, 1989.

Toshio Mori, "The Woman Who Makes Swell Doughnuts," from *Yokohama, California 1946* (Caxton Printers, Ltd., Caldwell, ID).

Anna Bart, "Ravioli," from *The Dream Book: An Anthology of Writings by Italian American Women*, Helen Barolini, ed. Schocken Books, 1985.

Amy Uyematsu, "Rice Planting," from *Invocation L.A.: Urban Multicultural Poetry*, pp. 38-40, Michelle T. Clinton et al, eds., copyright © 1989 by West End Press.

Samuel Allen (Paul Vesey), "To Satch: American Gothic," copyright © by Samuel Allen.

Nicholasa Mohr, *The English Lesson*, from *In Nueva York*. Reprinted by permissionn of Arte Publico Press, University of Houston, 1988.

ART ACKNOWLEDGMENTS

Page 6
Photographer unknown, Japanese-American Neighborhood, Sienaga, California, 1932. Courtesy of the Obata Family.

Page 46
Sargent Johnson, *Forever Free*, 1933. Lacquered cloth over wood, 36 x 11 1/2 x 9 1/2" (91.5 x 29.2 x 24.2 cm), San Francisco Museum of Modern Art, Gift of Mrs. E. D. Lederman.

Page 51
Malaquias Montoya, *Long Before—Long After*, 1992. Charcoal on paper with color pastel. Courtesy of Malaquias Montoya.

Page 61
Naomi Savage, *Mask*, 1965. Line-cut, photo-engraving on silver-plated copper, 18 3/4 x 14 1/2". Collection, The Museum of Modern Art, New York. Joseph G. Mayer Foundation Inc., Fund. Courtesy of Naomi Savage.

Page 63
Yreina Cervántez, *La Offrenda* (detail), 1989. Los Angeles mural, 16 x 52', A Neighborhood Pride/Great Walls Unlimited project. Photo by James Prigoff.

Page 67
Joel Meyerowitz, *Hartwig House, Truro, Cape Cod*, 1976. Extacolor RC print, 15 3/8 x 19 1/2". Milwaukee Art Museum, Floyd and Josephine Segel Collections, Gift of Wis-Pak Foods, Inc.

Page 73
Elizabeth Catlett, *Malcolm X Speaks For Us,* 1969. Linocut, 37 x 27". Courtesy of Elizabeth Catlett and SAMJAI Fine Arts, Inc., Culver City, California.

Page 82
Miguel Covarrubias, *Lindy Hop,* 1936. Lithograph on paper, 16 1/8 x 11 1/2". Philadelphia Museum of Art. Purchased: The Thomas Skelton Harrison Fund.

Page 99
Edward Curtis, *Prayer to the Stars,* n.d. Orotone (gold-tone print), 13 3/8 x 10 1/4". Collection of The Oakland Museum, Gift of Mr. & Mrs. Howard Willoughby. Photo by M. Lee Fatherree.

Page 115
Peace symbol and love beads. Courtesy of Gail Kefauver; Barbara Robinson.

Page 120
Sara Alexander, *Collage,* 1990. Courtesy of Barbara Anderson Gallery.

Page 123
Minor White, *Windowsill Daydreaming,* 1958. Reproduction courtesy the Minor White Archive, Princeton University. Copyright © 1982 by The Trustees of Princeton University. All rights reserved. Photo courtesy of The Minneapolis Institute of Art.

Page 131
Faith Ringgold, *Sunflowers Quilting Bee at Arles,* 1991. Painted story quilt, acrylic on canvas with pieced fabric, 74 x 80". Private Collection. © Faith Ringgold.

Page 170
Roman Vishniac, *Granddaughter and Grandfather, Warsaw,* 1938. Gelatin silver print. The Roman Vishniac Archives at the International Center of Photography.

Page 215
Miné Okubo, *Moving In (Topaz, Utah),* 1942. Tempera drawing. Courtesy of Miné Okubo.

Page 217
Morgan Paul (age 10), *Legs,* 1989. Silver print, 11 x 14", Reproduced in exhibition and book *Shoooting Back: A Photographic View of Life by Homless Children* © 1991. Courtesy Shooting Back, An Education & Media Center.

Page 227
Martin Luther King, Jr. in a Jefferson County Courthouse Jail Cell, Birmingham, Alabama, 1967. UPI/Bettmann Newsphotos.

Page 243
Flip Schulke, *Martin Luther King, Jr. with his Son,* c. 1963. Flip Schulke/Black Star.

Page 247
Victor Fan, *Chinese-American History* (detail), 1988. YMCA Playground, Los Angeles, Acrylic on concrete. Photo by James Prigoff.

Page 258
Ben Shahn, *Miners' Wives,* 1948. Egg tempera on board, 48 x 36". Philadelphia Museum of Art, Given by Wright S. Ludington.

Page 266
Emmi Whitehorse (Navajo), *Rincon Marquez's Renewal,* 1986. Oil on paper, 31 x 47 1/4". Courtesy of Emmi Whitehorse.

Page 279
Jacob Lawrence, *Harriet Tubman series No. 9: Harriet Tubman dreamt of freedom ("Arise! Flee for your life!"), and in the visions of the night she saw the horsemen coming. Beckoning hands were ever motioning her to come, and she seemed to see a line dividing the land of slavery from the land of freedom,* 1939-40. Casein on hardboard, 12 x 17 7/8". Hampton University Museum, Hampton, Virginia.

Page 283
Sophie Rivera, *Woman and Daughter in Subway,* 1982 . Silver gelatin print, 16 x 20". Courtesy of Sophie Rivera.

Page 288
Betye Saar, *Black Girl's Window,* 1969. Mixed media assemblage window, 35 3/4 x 18 x 1 1/2". Courtesy of Betye Saar. Photo by Frank Thomas.

Page 303
African-American Pilots in Italy during World War II. The Bettmann Archive.

Page 318
L. Tomi Kobara, *To Greatgrandmother,* 1988. Silkscreen print, 24 x 32". Courtesy of L. Tomi Kobara.

Page 335
Jeffrey M. Thomas (Onondaga/Cayuga), *4 Dancers, Niagara Falls, New York,* 1985. Black/white photograph, 7 x 10 3/4". Courtesy of Jeffrey M. Thomas.

Page 344
Amos Ferguson, *Beeded Hair,* 1984. Plio-lux enamel on cardboard, 35 3/4 x 29 3/4 ". Wadsworth Atheneum, Hartford, Connecticut. The Ella Gallup Sumner and Mary Catlin Sumner Collection.

Page 351
John Running, *Little Shell Pow Wow.* Courtesy of John Running.

Page 356
Frank LaPena (Wintu, Sacramento), *Big Head Spirit,* 1987. Wood engraving. Courtesy of Frank LaPena.

Page 376
Linda Lomahaftewa (Hopi/Choctaw), *Star Gatherers,* 1990. Monotype, 41 1/4 x 29 5/16". Courtesy of Linda Lomahaftewa. Photo by David Broda.